Chaos, Cosmos and Creation
in Early Greek Theogonies

Classical Literature and Society

Series Editor: David Taylor

Classics and the Bible: Hospitality and Recognition, John Taylor
Culture and Philosophy in the Age of Plotinus, Mark Edwards
Homer: The Resonance of Epic, Barbara Graziosi and Johannes Haubold
Juvenal and the Satiric Genre, Frederick Jones
Ovid and His Love Poetry, Rebecca Armstrong
Pastoral Inscriptions: Reading and Writing Virgil's Eclogues, Brian Breed
Pausanias: Travel Writing in Ancient Greece, Maria Pretzler
Propertius: Poet of Love and Leisure, Alison Keith
Silent Eloquence: Lucian and Pantomime Dancing, Ismene Lada-Richards
Statius, Poet Between Rome and Naples, Carole E. Newlands
The Myth of Paganism, Robert Shorrock
The Roman Book, Rex Winsbury
Thucydides and the Shaping of History, Emily Greenwood

Chaos, Cosmos and Creation in Early Greek Theogonies

An Ontological Exploration

Olaf Almqvist

BLOOMSBURY ACADEMIC
LONDON • NEW YORK • OXFORD • NEW DELHI • SYDNEY

BLOOMSBURY ACADEMIC
Bloomsbury Publishing Plc
50 Bedford Square, London, WC1B 3DP, UK
1385 Broadway, New York, NY 10018, USA
29 Earlsfort Terrace, Dublin 2, Ireland

BLOOMSBURY, BLOOMSBURY ACADEMIC and the Diana logo
are trademarks of Bloomsbury Publishing Plc

First published in Great Britain 2022
Paperback edition published 2023

Copyright © Olaf Almqvist, 2022

Olaf Almqvist has asserted his right under the Copyright, Designs
and Patents Act, 1988, to be identified as Author of this work.

For legal purposes the Acknowledgements on pp. vii–viii constitute an extension of this
copyright page.

Cover design: Terry Woodley
Cover image © *Chamber of the giants*, Giulio Romano, 1532. Palazzo Te, Mantua, Italy. ART
Collection / Alamy Stock

All rights reserved. No part of this publication may be reproduced or transmitted
in any form or by any means, electronic or mechanical, including photocopying,
recording, or any information storage or retrieval system, without prior permission
in writing from the publishers.

Bloomsbury Publishing Plc does not have any control over, or responsibility for,
any third-party websites referred to or in this book. All internet addresses given in
this book were correct at the time of going to press. The author and publisher
regret any inconvenience caused if addresses have changed or sites have ceased
to exist, but can accept no responsibility for any such changes.

A catalogue record for this book is available from the British Library.

Library of Congress Cataloging-in-Publication Data

Names: Almqvist, Olaf, author.
Title: Chaos, cosmos and creation in early Greek theogonies :
an ontological exploration / Olaf Almqvist.
Other titles: Classical literature and society.
Description: New York : Bloomsbury Academic, 2022. | Series: Classical literature and
society | Includes bibliographical references and index.
Identifiers: LCCN 2021033198 (print) | LCCN 2021033199 (ebook) |
ISBN 9781350221840 (hardback) | ISBN 9781350221864 (ebook) |
ISBN 9781350221888 (epub)
Subjects: LCSH: Cosmology, Ancient. | Creation–Mythology. | Greece–Religion.
Classification: LCC BL795.C68 A46 2022 (print) | LCC BL795.C68 (ebook) |
DDC 292.2/4—dc23
LC record available at https://lccn.loc.gov/2021033198
LC ebook record available at https://lccn.loc.gov/2021033199

ISBN:	HB:	978-1-3502-2184-0
	PB:	978-1-3502-2194-9
	ePDF:	978-1-3502-2186-4
	eBook:	978-1-3502-2188-8

Series: Classical Literature and Society

Typeset by RefineCatch Limited, Bungay, Suffolk

To find out more about our authors and books visit www.bloomsbury.com
and sign up for our newsletters.

Contents

Acknowledgements	vii
Abbreviations	ix
Introduction: Myth, Philosophy and Ontological Pluralism	1
Between myth and philosophy	7
Ontologies and theogonies	12
Summary overview	16
1 Cosmos and Chaos in Hesiod's *Theogony*	21
Etymologizing Chaos and the search for order	22
Cosmos and chaos in ancient cosmologies	27
The ontology of chaos	30
Rethinking the opening of Hesiod's *Theogony*	34
Ouranos and Kronos or how *not* to rule the cosmos	37
Zeus, Oedipus and the King of Fiji	41
Making a cosmos out of chaos	43
Conclusion	44
2 Beyond the Golden Age: Sacrifice, Sharing and Affinity in Hesiod's Mekone	47
Hesiod and human origins	47
Hesiod and ὁμόθεν	54
Affinity, consanguinity and the shared table of gods and men	55
Sacrifice between sharing and separation	62
The shared feast at Mekone	66
Conclusion: Sacrifice and cosmology	69
3 Orpheus and the Reinvention of the Cosmos	73
Orpheus amid the poets and philosophers	74
Reconstructing the beginning of the *Derveni Theogony*	78
Protogonos and the early gods in the *Derveni Theogony*	85
Zeus first, middle and last	90
Recreating the cosmos	94
Conclusion	96

4	Dionysus Dismembered	99
	Early Orphism and circumstantial evidence	100
	Making sense of murder	108
	Body and soul in early Orphism	112
	From soul to sacrifice	120
	Appropriate offerings to the gods	127
	Conclusion: Sacrifice as the pivot of the world	131

Conclusion: Protagoras and Greek Naturalism 133
   Naturalism and sophistic thought 134
   Protagoras' legacy 139
   Living in Protagoras' world 142

Appendix: Some Key Orphic Texts 145
Notes 153
Bibliography 205
Index Locorum 233
General Index 235

Acknowledgements

From the beginning of my PhD to the completion of this book, I have benefited from the help of countless friends, family members and colleagues. It is unlikely that this book would have seen the light of day without the eternal patience and support of my PhD supervisor, Dr Ashley Clements. I first met Ashley during my studies as an MPhil student in Trinity and was immediately impressed by his combination of classical and anthropological acumen. During my time as an MPhil and PhD student, I have had the pleasure of attending multiple classes under his guidance and have learned a great deal from his wide-ranging theoretical and linguistic knowledge. Alongside Ashley, I must thank the Irish Research Council for funding my doctoral research and the Trinity College Classics department and in particular Dr Shane Wallace and Dr Martine Cuypers for allowing me to sit in on their reading modules. This certainly made learning Greek a great deal more fun. Further, thanks are also due to Dr Christine Morris and Dr Shaul Tor for their astute and constructive criticism during my viva and countless referral letters thereafter.

During the course of my research, I have also benefited immensely from presenting and discussing my ideas at conferences. In particular, I would like to thank the organizers and participants of the Prometheus Trust conference on 'Immortality' for providing an opportunity to discuss my ideas on Hesiod and Empedocles, and Dr William Matthews for his organization of an interdisciplinary conference on divination hosted by the London School of Economics. I have also benefited from the weekly reading groups at the Trinity Plato Centre and offer thanks to Professor John Dillon, Dr Vasilis Politis and everyone else involved. I doubt that I would have discovered the riches of Plato's *Cratylus* without this group. I must also extend my warmest thanks to the staff and researchers at the Long Room Hub and especially Professor Jane Ohlmeyer and Dr Caitriona Curtis. The reading groups and weekly coffee mornings provided a welcome chance to discuss ideas in an interdisciplinary environment.

During the writing of this book, I have been fortunate enough to teach in University College Dublin, Trinity College Dublin and Maynooth University. In particular, I would like to thank Dr Alexander Thein, Dr Christopher Farrell, Professor Michael Lloyd, Dr Martin Brady, Dr Helen Dixon, Dr William

Desmond, Dr Gordon Campbell, and everyone else for their encouragement and support in my development as a lecturer.

Thanks are also due to everyone at Bloomsbury, including Lily Mac Mahon, Georgina Leighton, Alice Wright and Moira Eagling. I would like to thank the anonymous reviewers for their careful and sometimes critical advice, comments and observations.

Finally, none of this would have been possible without my friends and family. I regret that I can only mention a small fraction of them here. I would like to thank my brother Ragnar, his wife Ailbhe, my wonderful nieces Freja and Sadhbh, and my sister Marja and her family. Special thanks are due to my mother, Éilís, for her help, support, and reading of an early draft of this book. I also thank my Bulgarian family, my *shurey* Ivan, *tust* Nikolai and *tushta* Irina, who supported and cared for me and my family during this period. I cannot begin to say how grateful I am to my wife Nadezhda and our son Nikolai. Nikolai is not only one of my most attentive readers, he is a constant reminder of what is important in life. As for my wife Nadezhda, gratitude is too weak a term. This book would have been impossible without her.

Abbreviations

Abbreviations of ancient authors and works follow those of the *Oxford Classical Dictionary* 4th edition. Oxford. 1999.

DK	*Die Fragmente der Vorsokratiker*, 7th edition. Diels, H. ed. with additions and Nachträge by Kranz, W. Berlin. 1954.
FGrH	*Die Fragmente der Griecischen Historiker.* Jacoby, F. et al. eds. Berlin and Leiden. 1923.
GRBS	*Greek, Roman and Byzantine Studies.*
IG	*Inscriptiones Graecae.* Kirchhoff, A. et al. eds. Berlin, 1873–.
KRS	*The Presocratic Philosophers: A Critical History with a Selection of Texts.* Kirk, G. S., Raven, J. E. and Schofield, M. Cambridge. 1983.
LSJ	Liddell and Scott, *A Greek-English Lexicon*, 9th edition revised Stuart Jones, H. and McKenzie, R. Oxford. 1940.
MW	*Fragmenta Hesiodea.* Merkelbach, R. and West, M. eds. Oxford. 1967.
OF	*Orphicorum et Orphicis similium testimonia et fragmenta. Poetae Epici Graeci. Pars II. Fasc. 1. Bibliotheca Teubneriana.* Bernabé, A. ed. München/Leipzig. 2004.
OF K	*Orphicorum Fragmenta.* Kern, O. ed. Berlin. 1922.
PCG	*Poetae Comici Graeci.* Kassel, R. and Austin, C. Berlin. 1983–.
OH	*The Orphic Hymns.* Athanassakis, A. and Wolkow, B. Johns Hopkins. 2013.
SVF	*Stoicorum Veterum Fragmenta.* von Arnim, H. ed. Leipzig. 1903–5.
ZPE	*Zeitschrift für Papyrologie und Epigraphik.*

INTRODUCTION

Myth, Philosophy and Ontological Pluralism

ἓν ἀνδρῶν, ἓν θεῶν γένος: ἐκ μιᾶς δὲ πνέομεν
ματρὸς ἀμφότεροι: διείργει δὲ πᾶσα κεκριμένα
δύναμις, ὡς τὸ μὲν οὐδέν, ὁ δὲ χάλκεος ἀσφαλὲς αἰὲν ἕδος
μένει οὐρανός ἀλλά τι προσφέρομεν ἔμπαν ἢ μέγαν
νόον ἤτοι φύσιν ἀθανάτοις,
καίπερ ἐφαμερίαν οὐκ εἰδότες οὐδὲ μετὰ νύκτας ἄμμε πότμος
οἵαν τιν᾽ ἔγραψε δραμεῖν ποτὶ στάθμαν.

There is one race of men, and one of gods,
though from one mother we both draw our breath.
A division of power keeps us entirely separate:
the one is nothing, the other has an eternal home in the secure
brazen heaven.
Even so, we resemble the immortals in some respects,
in greatness of mind or of stature,
though we do not know by day or night
what finishing line destiny has marked out for us to run towards.

Pindar, *Nemean Six* 1–7[1]

The opening lines of Pindar's *Nemean Six* are as striking as they are unclear. Some translators argue that Pindar refers to two distinct races: 'there is one race of men, another race of gods'. Others, however, state the very opposite: 'there is one race of gods and men'.[2] This ambiguity is a problem that goes beyond Pindar's difficult syntax and strikes at the very core of the poem and the central investigation of this book. What precisely are human beings? What are gods? How do they interact with each other? In the course of this work, these questions – and some very different answers – will be explored through three detailed case studies: Hesiod's *Theogony*, the Orphic *Derveni Theogony*, and Protagoras' myth in Plato's eponymous dialogue. However, what will take me more than 200 pages, and a fair few digressions, Pindar does in fewer than eight lines. Indeed, after a puzzling opening, Pindar categorically states that gods and humans have one single divine mother. Although no specific title or epitaph is given, this is undoubtedly Gaia or Earth. In this reference at least, Pindar may suggest a single genealogical line for humans and gods. This is not, however, necessarily the case and for Pindar to say that Gaia is the mother of humans and gods may be no more an indication of a literal genealogy than Homer saying Zeus is the father of men and gods (*Il.* 1.544). Indeed, even if Pindar hints at a kinship connection through Gaia, the idea is one quickly replaced by an emphasis on distance and difference:

διείργει δὲ πᾶσα κεκριμένα
δύναμις, ὡς τὸ μὲν οὐδέν, ὁ δὲ χάλκεος ἀσφαλὲς αἰὲν ἕδος
μένει οὐρανός.

A division of power keeps us entirely separate:
the one is nothing, the other has an eternal home in the secure
brazen heaven.

This is both the longest and most definitive statement in Pindar's mini-theogony and there is little that suggests kinship in these lines. Indeed, the act of separation is enforced by two verbs διείργω ('kept asunder') and the perfective participle κρίνω ('having been separated'). This, to use Jean Pierre Vernant's famous phrase, is an 'uncrossable gulf' between mortals and immortals if ever there was one. Yet, after having clearly distinguished humans from gods, Pindar wavers again:

ἀλλά τι προσφέρομεν ἔμπαν ἢ μέγαν
νόον ἤτοι φύσιν ἀθανάτοις

Even so, we resemble the immortals in some respects,
in greatness of mind or of stature,

This resemblance considerably complicates Pindar's anthropology. Indeed, the previously cemented gulf now appears to admit a degree of likeness in respect of νόος and/or φύσις. Both of these terms create difficulties for translators. Νόος, the easier of the two words, may be roughly translated as 'mind', an inner reflective capacity. Φύσις is more obscure. Etymologically the word is derived from φύω to grow. For the Greek philosophers known as the φυσιολόγοι or natural philosophers, φύσις describes the nature and developmental growth of a particular thing.[3] However, the term is rare in early poetry and when it appears often has different connotations from its philosophical usage. For example, Homer uses φύσις only once in reference to a plant which will protect Odysseus from the treacherous magic of Circe. Hermes (*Od.* 10.303), explaining the φύσις of this plant to Odysseus, outlines the colour of its flower and roots and states its divine name, Moly. Although *Nemean Six* provides little clue on how we are to understand φύσις, elsewhere (*Isth.* 4: 49–50) Pindar uses the term to refer to an athlete's physical form or appearance.[4] If *Nemean Six* follows suit, φύσις refers to a physical aspect and is used to complement the inner disposition described by νόος.[5] In other words, gods and humans are compared in terms of their interior minds and their physical exteriors. This comparison is fitting and entirely in tune with other poetical comparisons. Hesiod (*WD* 129), for example, differentiates the Silver Race from the Gold, saying:

χρυσέῳ οὔτε φυὴν ἐναλίγκιον οὔτε νόημα.

It was like the golden race neither in body (φυὴν) nor in mind (νόημα).[6]

A similar contrast again appears in Xenophanes' (DK 21B 23) description of a super-deity who in respect to mortals is:

οὔτι δέμας θνητοῖσιν ὁμοίιος οὐδὲ νόημα.

neither alike in body nor mind.

Yet, if *Nemean Six* describes a resemblance between humans and gods in terms of their physical forms and inner dispositions, how Pindar contrasts these beings is obscure. Is the relation expressed in terms of both minds and bodies or minds alone? Perhaps, physical forms are what are shared, while divine minds remain unknowable?[7] Alternatively should we follow Pindar's earlier insistence on the presence of the insurmountable power which separates humans from the gods and understand that humans share no direct similarity but merely approach or resemble (προσφέρω) the gods in terms of their bodies and minds?[8]

What to make of Pindar's hesitations is unclear. Perhaps the poet was simply confused. Perhaps modern readers are misled by his impenetrable Greek. However, it is also possible that ambiguity was precisely what the Theban poet intended in this striking overture. Living from the late sixth to the mid-fifth century BCE, Pindar was a poet who looked both back to the earlier poetic traditions of Homer and Hesiod and forward to the metaphysical speculation of the Presocratic philosophers. In this respect, the plurality of views expressed in these few lines stands as testament to the countless theological and philosophical debates he undoubtedly witnessed, and which occasionally come to the fore in his praise poetry. For example, *Nemean Six*'s potential stress on the difference between gods and humans may well allude to Homer's and Hesiod's insistence on what I will describe as the ontological difference between humans and non-humans. Homer's Apollo (*Il.* 5. 441–2), for instance, states this distinction in categorical terms:

> οὔ ποτε φῦλον ὁμοῖον
> ἀθανάτων τε θεῶν χαμαὶ ἐρχομένων τ' ἀνθρώπων.
>
> Never the same is the tribe of gods
> who are immortal and men who walk the ground.[9]

Apollo's claim may seem puzzling in some respects. After all, the Greek gods are very close to mortals. Their appearance is human and their forms of feasting and recreation are nearly identical to those of their human counterparts.[10] Yet despite these similarities, Homer stresses that difference remains at a very basic level. A good example of this occurs when Aphrodite is injured by Diomedes on the battlefield of Troy and Homer (*Il.* 5. 339–42) describes how:

> ῥέε δ' ἄμβροτον αἷμα θεοῖο
> ἰχώρ, οἷός πέρ τε ῥέει μακάρεσσι θεοῖσιν·
> οὐ γὰρ σῖτον ἔδουσ', οὐ πίνουσ' αἴθοπα οἶνον,
> τοὔνεκ' ἀναίμονές εἰσι καὶ ἀθάνατοι καλέονται.
>
> and blood immortal flowed from the goddess,
> ichor, that which runs in the veins of the blessed divinities;
> since these eat no food, nor do they drink of the shining
> wine, and therefore they have no blood and are called immortal.[11]

In these lines Aphrodite's wound becomes a potent site for theological speculation. Indeed, Aphrodite as she descends on the battlefield only superficially resembles the warriors she fights. In reality, the goddess possesses blood that is not blood, eats food that is not food, and, as Vernant has memorably described it, possesses a body that is not a body.[12] In short, although humans and gods are analogously similar, they are ontologically distinct beings.

The idea that humans and gods are worlds apart is by no means limited to the *Iliad*. Indeed, it is a sentiment evident in the very word for the gods themselves: ἀθάνατοι, a term which literally means 'not mortal'. The theme is also demonstrably Pindaric. In *Isthmian* 5.14–16, for example, the poet warns:

> μὴ μάτευε Ζεὺς γενέσθαι· πάντ' ἔχεις,
> εἴ σε τούτων μοῖρ' ἐφίκοιτο καλῶν.
> θνατὰ θνατοῖσι πρέπει.

Do not seek to become Zeus; you have everything,
if a share of these fine things comes to you.
Mortal aims befit mortal men.[13]

In *Pythian Three* (59–62), the poet again reminds us that:

χρὴ τὰ ἐοικότα πὰρ δαιμόνων μαστευέμεν θναταῖς φρασίν,
γνόντα τὸ πὰρ ποδός, οἵας εἰμὲν αἴσας.
μή, φίλα ψυχά, βίον ἀθάνατον
σπεῦδε, τὰν δ' ἔμπρακτον ἄντλει μαχανάν.

Men should seek from the gods only what is consistent
with mortal minds,
knowing what lies before our feet, and the nature of
our destiny.
Do not, my soul, long for an immortal life,
but make the most of what you can realistically achieve.[14]

Given these repeated sentiments, it is tempting to assume that *Nemean Six* expresses a similar idea. However, we should be cautious in ascribing a single view to the Theban poet. Indeed, if Pindar frequently attempts to distinguish gods from humans, his poems at times introduce very different conceptions of what human beings are and what they can aspire towards. In *Olympian Two* (65–70), far from exhorting mortals to know their proper limits, Pindar even speaks of humans rejoicing in the company of the gods:

ἀλλὰ παρὰ μὲν τιμίοις
θεῶν, οἵτινες ἔχαιρον εὐορκίαις, ἄδακρυν νέμονται
αἰῶνα· τοὶ δ' ἀπροσόρατον ὀκχέοντι πόνον·
ὅσοι δ' ἐτόλμασαν ἐστρὶς
ἑκατέρωθι μείναντες ἀπὸ πάμπαν ἀδίκων ἔχειν
ψυχάν, ἔτειλαν Διὸς ὁδὸν παρὰ Κρόνου τύρσιν

Those who in life took pleasure in keeping oaths
pass their time without tears in the company of the
revered gods,
while the wicked endure a punishment too dreadful to behold.
But those with the courage to have lived three times in
either place,
keeping their hearts entirely free from wrongdoing,
travel the road of Zeus to the tower of Cronus[15]

Another fragment speaks of a payment to Persephone and the possibility of becoming holy heroes (*Fr. 133 Bergk*):

Φερσεφόνα ποινὰν παλαιοῦ πένθεος
δέξεται, εἰς τὸν ὕπερθεν ἅλιον κείνων ἐνάτῳ ἔτεϊ
ἀνδιδοῖ ψυχὰς πάλιν,
ἐκ τᾶν βασιλῆες ἀγαυοὶ
καὶ σθένει κραιπνοὶ σοφίᾳ τε μέγιστοι
ἄνδρες αὔξοντ᾽: ἐς δὲ τὸν λοιπὸν χρόνον ἥρωες ἁγνοὶ
πρὸς ἀνθρώπων καλεῦνται.

Persephone will return to the sun above in the ninth year
the souls of those from whom
she will exact punishment for old miseries,
and from these come noble kings,
mighty in strength and greatest in wisdom,
and for the rest of time men will call them sacred heroes.[16]

The precise message of these cryptic theologies will be discussed at length in later chapters. Presently, it is sufficient to note that in these lines, intersecting with ideas of reincarnation and even deification found in the thought of Pythagoras, Empedocles and the Orphics, Pindar strays far from the Iliadic ideal. In place of stern warnings to think mortal thoughts, humanity aspires to live in the company of gods and even become holy heroes (ἥρωες ἁγνοί). And with these sentiments, Pindar provides a very different context for interpreting the ambiguities of *Nemean Six*. If humans can return to the company of the gods, perhaps they were always part of a single genealogy? They may even share a common essence in terms of their minds and bodies. Indeed, for Lourenço, the opening of *Nemean Six* is anti-Iliadic and stresses that 'it is not outside the nature of human φύσις to become deathless and immortal'.[17]

Of course, what precisely Pindar intends to say in *Nemean Six* will remain debated. Perhaps his poem stresses a foundational ontological difference between men and gods, perhaps the very opposite. Perhaps Pindar points in both directions simultaneously. Indeed, given that Pindar's audience and patrons spanned the entire Greek world from Sicily to Aegina, it would hardly be surprising if his poetry also engaged with the lively debates that characterized mid-fifth-century Greece. This may even be expected. However, in his easy shift between mythic descriptions of ontological distance and continuity, Pindar's poetry also potentially does something more problematic. It blurs two disciplines some scholars have preferred to keep separate: myth and philosophy.

Between myth and philosophy

About a century after Hesiod and one before the birth of Pindar, the first philosopher Thales of Miletus was born. The life and philosophy of Thales is preserved by a patchwork of later sources and probably apocryphal anecdotes which collectively paint a vivid, if somewhat contradictory, portrait. One of the seven sages, Thales was a figure engaged as much with philosophy as he was with military, commercial and political activities. Sometimes these ideas were combined in surprising ways. Aristotle in *Politics* (1259a5–21), for example, describes how Thales through his careful observations of the heavens concluded that there would be a bountiful harvest in the coming year. He immediately bought all the olive presses in Miletus and Chios and a made a fortune selling them back when his celestial observations proved correct. Today, however, Thales is rarely remembered for his engineering expertise or economic acumen, but for the rather strange idea that everything is water. Like almost everything said or done by Thales, what precisely this enigmatic phrase means is unclear. On the one hand, it is possible that Thales was saying something quite commonplace. Indeed, watery beginnings are widespread in mythical accounts such as the Babylonian *Enûma Eliš* and Homer's description of the river gods Okeanos and Tethys as the father and mother of all the gods (*Il.* 14.200–4). However, for Aristotle, at least, Thales was not simply repeating these ancient stories but saying something new. Water was not only something closely associated with the beginning of the cosmos, it was a more fundamental essence, an ἀρχή or a first principle. As Aristotle explains in the *Metaphysics* (983b):

τῶν δὴ πρώτων φιλοσοφησάντων οἱ πλεῖστοι τὰς ἐν ὕλης εἴδει μόνας ᾠήθησαν ἀρχὰς εἶναι πάντων· ἐξ οὗ γὰρ ἔστιν ἅπαντα τὰ ὄντα καὶ ἐξ οὗ γίγνεται πρώτου καὶ εἰς ὃ φθείρεται τελευταῖον, τῆς μὲν οὐσίας ὑπομενούσης τοῖς δὲ πάθεσι μεταβαλλούσης, τοῦτο στοιχεῖον καὶ ταύτην ἀρχήν φασιν εἶναι τῶν ὄντων, καὶ διὰ τοῦτο οὔτε γίγνεσθαι οὐθὲν οἴονται οὔτε ἀπόλλυσθαι, ὡς τῆς τοιαύτης φύσεως ἀεὶ σωζομένης.

Most of the earliest philosophers conceived only of material principles as underlying all things. That of which all things consist, from which they first come and into which on their destruction they are ultimately resolved, of which the essence persists although modified by its affections – this, they say, is an element and principle of existing things. Hence they believe that nothing is either generated or destroyed, since this kind of primary entity always persists.[18]

For Thales, Aristotle argued, this underlying first principle was water, the source from which all things emerged and, in some sense, remained amid a change of myriad forms. And with this simple idea, the story goes, Thales invented philosophy.[19]

Thales' new style of analysis was quickly adopted and adapted by his compatriots. In place of water, Anaximander argued that the cosmos originated from an abstract concept referred to as the boundless (ἄπειρον) and shortly afterwards, Anaximenes proposed that the ἀρχή was air. Although the precise details of Milesian thought remain obscure, we are better informed regarding the related views of Heraclitus of Ephesus.[20] Heraclitus, like the Milesians, is best known for understanding the cosmos in terms of a first principle, fire (DK 22 B 30). However, while fire is often called an ἀρχή, it is arguably a great deal more. Indeed, Heraclitus, rather than describing fire as a stable entity, places the emphasis on process and transformation. Change is absolutely key to understanding Heraclitus' worldview and expressed in some of his most famous statements such as (DK 22 A6) 'you cannot step into the same river twice' (δὶς ἐς τὸν αὐτὸν ποταμὸν οὐκ ἂν ἐμβαίης).[21] Although this fragment is controversial, the idea of flux should not be and is a concept applied as readily to water as to the elements themselves (DK 22 B 36):

> ψυχῇσιν θάνατος ὕδωρ γενέσθαι, ὕδατι δὲ θάνατος γῆν γενέσθαι, ἐκ γῆς δὲ ὕδωρ γίνεται, ἐξ ὕδατος δὲ ψυχή.
>
> For souls it is to die to become water, for water it is to die to become earth, from earth water is being born, from water Soul.[22]

Heraclitus' emphasis on the continuity and change of a single underlying element is also of central importance for understanding his disagreement with the earlier assumptions of the poets. Indeed, in one of his few explicit criticisms of his predecessors, Heraclitus censors Hesiod for his problematic dualism (DK 22 B57):

> διδάσκαλος δὲ πλείστων Ἡσίοδος· τοῦτον ἐπίστανται πλεῖστα εἰδέναι, ὅστις ἡμέρην καὶ εὐφρόνην οὐκ ἐγίνωσκεν· ἔστι γὰρ ἕν.
>
> The teacher of the multitude is Hesiod; they believe he has the greatest knowledge – who did not comprehend day and night: for they are one.[23]

This passage strikes at the crux of the conflicting views of the older poets and the newer philosophers. In place of Hesiod's dualistic oppositions, Heraclitus stresses an ongoing transformation in terms of process or flow. As Drozdek describes it, just as water becomes earth, 'Night is always followed by day and vice versa, they constitute a unity, a whole, νυχθήμερον' [nightday].[24]

That Thales and his successors were formidable and original thinkers is clear. Indeed, Thales' monopoly on olive presses is enough to prove this. However, in the history of ideas, Presocratic thought is often elevated into a minor miracle and perceived as a decisive shift from the world of myth to reason. The classic formulation of this transition is expressed by Wilhelm Nestle in his *Vom Mythos zum Logos*, who interprets the Presocratic revolution as an escape from the obscurity of myth:

> Just as in the beginning the surface of the earth was completely covered by water, which only gradually receded and let islands and continents appear, so too for primitive man the world surrounding him and his own nature were covered over by a mythical layer of beliefs, which only over a long period of time gradually receded enough for bigger and bigger areas to be uncovered and illuminated by rational thought.[25]

Nestle was not alone in this assessment. Kirk, Raven and Schofield, for example, also describe the philosophical revolution as a dramatic shift from a 'closed traditional society ... towards an open society in which the values of the past become relatively unimportant and radically fresh opinions can be formed both of the community itself and its expanding environment'.[26] Guthrie is even more emphatic and sharply contrasts a transition from 'mythical expression' to 'a purely rational account of the origin and nature of the universe'.[27]

Although Guthrie and Kirk et al. concede that this intellectual shift did not take place overnight, they nonetheless insist that a transition between myth and philosophy remains a useful means for conceptualizing this period and, moreover, that myth and philosophy connote two distinct styles of thought.[28] Recently, however, what initially seemed like common sense has become increasingly debated.[29] What has emerged from a wealth of recent scholarship on the origins of philosophy and early Greece is a far messier picture than was previously realized. For a start, despite the supposedly detrimental effects of myth upon intellectual progress, it is clear that Greek thought prior to philosophy was far from static, traditional and unreflective. On the contrary, philosophy itself emerged from a period of innovation, travel and the adoption of technologies and religious concepts from Egypt and the Near East.[30] In fact, islands like Thales' Miletus were ideal sites for this rich influx of ideas and not only did Thales have Phoenician connections, he allegedly visited and learnt from the Babylonians and the Egyptians.[31] Nor should we downplay the continued importance of supposedly traditional Greek myth and religion upon the early philosophers. Indeed, with some few possible exceptions, the Presocratics did not so much turn away from myths and religious practices as develop and innovate upon an existing framework. Empedocles, for example, deserves to be placed on par with poets such as Hesiod and Homer for his detailed and imaginative works and Parmenides' discovery of logic was famously revealed by an underworld goddess.[32] Not all philosophers, of course, were equally indebted to myth. It is possible, for example, that Xenophanes (DK 21 A 33) may have engaged with empirical methods and thus paved the way for philosophy and science as disciplines. However, these activities were rare and whether Thales or Heraclitus, for example, sought empirical verification for their imaginative accounts is doubtful. Indeed, rather than inventing a new science, these thinkers were actively engaged in telling new stories about the gods. Thales' eternal and ever-changing water, for example, more than an element may have been understood as a divine force.[33] Elsewhere, Thales reportedly said that everything was full of gods, attributed souls to magnets, and may have described the cosmos itself as 'ensouled' (DK 11 A1). Similarly, for Anaximenes air was more than a physical entity; it was something closely identified with the soul (DK 13B 2):

οἷον ἡ ψυχὴ ἡ ἡμετέρα ἀὴρ οὖσα, συγκρατεῖ ἡμᾶς, καὶ ὅλον τόν κόσμον πνεύμα καὶ ἀὴρ περιέχει.

our soul, which is air, controls us, so do breath and air encompass the whole world-order.[34]

Although we rarely know as much about these early theologians as we would like, it is again with Heraclitus that this new theological orientation appears most clearly. In this case at least, the Ephesian's descriptions of fire and process are more closely related to theology than cosmology. His transformation of opposites that defines his world of flux, for example, was something intimately associated with a new kind of cosmic God (DK 22 B 67):

ὁ θεὸς ἡμέρη εὐφρόνη, χειμὼν θέρος, πόλεμος εἰρήνη, κόρος λιμός. ἀλλοιοῦται δὲ ὅκωσπερ ὁκόταν συμμιγῇ θυώμασιν, ὀνομάζεται καθ' ἡδονὴν ἑκάστου.

God is day night, winter summer, war peace, surfeit hunger. It alters as when mingled with perfumes, it gets named according to the pleasure of each.[35]

While I will return to these fragments in more detail in later chapters, my argument in short is that the Presocratics were less concerned with abandoning mythic frameworks than the creation of a new mythology – the creation of new understandings about what gods and humans are.[36] As Aryeh Finkelberg puts it:

> The early sixth century witnessed the emergence of a new religious attitude. The traditional 'religion of distance' began to yield to the belief in man's kinship with gods: the soul was identified with the individual's self and came to be seen as divine and only temporarily attached to the perishable body, a belief heavily loaded with eschatological implications.[37]

Of course, it may be pointed out that this new theology is in itself a clear indication of the innovative and original ideas of the Presocratics and that this new theology in itself marks a distinctive shift from the cosmos envisioned by the poetic worlds of Hesiod and Homer. Indeed, it does. However, this new direction cannot be called a departure from myth to philosophy for one very simple reason: myth continued to develop apace. This is not simply to say that philosophers such as Empedocles were mythmakers or that poets such as Pindar used myth to philosophize. Nor is it to repeat Lloyd's persuasive argument that some Presocratic and Hippocratic texts 'while different in *style* to be sure, are also very largely a product of his imagination'.[38] Both points are true and both problematize any simple shift from myth to reason. However, my claim is even more direct. The theological shift we see in Presocratic philosophy cannot be contrasted with myth for the simple reason that the stories of the mythmakers and poets also changed and developed during this period. Indeed, just as the Presocratics introduced monism and new conceptions of divinity, mythologists such as Pherecydes and the Orphics were equally busy rewriting mythology from within. While it is true that the style of the new mythologists was in some ways distinct from the often pared-down accounts of Presocratics such as Thales, it was no less innovative for that. In fact, in many cases, myth provides clearer illustrations of ideas such as monism than we can glean from the fragments of the early philosophers. An example I will later discuss at length is found in an early Orphic poem, which describes how everything in the cosmos grows into Zeus and he becomes alone (*Derveni Papyrus* 16.3–6). This is far from the only illustration and throughout this book I will argue that ideas such as monism, pantheism and new conceptions of the soul as air were all innovations as closely associated with mythology as they were with philosophy.[39] Of course, what the presence of these ideas in sixth-century myth tells us is open to debate. It is even possible to retain a contrast between the traditional conservative framework of

Homer and Hesiod and the new mythological orientation of the sixth century BCE. However, the case seems a good deal weaker than the grand contrast between Homer the mythmaker and Thales the rationalist. Indeed, to simply say that Orpheus was superior to Homer because they disagree on how the world works is somewhat akin to saying that Heraclitus is superior to Democritus. For this reason, rather than addressing issues of superiority, this book seeks to pass beyond the problematic transition between myth and philosophy, by outlining the ongoing and flourishing debate on gods, the cosmos and humanity that appears in early Greek theogonies.

Ontologies and theogonies

This book is an exploration of early Greek myth and thought. More specifically it is an exploration of three early creation myths and their underlying and competing ontological assumptions. My focus on creation myths is not coincidental. Creation stories are often considered to be the most philosophical of myths and to provide, as Gregory Schrempp argues, 'alternate, but parallel paths through the same terrain'.[40] Why creation myths and philosophy share this common terrain is not surprising. Indeed, whether we are writing a myth describing a self-sacrificing giant or a cosmos emerging from water, to account for origins at all demands that certain issues, if not necessarily be elaborated, at least be addressed. Can something emerge from nothing? How many components are necessary to invent a world? Was the world designed or did it emerge by chance? Whether we engage with Empedocles' philosophical cosmology or Hesiod's mythical counterpart, as anthropologist Michael Scott argues in a related context, these narratives provide ontological blueprints which 'not only offer accounts of the origin of all things, they also often explicitly formulate the relations and distinctions thought to exist in the cosmos'.[41]

In some respects, stressing the close association between philosophical cosmologies and creation myths may seem like well-worn terrain. As will be discussed in detail in Chapter 1, for over a century, classicists have referred to poems such as Hesiod's *Theogony* as predecessors to early philosophy and attempted to outline their underlying ontological assumptions. However, I will argue that the recognition of philosophical elements in early poetry is often partial and in many instances enforces rather than dissolves the distinction between myth and philosophy. As Scott points out, there is an overwhelming emphasis in comparative religion, anthropology and, indeed, classics on interpreting creation narratives as mono-ontological myths that 'assume the consubstantiality of all things as a result of their common origin'.[42] Furthermore, for many theorists it is often only mono-ontological myths that count as truly philosophical, while the rest remain confined to obscure recesses of mythological thought. Although I will argue that some Greek myths indeed exemplify mono-ontological assumptions, it is pivotal to point out that other stories illustrate very different understandings of how the cosmos works. In fact, many well-known creation stories in antiquity and the modern world emphasize the role of chaos as much as cosmos, and destruction as much as creation. Yet how to theoretically understand these accounts has received little analytic attention. As Johnathan Z. Smith notes:

> It strikes me that historians of religion have been weakest in interpreting those myths which do not reveal a cosmos in which man finds a place to dwell and on which he found his existence, but rather which suggest the problematic nature of existence and fundamental tension in the cosmos. I have in mind such traditions as dualistic creation myths, Earth-diver traditions, Tricksters, or the complex narratives of Corn or Rice Mothers who create by 'loathsome' processes (e.g., rubbing the dirt off their bodies, by defecation, secretion).[43]

This theoretical lack is fortunately currently being addressed and anthropologists have increasingly attempted to create robust frameworks for understanding how contrasting ontological debates come to the fore in mythical cosmologies. One of the most important theoretical steps towards this goal and a major influence for my own theoretical approach is found in Philippe Descola's *Beyond Nature and Culture*. Originally published in 2005, *Beyond Nature and Culture* is a dazzling study of the competing ontological assumptions found across the world. Descola, in what he refers to as 'relative universalism',[44] attempts to navigate a middle ground between cognitive universals and the diversity of views and configurations of humans and non-humans found in the ethnographic record. His starting point is the simple question of why certain societies that have no historical connections develop similar cosmologies and institutions but lack others. Why do the ancient Greeks and pre-Christian Hawaiians, for example, tell similar myths and sacrifice to highly structured pantheons of gods, whereas animist societies such as the Achuar lack rigidly hierarchal pantheons and sacrifice altogether? Victorian anthropologists and modern adherents of the Axial Age have argued that these represent stages of cultural development, which are passed through on the path to modernity.[45] Descola, on the other hand, does away with the ethnocentric idea of stages of development and instead sees these similarities in terms of spontaneous developments due to similar cognitive schemas or what he calls ontologies.

Echoing Pindar's ambiguous comparison between humans and gods, Descola's cognitive assumptions are founded upon a universal duality based on particular configurations of physicality and interiority.[46] These terms are deliberately general as to incorporate a wide range of conceptions, but for simplicity's sake one would not go far wrong in understanding them in terms of body and soul. This body/soul dualism, he argues, is not only well supported by developmental studies,[47] but, more importantly, is repeatedly adhered to in the languages and cultural practices of humans from all corners of the world. Although Descola argues that 'every human perceives himself or herself as a unit that is a mixture of interiority and physicality', not all societies understand this mixture in an identical way.[48] Rather, Descola outlines how various combinations of physicality and interiority result in four possible schemas or ontologies which he calls animism, analogism, naturalism and totemism. These can be illustrated on the following grid:*

• Similar interiorities (continuity of souls)	Animism	Totemism	• Similar interiorities (soul essences are identical)
• Dissimilar physicalities (discontinuity of forms)			• Similar physicalities (substance and behaviour are identical)
• Dissimilar interiorities (discontinuity of minds)	Naturalism	Analogism	• Dissimilar interiorities (gradual discontinuity of the components of existing beings)
• Similar physicalities (continuity of matter)			• Dissimilar physicalities (gradual discontinuity of the components of existing beings)

Naturalism posits a continuity of physicalities or bodies, which is common to humans and animals alike. Division, on the other hand, occurs in terms of interiorities or souls. This is the ontology prevalent in the West and is defined by the assumption that humans and animals possess similar bodies but are distinguished in terms of their interiorities or minds, which are reserved for

---

* Grid is adapted from Descola (2013) 233.

humans alone. Animism is the inverse of naturalism and posits a continuity of interiorities but discontinuity in terms of physicalities. In many Amazonian societies, such as the Achuar, animals, spirits and humans all have the same souls but are differentiated in terms of their physical forms. Totemism, like animism, is a rehabilitation of an older anthropological concept. Descola argues that totemism is an ontology where 'specific plant and animal species are believed to share with particular sets of humans an identical complex of essential qualities, but one that is absolutely different from other similar groupings'.[49] In other words, similarity occurs at the level of body and soul, but separation occurs between different groups. An Aranda member of the kangaroo totem, for example, can say 'this kangaroo is the same as me', but someone of the cockatoo totem would possess no connection to him in either his physicality or interiority. Finally, analogism is an ontology found in Polynesia, West Africa, Mesoamerica and the Andes. It was also prevalent in medieval Europe and is posited by Descola as the dominant ontology of the Greeks.[50] Analogism is the opposite of totemism and involves a separation in terms of both the interiority and physicality axes. Descola defines analogism as:

> A mode of identification that divides up the whole collection of existing beings into a multiplicity of essences, forms, and substances separated by small distinctions and sometimes arranged on a graduated scale so that it becomes possible to recompose the system of initial contrasts into a dense network of analogies that link together the intrinsic properties of the entities that are distinguished in it.[51]

A common expression of analogist cosmologies is found in the 'great chain of being'. In essence, the chain of being is an elaborate configuration that encompasses and orders the diverse and distinct components of the cosmos 'into a web of meaningful affinities and attractions that gives the appearance of constituting a continuity'.[52] In early Greece, this chain is found, for example, in the hierarchy of ontologically distinct animals, humans and gods.[53]

Although the schematic nature of Descola's model might be considered overly rigid and even reductionist, by focusing on basic cognitive assumptions it provides a means of understanding similar patterns found in many societies without imposing an overly systematic model on any. In this respect, it avoids the criticism often levelled against structuralists that the neat and tidy image of social organization they describe belies a more messy reality, which includes local and historical disagreements.[54] Parker, for example, argues that 'structuralism postulates a large database of theological knowledge in the mind of every Greek, and a willingness to be bound by its implicit rules'.[55] Even if we accept that these criticisms are true of the kind of structuralism often applied to the study of ancient Greece,[56] they do not apply to Descola's ontologies. In this respect, Descola's ontologies are comparable to Bourdieu's *habitus*.[57] Bourdieu was critical of mapping entire societies in terms of up/down, male/female, sun/moon, etc. His point was not that such associations are uncommon, but rather that these oppositions are not fixed totalities existing outside of historical circumstances. Instead, he advocated describing a more basic *habitus* or 'principles which generate and organize practices'[58] and shifted the emphasis from the finished project towards the structuring principles from which social relations emerge. Descola's ontological project is similar. In his own words, it is a little 'farther upstream' from *habitus* and 'enable[s] us', as Scott explains, 'to structure our perceptions, organize our actions, thoughts, and feelings according to relatively stereotyped scenarios, and interpret patterns of behaviour and events in terms of a shared framework'.[59] In other words, although the ontologies may initial seem rigid and inflexible, it should be stressed that in practice Descola's ontologies are not descriptions of precise cultural institutions and societies. Rather they provide the basic cognitive orientations from which, given suitable historical circumstances, similar ideas may emerge.

Summary overview

Adapting the language of Descola, this book is a study of competing ontological assumptions in three cosmological myths: Hesiod's *Theogony*, the Orphic *Derveni Theogony*, and Protagoras' myth from Plato's dialogue. In my discussion of these works, I will also engage with a wealth of other creation stories, including Pherecydes of Syros' prose theogony, Empedocles' philosophical cosmology, and non-Greek myths such as the Babylonian *Enûma Eliš* and the biblical Genesis. This work, however, is not a comprehensive guide of early accounts of creation, but a study of competing orientations in early Greek myth. Hesiod's *Theogony*, the Orphic *Derveni Theogony* and Protagoras' myth are all variations on the same mythical material and explorations on how mortals, animals and gods interact. However, although these narratives explore the same mythic material, I argue that they possess very different ideas about how the cosmos works and express contrasting ontological assumptions. This book attempts both to analyse these underlying assumptions and to describe the repercussions of these ontologies on ritual life. Towards this goal, this book will adopt and develop upon three key ontologies: Descola's analogism and naturalism, and a new ontological configuration referred to by William Matthews as homologism, but for reasons which I will outline in Chapter 3 I refer to as pantheism.[60]

In Chapter 1 I outline the ontological foundations of Greece's most famous cosmological text: Hesiod's *Theogony*.[61] Cosmologies, the world over, are predominantly studied in terms of their supposed descriptions of an inherent cosmic order which neatly unfolds from beginning to end. Hesiod's poem is no exception, and it is frequently discussed as a pivotal first step towards the rational cosmologies of later Greek philosophers. This chapter argues against this orthodoxy. Following some suggestive remarks by Aristotle (*Metaphysics* 14.1091a–b) and recent anthropological perspectives on analogist cosmologies, I argue that Hesiod's poem has little to do with monism and order. On the contrary, from the confusing initial divine triad of Chaos, Gaia and Eros to the countless battles of gods against gods, Hesiod consistently depicts a chaotic world composed of distinct and conflicting forces. I argue that unlike monistic cosmologies, Hesiod's analogist cosmology is based on ontological difference and antagonism. Cosmic order, of course, can be achieved in this world but only if imposed by an external force. In Hesiod's poem this task falls to Zeus who, in his battles against chaotic monsters, strategic marriages and extensive remodelling of the cosmos, finally unites the dissolute parts of the originally chaotic cosmos into a hierarchal totality. Although the end result of both monist and analogist cosmologies is an ordered totality, for Hesiod order is always temporary and chaos a potential threat.

An important argument in this book is that ontological assumptions have consequences for understanding ritual life. Chapter 2 discusses humanity's place within Hesiod's analogist cosmos through a close reading of the Promethean myth and humanity's separation from the table of the gods. I begin by challenging the idea that humanity once lived in a harmonious Golden Age where the boundaries between mortal and immortal blurred or collapsed entirely. The Golden Age myth, although known to Hesiod, is not found in the *Theogony* and nothing in the poem suggests the existence of a previous idyllic harmony of gods and humans. On the contrary, the rule of Kronos is consistently depicted in terms of tyranny, cruelty, and even cannibalism. Drawing on these complexities and the analogical ontological foundation outlined in Chapter 1, I suggest thinking beyond the Golden Age and, following Pausanias (8.2.4), I argue that humans and gods were never equals or kin, but guest-friends (ξένοι) united by difference. After exploring the importance of food in the creation of guest-friend kinship ties, I turn towards an exploration of the Promethean sacrificial shares and the nature of the relationship sacrifice creates between human and gods and, to a lesser extent, animals. I ask whether sacrifice forms a commensal relationship based on the shared meal, as Robertson Smith (1889) argued, or whether it emphasizes the fundamental difference between ontologically separate beings proposed by Vernant. Focusing on sacrifice through the mediating substance meat, I navigate a path between the separation of Vernant and sharing of Robertson Smith and offer a new theory of Greek sacrifice as a flexible and creative act where mortals and immortals approach each other neither as kin, nor as strangers, but through the ambiguous and dangerous relationship known as affinity.

Chapter 3 turns to theogonies associated with the mythical poet Orpheus. While Hesiod's *Theogony* remained the dominant cosmology of the ancient Greek world, the sixth century BCE witnessed some radically new views on the relations between gods, animals and nature. It also marked a shift in the understanding of the word cosmos from its original meaning as decoration to its new meaning as world order. Although this period is sometimes described as the Greek miracle and birth of science, I discuss it as a shift in ontological assumptions from the separation characteristic of analogism to the ontological continuity characteristic of pantheism. This new monistic orientation was not limited to philosophical speculation but was also evident in cosmological poetry, which developed upon Hesiodic themes. This chapter focuses in detail on the earliest surviving Orphic poem, the *Derveni Theogony* (c. sixth century BCE). I argue that through a process of omissions and additions to the basic Hesiodic narrative, the Orphic poet transforms and rewrites the ontological assumptions of Hesiod's cosmos. In place of ontological plurality we see a focus on monistic origins, and in place of an emphasis on difference we see a repeated focus on connections. One of the most obvious examples of these transformations occurs when the entire cosmos grows into Zeus, and after a period of temporary isolation, he creates the world anew (col. 6.3–6). Discussing a number of similar examples, I argue that in place of Hesiod's analogism, the Orphic poem is an example of what I call a pantheist ontology where the many-named gods are really refractions of a single deity and divinely ordered cosmos.

Chapter 4 explores Orpheus' variation of the Promethean division where the Titans gather and sacrifice the god Dionysus. Despite some notable differences in the plot, the Orphic myth, like Hesiod's, remains a meditation on the origin of human beings and their relations with animals and gods. After discussing the controversial evidence for the myth itself, I turn to analysing its divergent ontological assumptions and repercussions on theorizing sacrifice. I argue that whereas Hesiod's Mekone assumes a basic discontinuity between humans and gods and sees sacrifice as a means of making ambiguous connections between the ontologically distinct tribes of mortals and immortals, the Orphic myth emphasizes a foundational continuity between all beings. These ontological assumptions have important repercussions on ritual life and following Descola's observations on the absence of sacrifice in animistic societies, I argue that in a world based on a pre-existing connection, animal sacrifice becomes redundant and is consequently replaced with rituals based not on creating tentative ties with potentially hostile affines, but on sharing pure offerings with kin.

The final chapter turns to the sophist Protagoras and a new philosophical myth on the origins of humanity and Prometheus' theft of fire. This chapter examines the ontological assumptions of Protagoras' Promethean myth in terms of Descola's naturalism and contextualizes his narrative within the vibrant fifth century, where all three ontologies, naturalism, analogism and pantheism, coexisted and coalesced. I end by surveying the legacy of Protagoras' myth found in Western thought and briefly speculate on what we can learn from the presence of competing myths in the early Greek world.

1

Cosmos and Chaos in Hesiod's *Theogony*

Geoffrey Lloyd has stressed that 'there is no such thing as *the* cosmological model, *the* cosmological theory, of the Greeks'.[1] This is undoubtedly true, yet few cosmologies were as influential as Hesiod's description of the creation of the world and the birth of the gods in his *Theogony*. Hesiod composed his poetry between the eighth and seventh centuries BCE. This was a particularly vibrant period in Greek history and saw the early formation of the Greek city-state and the cultural, artistic and social institutions that were to define Classical Greece. Hesiod was a pivotal part of these cultural transformations. Indeed, not only was his poetry the cornerstone of a good Greek education, according to the historian Herodotus (2.53) Hesiod, alongside Homer, 'taught the Greeks the descent of the gods, and gave the gods their names, and determined their spheres and functions, and described their outward forms'.[2] Few philosophers and poets escaped his influence and over a thousand years after the *Theogony*, Hesiod's narrative remained the standard version of the Greek creation myth (Apollodorus 1.1-4). His influence even extended beyond Greece and when the Roman poet Ovid described the world's creation in his *Metamorphosis*, it was largely to Hesiod that he turned for inspiration. In this respect, if any single cosmology can be called the cosmology of the Greeks, it was not that of Plato or Aristotle, but that of the poet Hesiod.

Despite Hesiod's fame and influence, the little we know about him comes from his own words and even this information is open to doubt.[3] Hesiod describes himself as a shepherd from Boeotia (*Theog.* 22-23) who has a brother called Perses (*WD* 27-41). At some stage Hesiod won a prize for his poetry in Chalkis (*WD* 651-9). This may well have been awarded for the *Theogony*, a poem that Hesiod tells us was directly inspired by the Muses while tending his flocks on the foot of Mount Helicon. In Hesiod's words, the goddesses

ἐνέπνευσαν δέ μοι αὐδὴν
θέσπιν, ἵνα κλείοιμι τά τ' ἐσσόμενα πρό τ' ἐόντα,

καί μ' ἐκέλονθ' ὑμνεῖν μακάρων γένος αἰὲν ἐόντων,
σφᾶς δ' αὐτὰς πρῶτόν τε καὶ ὕστατον αἰὲν ἀείδειν.

breathed a divine voice into me, so that I might glorify what will be and what was before, and they commanded me to sing of the race of the blessed ones who always are, but always to sing of themselves first and last.

Theog. 31–34[4]

Yet Hesiod's poem is more than a description of the gods – it is a discussion about the origins of the world itself, of Gaia (Earth) and Ouranos (Sky), and of humanity. Because of this, Hesiod's poem is often considered to be the first Greek cosmology. Indeed, for scholars such as Cornford and Clay, Hesiod's poem even anticipates the ordered worlds of the first Presocratics, the Milesian monists.[5] In this chapter, I will argue against this view and propose that while Hesiod is indeed writing a cosmological poem, his notion of cosmos is worlds away from that of the Milesians. Far from the neatly unfolding monism of later philosophers, Hesiod's poem describes a world of conflicts, multiple genealogies and wayward kings, a fractured and volatile cosmos in need of imposed order. And nowhere is this clearer than in his description of the first-born god, Chaos.

Etymologizing Chaos and the search for order

After a lengthy description of his encounter with the Muses, Hesiod finally begins the cosmological section of his poem and makes the staggering revelation that (*Theog.* 116–20)

ἦ τοι μὲν πρώτιστα Χάος γένετ', αὐτὰρ ἔπειτα
Γαῖ' εὐρύστερνος, πάντων ἕδος ἀσφαλὲς αἰεὶ
ἀθανάτων, οἳ ἔχουσι κάρη νιφόεντος Ὀλύμπου,
Τάρταρά τ' ἠερόεντα μυχῷ χθονὸς εὐρυοδείης,
ἠδ' Ἔρος, ὃς κάλλιστος ἐν ἀθανάτοισι θεοῖσι

In truth, first of all Chaos came to be, and then broad-breasted Earth, the ever immovable seat of all the immortals who possess snowy Olympus' peak and murky Tartarus in the depths of the broad-pathed earth, and Eros, who is the most beautiful among the immortal gods.[6]

Gaia (Earth) and Eros (Love) are well-known gods intimately associated with creation, yet who or what precisely is Chaos and what is he doing at the beginning of the cosmos? Although later Greeks were often as puzzled about Chaos' presence as we are today, this did not stop them from talking about it. Indeed, Plutarch notes that Hesiod's Chaos was an extremely popular topic of discussion (Plu. *Mor.* 678 F).[7] More than an object of conversation, for many poets Chaos was an essential ingredient in a good theogony.[8] Yet despite its popularity, Chaos remains a very puzzling way to begin a cosmology. Indeed, the very word 'cosmology' is a near antonym. In Classical Greek, κόσμος is synonymous with order and a cosmology is an account of such order. As Socrates explains in Plato's *Gorgias* (507e–8d), wise men say that

> οὐρανὸν καὶ γῆν καὶ θεοὺς καὶ ἀνθρώπους τὴν κοινωνίαν συνέχειν καὶ φιλίαν καὶ κοσμιότητα καὶ σωφροσύνην καὶ δικαιότητα, καὶ τὸ ὅλον τοῦτο διὰ ταῦτα κόσμον καλοῦσιν, ὦ ἑταῖρε, οὐκ ἀκοσμίαν οὐδὲ ἀκολασίαν.
>
> heaven and earth and gods and men are held together by communion and friendship, by orderliness, temperance, and justice; and that is the reason, my friend, why they call the whole of this world by the name of order (κόσμος), not of disorder or dissoluteness.[9]

As Socrates stresses in this passage, a good cosmology consists of communion, friendship and above all else, order. Hesiod, however, by giving pre-eminence to Chaos, seems to entirely miss the point. This is not really surprising. When Hesiod wrote the *Theogony* the idea of a cosmology had yet to be invented. He was familiar with the word κόσμος but rather than understand it as world order, he uses it in the sense of adornment or decoration. For example, the word is used to describe the garlands and crown given to Pandora by the goddess Athena (*Theog.* 587).[10] However, if Hesiod had little notion that the world was a κόσμος, scholars are as quick to tell us that Chaos has no relation with its English homonym. Rather based on the root χα 'gap' and χάσκειν or χαίνειν 'to gap', it refers to yawning or gapping and in no way contains 'the idea of confusion or disorder'.[11] Although an etymological connection between Χάος and χάσκειν is plausible, we should remember that etymologies reveal linguistic histories rather than common understandings and these two aspects seem to have diverged widely. The cosmological poet Pherecydes of Syros appears to have equated Chaos with primal water, perhaps based on the verb χεῖσθαι to flow (DK 7 B 1). While this is often dismissed as a later addition by the Stoics, who similarly understood the word through the related verb χείομαι (SVF 1.103), I see no reason why the view cannot have been held by both Pherecydes and the Stoics. Wordplay is very common in early Greek poetry and the imagery of a watery beginning is well established in Mediterranean cosmologies.[12] Even Homer calls

Okeanos and Tethys the father and mother of all the gods (*Il.* 14.200–4). If Pherecydes' Chaos resided in the water, for others it was found in the underworld. Aristophanes in *Birds* (698) describes Chaos as the winged partner of Eros. While Chaos' wings may simply complement the play's feathered protagonists, when Chaos is said to mingle with Eros in a recess of Tartarus, it is unlikely that the audience envisioned a gap. Nor is the god happy to remain in a single location and elsewhere in *Birds*, Chaos appears in the sky (192). Aristotle differs again, interpreting Chaos in relation to making space, this time perhaps etymologizing it according to the verb χωρέω (*Phys.* 209a).[13] Moving effortlessly between flowing, gapping and making space, Chaos also at times appears to be exactly what so many scholars distance it from: disorder. Pseudo Lucian (*Amores* 32) describes:

> σὺ γὰρ ἐξ ἀφανοῦς καὶ κεχυμένης ἀμορφίας τὸ πᾶν ἐμόρφωσας. ὥσπερ οὖν ὅλου κόσμου τάφον τινὰ κοινὸν ἀφελὼν τὸ περικεί μενον χάος ἐκεῖνο μὲν ἐς ἐσχάτους Ταρτάρου μυχοὺς ἐφυγάδευσας ...

> For you [Eros] gave shape to everything out of dark confused shapelessness. As though you had removed a tomb burying the whole universe alike, you banished that Chaos which enveloped it to the recesses of farthest Tartarus ... .[14]

This too was the Chaos opted for in Latin by Ovid. In his *Metamorphosis*, Ovid (1.7–9) describes it as

> rudis indigestaque moles
> nec quicquam nisi pondus iners congestaque eodem
> non bene iunctarum discordia semina rerum.

> A shapeless, unwrought mass of inert bulk and nothing more, with the discordant seeds of disconnected elements all heaped together in anarchic disarray.[15]

This understanding also appears in some Egyptian translations and when the Gnostics searched for an equivalent for the Egyptian cosmological term Nun (the primal waters of disorder) they settled on Χάος.[16]

While we may rightly claim that these authors – some of them quite late – simply misunderstood the word, it is unclear why Hesiod was not equally susceptible to such a misunderstanding. Indeed, at the very least the widespread ancient confusion serves as a word of caution against an over-reliance on etymologies as vehicles for understanding historical usage.[17] Yet despite this ambiguity, not only do many scholars support reading Chaos as a gap, a number of translations go so far as to replace Hesiod's first god with a more neutral term such as chasm. Martin West, for example, translates 'ἦ τοι μὲν πρώτιστα Χάος γένετ᾽' as 'First came the Chasm' and Glen Most as 'In truth, first of all, Chasm came to be'. This substitution may seem innocent enough. However, etymologies have consequences, and it is important to stress just how central the reading has been in understanding how Hesiod's *cosmology* works.

The cosmological consequences of understanding Chaos as chasm are particularly clear in the pioneering work of Francis Cornford. Cornford was by no means the first or the last to speculate on the nature of Chaos. He was, however, the author of one of the most influential discussions on the subject in the English-speaking world and understanding Chaos as a gap was crucial to his discussion of Hesiod's important place in the history of philosophy.[18] When confronted with Hesiod's problematic overture, Cornford mused:

> 'First of all,' says Hesiod, 'Chaos came into being' – what does that mean? 'Chaos' was not at first, as we conceive it, formless disorder. The word means simply the 'yawning gap' – the gap we now see, with its lower part filled with air and mist and cloud between earth and the dome of heaven.[19]

It is important to stress that Chaos in this brief passage is not simply distanced from the idea of disorder, Cornford's gap rewrites the genealogical sequence in Hesiod's text and transforms Chaos into its very opposite: the first stage in an ordered cosmological sequence beginning with the separation of Heaven and Earth.

While Cornford's reconstruction may at first appear to be an unforgivable act of symbolic violence, there was a rather noble idea behind this correction. As is suggested by the title of his work *From Religion to Philosophy*, Cornford wished to move beyond the problematic primitivist views of early poetry and establish the necessary ties between the chaotic world of Homer and the rational cosmos of the Milesian philosophers. In this transition, for Cornford and a great many others, Hesiod's *Theogony* was the pivotal bridge. This claim is, of course, far from saying that Hesiod was a philosopher. Indeed, no one really doubted that in many respects the Boeotian poet remained trapped in the irrational world of fighting gods and men. He was, however, an advancement from the purely mythical world of his predecessors towards a world where myth was 'on the way to becoming metaphor and allegory'.[20] To make this argument, however, some small but perfectly logical corrections were necessary. Cornford argued that despite Hesiod's insistence on the absolute priority of Chaos, a gap presupposes that something has been divided. Accordingly, he corrected Hesiod's text, positing an original union, a kind of primal matter made of Ouranos and Gaia or Sky and Earth. From this point on, Hesiod's cosmos neatly unfolds in a series of sexual encounters and births, which eventually result in the world as we know it.

Cornford's originality and willingness to take early poetic texts seriously is praiseworthy and marks an innovative attempt to move beyond the rigid dichotomy between myth and reason. However, in many respects, this dichotomy was only partially bridged. Indeed, for Cornford, Hesiod's poem was philosophical only to the extent that it described an orderly cosmos in the spirit of the later Milesian philosophers. Moreover, to make this bridge, Cornford needed to substantially reinterpret and even rewrite Hesiod's text. For example, despite Cornford's assertions, Hesiod never says that Chaos was the gap between Gaia and Ouranos. Secondly, not only is Hesiod emphatic that Chaos preceded everything else, he directly contradicts Cornford's reading, explaining that far from the simultaneous birth of Gaia and Ouranos from a chasm, Ouranos was born at a later stage from Gaia (*Theog.* 126). Given these obvious shortcomings, it is surprising that Cornford's position has any adherents at all. However, either directly or in a modified stance, his claims are repeated in influential works from Kirk, Raven and Schofield's *The Pre-Socratic Philosophers* right up to Gregory's *Ancient Greek Cosmogony*.[21]

Although Cornford's views remain influential, his position has also attracted a fair number of critics who view Chaos in more ambiguous terms.[22] I will develop upon these positions shortly, yet if I have chosen to begin with Cornford and Kirk, it is not simply because they propose an untenable view, but to question what makes such an untenable view persuasive in the first place. Indeed, Kirk et al. openly acknowledge the weakness of the separation thesis and admit that explaining why Hesiod expressed his theory in this way

> would be, undoubtedly, a cryptic and laconic procedure; and it seems probable that something more complicated was meant by Χάος γένετ᾿ than simply, 'sky and earth separated' – though I am inclined to accept that this was originally implicit in the phrase.[23]

This admission, if initially mystifying, is at least partially explained when we consider Hesiod's pivotal role as a proto-philosopher and cosmologist.[24] Indeed, to make sense of the birth of philosophy, we first need to make sense of its Hesiodic origins, and this means downplaying or removing any signs of chaos that impede this understanding. In this at least, Cornford was incredibly influential and while the precise theory outlined above may be increasingly on the wane, Cornford's gap remains a symptom of something more pervasive: the assumption that Hesiod was writing about a cosmos rather than a chaos.[25] Indeed, even many authors who distance themselves from Cornford's gap happily accept this position. As Koning points out, Hesiod is variously described as 'defining, organizing, classifying, conceptualizing; systematic, rational, abstract, intellectual, analytical, even scientific' and adds that 'this particular view of the poet is in fact one of the very few constants in modern Hesiodic scholarship'.[26] A good example of this appears in Clay's penetrating and far-ranging study of Hesiodic poetry. Clay, it should be noted, does not see Chaos as a gap. Yet, she nevertheless distances Hesiod's first god from chaos, noting 'this is apparently not, as we might think, a jumble of undifferentiated matter, but rather its negation, a featureless void'.[27] From this starting point, her reading, following a generally Milesian pattern, searches for the underlying order of Hesiod's text.[28] Indeed, in some respects she goes further than Cornford and Kirk, seeing even in the many battles and rebellions a 'radically teleological'[29] scheme where 'from the beginning Hesiod alludes to the final disposition of the cosmos ... a disposition that is somehow immanent from the outset'.[30] In this respect, Hesiod not only anticipates the likes of Anaximander and even Plato in the opening cosmogony, but even in his most chaotic discussions of gods vying with gods, Clay detects a divine steersman at the helm.

Cosmos and chaos in ancient cosmologies

For Cornford, Hesiod was not the only mythmaker to anticipate the monism of the Milesians. On the contrary, to substantiate his claims, Cornford marshalled a vast array of comparative myths (and their interpretations) from Egypt, Mesopotamia and China. He also located Hesiod alongside later Greek examples such as Euripides' *Melanippie the Wise* (fr. 484) and Orpheus' song in Apollonius' *Argonautica* (1.496). Despite my reservations regarding Hesiod, many of these myths indeed offer compelling parallels with early Milesian philosophy. A creation myth from China, the *Pangu Kaitian* (220–80 CE), for example, begins with a confused state called Hundun. This is compared by Wang to 'an egg in a condition of chaos and indistinctness'.[31] The philosopher Huanzi interpreted Hundun as the primal matter of creation and described it as an 'uncarved block, not yet fashioned into things' and followed by a process of 'differentiation'. Afterwards Pangu, the primal deity, emerges from Hundun and begins a process of cosmic separation. When Pangu dies and his body is transformed into the myriad things, his breath becomes the wind, his voice thunder, his eyes the sun and the moon, etc. Ultimately the continuing unity of matter from Hundun onwards entails, as Wang outlines, that the 'analogy between parts of nature and the parts of the human body suggests that the world is conceived as a living organic whole on the model of a human body'.[32] In other words, the original unity of Hundun, according to Wang, ensures a total cosmic order and even pantheistic universe, which proceeds from the first act of separation to the current day.

The *Pangu Kaitian*, in its specific details and structure, is far from exceptional. Valerio Valeri similarly describes the Hawaiian *Kumulipo* as an evolutionary cosmogony based on 'the continuity of principle from the beginning to the end of the cosmogonic process'.[33] Indeed, not only have scholars overwhelmingly made sense of creation myths through monistic and orderly assumptions, the comparative theorist of religion Mircea Eliade has even described this kind of myth as a universal 'archaic ontology', arguing that

> a great number of creation myths present the original state – 'Chaos' – as a compact and homogenous mass in which no form could be distinguished; or as an egg-like sphere in which Sky and Earth were united, or as a giant man, etc. In all these myths Creation takes place by division of the egg into two parts, representing Sky and Earth – or by the breaking up of the Giant, or by the fragmentation of the unitary mass.[34]

It would appear then that Cornford's basic claim that a mythical cosmology could anticipate Milesian philosophical assumptions is well supported.[35] The problem, however, is that Cornford does not consider any alternatives. Indeed, despite the wide prevalence of monistic myths, Eliade's archaic ontology is by no means as universal as he imagines. As Puett and Smith have pointed out, this model has little to do with a vast number of totemist and animist myths, many of which are equally archaic.[36] Nor does it adequately describe many of the conflicting orientations found in early Mediterranean mythology, which often point towards chaos as much as cosmos.

A familiar starting point for approaching the diversity of cosmic assumptions in ancient Mediterranean cosmology is found in the biblical creation myth in Genesis. The opening of the King James translation is well known: 'In the beginning God created the heaven and the earth.' There could hardly be a clearer expression of an ordered beginning and the term 'created' strongly suggests the idea that this order proceeds *ex nihilo*. The Hebrew text, however, is more ambiguous and describes an initial formless waste (*tohu wabohu*) within chaotic waters (*tehom*). Furthermore, rather than an act of creation, the term *bara'* is closer to an act of separation or division of this pre-existing material.[37] Although the biblical narrative can hardly be described as a chaotic account, it is not entirely orderly either.[38] A similar position appears in Egypt, which again is often held as an exemplar of an ordered cosmos. However, disorder too plays an important role in the form of Nun. In the Heliopolis creation myth, the initial condition, Nun, is envisioned as a chaotic watery condition which eventually gives birth to Atum and an orderly cosmos. Like Hesiod's Chaos, Nun is a difficult word to define, moving between a watery abyss and the chaotic forces that threaten the state. Although some scholars do not strongly differentiate between Nun's two aspects, Assmann argues that the primordial Nun and the later negative or 'cratogonic chaos' are two separate phenomena which should not be confused.[39] This could be the case, yet it is possible that in Nun we see an ambiguous force which could be potentially drawn towards either order or chaos.[40]

Although the emphasis in the Genesis and Heliopolis creation stories remains by and large on the side of order,[41] other ancient models, including the Babylonian *Enûma Eliš*, the Hurro-Hittite *Song of Kumarbi*, and perhaps a Phoenician theogony later recounted by Philon of Byblos, shift the emphasis decidedly to chaos.[42] Like Hesiod's poem, these myths offer detailed descriptions of how the cosmos achieved its present state under the benevolent rule of a good king. However, this final harmony is often belied by more ambiguous beginnings under previously wayward rulers.[43] The starting point of the Mesopotamian *Enûma Eliš*, for example, is the mixing of Tiamat and Apsu which refuse to be separated:

> When the skies above were not yet named
> Nor Earth below pronounced by name
> Apsu, the first one, their begetter
> And maker Tiamat, who bore them all,
> Had mixed their waters together,
> But had not formed pastures, nor discovered reed beds;
> When yet no gods were manifest,
> Nor names pronounced, nor destinies decreed,
> Then gods were born within them.[44]

Tiamat, the primal deity, is not simply limited to the beginning of the account but a continuing force of destruction throughout the narrative until finally suppressed by the Babylonian Zeus, Marduk, who creates heaven and earth from the body of Tiamat.[45] In other words, rather than a neatly unfolding cosmos, the majority of the narrative describes a cosmic struggle – what Hermann Gunkel famously referred to as a *chaoskampf* – where, as Frankfort notes, 'the actual creation forms, not the beginning, but the end of the narrative'.[46]

The idea that the cosmos emerged from an earlier struggle is not only one which precedes Hesiod, it was also influential in the post-Hesiodic cosmology depicted in Ovid's *Metamorphosis* (1. 5–9):

> Ante mare et terras et quod tegit omnia caelum
> unus erat toto naturae vultus in orbe,
> quem dixere chaos: rudis indigestaque moles
> nec quicquam nisi pondus iners congestaque eodem
> non bene iunctarum discordia semina rerum.
>
> Before the seas and lands had been created, before the sky that covers everything,
> Nature displayed a single aspect only throughout the cosmos;
> Chaos was its name: a shapeless, unwrought mass
> of inert bulk and nothing more, with the discordant seeds of disconnected elements
> all heaped together in anarchic disarray.[47]

Ovid's Chaos entirely collapses Assmann's distinction between primordial and cratogenic chaos. Chaos is here unquestionably aligned with disorder, so much so that only through the help of god or nature is the condition resolved. Yet Chaos, as in Middle Kingdom Egypt, never quite disappears. According to Tarrant, 'Chaos in Ovid's Metamorphoses is not limited to the poem's opening episode but has a pervasive presence in the poem, both in the physical world and, more significantly, in the moral lives of human beings'.[48]

The ontology of chaos

Although the many links between Near Eastern cosmological accounts and Hesiod are well known,[49] the chaotic element in creation has not proven influential in modern interpretations. Instead, as we have seen, the majority of scholars have attempted to impose order upon Hesiod's poem and in particular to redefine his ambiguous descriptions of the first god. A notable exception, however, is found in Jean-Pierre Vernant, who staunchly rejected Cornford's association of Hesiod and the later Milesian monists.[50] In place of a neatly unfolding cosmos, Vernant argued that just as we have seen in poems such as the *Enûma Eliš*, Hesiod's early world is characterized by disorderly forces in need of an imposed order. According to Vernant, 'order did not emerge inevitably out of the dynamic play of the elements that made up the universe but was established in a dramatic fashion through the exploits of an agent' (that is, Zeus).[51] Vernant, however, does not present his theory as an alternative cosmological framework for understanding Hesiod's poem. On the contrary, Hesiod should not be understood in cosmological terms at all and Vernant places Hesiod's poem within an evolutionary scheme radically separating myth from philosophy. Hesiod's narrative, he argues, is 'a myth of sovereignty' and the poet 'remained a prisoner of its mythic framework'.[52] In this respect, Vernant's analysis ultimately falls within the same myth-versus-philosophy dichotomy that Cornford tried to escape from.

Despite Vernant's insistence on a dichotomy between myth and reason, I see no good reason why Hesiod's myth of sovereignty could not also reflect a particular cosmological understanding quite different from that argued for by the Milesians.[53] Indeed, Aristotle proposed just this in Book 14 of the *Metaphysics* (14.1091a–b) where he depicts two contrasting ways of worldmaking. The first group of cosmologists include the Persian Magi, the philosophical poet Pherecydes and the Presocratic philosophers Anaxagoras and Empedocles. In these cosmologies the Supreme Good is placed at the beginning of their cosmogonic accounts and the cosmologies describe harmonious and ordered accounts of cosmic development. Aristotle also includes his own prime mover within this category. The second group, on the other hand, do not start with the Good but place it at a later point in the narrative. In this group Aristotle may have Plato's nephew Speusippus and some Pythagoreans in mind. He definitely, however, also includes Hesiod and the earlier poets (14.1091b):

οἱ δὲ ποιηταὶ οἱ ἀρχαῖοι ταύτῃ ὁμοίως, ᾗ βασιλεύειν καὶ ἄρχειν φασὶν οὐ τοὺς πρώτους, οἷον νύκτα καὶ οὐρανὸν ἢ χάος ἢ ὠκεανόν, ἀλλὰ τὸν Δία.

The early poets agree with this view in so far as they assert that it was not the original forces – such as Night, Heaven, Chaos or Ocean – but Zeus who was king and ruler.[54]

Although both Aristotle and Vernant agree that Hesiod does not present a monistic and orderly cosmogony, Aristotle does not deny that Hesiod is a cosmological thinker. Instead, in this case at least, steering clear of the myth/reason dichotomy, Aristotle proposes that Hesiod's cosmogony depicts an alternate but coherent system where the Good is something secondary and imposed by Zeus upon an originally chaotic world.

Although Aristotle's reading of Hesiod has received a mixed reception among Hesiodic scholars, the narrative is not only consistent with a number of ancient Mediterranean cosmologies, but also anticipates recent debates among ontologically orientated anthropologists.[55] Creation myths, as noted in the introduction, play an important part in anthropological understandings of a particular society's underlying ontologies. In particular, Michael Scott has pointed out that many creation myths such as the *Pangu Kaitian* illustrate what he calls a mono-ontological orientation, a term that broadly overlaps with what I will discuss in Chapter 3 as pantheism or an ontology based on the double continuity of physicalities and interiorities. Scott outlines that the myths associated with this kind of ontology 'assume the consubstantiality of all things as a result of their common origin. Myths of mono-genesis represent processes of internal differentiation and separation within an original unity.'[56] Although mono-ontological creation myths are found the world over, they remain one variant among many. Philippe Descola, for example, argues that animist myths often reflect their ontological commitments to a continuity of souls and discontinuity of bodies, noting 'the question of the discontinuity of bodies is the obsessive theme that Amerindian myths convey at every opportunity'.[57] Descola makes a similar claim in relation to totemist myths such as the Australian Dreaming, which he argues are intimately related to their ontological assumptions of pluralism and difference. In Descola's words, these stories describe 'a world already divided into substantive essences that were actualized as classes of particular entities thanks to the intervention of the Dream-beings'.[58] When it comes to the Greeks, or indeed any analogist society, Descola unfortunately has less to say about how their creation stories align with their assumptions of ontological difference and discontinuity. Scott suggests that this curious omission may be because

> the cosmogonic myths of analogists are not always reliable indices of how analogism works; such myths often seem to present scenarios of original continuity in need of differentiation in ways that obscure rather than reveal the premises of double discontinuity Descola discerns in analogism.[59]

In other words, for Scott the issue has been sidelined because analogist cosmologies, rather than emphasizing discontinuity, often deceptively resemble pantheist or mono-ontological cosmologies.

Although it may sometimes be the case that analogist societies describe pantheist myths, it would be remarkable if not a single analogist creation story bore any resemblance to their more prevalent ontological assumptions. Nor would it lend much support for the utility of analogism as an ontological classification. An alternative possibility is that, just as we have seen in Cornford's reading, the similarities between analogist and pantheist creation accounts may have been exaggerated by a tendency to neglect chaotic elements and simply assume the presence of order.[60] Indeed, it may well be that poems such as the *Enûma Eliš* provide clear examples of analogist cosmological myths and have simply not been recognized as such. Although analogist creation myths have not received much analytic attention, a potential theoretical parallel is provided by Scott's description of poly-ontologies.[61] According to Scott, poly-ontologies, in contrast with mono-ontologies, understand 'the universe as the sum of multiple spontaneously generated and essentially different categories of being'.[62] Scott further outlines how poly-ontologies and mono-ontologies also have contrasting views on cosmic order. In mono-ontologies, order exists from the very beginning and often guides creation in a teleological manner. In poly-ontologies, no such overarching order exists. Instead, order appears as something secondary and imposed upon an earlier chaotic state. In the words of Valeri, this kind of cosmogony puts 'the parts ontologically before the whole' and moves from an initial diversity to a temporary unity. Consequently, order within poly-ontologies rather than an emergent and guiding force is seen as a secondary and 'reversible result'.[63] A good example of this kind of cosmogony appears in Gregory Bateson's summary of the New Guinea Iatmul creation myth:

> They say that in the beginning the crocodile Kavwokmali paddled with his front legs and with his hind legs; and his paddling kept the mud suspended in the water. The great culture hero, Kevembuangga, came with his spear and killed Kavwokmali. After that the mud settled and dry land was formed. Kevembuangga then stamped with his foot on the dry land, i.e., he proudly demonstrated 'that it was good'.[64]

Rather than a neatly unfolding flower petal in which order is implicit from the beginning, for the Iatmul, Bateson argues, order only appears if disorder is opposed.[65]

Although Scott, Bateson and Valeri are discussing totemist myths, I argue that many of the characteristics Scott attributes to poly-ontologies are also compatible with analogist cosmologies. Indeed, while there are certainly differences between the Solomon Islands and the Cyclades, poly-ontologies show a number of striking similarities to Vernant's and Aristotle's interpretations of Hesiod's poem. Moreover, these similarities are – ontologically speaking – not surprising, as both totemist and analogist ontologies have a complex history in

Descola's thought and originally shared a single schema.[66] While Descola has since revised this model, the ontological assumptions underlying totemism and analogism retain a similar focus on discontinuity and William Matthews has persuasively argued for revising Descola's fourfold classification scheme and relocating totemism 'as a genus of Analogism'.[67] I will return to this debate in Chapter 3. Presently, it is sufficient to note that given totemism's and analogism's shared stress on ontological difference, it would not be surprising if their respective cosmogonic myths showed certain similarities.

Rethinking the opening of Hesiod's *Theogony*

Descola's ontologies are, of course, ideals rather than realities. While they present a useful means of broadening our conceptual horizons and re-examining our underlying prejudices, their value ultimately lies in their potential to clarify the ethnographic material itself, and whether Hesiod's *Theogony* is best understood as an expression of an analogist or pantheist ontology awaits an analysis of the poem itself. In other words, we must go back to the very beginning of the world (*Theog.* 116–20):

> ἦ τοι μὲν πρώτιστα Χάος γένετ', αὐτὰρ ἔπειτα
> Γαῖ' εὐρύστερνος, πάντων ἕδος ἀσφαλὲς αἰεὶ
> ἀθανάτων, οἳ ἔχουσι κάρη νιφόεντος Ὀλύμπου,
> Τάρταρά τ' ἠερόεντα μυχῷ χθονὸς εὐρυοδείης,
> ἠδ' Ἔρος, ὃς κάλλιστος ἐν ἀθανάτοισι θεοῖσι

> In truth, first of all Chaos came to be, and then broad-breasted Earth, the ever immovable seat of all the immortals who possess snowy Olympus' peak and murky Tartarus in the depths of the broad-pathed earth, and Eros, who is the most beautiful among the immortal gods.

Despite the debates surrounding this passage, in one respect at least Hesiod's language is clear: Chaos comes first. The use of ἦ τοι μὲν not only conveys a contrast with the preceding figures but imbues the words that follow with conviction.[68] Πρώτιστα signifies not simply first but absolutely first or very first.[69] Γένετ' may be translated as 'came into being' or 'was born'.[70] And just to make sure we understand the order of this sequence, the firstness of Chaos is complemented by αὐτὰρ ἔπειτα, a traditional couplet used to mark temporal sequences.[71] The usual translation of αὐτὰρ ἔπειτα is something like 'only then', 'thereafter'. In short, Chaos is not preceded by primal matter, as Cornford said, nor is he symbolically first but really second, as Miller argues.[72] Chaos is simply first and Hesiod provides a number of complementary terms within a temporal sequence to reinforce this point. We may then literally read these lines as: 'In truth, Chaos was born absolutely first, and then afterwards came broad-breasted Gaia.'

If Chaos is born first, he is, however, shortly followed by Gaia, Tartarus and Eros. Here we again encounter further interpretative problems and there is no consensus on how to understand Hesiod's primordial deities, or even which gods count as primordial. Theories range from excluding Tartarus, to seeing him as an important cosmological principle. Miller, for example, places Tartarus and Gaia as the central protagonists in his interpretation. However, I am inclined to read the unusual form Τάρταρα (119) not as a nominative but as an accusative and a location within Gaia.[73] This still leaves us with a triad comprised of Chaos, Eros and Gaia. Although secondary, Hesiod does not describe these gods as the children of Chaos. In fact, they simply appear as inexplicably as Chaos did before them. In other words, they have separate origins.[74] Given the predominantly monistic interpretations imposed on Hesiod, the idea that the world starts with three separate divine beings may seem rather strange. Greek cosmological speculation, however, at some point or other attempted almost every possible combination of beginnings. In Pherecydes' cosmological account (DK 7 B1), for example, we see a primal triad of Chthonie (chthonic Earth) and two forces, Zas (similar to Zeus) and Chronos (time).[75] Parmenides (DK 28 B 9) discusses the cosmos in terms of the interplay of two elements, light and night, and Empedocles (DK 31 B 17) in terms of the four roots and Love and Strife.

Given the widespread occurrence of poly-ontological starting points in ancient Greece, there is no reason not to follow Hesiod's text to the letter at this point. However, while accepting multiple points of origins certainly complicates our interpretation, it should be stressed that it in no way excludes that Hesiod's poem shows mono-ontological characteristics. This is arguably the case with Pherecydes' theogony, where three primal gods work together to form a harmonious world. Similarly, Hesiod's triad of Chaos, Gaia and Eros could be interpreted as co-creators of an ordered totality. As Clay puts it, 'the *Theogony* constitutes an attempt to understand the cosmos as the product of a genealogical evolution and a process of individuation that finally leads to the formation of a stable cosmos and ultimately achieves its telos under the tutelage of Zeus'.[76] Chaos, in this reading, is a mysterious starting point. Gaia, playing a much more active role, is a kind of material principle and mother of almost everything. A versatile goddess, she is simultaneously the ground on which mortals walk, the mother of nearly everything, and an agent who can offer counsel and advice to Zeus. How we are to understand Eros is less clear. Hesiod says almost nothing about him, yet given his prominent place in the *Theogony* it is likely that he is introduced as an initiator of sexual relations.[77] According to Calame, 'Eros was thus at once a primordial deity and a metaphysical principal, a generating power that constructed and animated the relations between things, between men, and between gods'.[78] This view is certainly how later interpreters appropriated Hesiod's Eros and it makes sense of the sexual relations which follow the god's appearance.[79] In this way, it may be supposed that these three divinities – through a long genealogy of gods including Kronos, Zeus and Apollo – generate the harmonious world we know today.

The cosmos as a happy family tree is an attractive interpretation and one that resonates with many anthropological understandings of comparative mythical material. Valeri, for example, in relation to Hawaiian cosmogonies, has argued that 'reducing the entire cosmos to genealogy is the most elementary and persuasive way to represent the unity of the world as the expression of a single order'.[80] However, although many analogist cosmogonies do depict extensive family trees, in practice Valeri admits that these myths are often more complex. Hesiod's *Theogony* is no exception. Indeed, for Hesiod the cosmos is not the product of a single genealogy but of two extensive lineages that never intersect. While the illustrious family of Gaia including the Titans and Olympians is well known, the salient fact that Chaos also has an extensive family tree has received comparatively little attention from Hesiodic scholars, who either etymologize Chaos away as a gap or see him more generally as an ambiguous starting point with little importance in the later narrative. For Hesiod, however, Chaos was not only honoured as the firstborn deity, he was the father of a long lineage that rivals that of Gaia and perpetually threatens cosmic stability.

The rival genealogies of Chaos and Gaia often occupy little role in philosophical discussions of Hesiod's poem. Indeed, after the triad of Chaos, Gaia and Eros, Hesiod's account shifts from abstract and ambiguous gods to a more familiar mythic narrative describing struggles among anthropomorphic deities. And with this mythical turn many philosophical interpreters lose interest and consider that Hesiod abandons his philosophic narrative for the sake of a more conventional (and non-philosophic) account.[81] This is unfortunate, as it is only at this point that Hesiod begins to describe the actual roles of these beings and provide us with any clear means of making sense of them. Eros, perhaps taking charge of sexual relations, is not spoken of anymore and the narrative turns to Gaia, who bears Ouranos and in turn a long genealogy of gods, culminating in

Zeus. I will return to this genealogy shortly. Presently, however, it is worth noting that Gaia is not the only figure with an impressive lineage and Hesiod also recounts how Chaos is the father of a long genealogy which never intersects with that of Gaia.[82] This rival genealogy starts when Chaos, by himself, gives birth to Erebus and Night. The pair in turn, in the only sexual relation among the children of Chaos, bear their opposites, Aither and Day. Afterwards Night produces a formidable list of predominantly negative forces including Resentment, Deceit, Old Age and Strife. Night's child Strife, continuing this long list of plagues, bears 'Toil and Forgetfulness and Hunger and tearful Pains, and Combats and Battles and Murders and Slaughters, and Strifes and Lies and Disputes, and Lawlessness and Recklessness, much like one another' (226–30).[83]

Although these figures are often downplayed, abstract gods play a very important role in Hesiod's poem and throughout the *Theogony* Hesiod introduces them at pivotal points in the narrative as a means of expressing underlying problems or solutions.[84] While I will discuss several examples of Hesiod's strategic use of abstractions in time, the first and longest example of his strategic use of abstract gods appears in Chaos' descendants, which emerge as a problematic group continuously threatening to destroy the cosmos. In this respect, Chaos, far more than a gap or an ambiguous starting point, appears as a continuing disorderly force which is felt throughout the narrative. This makes Chaos and his children a kind of counterpart to the unions created by Eros. As Miller puts it, 'whereas Χάος signifies breach and separation, Ἔρος signifies attraction and coming-together'.[85] In other words, Chaos and Eros are integral components of the cosmos and opposing gods. And just as we may interpret Eros' influence at the basis of every sexual union, in each instance of strife, war and enmity, we see the continuing power of Chaos.

Ouranos and Kronos or how *not* to rule the cosmos

Despite efforts to cleanse Hesiod's poem of Chaos, as the narrative moves towards what West calls 'the backbone of the *Theogony*', this possibility collapses altogether.[86] Indeed, at this point even sympathetic readers of Hesiod are inclined to agree that the poet abandons his truly philosophic interests in favour of mythical stories.[87] Other than a deeply held and somewhat arbitrary association between anthropomorphic gods and irrationality, there is no real reason why an exclusively mythic narrative should be considered less philosophically interesting than the opening cosmogony.[88] Indeed, Aristotle in the *Metaphysics* (14.1091a–b) not only made no such division, but saw in the conclusion of the mythical fights the expression of Hesiod's concept of the Good.[89] Following in his footsteps, I will argue that the myth of succession is Hesiod's clearest expression of the cosmos as a problem. The myth of succession begins when Gaia bears Ouranos, one equal to herself (ἶσον ἑαυτῇ) (126–7). This pair provides an excellent example of the dual influence of Eros and Chaos. Initially split by chaotic division, Eros attempts to reconcile this division by inspiring Ouranos to literally wrap himself around Gaia. Through this act of love, Ouranos plunges the world into darkness and reverses the very differentiation that first bore him. However, this erotic union, which initially hinders the development of the cosmos, has the side effect of producing diversity and Gaia bears the Titans. Ouranos, despising his own offspring, forces the Titans under the earth. Gaia in retaliation attempts to punish this behaviour by urging her children to castrate their father. Kronos, the youngest, agrees and having defeated Ouranos, casts his testicles into the sea. In this way, Kronos' ascension reinstates the initial division between Ouranos and Gaia and once more separates the heaven from the earth. However, the new king is no wiser than his father. After copulating with another feminine power closely associated with earth, Rhea, Kronos is warned that his children will one day overthrow his rule. To avoid this disaster Kronos, rather than force his children under the ground, eats each child as soon as they emerge from Rhea's womb. In other words, Kronos' behaviour simply repeats the scandalous acts of his father.

While this narrative has proven so abhorrent to philosophers, this series of kings and conquerors is in fact the closest thing we have to a repeated and ordered pattern in the *Theogony*. Moreover, this pattern is by no means unique to Hesiod and appears in a number of related myths such as the Babylonian *Enûma Eliš*, the Hurro-Hittite *Song of Kumarbi* and the Phoenician theogony recounted by Philon of Byblos.[90] Littleton has proposed that all these variations follow a single pattern:

> (1) *generations are born*, (2) *parents aggress against their offspring*, (3) *offspring aggress against their parents*, and (4) *offspring replace their parents*. The first category introduces the idea of succession; the second category states a thesis; the third category serves as its antithesis; and the final category can be viewed as a synthesis.[91]

In Littleton's somewhat Hegelian pattern, a structurally inclined analyst might note a neat set of oppositions such as sky/earth, male/female, parents/children governed by Chaos and Eros. Indeed, many interpreters have attempted to find such an underlying developmental pattern in this sequence. However, despite the real presence of oppositions such as male and female, Hesiod's characters rarely neatly align with these classificatory categories. Kronos, for example, is initially associated with female powers such as Gaia. However, after defeating Ouranos, he occupies a male role, only to alternate again when defeated by Zeus. For this reason, rather than a developing order, I argue that these conflicts are illustrations of a cosmos unable to get started. This is not to deny that the world increasingly develops and diversifies. Indeed, as each generation advances, the cosmos proliferates with beings and erotic partnerships. My point is simply that development is not synonymous with teleology and from the first batch of children on, the world gets increasingly strange as hybrid beings with hundreds of hands and almost as many heads emerge and populate the earth.

Hybrids present a particular problem for theorizing Hesiod's poem as an example of ordered and neatly unfolding patterns. Clay, for example, describes hybrids as essentially disruptive creatures who 'violate the classificatory system of the *Theogony* and subvert the process of individuation and articulation that underlies the Hesiodic scheme of evolution'.[92] This view, however, is not really supported by the text. The Hundred Handers are fearsome gods, yet far from disrupting the order of the cosmos, they are the allies of Zeus. The Titans, on the other hand, are anthropomorphic beings, yet appear as disruptive forces. If hybrids seem to straddle the sides of order and disorder simultaneously, it is somewhat arbitrary to see them as subverting 'the process of individuation and articulation'. Instead, I propose that hybrids exemplify the current cosmic situation, not as one whose teleological scheme is hindered, but as one which refuses categorization altogether.[93] Rather than an ordered system, what Hesiod presents is a world defined by contradictions.

Despite the scholarly preference for neatly unfolding narratives, that Ouranos and Kronos rule over chaotic rather than progressive kingdoms should hardly be surprising. Indeed, it was taken for granted by both Homer (*Od.* 19.109–14) and Hesiod (*WD* 225–40) that the character of kings produces analogous effects on the surrounding environment. For the early poets, a good king does more than encourage a city to flourish; his rule analogously extends to fertile crops, rich herds, and wives who 'give birth to children who resemble their parents'. On the other hand, even a single bad man 'who sins and devises wicked deeds' can be the downfall of a whole city (*WD* 239–40). There is no better example of Hesiod's problematic cosmos and wayward king than the paradoxical god and ruler Kronos. Indeed, for Hesiod and the Greeks at large, Kronos is a rather strange deity – at times characterized as the eater of children (*Theog.* 473), at others as the benevolent leader of a utopian afterlife (*WD* 110–20). As Henk Versnel notes in his influential treatment of Kronos in myth and ritual, Kronos' rule is one of patricide, infanticide and cannibalism and shows 'a complete absence of moral standards'.[94] As a result, the cosmos Kronos rules is also one marked by ambivalence, including the birth of hybrid and monstrous beings such as the Echidna, whom Hesiod describes as 'not at all similar to mortal human beings or to the immortals gods … half a quick-eyed beautiful-cheeked nymph, but half a monstrous snake, terrible and great, shimmering, eating raw flesh, under the hidden places of the holy earth' (*Theog.* 296–9). The association between Kronos and confusion was long-lasting and appears, for example, in the Athenian *Kronia*, a festival much like the better-known Roman Saturnalia, where masters and servants ate side by side. Versnel, neatly capturing these contradictory images, describes the Kronia as a period of 'marked ambivalence in the Greek concept of harmony: the ideal of freedom and abundance is unstable, it cannot last, because it carries the real seed of social anomie and anarchy'.[95]

Kronos' rule and his relationship with early humanity will be discussed in more detail in the following chapter. Presently, it is sufficient to note that the rules of Ouranos and Kronos are decidedly anti-cosmic and that their disorderly conduct and kinship extends not only to the inhabitants of the world, but to the cosmos as a whole. This is a period where rulers repeatedly change hands and even the separation between heaven and earth refuses to remain in place. Indeed, when precisely Gaia and Ouranos are distinguished is far less clear than is often realized. In some respects, we may see this occurring when Gaia gives birth to Ouranos (126). Yet immediately after this Kronos must differentiate them again by castrating his father (164–82). Even at this stage the division is incomplete and full differentiation awaits Zeus' appointment of trusty Atlas, who places Ouranos on his shoulders and stands at a pivotal and newly built intersection of the gates of Night and Day. The question of how Ouranos, Gaia, Night and Day existed before these clear divisions were put in place is not answered. Like Kronos' combination of peace and love, the scene is unimaginable and nicely encapsulates Hesiod's early cosmos as a world of ambiguity, ever on the verge of collapsing, yet never doing so. This unimaginable world comes to its climax with Typhoeus, the seven-headed dragon Clay dubs '*acosmia* incarnate'.[96] In this monumental battle nothing is clear. Zeus or Typhoeus may win and rule over very different worlds. Indeed, even when Zeus defeats his enemy and secures his reign, the image is bleak. The world is all but destroyed in an apocalyptic conflagration (860–8). This conflagration, however, also has a positive side: Zeus' rule effectively begins with a blank canvas.

Zeus, Oedipus and the King of Fiji

I have argued so far that the early cosmos appears not as a neatly unfolding order but as a problem. Ouranos and Kronos recognize this situation but fail in their different attempts at subduing their children. The idea that the world is something that needs to be solved could be seen as an example of a philosophical *aporia*, yet I would instead like to examine it in terms of another, perhaps equally arbitrary category: the riddle.[97] While there is no shortage of riddles in Greek mythology, easily the most famous was that set by the Sphinx. According to Apollodorus (3.5.8), prior to eating her interlocutor she would ask:

τί ἐστιν μίαν ἔχον φωνὴν τετράπουν καὶ δίπουν καὶ τρίπουν γίνεται;

What is that which has one voice and yet becomes four-footed and two-footed and three-footed?[98]

While the question seemingly presents a series of bizarre hybrid beings which confound all reason – arguably an appropriate description of the Sphinx herself – the initial plurality is reducible to a unity. The answer, as is well known, is man moving through infancy, maturity and old age. Oedipus not only unravels this mystery but in doing so takes the crown. Hesiod's Zeus, in many respects, finds himself in a similar situation to Oedipus. His story begins as an underdog. Kronos is now in charge and fearing that he will be replaced by one of his children, he eats them as soon as they are born. When Zeus is born, his mother Rhea hides him under the earth and offers a stone to Kronos in place of the child. Zeus himself is raised in seclusion and once fully grown, enlists the help of the previously persecuted Hundred Handers, overthrows Kronos and takes his place. At this point there is no indication that Zeus' tale will be any different from his predecessors. Like Ouranos and Kronos, he too is warned of an impending threat to his kingdom. Yet Zeus avoids this by correctly solving the riddle. Rather than wait to eat his superior child, Zeus eats the mother, Metis.

At first glance, Zeus' violent act of cannibalism may seem to have little in common with Oedipus' wit, yet as astutely described by Detienne and Vernant, the narrative, like the Sphynx's riddle, is a play on words.[99] I noted earlier that Hesiod introduces abstractions to make definite points. In particular, I argued that the children of Chaos are not definite personalities in the narrative but utilized to express the problematic state of the world. This is also the case for the goddess Metis who is first introduced at this point. Her name literally means cunning intelligence, which is an attribute of pivotal importance to Hesiod's narrative. Indeed, it was precisely through such an act of *metis* that Rhea tricked

Kronos into eating a stone instead of Zeus (471). Detienne and Vernant describe these details as part of a larger opposition between male force βία versus female intelligence expressed by the terms μῆτις and δόλος. However, although there is a general male/female opposition in the scheme of the *Theogony*, a similar kind of cunning intelligence also appears in relation to males such as Kronos (495) and Prometheus (547, 559). In this respect, instead of a strictly gendered binary opposition, μῆτις is perhaps better viewed as a perennial problem in the cosmos which appears in challenges to the king's rule. Despite this, Detienne and Vernant's larger point holds; Zeus' act is not simply a case of eating a goddess, but of eating a word, an abstract force which caused the downfall of the previous kings. In doing so he combines within himself the power and intelligence that will ensure the continuity of his rule.[100]

The idea of a god or king consolidating power through the encompassment of another force is not only a common Greek and Near Eastern trope, it is found in analogistic societies the world over.[101] Marshall Sahlins refers to it as the myth of the stranger king, a narrative where a foreign or external power exerts his authority upon initially egalitarian oppositions. In doing so, the king combines the previous oppositions of the conquered people and himself into a single person. In Sahlins' words, the king becomes a 'conjunction of chief and people, sea and land, [and] generates a synthetic term, the sovereign power: itself male and female, a combination of *celeritas* and *gravitas*'.[102] The reference to '*celeritas* and *gravitas*' emphasizes Sahlins' debt to comparativist and classicist Georges Dumézil, yet there is also a clear resonance here with anthropologist Louis Dumont's idea of hierarchy as 'the encompassment of the contrary'.[103] The classic example Dumont uses is that of Adam and Eve:

> God creates Adam first, the undifferentiated man, the prototype of 'mankind'. In a second stage, he extracts a different being from this first Adam. In this strange operation, on the one hand, Adam has changed identity; from being undifferentiated, he has become male. On the other hand, a being has appeared who is both a member of the human species and different from the main representative of the species. In his entirety, Adam – or 'man' in our language – is two things in one: the representative of the species mankind and the prototype of the male individuals of this species ... This hierarchical relation is, very generally, that between a whole (or a set) and an element of this whole (or set).[104]

In other words, the encompassing relation, male, contains both male and female oppositions in one, and thus moves from the equal and problematic male/female opposition to the male or female part against a male–female whole. If in the above example Dumont presents the relation as something innate from the very creation of woman, what is interesting in Sahlins' description is the presence of two contrastive stages, disorder and order,[105] or an initial riddle concerning ambiguous relations and a solution that unifies the many into an ordered hierarchal whole.[106] In Hesiodic terms, this appears as a shift from the cosmos and problematic relations of force (βία) and intelligence (μῆτις) as separate and problematic relations that prevent cosmic growth, to a new hierarchal order that encompasses force and intelligence into a new totality: Zeus.[107] It is only with the introduction of hierarchal relations that we can speak of anything approaching cosmic order.

Making a cosmos out of chaos

While the symbolic significance of Zeus' ingestion of Metis is a familiar point, only rarely is the essential inconsistency between the early and later stages of Hesiod's cosmos stressed. For example, Clay mentions the key differences between Zeus and the previous rulers, yet nonetheless sees this as the expression of the cosmos' *telos*.[108] This is a somewhat strange conclusion and arguably the radical innovations of Zeus' rule stress precisely the opposite: discontinuity with all that went before. The point I wish to stress in this chapter is that there is no cosmos prior to the rule of Zeus and even afterwards, Zeus' power has limitations. Indeed, Zeus, rather than a creator god, is an organizer, obsessed with dividing portions in a contested and fragile world. In stark contrast to the tyrannical rule of his ancestors, Zeus' early reign is associated with negotiating and bestowing honours διέταξεν ὁμῶς καὶ ἐπέφραδε τιμάς (73, 855) apportioning shares μείρομαι (411–15, 424–8) and repeatedly in terms of allotting honours γέρᾶ (393, 396, 427).[109] This language, as I will explore in more detail in the next chapter, is not so much that of creation as of a king's skilful distribution at a feast. Moreover, if there is no real creation, neither is there any destruction and even rival gods such as Typhoeus and the Titans are imprisoned and encircled by a substantial bronze fence in the underworld rather than eliminated (746–51). Indeed, in his famous underworld description, Hesiod is at pains to describe how everything, even Chaos, receives a proper place in Zeus' cosmos.[110] As Bruce Lincoln stresses:

> The primal near-emptiness has been annexed, repositioned and put to new use. Now situated between the above and the below, the emptiness of Chaos

constitutes an uncrossable barrier that will keep the vanquished in their prison and Zeus on his throne.[111]

This relocation is something that should be stressed. In Hesiod's world, Chaos is not something that can ever be surmounted. It can, however, be utilized. This reflects a general theme on good and evil in Hesiodic poetry. Strife is admittedly bad. Yet at the same time there exists another Strife which, if properly used, is beneficial. Hesiod's description of two Strifes in the *Works and Days* (11–24) indicates the potential of utilizing even negative qualities towards positive ends. Indeed, in the *Theogony* not only does Zeus safely relocate and utilize Chaos, he proves himself equally adept at strategic marriages and his mastery of Eros gives birth to the most famous Olympian gods including Apollo, Artemis, Ares and Dionysus. In his description of this harmonizing, Hesiod (*Theog.* 901–2) once again turns to his favourite device, abstract gods, narrating how Zeus in his marriage to Right (θέμις) fathers the Seasons ("Ώρας), Good Order (Εὐνουμίην), Justice (Δίκην) and Peace (Εἰρήνην). As Clay stresses, these abstract deities form clear contrasts to the earlier Strife, Disorder and Battles associated with the offspring of Chaos.[112] These are the gifts that Zeus bestows upon mortals, which, while never quite removing their suffering, will potentially allow brief respite from a mostly hostile world. Emblematic of the fundamentally new order introduced by Zeus is the second birth of the Moirai. This second birth has been interpreted as an oversight of Hesiod, a slip in his vast series of genealogies.[113] However, given the context of Zeus' reordering of the universe and use of abstract deities throughout the poem, there could be no more appropriate illustration of the cosmos' new-found stability than a description of a second generation of goddesses signifying order, apportionment and destiny.[114]

Conclusion

In this chapter I have discussed Hesiod's *Theogony* as an analogist cosmology which places disorder at the heart of Hesiod's vision of creation. In this respect, I have departed from the dominant monistic interpretations. However, it might be noted that if the chaotic journey I have described differs from teleological interpretations, the endpoint remains the same. Indeed, we might be tempted to see the riddle solver Zeus as a kind of *deus ex machina* resolving all the contradictions that preceded him and finally creating a permanently ordered world.[115] While this is certainly hammered home in the text where 'it is not possible to deceive or go beyond the will of Zeus' (*Theog.* 613), there is a good deal that suggests that Chaos is a riddle never fully resolved. First, Zeus does not destroy his enemies, he simply relocates them. Secondly, Zeus envisions that his order may be breached and takes the precaution of making the gods swear an oath on the River Styx and outlines severe punishments if any should resist his rule (793–806). Although no acts of disobedience occur in Hesiod's *Theogony*, which is hardly the place to question Zeus' authority, there are many references in Homer and later poetry to such a possibility. For example, in the *Iliad* we are told that Hera, Poseidon and Athena once attempted to overthrow Zeus (1.396–406). This is a theme which is given full force in Aeschylus' *Prometheia* where the danger of succession appears again and we are told that Zeus, like Kronos, 'shall bear a son mightier than his father' (755–75). The potential instability of the cosmos is a reflection of the world's fragile harmony and underlying ontological assumption of difference. Although Greek scholarship has attempted to downplay the extent of everyday chaos, in Babylon we find clearer examples of chaos' potential return. Indeed, while the rule of the Babylonian Zeus, Marduk, remains the ideal, events frequently intervene that challenge this, including his imprisonment during the New Year festival. These myths indicate that order in Babylon was not a given, but an agreement constantly renewed. In Marduk's case this renewal was re-enacted yearly during the Atiku festival, an event that symbolized the recreation of the cosmos and Marduk's continuing triumph over disorder. According to Somer, 'the Babylonian Akitu brought back chaos in order that chaos could be expelled'.[116] Greece, of course, is not Babylon, and the full force of chaos is never stated so strongly. Yet, its power remains. Indeed, in both Greece and Babylon, chaos appears as a force that can never be eradicated but only suppressed. While Zeus, of course, is the archetype cosmic negotiator, humans also play a part in maintaining this tentative harmony. Their place in this world and their contribution to maintaining cosmic order is the subject of the next chapter.

2

Beyond the Golden Age: Sacrifice, Sharing and Affinity in Hesiod's Mekone

If Hesiod's *Theogony* describes an initially chaotic cosmos where gods fought with gods and hybrid monsters populated the earth, these horrors seem to have had little impact on humanity. Indeed, in dramatic contrast to the sufferings of the Olympians, humans are often described as living within a Golden Age, a wondrous period where even the rigid boundaries between mortal and immortal blurred and in some readings dissolved completely.[1] This utopic existence we are told came to an end in Mekone when Prometheus and Zeus negotiated man's destiny over the body of a sacrificial ox. Humans left the table of the gods to toil in the fields, and the gods ascended to the sky. In this chapter, I will argue that this well-known story is nowhere found in the poetry of Hesiod. It is a narrative woven out of multiple poems and stitched into a tragic tale of loss and separation. By placing Mekone within its wider theogonic context, I argue for a very different understanding of the Golden Age, sacrifice and humanity's relationship with the gods. Rather than interpreting Prometheus' encounter with Zeus in terms of a fall and the establishment of an unbridgeable chasm between mortals and immortals, I argue that the myth describes the creative potentials of sharing food and the negotiation of a complex affinal tie between humans and gods through sacrifice.

Hesiod and human origins

Humanity's loss of immortality and expulsion from the company of the gods was a theme Lévi-Strauss repeatedly returned to in his discussions of American mythology. In his *Mythologies* he recounts a Tenetehara myth describing how

> the first man, created by the demiurge, lived in innocence, although his penis was always in a state of erection. He tried in vain to induce detumescence by

sprinkling it with a manioc beverage. The first woman, having been instructed by the water spirit (who had subsequently been castrated and killed by her husband), taught the man how to soften his penis through copulation. When the demiurge saw the limp penis, he became angry and said: 'Henceforth your penis will be soft, you will make children, and then you will die: later when your child grows, he will make another child, and in turn he will die'.

M77. Tenetehara. 'How men lost immortality'[2]

The story of innocence, deceit, and ultimately the loss of paradise is not only common among the indigenous people of Brazil, it is found the world over. In *The Yearning for Paradise in Primitive Tradition* the comparative theorist of religion, Mircea Eliade, describes a universal longing for a lost world, a return to a place outside time or an *illud tempus* 'which is always the same, which belongs to eternity'.[3] The earliest literary description of paradise is sometimes linked to the Sumerian Dilmun, a site of creation described as 'a land that is "pure", "clean" and "bright"; a "land of the living" which knows neither sickness nor death'.[4] Yet we find perhaps the most famous variation on this theme in the book of Genesis where Adam and Eve are said to freely converse with God and enjoy the bounties of the earth without labour (Genesis 2.7–9). In some paradise myths, the easy relation between humans and god/s is even extended to animals who can speak.[5] However, despite the many variations these myths present, they often take a similar turn; human nature proves imperfect or a non-human agent proves ambivalent and paradise is lost.[6]

It may come as little surprise to hear that the Greeks told similar stories. In fact, they told dozens of them. Plato, for example, in the *Statesman* describes a utopic existence during the age of Kronos where gods and humans live in close community, crops shoot out of the earth without labour, and animals speak (*Politicus* 272c).[7] Similarly, in a myth we will discuss in more detail in Chapter 4, the philosopher Empedocles recounts a time when humans, gods and animals lived in close proximity during the Age of Cypris or Aphrodite. However, as is usually the case, Empedocles' paradise was short-lived, and a fall was enacted through humanity's greed and the sacrifice of a bull (DK 31 B 128):

ταύρων δ' ἀκρήτοισι φόνοις οὐ δεύετο βωμός,
ἀλλὰ μύσος τοῦτ' ἔσκεν ἐν ἀνθρώποισι μέγιστον,
θυμὸν ἀπορραίσαντας ἐέδμεναι ἠέα γυῖα.

The altar was not moistened with the pure blood of bulls,
but this was the greatest abomination to men,
to take away their life and devour their goodly limbs.[8]

This transgression leads to the hardships that characterize the human condition and the dissolution of the once close bonds between mortals, animals and gods. Although Empedocles' myth was idiosyncratic in certain details, it was far from unique. Indeed, Plato, Empedocles and most other classical descriptions of paradise developed their stories in reference to the poetry of Hesiod and his famous description of the first sacrifice at Mekone (*Theog.* 535–47):

> καὶ γὰρ ὅτ' ἐκρίνοντο θεοὶ θνητοί τ' ἄνθρωποι
> Μηκώνῃ, τότ' ἔπειτα μέγαν βοῦν πρόφρονι θυμῷ
> δασσάμενος προέθηκε, Διὸς νόον ἐξαπαφίσκων.
> τῷ μὲν γὰρ σάρκας τε καὶ ἔγκατα πίονα δημῷ
> ἐν ῥινῷ κατέθηκε καλύψας γαστρὶ βοείῃ,
> τῷ δ' αὖτ' ὀστέα λευκὰ βοὸς δολίῃ ἐπὶ τέχνῃ
> εὐθετίσας κατέθηκε καλύψας ἀργέτι δημῷ.
> δὴ τότε μιν προσέειπε πατὴρ ἀνδρῶν τε θεῶν τε:
>
> Ἰαπετιονίδη, πάντων ἀριδείκετ' ἀνάκτων,
> ὦ πέπον, ὡς ἑτεροζήλως διεδάσσαο μοίρας.

> For when gods and mortal men were reaching a settlement in Mekone, with eager spirit he [Prometheus] divided up a great ox and, trying to deceive Zeus' mind, set it before him. For he set down on the skin before him the meat and the innards, rich with fat, hiding them in the ox's stomach; and then he set down before him in turn the ox's white bones, arranging them with deceptive craft, hiding them with gleaming fat.

> Then the father of men and of gods addressed him: 'Son of Iapetus, eminent among all rulers, my fine fellow, how unfairly you have divided up the portions!'[9]

Following the Titan's attempt to deceive Zeus with two unequal shares of meat, the king of the gods is asked to choose. Given the options, we might expect Zeus to either anticipate Prometheus' plan and take the superior share of meat despite its unattractive covering, or to be fooled by the cunning Titan and choose the inferior but aesthetically more pleasing cut. Surprisingly, he does neither and Zeus, we are told, perceiving Prometheus' trick, deliberately chooses the animal's bones. The episode concludes with an aetiological note that from this day on humans sacrifice to the gods in this manner (556–7).

Although it is clear that humanity's fate is intimately linked to Prometheus' deception, many puzzles continue to surround Hesiod's paradise myth. Indeed, both ancient and modern commentators have endlessly asked why humans receive the superior share of meat yet the worse destiny.[10] Equally puzzling is

Zeus' reaction; if Prometheus' trick was really unsuccessful, why does he get so angry about it?[11] Yet perhaps the most debated aspect of all is what precisely Hesiod means by the expression 'ἐκρίνοντο θεοὶ θνητοί τ' ἄνθρωποι'. Glenn Most deciphers Hesiod's cryptic statement as 'when gods and mortal men were reaching a settlement'. However, as κρίνω could equally mean 'distinguishing', 'separating', 'deciding', 'settling', or 'judging', it is far from clear whether we should understand this episode as one of separation or negotiation.[12] Indeed, given the obscurity of Hesiod's text, it is perhaps tempting to agree with Walter Burkert that the myth was 'puzzling' even to the Greeks themselves.[13] Others, however, have been more sympathetic. The most influential commentator on Hesiod's myth, Jean-Pierre Vernant, has presented a compelling defence for the coherence of Hesiod's narrative and the rationale behind the different sacrificial shares.[14] For Vernant, Hesiod's myth if correctly analysed presents a pivotal insight into the most important ritual institution in the Greek world, sacrifice, and 'a valuable key to the mental system to which the ritual refers and the vast network of meanings that it bears'.[15]

The existence of scholarly debates surrounding Hesiod's poem is not surprising. Indeed, when dealing with such a terse and difficult text, debate is to be expected. What is, however, a real puzzle is the widespread agreement about what Hesiod leaves out. Indeed, despite any clear affirmative statement in Hesiod's poem, we are repeatedly told that prior to Mekone humans lived a paradise-like existence during a Golden Age. Vernant describes that 'Mecone can represent that place where men and divinities still living side by side used to be seated at the same tables, feasting together at banquets and eating identical food'.[16] Wirshbo describes how 'a golden age must be understood to exist at the time of the banquet described at 535ff. There is an easy conversance between gods and men, to the point of their both sharing in a common feast'.[17] Dougherty argues that Mekone recalls 'a memory of gods and men living side by side ... [and] of bountiful plenty, a golden-age world of effortless plenitude and fertility'.[18] Gera refers to 'an original state of happy communion with the immortals'.[19] Indeed, Dillon in his excellent discussion of Golden Age imagery in Plato is even more explicit in his paradise imagery, arguing that in Hesiod's description of Mekone 'the concept of a period when gods and men lived in some sort of communion, in what would necessarily be some sort of primitive paradise, does seem to have a place in his thought, as has the notion that this period was ended by some sort of primeval sin'.[20]

Despite a great many differences, all of the above interpretations are united by the common assumption that Hesiod's myth depicts a fall from an original community of gods and the dissolution of an original unity. That Hesiod understood the Promethean episode in this way is entirely possible. The myth, after all, was widespread in Greece and at least some of the elements are present in the Mekone episode. Indeed, while no clear reference to a Golden Age is found in the *Theogony*, there is a contrast implied between a time before and a time after sacrifice. Moreover, in Prometheus we certainly find a trickster whose actions, whatever their original intentions, lead to human suffering.[21] Yet for all the small similarities, there remain, as Jenny Strauss Clay has astutely analysed, a great many differences.[22] Unlike the book of Genesis, the *Theogony* offers no account of human origins, nor any details of mankind's early life. Indeed, Hesiod's supposed tale of separation simply begins *in medias res* describing how gods and men distinguished their honours through an obscure and obsessive account of sliced meat. Nor is it particularly clear how this transition from unity to plurality fits within the wider poem's description of divine conflicts and chaotic conditions. What results then is a strange, truncated paradise myth within a broader narrative concerned with chaos.

Of course, despite Hesiod's many omissions, the meaning of the story may well have been perfectly clear to the poet and his original audience. Some of these details may have been so well known that they simply did not require any further explanation. For example, the idea that humans and Kronos once shared a meal was a myth repeated throughout antiquity and even, as noted in the previous chapter, ritualized in an event known as the Kronia where masters and slaves shared a single table.[23] Yet perhaps most importantly of all, there is no doubt that Hesiod himself was familiar with this kind of myth. In fact, the earliest surviving Greek version of a Golden Age is preserved in Hesiod's own poetry. In the *Works and Days* (109–18) we are told how

χρύσεον μὲν πρώτιστα γένος μερόπων ἀνθρώπων
ἀθάνατοι ποίησαν Ὀλύμπια δώματ' ἔχοντες.
οἳ μὲν ἐπὶ Κρόνου ἦσαν, ὅτ' οὐρανῷ ἐμβασίλευεν·
ὥστε θεοὶ δ' ἔζωον ἀκηδέα θυμὸν ἔχοντες
νόσφιν ἄτερ τε πόνων καὶ ὀιζύος· οὐδέ τι δειλὸν
γῆρας ἐπῆν, αἰεὶ δὲ πόδας καὶ χεῖρας ὁμοῖοι
τέρποντ' ἐν θαλίῃσι κακῶν ἔκτοσθεν ἁπάντων·
θνῇσκον δ' ὥσθ' ὕπνῳ δεδμημένοι· ἐσθλὰ δὲ πάντα
τοῖσιν ἔην· καρπὸν δ' ἔφερε ζείδωρος ἄρουρα
αὐτομάτη πολλόν τε καὶ ἄφθονον· οἳ δ' ἐθελημοὶ
ἥσυχοι ἔργ' ἐνέμοντο σὺν ἐσθλοῖσιν πολέεσσιν.
ἀφνειοὶ μήλοισι, φίλοι μακάρεσσι θεοῖσιν.

Golden was the race of speech-endowed human beings which the immortals, who have their mansions on Olympus, made first of all. They lived at the time of Cronus, when he was king in the sky, just like gods they spent their lives, with a spirit free from care, entirely apart from toil and distress. Worthless old age did not oppress them, but they were always the same in their feet and hands, and delighted in feasts, lacking in all evils; and they died as if overpowered by sleep. They had all food things: the grain-giving field bore crops its own accord, much and unstinting, and they themselves, willing, mild-mannered, shared out the fruits of their labours together with many good things, wealthy in sheep, dear to the blessed gods.[24]

Hesiod's description of the Golden Race presented in the *Works and Days* has every right to be described as paradise. Indeed, the lives of these early humans are even more spectacular than those enjoyed by Adam and Eve. Hesiod's Golden Race possess 'unpained hearts' (ἀκηδέα θυμὸν), perpetual feasts and even freedom from old age. Moreover, not only do they live with the gods, they closely resemble the Olympians themselves.[25] Although these details are not found in the *Theogony*, Hesiod was evidently fascinated by the image of mortal eating with immortal and in his fragmented *Catalogue of Women* he again describes a utopic time before the current day where humans and gods shared meals, seats and even women (fr. 1.1–7 M.W.):

Νῦν δὲ γυναικῶν φῦλον ἀείσατε, ἡδυέπειαι
Μοῦσαι Ὀλυμπιάδες, κοῦραι Διὸς αἰγιόχοιο,
αἵ ποτ᾽ ἄρισται ἔσαν[
μίτρας τ᾽ ἀλλύσαντο [
μισγόμεναι θεοῖσ[ιν
ξυναὶ γὰρ τότε δαῖτες ἔσαν, ξυνοὶ δὲ θόωκοι
ἀθανάτοις τε θεοῖσι καταθνητοῖς τ᾽ ἀνθρώποις.

Now the tribe of women sing, sweet-talking,
Olympian muses, daughters of Zeus who holds the Aegis,
[tell me] of the noble women,
loosening their belts as
they mixed with the gods. Because then,
men and gods had common feasts, common seats.[26]

Given Hesiod's knowledge and interest in the original communion between gods and men, it is understandable why these passages are often introduced to shed light on the ambiguities of Hesiod's *Theogony*. However, while there is certainly room for comparison, we must be equally wary of the many incompatibilities between the mythic material. This is particularly clear with the

Catalogue of Women where the context of the shared feast has shifted from the transition between the rules of Kronos and Zeus to the Age of Heroes, which takes place long after. The *Works and Days*, though overall a better fit, is in many details equally difficult to square with the plot of the *Theogony*. For example, in place of the sequence of changing rulers and cosmic battles described in the *Theogony*, in the *Works and Days* Hesiod lists a succession of five races, Gold, Silver, Bronze, Heroes and Iron, created by Zeus. Moreover, if the *Works and Days* presents a compelling portrait of a Greek paradise, it excludes any account of the fall and leaves no room whatsoever for Prometheus' trick; Hesiod simply describes how the Golden Race is buried under the earth (*WD* 121). Yet perhaps the most glaring inconsistency is found in the very different characterizations of the god, Kronos. The myth in the *Works and Days* provides no backstory. Nothing is said of Ouranos and Gaia, nothing is said of early cosmic struggles. We are simply introduced to Kronos, who is depicted as a benevolent father presiding over an orderly and idealized cosmos. The Kronos of the *Theogony*, as explored in the previous chapter, is completely different. Far from a utopian father figure, he is part of a succession of crooked kings whose reigns are defined by acts of patricide, infanticide and cannibalism. Indeed, given these antithetical characterizations, it is little wonder then that Hesiod (*WD* 106) specifically contrasted his description of the Golden Age in the *Works and Days* to the *Theogony* as another story (ἕτερόν λόγον).

Although the significant narrative differences in Hesiod's myths may warn against comparison, the problem is not comparison itself. Myths are flexible and variations the norm. There is no doubt that in the *Theogony* the rule of Kronos precedes that of Zeus and given the ubiquity of Kronos' association with the first human beings, it is entirely possible that Hesiod assumed that a period of closer relations existed prior to the Promethean divide and humanity's transition to the hardships of the current day. Indeed, it is very hard to make sense of the Promethean myth in any other way. However, filling mythical lacunae should not be done at the expense of what is clearly stated in the text. Humans could well have eaten with gods, or at least with the Titans, yet if they did so, they shared their meals within a period characterized by uncertainty and any comparison we make between Hesiod's two texts cannot ignore the more complex context of the *Theogony*. This was a world of ambiguity, a time when day blurred with night, Ouranos with Gaia, and gods vied with gods. A world of chaos until Zeus imposed order and safely demarcated the roles of the gods and the cosmic bodies as a whole.[27] As Versnel summarizes it, Kronos' reign was primarily one of ambivalence where primeval chaos manifests itself as a temporary elimination of all contours, a return to a state undefined by bounds and moral standards, expressing itself in the creation of monsters and monstrosities; a period of total freedom manifesting itself in both total lawlessness and total abundance.[28]

In short, Kronos' rule, far from golden, was one of contradictions, and no contradiction was greater than the meeting of humans and gods.

Hesiod and ὁμόθεν

Golden Age mythology is often more than a discussion of origins, but also of kinship and in many instances presents the key to understanding how humans and gods relate to each other in both the early cosmos and the world thereafter. In this spirit, Hesiod's Golden Age is often assumed to imply that an original closeness and even identity once existed between humans and gods. Indeed, Lorenzo Garcia has argued that prior to Mekone mortals and immortals displayed 'a similarity both in terms of spatial position and ontological status'.[29] While not all scholars would agree with this claim, the common assumption that Prometheus' deception resulted in the differentiation of humans and gods carries with it the implicit or explicit belief that these beings were initially connected. Although, the presence of this kinship is nowhere clearly confirmed or rejected in Hesiodic poetry, a critical element of this debate is found in Hesiod's puzzling phrase that humans and gods come from a common source (ὡς ὁμόθεν γεγάασι θεοὶ θνητοί τ' ἄνθρωποι) (WD 109).[30] Like many pivotal passages in Hesiod, the text has produced almost antithetical readings.[31] ὁμόθεν is a combination of ὁμός 'the same' and the locative θεν meaning 'from'. Thus 'from the same source' or 'place' is a safe translation. This is how it appears in the *Odyssey* where Homer (*Od.* 5.451) describes two different trees that grow from a single place. Others argue that when ὁμόθεν is coupled with γίγνομαι as it is used, for example, in the *Homeric Hymn to Aphrodite*, the meaning connotes 'born from the same source'.[32] Garcia for this reason argues that Hesiod's phrase suggests a 'blood relationship'.[33] Graf and Johnston also suggest that Hesiod's use of ὁμόθεν could indicate a literal genealogical relation through Gaia and cite Pindar's *Nemean Six* as a possible parallel (6.1).[34] This idea, as will be discussed in later chapters, was appealing to later poets and, if valid, would strongly support the idea that human/divine difference was something introduced only after Mekone. Unfortunately, a genealogical relationship makes little sense of Hesiod's text.

ὁμόθεν may indicate more than place, yet a genealogical tie makes no sense of a text that specifically states that the Golden Race were made (ποιέω) by the gods.[35] Humanity's origins in the *Theogony* are less clear and although it is sometimes claimed that humans are obliquely integrated into the wider genealogy of the gods, the idea is one weakly supported in the text. Indeed, based on the most common versions of the myth, including those known to Hesiod, it is likely that humans were also made by the gods (Apollodorus 1.7.1).[36] If Hesiod's exact thoughts on human origins will remain obscure, there is, however, no doubt that he considered humans and gods to be ontologically distinct beings. Indeed, while it is true that Hesiod describes early men as godlike in some respects, he is also very careful to point out that they die (*WD* 116):

θνῆσκον δ᾽ ὥσθ᾽ ὕπνῳ δε δμημένοι.

When they died, it was as though they were overcome with sleep.

This was admittedly a peaceful death, but death nonetheless, and confirms that the central ontological division between mortals and immortals was always in force.[37] The same idea appears in the *Catalogue of Women* (fr. 1.1–7 M.W.) and Hesiod stresses that despite sharing tables and meals, humans and gods 'were not of equal life spans (ἰσαιωνες)'.[38] The mortal difference is also something we see in later descriptions of humans who continue to share tables with the gods such as the Ethiopians (*Od.* 1.25) and the Phaeacians (*Od.* 7.201–5). Again, these societies are certainly superior to ordinary mortals, yet they are far from gods. In short, there is little reason to suggest that shared meals during Hesiod's Golden Age should be interpreted as an expression of ontological identity and in this critical detail we see an important difference from many paradise myths. For example, in the Tenetehara myth quoted above, the focus was not simply upon the loss of paradise but of immortality itself.[39] Hesiod, however, never makes this claim and from the Golden Age to the Age of Iron, he consistently describes humans as human, and gods as gods. And here we have a problem. Indeed, if humans and gods were always ontologically different, the question becomes not what was separated in Mekone, but how such different beings ever shared a table in the first place?

Affinity, consanguinity and the shared table of gods and men

What connects ontologically distinct humans and gods during the Golden Age is not something often asked. Indeed, both the widespread assumptions of an ambiguous unity and common analytic focus on humanity's departure from the table of the gods have obscured just how problematic the shared table really was. This problem, however, was not overlooked by the Greeks and addressing the scepticism surrounding the once closer ties between mortals and immortals, the second-century CE geographer Pausanias argues (8.2.4) that humans and gods could well have shared a table:

οἱ γὰρ δὴ τότε ἄνθρωποι ξένοι καὶ ὁμοτράπεζοι θεοῖς ἦσαν ὑπὸ δικαιοσύνης καὶ εὐσεβείας, καί σφισιν ἐναργῶς ἀπήντα παρὰ τῶν θεῶν τιμή τε οὖσιν ἀγαθοῖς καὶ ἀδικήσασιν ὡσαύτως ἡ ὀργή

For the men of those days, because of their righteousness and piety, were guest-friends (ξένοι) and table companions (ὁμοτράπεζοι), eating at the same board; the good were openly honoured by the gods, and the unjust were openly visited with their wrath.[40]

Although it may seem that Pausanias simply repeats the Hesiodic theme that mortals and immortals shared the same table, he is in fact offering an explanation as to how this unusual situation was possible in the first place. Humans and gods shared a table not because they were initially similar but because they were ξένοι (guest-friends) and ὁμοτράπεζοι (table companions). Neither of these words refers to a genealogical tie or blurred relations. Indeed, in some respects they refer to the very opposite and the word ξένοι, as I will discuss at length, can refer to strangers as much as honoured guests. However, despite this lexical ambiguity, both words remain important kinship ties in the ancient world, which force us to rethink human and divine relations beyond identity and similarity to a relationship built on difference.

Kinship among strangers may sound like a paradoxical idea. However, as Marshall Sahlins has recently argued, kinship entails far more than blood. Kinship concerns 'mutuality of being' and 'kinfolk are persons who participate intrinsically in each other's existence; they are members of one another. "Mutuality of being" applies as well to the constitution of kinship by social construction as by procreation.'[41] Pausanias' use of ξένοι (guest-friend) and ὁμοτράπεζοι (table companions) refer precisely to two key examples of long-standing socially constructed kinship relations established through ritualized eating. Although Pausanias was writing almost a millennium after Hesiod, when it comes to making sense of Hesiod's poetry his classification is perceptive. Indeed, in all three of Hesiod's major descriptions of early humans we see close relations between gods and humans expressed not through blood or genealogy, but through food and feasting. The *Theogony* describes the creation of humanity's new portion in the feast and the *Catalogue* how humans and gods sit at the same table on common seats. Finally, in the *Works and Days* mortals are said to feast with Kronos and even to eat special foods such as 'automatic grain' (*WD* 117–8).[42] Moreover, Hesiod in these descriptions treads well-worn territory and in Homer's depictions of godlike men such as the Ethiopians or the Phaeacians, we encounter remarkably similar humans who both eat a diet of 'unperishing fruit' (οὔ ποτε καρπὸς ἀπόλλυται) (*Od.* 7.117) and feast at a single table with the gods (*Od.* 7.201–5):

αἰεὶ γὰρ τὸ πάρος γε θεοὶ φαίνονται ἐναργεῖς
ἡμῖν, εὖθ' ἔρδωμεν ἀγακλειτὰς ἑκατόμβας,
δαίνυνταί τε παρ' ἄμμι καθήμενοι ἔνθα περ ἡμεῖς.
εἰ δ' ἄρα τις καὶ μοῦνος ἰὼν ξύμβληται ὁδίτης,
οὔτι κατακρύπτουσιν, ἐπεί σφισιν ἐγγύθεν εἰμέν,
ὥς περ Κύκλωπές τε καὶ ἄγρια φῦλα Γιγάντων.

Always, up to now, they came to us face-to-face
whenever we'd give them grand, glorious sacrifices –
they always sat beside us here and shared our feasts.
Even when some lonely traveller meets them on the roads,
they never disguise themselves. We're too close for that,
close as the wild Giants are, the Cyclops too.[43]

Homer's description of the Phaeacians has a great deal in common with Hesiod's early humans. Indeed, not only are shared seats and banquets mentioned, Homer even stresses the close relationship between mortals and immortals by using ὁμόθεν's kindred term ἐγγύθεν (from a near place), again stressing a relationship not of blood but of proximity.

That eating creates and fosters kinship relations is not a new idea. For decades anthropologists have explored the close relationship between sharing meals and the creation of kinships ties.[44] Aparecida Vilaça, for example, argues that among the Amazonian people, the Wari, 'food is central to defining identity. People who eat together (or consume the same type of food) become similar', while those who eat apart gradually lose their relations. Indeed, by eating and living with a local family, the Wari insisted that Vilaça literally became their kin.[45] The close connection between eating and kinship relationships also has a long legacy in the study of the ancient world. Numa Denis Fustel de Coulanges in his classic work, *The Ancient City,* makes a similar point about the role of the hearth in creating patrilineal groups in Rome. He even reverses our expectation on kinship, claiming that 'it was not by birth, it was by the cult alone that the agnates were recognized'.[46] It is not a huge leap from the hearth to the table and William Robertson Smith, in a theory I will later explore in more detail, made commensal relations central to his understanding of Hebrew sacrifice, describing how

> after the child is weaned, his flesh and blood continued to be nourished and renewed by the food which he shares with his commensals so that commensality can be thought of (1) as confirming or even (2) as constituting kinship in a very real sense.[47]

Although these ideas were somewhat sidelined in classical studies, recently a similar position has been revived and Stowers and Stocking, both drawing theoretical inspiration from Nancy Jay, emphasize that patrilineal kinship is 'constructed and negotiated through rituals of sacrifice and commensality'.[48] Alongside these ritual examples of socially constructed relationships, the close connection between food and kinship was also something testified by a rich lexicon of everyday kinship terms. Σύντροφος 'being reared' or 'fed together', for example, refers to a relationship created through shared meals and ὁμεστίοι to kinship created through the sharing of the same hearth.[49] In addition to these, Aristotle (*Pol.* 1.1252b) describes a list of less common words including ὁμοσίπυος ('sharing the same meal tub') and ὁμόκαποι ('those eating in the same manger') as equivalents for the common Athenian household.[50] In the same passage Aristotle also mentions the interesting term ὁμογάλακτες. The meaning of this word is not explained by Aristotle, but etymologically it appears to focus on the common European (and indeed world) practice of kinship through shared breast milk.[51] As this vocabulary suggests, shared meals and in particular grain was a key site of creating and strengthening kinship ties among family members. Indeed, for the Greeks, even to raise and educate children was synonymous with nourishing them (τρέφω).[52]

Although the precise meaning of some of these kinship terms remains obscure, the association between diet and being is also a central and repeated obsession in early epic. Indeed, mortals, as Homer and Hesiod never tire of reminding us, are bread eaters.[53] Barley or bread is not only a characteristic of their diets, ἄλφιτον is literally the marrow of men (μυελὸν ἀνδρῶν) (*Od.* 2.290; 20.108). Richard Onians argues that marrow is one of the central human components in Homer's anthropology and is something equated with the very life (αἰών) of human beings.[54] Moreover for Homer, αἰών appears to have a very concrete meaning, appearing as a fluid that emerges from tears (*Od.* 5.151-3). Elsewhere (*Il.*19.27) it is said that 'the αἰών is slain out [of the man], and accordingly the flesh will rot' (ἐκ δ'αἰὼν πέφαται, κατὰ δὲ χρόα πάντα σαπήῃ).

Following the Homeric scholia on this line, Onians has identified αἰών as bone marrow and directly connected this 'stuff of life' with the bread mortals eat.[55]

If humans are bread eaters, the gods also possess their own distinct foods. In Book 5 of the *Odyssey*, Homer describes how Odysseus and Calypso sit at the same table but eat very different things (5.196-9):

Νύμφη δ᾽ἐτίθει πάρα πᾶσαν ἐδωδήν,
ἔσθειν καὶ πίνειν, οἷα βροτοὶ ἄνδρες ἔδουσιν·
αὐτὴ δ᾽ἀντίον ἷζεν Ὀδυσσῆος θείοιο,
τῇ δὲ παρ᾽ἀμβροσίην δμῳαὶ καὶ νέκταρ ἔθηκαν.

While the nymph set out before him every kind
of food and drink that mortal men will take.
Calypso sat down face-to-face with the king
and the women served her nectar and ambrosia.[56]

These are key examples of analogically similar but ontologically opposed foods.[57] Ambrosia is self-referential and literally means 'not mortal'.[58] The closely related foodstuff nectar is more opaque but has been etymologically linked with 'getting across death'.[59] In both cases the transformative power of these foods is abundantly testified. In the *Iliad*, Hera applies ambrosia to her skin and becomes more beautiful (14.170). Elsewhere wounds are healed with this miraculous substance (*Il*.14.170-2). In the *Homeric Hymn to Delian Apollo* (124-30), the infant Apollo is fed ambrosia and instantly outgrows his clothing, walks and talks. One of the most eloquent expressions of the effects of ambrosia appears when Aphrodite is wounded by the mortal hero Diomedes. Homer informs us in one of his ethnographic asides that rather than blood, ἰχώρ flows through the veins of the goddess. He even offers an explanation why (*Il*. 5. 339-42):

ῥέε δ᾽ἄμβροτον αἷμα θεοῖο
ἰχώρ, οἷός πέρ τε ῥέει μακάρεσσι θεοῖσιν·
οὐ γὰρ σῖτον ἔδουσ᾽, οὐ πίνουσ᾽αἴθοπα οἶνον,
τοὔνεκ᾽ἀν αἱμονές εἰσι καὶ ἀθάνατοι καλέονται

and blood immortal flowed from the goddess,
ichor, that which runs in the veins of the blessed divinities;
for they eat no bread, nor do they drink of the shining
wine, and therefore they have no blood and are called immortal.[60]

While it is possible to read this passage as one which simply distinguishes gods from men, Homer is also offering an explanation.[61] This is stressed through the use of the explanatory γὰρ, *'for* they do not eat or drink mortal food' and reinforced by τοὔνεκα, '*therefore* they are immortal'. In this case ἰχώρ is not simply an attribute of the gods but one that is intimately related to their diet. Although it is not literally said that ambrosia creates immortal blood, it is difficult to read ἄμβροτον αἷμα without immediately thinking of the nearly identical term, ambrosia.[62] Onians, in this respect, may not be far off the mark when he likens this immortal food to the αἰὼν of the gods.[63]

In short, for the early poets food is something that creates flesh, separates those who eat apart, and unites those who eat together. This miraculous propensity for creating and breaking kinship ties makes it an ideal medium for understanding not only how humans and gods can be distinguished through antithetical diets, but also how the ontologically distinct tribes of mortals and immortals could ever relate. And it is precisely for this reason that Pausanias' comments on the early shared feasts are so valuable. Indeed, nothing in Hesiod's poetry suggests that humans and gods associated as blood relatives, rather they met as opposites or in Pausanias' terminology as ξένοι and ὁμοτράπεζοι. As noted, both of these terms emphasize a relationship created through shared meals and feasting rather than shared blood.[64] In this respect both can be defined as forms of affinity rather than consanguinity. This is particularly clear with ξενία, a term often awkwardly translated as guest-friendship, which describes a social bond based on feasting, hosting and the exchange of gifts. Ξενία, however, was much more than friendship. It was a sacred pact which could be formed between individuals, families, and even ethnic groups such as the Persians and the Arabs (Hdt. 3.88). Indeed, given its central importance in the ancient world, it would not be misleading to classify ξενία as an affinal tie on par with marriage.[65] Vernant, for example, argues that 'the bonds between the man and his wife are the same as those which unite two antagonistic groups who become guest-friends'[66] and for Hesiod breaches of ξενία appear alongside patricide and incest (*WD* 327).[67] Indeed, so strong were ξενία ties that the Phaeacian king Alcinous describes them as equal to those of consanguineous kin (*Od.* 8.546–7), declaring that a 'ἀντὶ κασιγνήτου ξεῖνός θ' ἱκέτης τε τέτυκται ἀνέρι' (a ξένος and a supplicant are equal to a brother to a man).

Although there is no shortage of examples that relate eating to the creation of kinship in Greece, not all scholars are convinced that ritual can foster a genuine tie. Gabriel Herman in his study of guest-friendship, for example, argues that ξενία merely 'mimicked aspects of kinship relations', and that 'real kinship is given: it follows from birth. Ritual friendship was an acquired relationship.'[68] In other words, ritually acquired relationships are pale imitations of genuine kinship ties based on blood and birth. Although Herman is certainly correct to differentiate kin by birth from acquired kinship, his distinction between real and imitative kinship is problematic in a society where a child's relationship to his mother was debated and ξενία ties were transmitted through birth.[69] Indeed, in the Greek world kinship was a complex mix of nature and nurture and even if a person was born with fixed consanguineous ties, they were not born complete. Just as an aristocratic child needs to be shaped and moulded into their proper form, the greater part of kinship takes place well after birth through incorporation into demes, phratries and extended affinal ties.[70] The same is true of marriage. Indeed, spouses might start out as strangers yet, as Wilgaux notes, through their mutual intercourse and the process of σύμφυσις 'growing together' they become kin in a very real sense (cf. Pl. *Sym.* 189d).[71] For the Greeks, eating involved a similar growing together and, like marriage, it was an act that creates and changes the very bodies of those who share. This can certainly be called an acquired relationship, yet it was no less real for that. Indeed, while it is often difficult to literally see the relationship growing between strangers who share meals, we find a vivid illustration of the transformative powers of food during the Golden Age described in the *Works and Days*, where humans and gods not only symbolically expressed their ξενία tie through shared meals, but their very bodies were also transformed in the process.

Although food was clearly a powerful means of making connections, eating in Greece had its limits. Vilaça, as noted above, describes how among the Wari those who share food become similar while those who eat apart gradually lose their relations.[72] This idea would have proved surprising to most Greeks. Eating may create closer ties, it may change the bodies of those who share food, yet it never overwrites ties created by birth. To understand the limitations of food in Greece we need only think about Oedipus, a child raised apart from his family, nourished in a foreign land, yet tragically unable to overwrite his natal ties. In other words, although guest-friendship could create kinship ties among strangers, no Greek imagined that ritualized feasts could overwrite kinship by blood. In this respect consanguines and affines were sharply differentiated. Indeed, if kin by birth were, as Aristotle (*Nic. Eth.* 1161b) described them, united by similarity, guest-friends and affines more generally were, to adopt Sahlins' phrase, 'united by a difference'.[73] The alterity Sahlins associates with affines is a common observation. Indeed, Helms, in an important work dedicated to the comparative study of affinal ties, describes how affines or potential affines are depicted the world over as 'foreigners, outsiders, opposites, enemies, strangers, or sojourners'.[74] In Greece the idea of the dangerous affine is recurrent among wives and ξένοι alike. Greek wives in literary depictions are frequently the subject of suspicion and the foreigner Medea epitomizes the element of fear present in every act of incorporating the Other through marriage.[75] If no wife is above suspicion, ξενία is even more emphatic in its emphasis on Otherness and potential treachery. Although ξενία is often awkwardly translated as guest-friendship, this hardly encapsulates the meaning of a particularly rich term that carries two antithetical meanings, 'stranger' and 'honoured guest'.[76] Moreover, these two meanings frequently intersect; Paris' violation of Menalaus' ξενία, for example, started the Trojan war. This double meaning, far from being idiosyncratic, is a surprisingly common designator of affines across the globe.[77] Viveiros de Castro, for example, explains how the Tupinambá word *tovajar* means both brother-in-law and enemy and 'expressed both friendly alliance within and deadly enmity without, and very probably vice versa. It approximated and opposed in one fell swoop.'[78] This is also true of ξένος and while it is common to translate it as either stranger or guest, arguably there is a sense of ambivalence in every use of the term.[79]

Sacrifice between sharing and separation

The transformative role of food is not only central to understanding everyday kinship relations in Greece, it is the key to understanding Hesiod's descriptions of early humans and their ties to the gods. I have described above how for the Greeks sharing food among kin and strangers creates a relationship. It changes the flesh of those who share and brings those who eat the same food closer together. Its transformative potential was incredibly diverse and just as early humans ate with the gods and expressed their affinal ties, so too could mortals during the Age of Iron establish their kinship with strangers through shared meals. Yet curiously, when it comes to understanding the sacrificial divisions at Mekone and Prometheus' creation of two unequal shares of meat, far from stressing the creation of a bond, we repeatedly encounter the very opposite claim: sharing emphasizes separation. As Vernant argues, 'the division of the animal both provokes and reflects the opposition between the two respective parties. The distance separating mortals from immortals is begun in sacrifice and perpetuated by sacrifice.'[80] Vernant, in short, argues that the Promethean division initiates the separation of two tribes and the creation of distinct diets and lifestyles.[81]

Vernant's interpretation has been deservedly influential, and I entirely agree that the Promethean episode describes the creation of a new status for humanity.

Indeed, the myth as a whole, from the duplicity of the Titan to the punishment of mankind through the creation of woman, clearly stresses a distinction between the reign of Kronos and that of Zeus. Moreover, Vernant makes a compelling case that this distinction is expressed through Prometheus' two unequal shares of meat. However, Vernant does not simply argue that the two shares initiate a new kind of relationship, he argues that they dissolve a previous tie based on equality.[82] This makes Prometheus' two shares the equivalent of bread versus ambrosia, two antithetical foods for two antithetical beings. In Vernant's words, in Mekone humans receive meat and 'recognize the inferiority of their mortal condition and confirm their complete submission to the Olympians'.[83] The gods, on the other hand, receive 'the very life of the animal, released from the bones, in short, those parts of the animal that, like the aromatics with which they are burned, escape the putrefaction of death'.[84] The end result of Vernant's study is that Mekone is a myth on the 'origin of separation' and sacrifice is a commemorative rite where

> communication is founded upon a religious ritual which, by memorializing Prometheus's error, reaffirms on every occasion of its performance the existence of that uncrossable gulf. And it is the purpose of the myth, as told by Hesiod, precisely to lay bare the origins of the separation and to make plain its dire consequences.[85]

In other words, sacrifice is an act of nostalgia where humanity mourns its loss of the Golden Age.

Although there is little in this chapter which is not influenced by Vernant, it should be pointed out that with few exceptions, the idea that sacrifice emphasizes difference is at odds with almost every description of the ritual in ancient literature.[86] As Parker stresses, in most cases the goal of sacrifice, far from stressing distinctions, was about sharing and an effort 'to communicate with the gods across the great divide'.[87] Indeed, at times sacrifice is even described as part of a ξενία relationship. The most overt example of this is the classical ritual known as θεοξένια. This, as the name suggests, was an act of ξενία to the gods and involved setting aside a meal for a divine guest at a mortal feast.[88] Although this is a rather specialized case, I argue that it was unique only in its ambition. Indeed, the idea that sacrifice was predominantly viewed as a shared meal among gods and humans is one advocated from Homer's Zeus (*Il.* 24.69)[89] to Saint Paul's first letter to the Corinthians (10.18–20) and the apostle's warning against the danger of becoming companions of demons/gods (κοινωνοὺς τῶν δαιμονίων γίνεσθαι). Despite Vernant's insistence on the antithetical nature of the shares, that sacrifice was primarily about connecting over the butchered animal is something repeatedly confirmed in the increasing research on literary and epigraphical sources.[90] Vernant, in fact, was aware of the weaknesses of his argument in respect to Homeric descriptions of sacrifice. In a footnote, he recognizes the ambiguity of the σπλάγχνα (innards): 'although food for humans, the splankna organ filled with blood, roasted directly over the flames of the altar, have a status that puts them more on the side of the gods and makes the gap separating the two forms of existence less acute.'[91] While this might seem to strike a fatal blow to the strict mortal/immortal divide in the Mekone episode, Vernant insists that the problem is Homer's and Hesiod, by eliminating the innards from his sacrificial narrative, 'in some way banishes the problem'.[92] However, even in this less than satisfactory evasion a strict dichotomy is not clear. Although the god's share certainly contains less meat, both divisions contain fat (δημός). In the mortal case this is present in the fat disguised in the ox's belly. For the gods, the bones are concealed in shining fat (538–41). In short, even in Vernant's key example there is greater overlap than he would like.

The increasing awareness of the complications of the sacrificial evidence has led to a general reassessment of Vernant's thesis and a turn from interpreting sacrifice as separation towards sacrifice as sharing. This theoretical position also has a long legacy. Indeed, as early as 1889, Robertson Smith famously argued:

> The one thing directly expressed in the sacrificial meal is that the god and his worshippers are *commensals*, but every other point in their mutual relations is included in what this involves. Those who sit at meals together are united for all social effects, those who do not eat together are aliens to one another, without fellowship in religions and without reciprocal social duties.[93]

For Robertson Smith sacrifice is an act of communication where humans and god/s emphasize their shared kinship and reciprocal obligations through a shared meal. This idea was in turn adapted by Hubert and Mauss in their influential work on sacrifice. In their words, sacrifice 'consists in establishing communication between the sacred and profane worlds through the mediation of a victim – that is, of something destroyed in the course of the ceremony'.[94] More recently a related idea has also been proposed by Philippe Descola in his adaption of Lévi-Strauss' position where he argues that sacrifice is

> a means of action developed within the context of analogist ontologies in order to establish an operational continuity between intrinsically different singularities. For this purpose, it makes use of a serial mechanism of connections and

disconnections that functions either as an attractor – to establish a connection with something else – or as a separator – to break a connection that already exists at a different level and that one seeks to dissolve.[95]

In other words, like the shared meals eaten by gods and men during the ambiguous Golden Age, sacrifice is a means of connecting two ontologically distinct groups through the use of an intermediary animal, which allows each tribe to connect while retaining their distinctions. Although this understanding of sacrifice might sound suspiciously modern, it is in many respects similar to that expressed by Socrates in his recitation of Diotima's speech in the *Symposium* (202e–203a) and his discussion of the daemon and intermediary Eros who is responsible for:

ἑρμηνεῦον καὶ διαπορθμεῦον θεοῖς τὰ παρ' ἀνθρώπων καὶ ἀνθρώποις τὰ παρὰ θεῶν, τῶν μὲν τὰς δεήσεις καὶ θυσίας, τῶν δὲ τὰς ἐπιτάξεις τε καὶ ἀμοιβὰς τῶν θυσιῶν, ἐν μέσῳ δὲ ὂν ἀμφοτέρων συμπληροῖ, ὥστε τὸ πᾶν αὐτὸ αὑτῷ συνδεδέσθαι. διὰ τούτου καὶ ἡ μαντικὴ πᾶσα χωρεῖ καὶ ἡ τῶν ἱερέων τέχνη τῶν τε περὶ τὰς θυσίας καὶ τελετὰς καὶ τὰς ἐπῳδὰς καὶ τὴν μαντείαν πᾶσαν καὶ γοητείαν. θεὸς δὲ ἀνθρώπῳ οὐ μείγνυται, ἀλλὰ διὰ τούτου πᾶσά ἐστιν ἡ ὁμιλία καὶ ἡ διάλεκτος θεοῖς πρὸς ἀνθρώπους <καὶ πρὸς θεοὺς ἀνθρώποις>, καὶ ἐγρηγορόσι καὶ καθεύδουσι·

Interpreting and transporting human things to the gods and divine things to men; entreaties and sacrifices from below, and ordinances and requitals from above: being midway between, it makes each to supplement the other, so that the whole is combined in one. Through it are conveyed all divination and priestcraft concerning sacrifice and ritual and incantations, and all soothsaying and sorcery. God with man does not mingle: but the spiritual is the means of all society and converse of men with gods and of gods with men, whether waking or asleep.[96]

This passage describes how the cosmos is comprised of two separate domains, mortal and immortal, which are entirely distinct. However, between these worlds is an intermediary god, Eros, who allows these domains to form a continuous whole (τὸ πᾶν αὐτὸ αὑτῷ συνδεδέσθαι) while simultaneously not mixing (οὐ μείγνυται). This idea is moreover offered as an explanation for a wide range of cognate institutions including sacrifice, augury, magic, divination, all of which work upon the presence of an intermediary between humans and gods. Sacrifice, in this description, takes place at the point of contact between gods and humans where status and relationships are negotiated without encroaching on the ontological distinctions of the categories themselves.

The shared feast at Mekone

While sharing is clearly a useful means for understanding many acts of sacrifice in ancient Greece, it may remain unclear how this model can be applied to Mekone. After all, does not the myth depict the very opposite and chart the dissolution of a previously closer tie? The answer is yes and no. The new sacrificial divisions in Mekone indeed create greater distance between humans and gods, yet they remain an act of sharing between affines for all that. As noted earlier, there is no reason to imagine equal relations were ever present during the reign of Kronos. Better shares and superior food existed, yet Hesiod in all his descriptions of early humans insists on the ontological difference between humans and gods. In this light, the new divisions established by Prometheus in Mekone describe a change in degree not kind, a transition from the close affinal ties which characterized the shared table to an increasingly hierarchical relationship.[97] This new hierarchy is perfectly encapsulated in the Hesiodic share referred to as ἑτερόζηλος 'zealous for one side'.[98] Hierarchy, of course, expresses difference, as Vernant argued. However, as Valerio Valeri astutely notes in his discussion of Hawaiian sacrifice, hierarchy 'involves distinction as much as connection'.[99] In other words, hierarchy is a term which looks both ways, a connection based upon inequality, and in this respect it presents a robust means of theorizing Greek sacrificial relations beyond the creation of difference. Indeed, although it is clear that there was no single way of sacrificing in ancient Greece and that no theory can encompass all instances of sacrifice, the idea that sacrifice establishes an affinal relation among hierarchically distinct groups is remarkably flexible.[100] Hierarchal connections, as we have seen, can be expressed in two shares of meat, yet the Greeks were creative and the animal including skin, flesh, fat, bones and innards was as rich as the butcher's imagination.[101] Indeed, whether we refer to two or twenty shares, I argue that Greek sacrifice works on identical principles: it was a means of connecting opposing groups through an intermediary animal. The intermediary nature of the sacrificial animal, as well as the flexibility of this theoretical model, is nicely illustrated in one of most extensive sacrificial scenes in archaic literature – the sacrifice performed by Odysseus' swineherd Eumaeus (*Od.* 14. 418–38):

ὣς ἄρα φωνήσας κέασε ξύλα νηλέϊ χαλκῷ,
οἱ δ' ὗν εἰσῆγον μάλα πίονα πενταέτηρον.
τὸν μὲν ἔπειτ' ἔστησαν ἐπ' ἐσχάρῃ· οὐδὲ συβώτης

Beyond the Golden Age: Sacrifice, Sharing and Affinity in Hesiod's Mekone

λήθετ᾽ ἄρ᾽ ἀθανάτων: φρεσὶ γὰρ κέχρητ᾽ ἀγαθῇσιν:
ἀλλ᾽ ὅγ᾽ ἀπαρχόμενος κεφαλῆς τρίχας ἐν πυρὶ βάλλεν
ἀργιόδοντος ὑός, καὶ ἐπεύχετο πᾶσι θεοῖσιν
νοστῆσαι Ὀδυσῆα πολύφρονα ὅνδε δόμονδε.
κόψε δ᾽ ἀνασχόμενος σχίζῃ δρυός, ἣν λίπε κείων:
τὸν δ᾽ ἔλιπε ψυχή. τοὶ δ᾽ ἔσφαξάν τε καὶ εὗσαν:
αἶψα δέ μιν διέχευαν: ὁ δ᾽ ὠμοθετεῖτο συβώτης,
πάντων ἀρχόμενος μελέων, ἐς πίονα δημόν,
καὶ τὰ μὲν ἐν πυρὶ βάλλε, παλύνας ἀλφίτου ἀκτῇ,
μίστυλλόν τ᾽ ἄρα τἆλλα καὶ ἀμφ᾽ ὀβελοῖσιν ἔπειραν,
ὤπτησάν τε περιφραδέως ἐρύσαντό τε πάντα,
βάλλον δ᾽ εἰν ἐλεοῖσιν ἀολλέα: ἂν δὲ συβώτης
ἵστατο δαιτρεύσων: περὶ γὰρ φρεσὶν αἴσιμα ᾔδη.
καὶ τὰ μὲν ἕπταχα πάντα διεμοιρᾶτο δαΐζων:
τὴν μὲν ἴαν νύμφῃσι καὶ Ἑρμῇ, Μαιάδος υἱεῖ,
θῆκεν ἐπευξάμενος, τὰς δ᾽ ἄλλας νεῖμεν ἑκάστῳ:
νώτοισιν δ᾽ Ὀδυσῆα διηνεκέεσσι γέραιρεν
ἀργιόδοντος ὑός, κύδαινε δὲ θυμὸν ἄνακτος:

Calling out
as he split up kindling now with a good sharp ax
and his men hauled in a tusker five years old,
rippling fat, and stood him steady by the hearth.
The swineherd, soul of virtue, did not forget the gods.
He began the rite by plucking tufts from the porker's head,
threw them into the fire and prayed to all the powers,
'Bring him home, our wise Odysseus, home at last!'
Then raising himself full-length, with an oak log
he'd left unsplit he clubbed and stunned the beast
and it gasped out its life ...
The men slashed its throat, singed the carcass,
quickly quartered it all, and then the swineherd,
cutting first strips for the gods from every limb,
spread them across the thighs, wrapped in sleek fat,
and sprinkling barley over them, flung them on the fire.
They sliced the rest into pieces, pierced them with skewers,
broiled them all to a turn and, pulling them off the spits,
piled the platters high. The swineherd, standing up
to share the meat – his sense of fairness perfect –
carved it all out into seven equal portions.
One he set aside, lifting up a prayer

to the forest nymphs and Hermes, Maia's son,
and the rest he handed on to each man in turn.
But to Odysseus he presented the boar's long loin
and the cut of honor cheered his master's heart.[102]

Despite its complexity, Eumaeus' sacrifice is no different from the shared tables during the Golden Age or the two unequal shares laid out by Prometheus. It is a multifaceted act involving the organizing of a previous whole into a complex series of parts in an effort to honour gods, make requests, and feed human and divine participants. The first offering (ἀπαρχή) is the animal itself, represented by the hairs from the live animal and a prayer to all the gods. At this point a request is made. The swineherd then continues to divide the gods' special share through the act of ὠμοθετεῖν. The name refers to a special share created from raw meat from all the limbs and is offered alongside barley. Suk Fong Jim plausibly argues that this share represents the animal as a whole.[103] Following this, Eumaeus divides the animal into seven portions and sets one aside for Hermes and the Nymphs. While this portion is burnt and offered as smoke not meat, the cut suggests a hierarchy among the gods in which Hermes and the Nymphs, because of both their contact with the earth and mortals, are closer to men than Zeus. Indeed, like the θεοξένια rituals mentioned above, Hermes appears as a kind of divine ξένος at Eumaeus' table.[104] Apart from honouring Hermes, the meal is also an example of the extension of ξενία to the disguised Odysseus, who in this case presents himself as an outsider. Indeed, Odysseus as a ξένος receives the reverence accorded to a god and similarly his share, the prized γέρας, is specified as the 'unbroken back' (νῶτον διηνεκής). Like the gods' ὠμοθετεῖν, the reference to unbrokeness or continuity may represent another case of a stress on totality against the divided parts. This single process of complex divisions, uniting gods, more ambiguous figures such as Hermes and the Nymphs, superior men like Odysseus, and commoners like Eumaeus, combines to form the hierarchal kinship chain that is the equal feast.[105]

Although Eumaeus' feast has some idiosyncratic details, the basic idea that the apportionment of sacrificial shares creates hierarchal relations is clear in the majority of extensive discussions of sacrifice in early literature and whether we refer to the shared table, Mekone's two unequal shares, or the multiple shares in Eumaeus' sacrifice, all these scenes follow an identical logic where the ontologically distinct tribes of humans and gods come together and express their affinal tie through the intermediary powers of meat. As the complexities in the swineherd's sacrifice display, the sacrificial feast can express close relations as easily as it can distant ones. It can even combine both. However, following Prometheus' ruse, sacrificial shares predominantly reflect a hierarchal 'chain of honour' where gods are at the apex and men well below.[106] This is undoubtedly a more distant relation from that humans knew during the reign of Kronos, but it remains a relation nonetheless. And both are based on affinity rather than blood.

Conclusion: Sacrifice and cosmology

I have argued in this chapter that there was no Golden Age in the *Theogony* – or at least there was no simple one. Although humans likely once sat alongside Kronos and in some respects lived better lives than today, for all that, the cosmos as a whole was far from golden. Indeed, the same benevolent father who dined with mortal men, dined on Olympian gods such as Zeus. Nor is the idea of a fall clear in Hesiod's tale of paradise lost and while the meeting between Prometheus and Zeus certainly results in a change of status, humanity's loss was the cosmos's gain.[107] Although it is always possible to shoehorn the Promethean myth into the mould of Eden, our analysis should ultimately be based not on what Hesiod omitted from his poem, but on the details he chose to include. And it is of at least some significance that rather than an idealized image of paradise, in the *Theogony* Hesiod chose to emphasize the dissection of an ox. If this gory detail makes for a rather odd Eden, it does, however, point to another common kind of myth sometimes known as 'creation by sacrifice'.[108] I will return to this myth type in more detail in Chapter 4 in relation to the Orphic anthropogony. Presently it is sufficient to note that the central feature of 'creation by sacrifice' myths is a description of how 'a primordial being is killed and dismembered, and from his body the cosmos is fashioned'.[109] The myth is widespread and appears, for example, in the Vafþrúðnismál poetic Edda, where the gods fashion the earth from the body of the giant Ymir.[110] The most famous example, however, comes from the Vedic *Purusha-Sutka* (10.90). In this poem the self-sacrifice of the primordial god Purusha leads to the formation of the world and human and divine social divisions (12–13):

> His mouth became the Brahmin, his arms were made into the warrior, his thighs the People, and from his feet the Servants were born.
> The moon was born from his mind; from his eye the sun was born.[111]

The cosmic shares of Purusha could be interpreted in terms of loss. Indeed, that the Brahmins fared better than the Servants is not in doubt. Yet the myth, rather than a reflection on human suffering, shifts our attention to cosmic order and in particular towards the idea of ordered distinctions emerging from a sacrificial act, which is moreover recreated and reinforced in all subsequent performances of the rite. The myth then has a dual function describing, as Lincoln notes, both 'the origin of the world and also of the origin of the most important human institution – sacrifice'.[112] Although Hesiod also recounts a myth that simultaneously aetiologizes sacrifice and defines the human condition, the idea that Mekone describes an act of creative sacrifice has received a mixed reception. Robert Parker, for example, warns against the dangers of Vedianizing Greek myth, noting that 'Greek sacrifice was entirely unaccompanied by exegesis; there is no reason to think that it was perceived as repeating a world-ordering act'.[113] Yet this is only partially true. Greek sacrifice may have been unaccompanied by the recital of a cosmological myth, yet Hesiod's cosmology was certainly accompanied by a description of sacrifice. Indeed, while significant differences exist between Hesiod's Mekone and the *Purusha-Sutka*, the comparison presents ample potential to rethink the many ambiguities of a myth where the first sacrifice is simultaneously the creation of the hierarchal distinctions between humans and gods. Indeed, everything in the myth suggests that we read it as such. Nestled within a cosmological narrative describing Zeus' triumph over the forces of chaos, the Promethean divide is a key example of Zeus' cosmic allotments. Furthermore, in one of the few non-Hesiodic sources to mention Mekone, the poet Callimachus even specifies that it was this very place where the gods 'cast lots and distinguished their honours'.[114] In other words, Mekone was not simply the location where humans were distinguished from the gods, but it was the site where Zeus reorganized the cosmos as a whole. Although Callimachus was writing well after Hesiod, the idea that Hesiod understood Mekone to be part of Zeus' cosmic divisions is also something well supported by his poetry. Indeed, the very language of the sacrificial divisions repeatedly echoes that of Zeus' other cosmic distributions and the use of terms such as μείρομαι 'to receive portions' (*Theog.* 411–15, 424–8), γέρας 'honoured share' (*Theog.* 393, 396, 427) and τιμάς (e.g. *Theog.* 75, 855) are as appropriate to describing shares of meat as they are cosmic allotments.[115] For example, when Hesiod refers to Prometheus' act of διεδάσσαο μοίρας ('he divided the pieces of meat'), the phrase is almost identical to Zeus' allotment of destinies μοῖραν ἐδάσσατο described just twenty or so lines earlier (*Theog.* 520).[116] Similar ambiguities also surround the troublesome word κρίνω. The word, as noted earlier, can be translated as 'separating' but equally as 'deciding', 'settling', 'judging', or more concretely 'the act of dividing itself'.[117] Although some interpreters favour the idea of separating humans and gods, given the context of a sacrificial act it may be more appropriate to understand κρίνω as an act of apportionment.[118]

Understanding Mekone as a myth of creation through sacrifice does not, of course, surmount the many complications of the scene. Indeed, there are certainly elements of Eden in Mekone and Hesiod was well aware of them. However, humanity's occasional nostalgia for the past does not change the fact that the sacrificial division, rather than separating humanity from the gods, integrated mortals into a new world order. Nor should we forget that Prometheus did not initiate humanity's distinction from the gods. Not only were mortals and immortals already ontologically separate, but Zeus' apportionment was in motion prior to Prometheus' deceit. Had Prometheus played fair, humans may have received a better lot, but there was never a question that they could remain in their previous ambiguous state. Mortals, like everything else in the cosmos, had a proper place and this is what was decided in Mekone.[119] In this respect, humanity's destiny contained both positive and negative aspects where cosmic order was attained at the expense of their labour. This message is echoed in all subsequent acts of sacrifice and from the allotments of Mekone to Eumaeus' feast we have repeatedly seen that sacrifice is an act based on incorporating its participants into a larger social hierarchy. This was more than a metaphor of integration; the sacrificial shares changed the very flesh of the participants and united their differences through very real kinship ties. Although different shares may create different kinds of being and foster different bonds, all participants were united through the animal as a whole. In this respect sacrifice was a cosmological act where, as McClymond argues in a more general context, the sacrificial divisions

> are physically manipulated and distributed to different parties, so they are ordered in a new *spatial* arrangement or pattern. Thus, apportionment takes a ritually chaotic victim's body and organizes that body into a ritually ordered microcosm. Chaos (the natural animal body) is transformed into ordered substance (the ritually arranged body).[120]

In a Greek context sacrifice was an effort to inscribe order upon human and non-human participants. It was an event where aristocrats, commoners, priests and gods came together and expressed their affinal ties through a complex series of divisions. Within these divisions humans certainly emerge on a lower link in the hierarchal chain, yet their place in this chain nevertheless implies a real relationship. Indeed, in every act of sacrifice humans call upon their affinal kin to share a meal and remind the gods of the order of the cosmos and the honours they agreed upon when Prometheus and Zeus first divided the sacrificial ox.

3

Orpheus and the Reinvention of the Cosmos

That theogonic poems other than Hesiod's existed in the ancient Greek world was always known. Homer, for example, refers to an alternate tradition beginning with Okeanos and Tethys (*Il.* 14.200–4) and in the sixth century BCE Pherecydes of Syros wrote a prose theogony starting with Chthonie (chthonic Earth), Zas (similar to Zeus) and Chronos (Time). Yet, the majority of Hesiod's competitors remain unknown, lost amid the fragments and summaries from authors of a much later age. Not everything, however, in ancient Greece remains in the past and in 1962 archaeologists uncovered the charred remains of an ancient scroll. Its survival was a remarkable accident, an almost paradoxical instance where the destructive flames were the creative force that preserved this document for the ages. The content of the book was almost as surprising as its survival. The scroll, now known as the Derveni papyrus, seemingly indifferent to the distinctions between myth and philosophy, was comprised of a philosophical commentary on a poem attributed to the mythical singer Orpheus.[1] The commentary, most likely dating to the fourth or fifth century BCE, is an exegetical work, an etymological reading of a poem in terms of cosmological processes. This in itself provides a fascinating glimpse into the early allegorical tradition. Yet even more exciting than the philosophical treatise was what lay hidden within this commentary: a small but significant number of lines of a theogony attributed to the mythical poet Orpheus.

The poem, perhaps dating as early as the sixth century BCE, may initially appear unremarkable. Indeed, in many respects it tells a story very similar to that of Hesiod's *Theogony*.[2] In both poems we see how a succession of the royal gods, including Ouranos and Kronos, culminates in the victory of Zeus. Yet, despite the familiarity of these details, Orpheus' theogony is remarkable for its innovations, omissions and emendations to Hesiod's well-known narrative. In place of Chaos, Orpheus begins with a creator god Protogonos. In place of multiple and non-intersecting genealogies, Orpheus describes a single lineage. Finally, where Hesiod's Zeus establishes his power through imposing order upon the chaotic elements of the cosmos, Orpheus' Zeus eats the entire world and becomes one with it. The end result is a poem which, though superficially similar to Hesiod's narrative, fundamentally transforms his vision of the cosmos. As anthropologist Frédéric Laugrand notes in a cosmologically related context, Orpheus' poem creates a 'complete transformation of the ontological and cosmological systems' of Hesiod's narrative.[3] This chapter will explore Orpheus' ontological transformation of Hesiod's poem, describing how through a process of substitutions and additions Hesiod's analogist world is redefined as an organic totality identified with a pantheistic god.

Orpheus amid the poets and philosophers

In antiquity it was common to utter the names Orpheus, Homer and Hesiod in a single breath (Plato *Ion* 536b). However, Orpheus was quite different from the other poets. Indeed, his very life is part of the same mythical fabric as the poems he wrote and both his mythical and literary origins remain obscure. Although Orpheus is absent from the poetry of Homer and Hesiod, by the mid-sixth century BCE the poet Ibykus can refer to him as Orpheus of the renowned name.[4] From this point on, his status in the Greek world continued to grow and his life can be pieced together through scattered references in tragedies, epics and his own poetic works.[5] Born of a Muse and a Thracian King, or in some versions the god Apollo, he was a bard whose song enchanted humans, animals, and even stones. As one of the Argonauts in Apollonius' *Argonautica* he sat shoulder to shoulder with Herakles and Jason in their search for the Golden Fleece. Orpheus' influence was, however, by no means confined to myth. He was also said to be the creator of religious innovations closely associated with Bacchic rites, the rejection of animal sacrifice, and the immortality of the soul. These views are expressed across a range of materials including gold tablets buried with Orphic initiates, fragmented poetry and philosophical discussions which seamlessly blur the supposed divide between myth and philosophy in the early Greek world.[6] The Derveni papyrus is an excellent example of these varied interests. Probably written by an Orphic priest or initiate, the text includes a combination of poetry and philosophical analysis.[7] Although I will repeatedly refer to this diverse range of Orphic sources in my arguments, I am primarily interested in analysing Orpheus' theogonies and in particular Orpheus' earliest known poem, the *Derveni Theogony*, a remarkable text which I argue provides a window on early Orphic thought and an innovative new ontological orientation I call pantheism.

That the earliest surviving Orphic text is a theogony is no coincidence. Indeed, ancient theogonies were closely associated with the name Orpheus and appear to have been written throughout antiquity. Some, such as the *Eudemian Theogony*, are practically unknown, while others, such as the *Rhapsodies*, are quoted more abundantly. Although no two poems share precisely the same details, they are united by a peculiar mix of tradition, innovative additions and what Edmonds refers to as their 'strangeness'.[8] In this chapter, I will argue that Orpheus' poems simultaneously adapt Hesiod's language and narratives and rewrite his ontological assumptions in ways that are reminiscent of the monism adhered to by Presocratic philosophers such as Anaximenes and Heraclitus. Indeed, at times Orphic poetry was so close to the words of Heraclitus that some Greeks accused the philosopher of plagiarizing Orpheus' words (DK 22 B 36; Clem. *Strom.* 6.2.17). However, while some Orphic fragments are strikingly close to the words of the philosophers, Orphic poetry also expresses itself in its own language and imagery. Indeed, rather than speaking of transforming elements, Orphic pantheism is often manifested through discussions of genealogies and the introduction of strange new gods. Though late, a good example of what I call Orphic poetic pantheism appears in an Orphic hymn preserved by Macrobius (*Sat.* 1.23.21):

τήκων αἰθέρα δῖον ἀκίνητον πρὶν ἐόντα ἐξαν
ἔφηνε θεοῖσιν Ἔρων κάλλιστον ἰδέσθαι.
ὃν δὴ νῦν καλέουσι Φάνητά τε καὶ Διόνυσον
Εὐβουλῆά τ' ἄνακτα καὶ Ἀνταύγην ἀρίδηλον·
ἄλλοι δ' ἄλλο καλοῦσιν ἐπιχθονίων ἀνθρώπων.
πρῶτος δ' ἐς φάος ἦλθε, Διώνυσος δ' ἐπεκλήθη,
οὕνεκα δινεῖται κατ' ἀπείρονα μακρὸν Ὄλυμπον·
ἀλλαχθεὶς δ' ὄνομ', ἔσχε προσωνυμίας πρὸς ἑκάστων
παντοδαπάς, κατὰ καιρὸν ἀμειβομένοιο χρόνοιο.

Melting the bright ether that was before now unmoved,
he revealed to the sight of the gods most beautiful Eros,
who now they call Phanes and Dionysus.
Sovereign Euboules and Antauges seen from afar:
among men who dwell on earth, some give him one name other another.
First he came into the light, and was named Dionysus,
because he whirls along the limitless length of Olympus;
but then he changed his name and took on forms of address of every sort
from every source, as suits the alternating seasons.[9]

Although written centuries after the *Derveni Theogony*, many of the philosophical ideas expressed in this poem can be traced to the Derveni commentator in the fourth or fifth century BCE and, as I will soon discuss, to the *Derveni Theogony* itself. For example, one of the central characteristics of Orphic poetry is its insistence that nominally distinct gods are in fact the same. In this case, the poet specifically tells us that the beautiful god Eros is known by many names including Phanes, Dionysus, Eubouleus and Antauges. A second key characteristic is that these names are as much proper nouns as they are descriptions of processes and events. This is entirely transparent with Phanes and Antauges, whose names both signify 'come to light' or 'shine'.[10] Other names are revealed through etymological readings and Dionysus, for example, is given an interesting interpretation from the verb δινεύω. This term is a characteristic description of Orphic gods such as Phanes elsewhere (e.g. *OH* 6.7) and refers to a whirlwind-like movement that sets everything in motion. Finally, we are given an explanation regarding the unity of these gods:

ἀλλαχθεὶς δ' ὄνομ', ἔσχε προσωνυμίας πρὸς ἑκάστων
παντοδαπάς, κατὰ καιρὸν ἀμειβομένοιο χρόνοιο.

But then he changed his name and took on forms of address of every sort
From every source, as suits the alternating seasons.

Like Heraclitus' evocation of a pantheistic god described as 'day night, winter summer, war peace, surfeit hunger' who 'alters as when mingled with perfumes, it gets named according to the pleasure of each' (DK 22 B 67), this passage explains that the many-named deities in this passage are really a single form with manifold aspects, alternating with the changes of time.[11] In this model, the one god is ever-present and never truly cedes power to another. Rather first, middle and last, the god appears in the process of becoming.[12] In short, Orpheus describes in this poem what Rowe defines as a 'typical Greek "pantheistic" view'.[13]

Although the precise boundaries between philosophy and myth continue to be debated, describing Orphic poetry, early or late, as pantheistic is nothing new. Finkelberg, for example, describes how Orpheus' 'pantheistic feeling' applies to the earliest poetic fragments.[14] Betegh comments that early Orphic poetry expresses pantheism in 'embryo'[15] and indicates 'a move towards a more abstract conception of divinity'.[16] Alderink summarizes Orphic poetry in general as 'monistic'.[17] It may be noted here that although Betegh and others attribute pantheistic qualities to Orphic poetry, they are somewhat hesitant to describe Orphic poetry as an expression of pantheism full stop. Rather, Orpheus anticipates aspects of pantheism without fully articulating a true pantheist position. As Burkert puts it, in early Orphic poetry we see the beginnings of 'the philosophical speculation which culminated in the pantheism of the Stoics'.[18]

By the end of this chapter, I hope to have demonstrated that the hesitancy to attribute a consistent philosophical stance to Orpheus is misplaced and that Orphic poetry from the *Derveni Theogony* on can rightfully be said to express a coherent pantheist position. However, before attempting to analyse the poem through the prism of pantheism, it is worth dwelling on the admittedly vague term 'pantheism' itself. Indeed, although widely used, what pantheism precisely means is rarely specified. For its critics, it is often taken as the absolute ontological identity between the world and god.[19] Drozdek for this reason argues against identifying Heraclitus as a pantheist, noting 'although Heraclitus' god is immanent in the world, he is not – as is often assumed – a proponent of pantheism. God-Logos is in full control of the events in the world, but identification of God with the world is inadmissible.'[20] This understanding of pantheism is common, yet modern proponents of pantheism often avoid it and argue more cautiously that 'although pantheists differ amongst themselves at many points, they all agree in denying the basic theistic claim that god and the world are ontologically distinct'.[21] In other words, the key feature of pantheism is not an absolute identification between god and the world so much as a stance against the ontological distinction between the world and god. A related view is sometimes specified as 'pan*en*theism' which allows for more nuanced positions, such as those proposed by the Stoics, where god permeates the world as a whole but is not identical with it.

Although pantheism has been applied to a wide range of cosmological positions in Greece, I argue that these differences emerge from a more basic set of shared assumptions and in this and the following chapter, I will refer to pantheism specifically as an ontological classification akin to Hesiod's analogism. Defining pantheism as an ontology alongside analogism, it may be noted, requires an emendation to Descola's four ontologies: naturalism, totemism, animism and analogism. Although redefining Descola's model entails problems of its own, the shift is one justified by both the Greek evidence and a set of wider criticisms raised by some anthropologists against Descola's model. As alluded to in the introduction, Descola's model has particular difficulty accommodating for societies which appear to mix analogist and animist tendencies. Many societies from Southeast Asia and Mongolia, for example, have been referred to as transcendental animism and hierarchal animism and discussed as hybrid ontologies.[22] A similar mix of animism and analogism is also something noted in China.[23] Although Descola has repeatedly referred to his ontologies as 'ideal types' rather than social realities,[24] the ubiquity of these hybrids seems to undermine even the heuristic value of his model. Indeed, Scott and Matthews argue that rather than hybrid ontologies, at least some of these exceptions may be better viewed as alternative ontologies in their own right. Scott describes that analogist systems in some cases 'as a result of their own efforts to embed entities in relations, have transformed themselves so completely that they now constitute a mode of identification not recognized in Descola's set of four permutations'.[25] Matthews, developing upon this idea, has specifically referred to this ontology as 'homologism' and discusses it in relation to Chinese divination practices.[26] He further argues that homologism should displace Descola's totemism, which should be reclassified in terms of its internal divisions as a subdivision of analogism 'albeit a highly derived one'.[27] The specifics of this debate and the ontological status of totemism are not important for my argument. Indeed, my point is not driven by a wish to redefine Descola's model, but by the Greek evidence. For this reason, following the work of Scott and Matthews and my own study of the Greek material, I propose the presence of an alternate ontology based on a double continuity of interiorities and physicalities. Although this ontological configuration can be referred to as homologism, given the existing Greek debates and philosophical nomenclature, I refer to this ontology as pantheism. Furthermore, although Descola's ontological models may seem reductionist, I wish to stress that my use of ontological pantheism is not intended as a means of glossing over the many differences between the philosophical and poetical models gathered under this classification. On the contrary, I stress that pantheism is not a concrete philosophy or theology but a basic set of assumptions which may show significant differences in practice. Thales' pantheism, for example, may be more concerned with eclipses than religious cults, while Empedocles' might focus on the relations between animals, men and gods. Yet despite these clear differences, I argue that they both share basic ontological assumptions that emerged as a rejection of Hesiod's stress on the foundational difference between humans and gods. This newfound orientation could be expressed in Thales' ensouled magnets (DK 11 A 22) or Orpheus' enchanted stones (Ap. Rhod. Argon. 1.26–30), but in both cases we see repeated common themes: unity over diversity, kinship over affinity, cosmos over chaos.[28] And it is also through these assumptions that we can understand how the *Derveni Theogony* rewrites Hesiod's poem.

Reconstructing the beginning of the *Derveni Theogony*

Examples of Orphic pantheism are found throughout the sparse fragments of the *Derveni Theogony*. The most frequently cited example appears when Zeus ingests the cosmos and becomes alone (col. 16). As Finkelberg notes, the pantheism expressed in this scene is 'obvious'.[29] However, this is far from an isolated example. Equally important is the theogony's opening scene and the birth of the god Protogonos. The Orphic poet's emphasis on origins is perhaps something to be expected. Indeed, origins are essential to understanding the ontological assumptions of countless cosmologies. Hesiod's *Theogony*, as we have seen, began with three distinct and independently born gods, Chaos, Gaia and Eros. This marked an essential and enduring conflict in the cosmos, which can be only tentatively united under the rule of Zeus. This conflict has no place in Orphic pantheism and in one of the most innovative transformations of its Hesiodic predecessor, the *Derveni Theogony* displaces this cosmic triad by giving pre-eminence to a new god, the 'reverend king Protogonos' (Πρωτογόνου βασιλέως αἰδοίου) (col. 16.3).

In many respects, the discovery of the name Protogonos (literally the firstborn) in the *Derveni Theogony* is hardly surprising. Indeed, Protogonos occupies a central position in early and late Orphism. While his precise characteristics vary, some of the god's key attributes are nicely summarized in his eponymous Orphic hymn:

Πρωτόγονον καλέω διφυῆ, μέγαν, αἰθερόπλαγκτον,
ᾠογενῆ, χρυσέαισιν ἀγαλλόμενον πτερύγεσσι,
ταυροβόαν, γένεσιν μακάρων θνητῶν τ' ἀνθρώπων,
σπέρμα πολύμνηστον, πολυόργιον, Ἠρικεπαῖον,
ἄρρητον, κρύφιον ῥοιζήτορα, παμφαὲς ἔρνος,
ὅσσων ὃς σκοτόεσσαν ἀπημαύρωσας ὀμίχλην
πάντη δινηθεὶς πτερύγων ῥιπαῖς κατὰ κόσμον
λαμπρὸν ἄγων φάος ἁγνόν, ἀφ' οὗ σε Φάνητα κικλήσκω
ἠδὲ Πρίηπον ἄνακτα καὶ Ἀνταύγην ἑλίκωπον.
ἀλλά, μάκαρ, πολύμητι, πολύσπορε, βαῖνε γεγηθὼς
ἐς τελετὴν ἁγίαν πολυποίκιλον ὀργιοφάνταις.

I call upon Protogonos, first born and of a double nature, great, roaming in Ether,
Born from an egg, exulting in his golden wings,
Bellowing like a bull, origin of the blest and of mortal men,
Seed full of memory, honoured in many secret rites, Ericepaios
The unspeakable, hidden and whizzing, all-shiny shoot,
You who removed the dark mist from the eyes,
And swirl everywhere in the kosmos with the beating of your wings,
Bringing bright and pure light: wherefore I call thee Phanes,

Lord Priapus and quick glancing Antauges,
But, blessed, full of wile and full of seed, come rejoiced
To this pure festival, full of variety, for those who reveal the mysteries.[30]

The hymn, dating to around the first century CE, lists many of Protogonos' most memorable features, including the many-named god's miraculous birth from an egg, his golden wings and dual sex, and his dizzying motion as he swirls around the cosmos.[31] Although the most detailed descriptions of Protogonos are found in late works such as the *Hymns*, there is no doubt that Protogonos is an early god. Indeed, many of his most important attributes can be dated to either the early Hellenistic or classical periods. *Erikapaios*,[32] one of Protogonos' few non-Greek titles, appears in the third century BCE Gurob papyrus (col. 1.22) and a form of the name is possibly referenced in a fourth-century gold tablet from Pherai (L 13 OF 493) where it is potentially etymologized as a mini-sentence: Ανδρικεπαιδόθυρσον.[33] Phanes, a far more common name for the god, is first recorded in the fourth century BCE Timpone Grande gold tablet (L 12 OF 492). Alongside Phanes, the Timpone Grande tablet also clearly mentions the name Protogonos.[34] Furthermore, a theogony-like fragment from Euripides' *Hypsipyle*, plausibly delivered by Orpheus himself, places Eros, Protogonos, Night and perhaps Aither in close succession:

ᾦ πότνια θεῶ[ν
φ]άος ἄσκοπον [αἰ-
θέ]ρι πρωτόγονο[
ἤ]θελ᾿ Ἔρως ὅτε Νὺ[ξ.

Queen of the gods
Unintelligible light [Aither]
Protogonos
Eros wished, then Night.[35]

Alongside these clear testaments for the god's early existence, Aristophanes' Orphic inspired parody in the *Birds* (693–7) describes a winged god born from an egg:

Ἐρέβους δ᾿ ἐν ἀπείροσι κόλποις
τίκτει πρώτιστον ὑπηνέμιον Νὺξ ἡ μελανόπτερος ᾠόν,
ἐξ οὗ περιτελλομέναις ὥραις ἔβλαστεν Ἔρως ὁ ποθεινός,
στίλβων νῶτον πτερύγοιν χρυσαῖν, εἰκὼς ἀνεμώκεσι δίναις.

Firstly, blackwinged Night laid a germless egg in the bosom of the infinite deeps of Erebus, and from this, after the revolution of long ages, sprang the graceful Eros with his glittering golden wings, swift as the whirlwinds of the tempest.[36]

Although neither Protogonos nor Phanes are named in this passage and a definite Orphic identification remains uncertain, many of these details are strikingly reminiscent of the Orphic god. Indeed, Eros is among Protogonos' many names in later poetry and the egg from which the god bursts out, his impressive golden wings, and whirlwind-like movement are ubiquitous Orphic details.[37] Santamaría has also more tentatively suggested that Protogonos' dual sex is an early attribute and can be inferred from specific details in Aristophanes' speech in Plato's *Symposium*.[38] Another tentative clue for this attribute may appear in Empedocles' negative description of the divine Sphere (DK 31 B 29): 'two branches [wings?] do not shoot out of his back, nor feet or swift knees, neither generative organs' (οὐ γὰρ ἀπὸ νώτοιο δύο κλάδοι ἀίσσονται, οὐ πόδες, οὐ θοὰ γοῦν(α), οὐ μήδεα γεννήεντα).[39] Empedocles does not say wings in this passage but 'branches' (κλάδοι).[40] Nor does he specify that his god lacks male and female genitalia. Nonetheless, why someone would describe a god as not possessing these features is very strange, unless we assume another influential god did, and Orpheus' Protogonos is a likely suspect.[41] Although the few hints and allusions to Protogonos' characteristics in the classical period may seem slight, some are secure and given Euripides' and Aristophanes' testimony alongside the Timpone Grande gold tablet, they suggest that Protogonos was not only present but was an important and impressive god in early Orphism.[42]

The best and the earliest source for Protogonos is, of course, the *Derveni Theogony* itself. In this poem the name Protogonos is present within a theogonic context almost identical to that preserved in later poems such as the Orphic *Rhapsodies*. However, reconstructing ancient documents is never a simple task and the presence of Protogonos in the *Derveni Theogony* is also one of the most controversial issues in early Orphism. Indeed, despite the clear presence of the word 'protogonos' in the surviving text, its meaning is not agreed upon. Some scholars, for example, point out that although 'protogonos' may be a proper name, it literally means firstborn and could refer to any firstborn god.[43] Moreover, since Ouranos is said to rule first (col. 14.6), it is possible that the epitaph Πρωτογόνου βασιλέως αἰδοίου or 'reverend firstborn king' refers to him.[44] This argument, however, is only the tip of the iceberg and even more controversy surrounds the translation of the term αἰδοίου. Some read it as the masculine adjective αἰδοῖος 'reverend', others as a neuter noun αἰδοῖον 'phallus'. This reading entirely transforms the sentence from 'the reverend firstborn king' to the new and strange phrase 'the phallus of the firstborn king'.[45] This may seem like a very odd translation. Indeed, if we were reading a fragment from Homer or any other poet from the period, it would be immediately rejected in favour of the common expression 'the reverend king'.[46] However, the translation is not simply the product of modern scholarship's overactive imagination but a view that goes back to the papyrus itself, where the philosophical commentator stresses that Orpheus understands this word as a phallus (13.7–10). Ordinarily the commentator's interpretation would hold little weight; indeed, many of his arguments are far removed from the text of the poem. However, largely because of the fragmented condition of the papyrus, it is unclear whether this is part of the commentator's unusual interpretative procedure or a detail present in the poem itself.[47] This has led to two widely diverging readings of the text. For Betegh and Bernabé, among others, the passage refers to the phallus of the firstborn king Ouranos, whereas for Parker and West, the text refers to the reverend king and demiurge Protogonos.[48]

Despite the subtle arguments made by both sides, there are some strong reasons for associating αἰδοῖος/αἰδοῖον with the god Protogonos rather than the phallus. In col. 13.4 the term αἰδοῖος/αἰδοῖον is used to refer to the time when Zeus swallows something:

αἰδοῖον κατέπινεν, ὃς αἰθέρα ἔκθορε πρῶτος.

he [i.e. Zeus] swallowed down the reverend one, who was first born from/in the aither.[49]

The idea of being born from the Aither strongly associates the term with the god Protogonos who is frequently associated with divine Aither.[50] In Proclus (OF 124–5) Protogonos is called the 'very beautiful son of Aither' (περικαλλὴς Αἰθέρος υἱός).[51] In the *Hymns* (6.2) he is called 'aither-roaming' (αἰθερόπλαγκτον). Damascius (OF 121) even uses the same verb when he describes the cloud from which Protogonos is born or leaps out from (ἐξέθορε).[52] In col. 13.4 of the Derveni poem, apart from the reference to a birth from Aither, the use of the masculine pronoun ὅς suggests an agreement with αἰδοῖον (reverend) and thus rejects the phallus reading, which requires a neuter pronoun. However, Betegh and others circumnavigate this problem by reading ὅς as a 'possessive genitive, subordinated to the neutral noun αἰδοῖον'.[53] While this assumption permits an identification with the god Ouranos, it does not cohere with the fact that the god in question is said to have been born from the Aither. The possibilities are limited and this certainly cannot apply to Ouranos who is the son of Night (col. 14.6). Nor does the idea make much sense in regard to the phallus of Ouranos. It does, on the other hand, nicely dovetail with later descriptions of Protogonos' birth from the Aither.

In response to these arguments, the phallus reading gets even stranger and Burkert and Bernabé adopt an unconventional reading of θρῴσκω as 'ejaculate' rather than 'to be born'. The sentence now refers to the phallus 'who *first ejaculated* the ether'.[54] This is certainly a possible and fascinating reading which, as Burkert points out, is paralleled by the Egyptian sky god Anum's ejaculation into the upper air. There is, however, a general consensus that θρῴσκω as 'ejaculate' is a rare reading whereas the meaning 'to leap out' or, especially concerning the birth of a god, to be born is common and intuitive.[55] Indeed, if the passage refers to a god born from the Aither, the most likely candidate is not Ouranos, son of Night, but aither-roaming Protogonos. In other words, the most intuitive reading, supported by classical and later texts, is also the most consistent with the fragmented papyrus itself. The debate, unfortunately, does not end here and if my reading solves one set of textual problems, it too necessitates creatively reading the clear statement that Ouranos is said to be the first god to reign (col. 14.6). Although this is certainly a problematic line, it can be circumnavigated. For Parker, the idea of first is here 'used loosely, as a mere title of respect', while others have pointed out a potential solution in a fragment (OF 174) cited by an Aristotelian scholiast where Ouranos is described as the god 'who ruled first among the gods after his mother Night' (ὃς πρῶτος βασίλευσε θεῶν μετὰ μητέρα Νύκτα).[56]

The debate surrounding Protogonos, of course, exists for good reason and no interpretation is problem-free. However, it is imperative to realize that there is no single coherent way of reconstructing the fragmented text and whether we place Protogonos first, Ouranos, or the phallus of Ouranos, we must choose from conflicting fragments. In this respect, the likelihood of any reconstruction must be judged by an external standard, the comparative material, and here the Protogonos reading is far more convincing. The comparative argument for the phallus reading rests almost entirely on a non-Greek poem, the Hurro-Hittie *Kumarbi* epic.[57] A phallus is indeed swallowed in this poem, yet not only are the narrative details different, but how a poem dating to the thirteenth or fourteenth century BCE exerted influence on Orphic authors in the sixth century is entirely unexplained. Nor is it clear why this very particular and memorable narrative simply disappeared after the Derveni poem, never to be repeated or even alluded to by later Orphic poets or Christian critics.[58] The Protogonos reading, on the other hand, is well supported. Not only is the god mentioned as early as the classical period, in later texts including the *Orphic Hymns*, the *Hieronymian Theogony* and the *Rhapsodies* he is among the most frequently described of Orphic gods.[59] Although the use of later texts to support earlier readings is sometimes viewed suspiciously, later Orphic texts surely have a superior claim in this debate than Hurro-Hittite material. While no two Orphic theogonies are the same,[60] the differences between Orphic accounts should not be exaggerated.[61] Indeed, many of the greatest divergences emerge from the texts we know least about. The Derveni poem, for example, is often compared with a theogony known to Aristotle's pupil, Eudemus. However, despite imaginative reconstructions, all that is known securely about this poem is that it started with Night.[62] On the other hand, the more detailed Orphic theogonies such as the *Rhapsodies* and the theogony associated with Hieronymus and Hellanicus substantially agree in the main narrative details.[63] Both start with primordial deities such as Night and Aither. Both give a central position to Protogonos–Phanes and his miraculous birth from an egg. Both describe the struggles for authority that follow until finally Protogonos–Phanes is swallowed by Zeus. Finally, both describe how Zeus after swallowing Protogonos recreates the cosmos.[64] With the discovery of the Derveni papyrus, which undeniably agrees in part with these narratives, the antiquity of Orphic poetic ideas became apparent. West was so confident regarding the close relation between these poems that he proposed a hypothetical urtext from which all other Orphic poems derive, the *Protogonos Theogony*.[65] Others are more sceptical of this methodology and while there is always a danger in reconstructing earlier poetic material from later sources, at times the correspondences are too close to be ignored.[66] In the *Rhapsodies* we are told how Zeus swallows Protogonos (OF 241):

ὣς τότε πρωτογόνοιο χαδὼν μένος Ἠρικεπαίου
τῶν πάντων δέμας εἶχεν ἑῇ ἐνὶ γαστέρι κοίλῃ,
μεῖξε δ' ἑοῖς μελέεσσι θεοῦ δύναμίν τε καὶ ἀλκήν,
τοὔνεκα σὺν τῶι πάντα Διὸς πάλιν ἐντὸς ἐτύχθη,
αἰθέρος εὐρείης ἠδ' οὐρανοῦ ἀγλαὸν ὕψος,
πόντου τ' ἀτρθγέτου γαίς τ' ἐρικυδέος ἕδρη,
Ὠκεανός τε μέγας καὶ νείατα Τάρταρα γαίης
καὶ ποταμοὶ καὶ πόντος ἀπείριτος ἄλλα τε πάντα
πάντες τ' ἀθάνατοι μάκαρες θεοὶ ἠδὲ θέαιναι,
ὅσσα τ' ἔην γεγαῶτα καὶ ὕστερον ὁππόσ' ἔμελλεν,
ἓν γένετο, Ζηνὸς δ' ἐνὶ γαστέρι σύρρα πεφύκει.

And so, swallowing the strength of first-born Erikepaios [another name for Phanes]
he had the body of everything inside his own hollow belly
and he mixed into his own limbs the god's power and strength.
And so along with him everything was fashioned again inside Zeus

the gleaming height of the broad aither and heaven,
the seat of the unharvested sea and glorious earth,
great Ocean and Tartarus, depth of the earth,
and rivers and the boundless sea and all other things
and all the immortal blessed gods and goddesses
all things that existed and would exist later,
became one, having grown together in the stomach of Zeus.[67]

It is a remarkable coincidence that this passage shows some striking similarities with the best-preserved and longest fragment from the *Derveni Theogony* found in col. 16.3–6:

Πρωτογόνου βασιλέως αἰδοίου· τῶι δ' ἄρα πάντες
ἀθάνατοι προσέφυν μάκαρες θεοὶ ἠδὲ θέαιναι
καὶ ποταμοὶ καὶ κρῆναι ἐπήρατοι ἄλλα τε πάντα,
ἄσσα τότ' ἦν γεγαῶτ', αὐτὸς δ' ἄρα μοῦνος ἔγεντο

Of Protogonos the reverend one, and on him (Zeus) all
the immortals grew, blessed gods and goddesses
And rivers and lovely springs and everything else
That had been born then; and he himself became solitary.[68]

There is no doubt that these two texts, one from as early as the sixth century BCE, another recorded in the fifth century CE, are closely related. As Parker points out, in addition to the similar events, the presence of the identical phrases μάκαρες θεοὶ ἠδὲ θέαιναι; ἄλλα τε πάντα; and the close ἄσσα τότ' ἦν γεγαῶτ' 'prove that the second passage in fact ultimately derives from the first'.[69] Parker concludes that 'it is natural to suppose that the original context was the same'.[70] Indeed, while the *Rhapsodies* were written a good deal earlier than Damascius' citation, the continuity we see between texts dating nearly a thousand years apart is compelling testament to the stability of the Orphic poetic tradition.

Protogonos and the early gods in the *Derveni Theogony*

Although little concrete information is given about the nature of Protogonos in the *Derveni Theogony*, from direct and indirect references it is possible to reconstruct some of his key characteristics and biographical details. First, unlike some later Orphic poems, Protogonos does not appear to have been born from an egg in the *Derveni Theogony*. The god was, however, definitely associated with an impressive birth from divine Aither (13.4):

αἰδοῖον κατέπινεν, ὃς αἰθέρα ἔκθορε πρῶτος.

he drank the reverend one, who was born from/in the Aither first.[71]

While I have translated θρῴσκω as birth, the word really refers to an astonishing leaping into existence that demarcates this divine birth as something exceptional. In the *Homeric Hymn to Apollo*, for example, we are told how Apollo (119):

ἐκ δ᾽ ἔθορε πρὸ φόωσδε· θεαὶ δ᾽ ὀλόλυξαν ἅπασαι.

From (Leto) leapt towards the light and all the goddesses let out a cry.[72]

Although Protogonos' emergence from the Aither may seem to detract from the priority of the firstborn god, his close association with earlier divinities was far from unusual in the Orphic tradition. As explained in the *Etymologicum Magnum*, 'they call him Phanes and Protogonos because he became the first one visible (φαντός) in Aither'.[73] Indeed, alongside Aither, Orphic poetry frequently places cosmic forces such as Chronos (time), Night and even Chaos prior to Protogonos' birth. Though fragmented, the *Derveni Theogony* roughly follows this model. Indeed, it is possible that alongside Aither, Night also preceded Protogonos. The issue, however, is unclear due of the multiple births of Night described in later Orphic poems.[74] No evidence either supports or rejects the presence of other primordial gods, but it is certainly possible that figures such as Chronos were also present at this stage.[75] The possible presence of multiple primordial beings in no way diminishes the grandeur of Protogonos. Indeed, it should be stressed that in the Greek tradition, creation was rarely *ex nihilo* and figures like Aither are arguably more prerequisites that allow creation to take place than rivals to Protogonos' power.[76] In later poems, for example, Aither was even described as without motion before the birth of Protogonos (OF 539).[77] In other words, literal priority is secondary here and the title firstborn indicates that cosmos and creation really begin with this figure. Indeed, while the actual creation is not described in the surviving fragments of the poem, there is some strong evidence that Protogonos was a creator god in the *Derveni Theogony*. This idea is suggested in a later episode when Zeus swallows Protogonos. The poem describes how Zeus' swallowing of the firstborn god is simultaneously the swallowing of rivers and springs, gods and goddesses, and in short of 'everything that had come into being then' (ἄσσα τότ᾽ ἦν γεγαῶτ᾽) (col. 16.6). I will return to this passage in more detail shortly. Presently, I wish to emphasize the taken-for-granted assumption that by swallowing Protogonos, Zeus also swallows everything else that came into being at that time (τότ᾽). In other words, we see here an allusion to a previous creation in the past and a remaining close, even inseparable, connection between Protogonos and the cosmos he first created. The precise method of Protogonos' creation will likely remain unknown. Indeed, these details are unclear even in the later and better-preserved poems. We can, however, speculate on the early genealogical line. In the *Rhapsodies*, for example, Protogonos starts by mating with himself and giving birth to Night, whom he in turn impregnates to produce the other gods.[78] This detail is neither confirmed nor contradicted by the Derveni poet, but I propose we take it as one possible guideline. An important consideration is whether we accept the evidence for Protogonos' male and female genitalia discussed above. If this detail was present from an early date, it presumably played a role in the narrative and suggests, as in other versions, that Protogonos creates all subsequent generations by mating with himself.[79]

After his probable creation of the cosmos, Protogonos, as in the later *Rhapsodies*, concedes his power to Night and recedes to the background until his later encounter with Zeus. Like Protogonos, Night is a pivotal deity in the *Derveni Theogony*, who again offers an important transformation of the Hesiodic narrative.[80] Night, as we have seen, is a formidable deity in Hesiod's poem. In the *Theogony*, she is the daughter of Chaos and mother and grandmother of a long lineage of destructive forces including Strife, Toil, Forgetfulness, Famine, and tearful Sorrows, Fighting, Battles, Murders, Manslaughters, Quarrels, Lying Words, etc. (*Theog.* 210–40). These abstract gods were exemplary of Hesiod's emphasis on the disorderly forces that plague the cosmos prior to the reign of Zeus. The descendants of Chaos were also, I argued, illustrative of Hesiod's analogist assumptions and insistence on multiple genealogical lines. In the *Derveni Theogony*, on the other hand, Hesiod's dualism is collapsed, and Night is integrated into a single genealogical line. Alongside this transformation, Night's terrible character is also reformed. Far from threatening the stability of the cosmos, the Orphic Night takes on many attributes associated with Hesiod's Gaia and is given a nurturing role illustrated by the epitaph 'nurturer' 'τροφός' (col. 10.11).[81] This characteristic is also reflected in her peaceful relations with the other gods whom she continues to assist by proclaiming oracles from her shrine (col. 11.1). Finally, in a further example of Night supplanting Gaia's position, the goddess is transformed into the mother of Ouranos (col. 14.6) and gives rise to the third generation of the gods.

Other than his close relation to Night, not much is said of Ouranos in the *Derveni Theogony* and even the identity of his father remains unclear.[82] Bernabé argues that the use of the matronymic Εὐφρονίδης indicates Ouranos has no father.[83] This is possible but not convincing. Indeed, in Homeric poetry both Apollo (*Hymn Merc.* 513) and Hermes (*Hymn Merc.* 42) are both frequently given matronymics despite being the children of Zeus.[84] Although the text is too fragmented to say anything with certainty, it is likely that Ouranos' father is Protogonos. It is also possible, though tentative, that through a union between Night (either a primordial Night or a second-born Night) and Protogonos the gods Gaia, Okeanos and the Moirai are born.[85] Whatever the precise details, these early gods are present in the poem and collectively set the stage for the more familiar Hesiodic genealogy which defines the mid-sections of Orpheus' narrative. Kronos, Rhea and the other Titans, although not specifically stated, are most likely born, as in Hesiod, from a union between Gaia and Ouranos. At this point, the usually opaque narrative becomes somewhat clearer. Column 14 refers to a great deed (μέγ' ἔρεξεν) committed by Kronos. From both the poetic fragments and the commentary, it is clear that this deed refers to the castration of Ouranos by Kronos. A later reference to heavenly Aphrodite also suggests that from Ouranos' severed phallus the goddess of love was born (col. 21. 5).

Although the many lacunae in the early sections of the Orphic poem prevent a secure reconstruction of the details, even these few surviving fragments indicate several key divergences from Hesiod's analogist narrative and a clear shift towards a pantheistic poem. The most notable example of an Orphic transformation found in the early verses is the elimination of Hesiod's dualistic and conflicting lineages into a single genealogy beginning with Protogonos. This emphasis on a single genealogy emphasizes the continuity and underlying kinship found in the cosmos as a whole. Indeed, more than simply stressing a close connection, Orphic genealogies emphasize as far as possible how nominally distinct gods and goddesses share a common identity.[86] This tendency is often expressed very directly in Orphic poetry and philosophical speculation. In column 14.7 of the philosophical Derveni commentary, for example, the commentator etymologizes the name Kronos as the striking mind of the supergod: 'naming the Mind that strikes things against each other Kronos' (κρούοντα τὸν Νοῦν πρὸς ἄλληλ[α] Κρόνον ὀνομάσας).[87] In other words, Kronos is not a distinct god but an aspect of a pantheistic divine Mind. This strategy is even more transparent in column 22.7–15 where the commentator tells us that the goddesses Gaia, Rhea, Demeter and Hera are really the same (ἡ αὐτή). In this case, however, the idea is not simply an example of the commentator's interpretative procedure but one he supports with a quotation from a poem by Orpheus (22.12):

Δημήτηρ [Ρ]έα Γῆ Μήτηρ Ἑστία Δηιώι.

Demeter Rhea Ge Meter Hestia Deio.[88]

While the lack of punctuation in this list potentially suggests the unity of these figures, the line does not specifically state that these goddesses are identical.[89] Fortunately we possess independent confirmation for this reading and a similar idea was noted by Philochoros in the late fourth century BCE. The testimony is reported by Philodemus, who writes: 'in the *Hymns* Orpheus in Philochorus (says) that Ge and Demeter are the same as Hestia.'[90] This tendency to identify the myriad gods as the same is also arguably expressed through the prominent place of incestuous relations in the divine successions in Orphic poetry. In the *Rhapsodies*, for example, Protogonos mates with himself and produces Night, who alongside Protogonos later begets Ouranos. This may seem in some respects comparable with Hesiod's narrative where Gaia by herself bears Ouranos and in turn Ouranos and Gaia produce the second generation of gods together (*Theog.* 125–50). Indeed, this general similarity is not surprising and in most polytheistic narratives the possibilities of partnerships are severely limited in the early stages of the cosmos. There are, however, some notable differences between incest in Hesiodic and Orphic poetry. In Hesiod, Gaia does not mate with herself but simply gives birth to Ouranos, perhaps by splitting herself in two. Following from this, the relations between Gaia and Ouranos are immediately hostile and illustrate the first step in a series of beings increasingly divided and genealogically distant. Orphic incestuous unions, on the other hand, are peaceful and importantly appear as a device which is repeatedly used at strategic points in the narrative. Skipping ahead a little in the plot, Zeus, after his recreation of the cosmos, mates with his own mother (col. 16). It is important to note that the act of incest is even more complex considering that he has just given birth to her. Although the detail is not present in the Derveni poem, in later versions, following this union Zeus mates with his daughter, Persephone. Persephone in turn gives birth to the most complex of all Orphic gods, Dionysus. These incestuous acts horrified many Greeks, and even the Derveni commentator was suspicious of their moral content.[91] Nevertheless, the confusing kinship relations they create point towards the underlying unity of the gods. As Sahlins explains:

> as a social reproductive capacity, incest is a modality of the famous autonomy of the Olympian gods, their self-sufficiency, of which their freedom from labor is another. In social terms, incest is a denial of dependence on others for reproduction, hence another aspect of immortality. And as it is among humans a

crime against kinship, a transcendent anti-structural act, it becomes for the gods the proof that they are stronger than society – and thus able to constitute it.[92]

In other words, Olympian incest produces a society of gods who are independent from mortals. Orphic genealogies do something even more extreme. Rather than differentiating two societies, mortal and immortal, the emphasis is on collapsing genealogy altogether. Protogonos reproduces entirely from himself and mates with his own offspring to become the grandfather, grandmother, father, mother, uncle, aunt, and brother and sister of Ouranos. This dazzling complexity of relations circumnavigates the distance usually created through genealogies and stresses once again the Orphic emphasis on identity over distinction. In other words, Orphic genealogies, rather than fork out as we see in Hesiod, fold in upon themselves, blurring the one and the many into a single being. All of these details amount to a distinctly new image of the cosmos, one shaped not by conflicting forces but by a single genealogical line. The best illustration of this genealogical monism, however, is not in the fragmented early sections but in the rich characterization of Zeus, the single clearest example of Orphic poetic pantheism in the surviving poem.

Zeus first, middle and last

That the best-preserved fragments in the *Derveni Theogony* describe the god Zeus is unlikely to be coincidental. Indeed, although often referred to as a theogony, the Derveni poem is equal parts hymn to the glory of Zeus. However, a pantheistic theogony glorifying the power of Zeus faces one serious obstacle: Zeus is a latecomer. Orpheus was not the only Greek concerned with this deficiency. Orphic theogonies were written during a period when both Zeus' behaviour and late birth were perceived as somehow incompatible with newly introduced ideas of god and order. One solution was simply to rewrite the divine history and place a powerful and often nameless deity at the forefront. Pherecydes called his Zeus Zas (DK 7 B 1). Anaxagoras adopted a more neutral name: Nous or Mind (DK 59 B 12). Xenophanes (DK 21 B 23) simply called his divinity the God. Orpheus' solution, as was often the case, was both traditional and innovative. Like his Presocratic peers, he too introduced a divine steersman at the beginning of his cosmology: Protogonos. Orpheus, however, did not wish to dismiss Zeus either and in a remarkable example of having his cake and eating it too, the Thracian poet composed a narrative that stretches the imagination of its readers to its limits. True to Hesiod's poem, Zeus would remain a latecomer. However, he would also be first, middle and indeed, last:

Ζεὺς πρῶτος γένετο, [Ζεὺς ὕστατος ἀργικέραυνος]
Ζεὺς κεφαλή, Ζεὺς μέσσα, Διὸς δ' ἐκ πάντα τέτυκται.

Zeus was born first, Zeus bearer of lighting is last
Zeus is the head, Zeus the middle, from Zeus are all things made.[93]

The above verse is identical with a later Orphic *Hymn to Zeus* and may have continued with:

Ζεὺς πνοιὴ πάντων, Ζεὺς πάντων ἔπλετο μοῖρα
Ζεὺς βασιλεύς, Ζεὺς δ' ἀρχὸς ἁπάντων ἀργικέραυνος.

Zeus is breath of all, Zeus the fate of all,
Zeus King, Zeus bearer of lighting is the ruler of all.[94]

Zeus as simultaneously the beginning and the end is a riddle at the very core of the poem and the key to its ontological orientation.

Orpheus' initial description of Zeus' ascent to the throne remains faithful to Hesiod. As in Hesiod, Zeus defeats his father Kronos and takes the crown. At this point he must solidify his rule. So far, so Hesiodic. However, to consolidate his rule, Zeus does not swallow the goddess Metis and combine intelligence and force in his single person. Rather, Zeus swallows the firstborn god Protogonos. The most plausible reconstruction of the surviving poetic fragments recounts how Zeus takes Protogonos into his hands and (13.4, 16.3–6)

αἰδοῖον κατέπινεν, ὃς αἰθέρα ἔκθορε πρῶτος.
...
Πρωτογόνου βασιλέως αἰδοίου· τῶι δ' ἄρα πάντες
ἀθάνατοι προσέφυν μάκαρες θεοὶ ἠδὲ θέαιναι
καὶ ποταμοὶ καὶ κρῆναι ἐπήρατοι ἄλλα τε πάντα,
ὅσσα τότ' ἦν γεγαῶτ', αὐτὸς δ' ἄρα μοῦνος ἔγεντο.

He [i.e. Zeus] swallowed down the reverend one [i.e. Protogonos], who was first born from the aither.
...
Protogonos the reverend one. And on him [i.e. Zeus] all
The immortals grew, blessed gods and goddesses
And rivers and lovely springs and everything else
That had been born then [i.e. the original creation of Protogonos] and he himself was alone.[95]

The scene occupies a pivotal role in the *Rhapsodies* and the *Hieronyman Theogony*[96] and that it happens to be the best-preserved fragment of the papyrus is no accident. It is likely that the commentator, like later writers, quoted this passage at length because of its clear philosophical significance and basic agreement with his own pantheistic interpretive strategy. Indeed, in this passage we see not only how Zeus eats the original creator Protogonos, but with him he swallows all the gods and goddesses, rivers and springs, and in short 'everything that had been born then' and becomes alone (μοῦνος).

As noted earlier, a great deal of scholarly debate hinges on whether Zeus swallows the phallus of Ouranos or the reverend Protogonos. However, despite this dispute, there is a broad consensus on the significance of this act. For Bernabé, Zeus swallows 'the immense generating capacity of Sky's penis'.[97] Betegh takes the idea further, arguing that the phallus is not simply a generating capacity but 'can easily be seen as some kind of origin or principle of all generation'.[98] As Edmonds puts it, whether Zeus swallows Protogonos or a phallus 'in either case the idea is the same: Zeus incorporates within himself the generative principle, whether it is the hermaphroditic Phanes who generates the other gods by copulating with himself/herself or it is the generative member of the oldest god, Ouranos'.[99] Despite the overall consensus on the meaning of the act, I am far from convinced that to swallow a phallus and to swallow the firstborn god Protogonos are actually equivalent acts. Although the idea that the phallus represents a generative principle is an association clearly made by the commentator, it is one weakly supported by the poem itself. Ouranos, it should be noted, in any interpretation is not the oldest god, but the son of Night (col. 14.6). In the narrative he probably mates with his sister Gaia, who in turn gives birth to Kronos and the other gods. In this respect, the phallus of Ouranos as a 'principle of all generation' has a partial claim at best. At worst it is an unclear metaphor, which although not literally responsible for the creation of everything, somehow stands in as a symbol for this act.[100] It is also for these reasons a weak answer to the riddle of how Zeus achieves the status first, middle and last. In contrast, Zeus achieving priority by swallowing the firstborn god Protogonos is a simpler, more profound and a more satisfying answer to the Orphic paradox.

It might help clarify my point by reflecting on Hesiod's description of Zeus' encompassment of Metis. In Chapter 1, I argued that Hesiod's poem can be read as a kind of riddle focusing on how Zeus can achieve stable power in an unstable world. The solution involved swallowing Metis, the personification of cunning intelligence. This was not a metaphorical eating of a female power, but the literal ingestion of a goddess and the capacities she personifies. This same transparency also applies to the poem of Orpheus. In both cases a problem arises concerning how Zeus can succeed where others failed. And in both cases, the poets utilize clear and unambiguous personifications to solve these problems.[101] In neither account does Zeus swallow a metaphor, he swallows a god who is simultaneously an attribute, capacity and a word. Metis is cunning intelligence and Zeus absorbs this goddess into himself and takes on this power/word. Similarly, in the Derveni poem, Zeus can become first, middle and last because he swallows a god who is simultaneously a personification/power/word: Protogonos or priority.

In other words, I argue that Zeus is first not because he eats a symbol that represents a creative power, but because he eats priority itself and by doing so literally unites first, middle and last.[102] This marks a remarkable transformation of Hesiod's poem. Indeed, the Orphic Zeus' answer to the problem of priority is not the imposition of a new relation on a previously chaotic cosmos as much as the closing of a circle and repetition of a process starting with Protogonos' birth from Aither. This cyclical nature is emphasized in the poet's insistence that Zeus not only swallows Protogonos, but that with him he simultaneously swallows all the gods, rivers, springs, and everything else that was born at that time. The poet's use of the word προσφύω provides an important clue as to why Protogonos is so closely associated with the cosmos as a whole. West translates it as 'become one with' though notes that the meaning is more literally 'grow towards'.[103] In this respect, the poetic imagery of Zeus eating Protogonos is somewhat akin to a tree with diverse branches and roots growing backwards into a seed. That this idea is intended as more than a metaphor is made clear when the text specifically states that everything literally grows into Zeus until he becomes solitary (μοῦνος ἔγεντο). If everything grows into Zeus when he eats Protogonos, the implication is that the cosmos first grew out of Protogonos.[104] Zeus, in this respect, by eating Protogonos, is not so much eating something separate from himself, but is eating his own roots and literally joining last to first, very much in the spirit of the ouroboros or the serpent that eats its own tail.[105]

The implications of Zeus' cosmic ingestion are wide-ranging and point towards a novel and somewhat paradoxical expression of a cyclic cosmos where, as Heraclitus describes it, beginning and end are common (DK 22 B 48). It might help to understand this event in terms of the bootstrap paradox. This is a popular science fiction plotline where the protagonist goes back in time and impregnates an ancestor. This paradox raises the strange idea that if the person is to be born at all, it means he has already gone back in time and begotten himself. Yet, to father himself in the first place he must have been born. In Orphic terms Zeus, the great-grandson, by swallowing Protogonos and recreating the cosmos, actually becomes Protogonos, the firstborn god, and the circle is complete.[106] The *Derveni Theogony* does not of course describe a literal act of time travel, yet nonetheless the bootstrap paradox is a useful means of conceptualizing the equally paradoxical idea of a god eating his own roots and becoming first, middle and last. It also helps make sense of the repeated emphasis in the *Hymns* and later poems that the many gods are really the same. Although in the *Derveni Theogony* Zeus is not identical with Protogonos, later Orphic poetry does strongly suggest this reading. In an Orphic *Hymn to Zeus* recorded by Porphyry, Zeus' description during his cosmic creation closely echoes earlier depictions of Protogonos (OF 243) and Zeus is said to possess golden horns (χρύσεια κέρατα) and wings. Through this shared imagery, the poet hints that Protogonos and Zeus are not only the same through a mystic identification but through a kind of temporal loop where linear time gives way to a vision where future, past and present exist simultaneously.[107] The author of the Derveni poem may not have extended the logic of the act to this extreme, yet the basics of this reading are evident and it is unlikely to be a coincidence that the idea of a cyclical cosmos is also expressed in the Derveni commentator's reading. In column 17.7–9, the commentator describes a cyclic cosmos in relation to the passing and eternal return of the elements, noting that the name Zeus

> καὶ τοῦτο αὐτῶι διατελεῖ ὄνομα ὄν,
> μέχρι εἰς τὸ αὐτὸ εἶδος τὰ νῦν ἐόντα συνεστάθη
> ἐν ὧιπερ πρόσθεν ἐόντα ἠιωρεῖτο.
>
> will continue to be his name until the things that are now have got set together in the same form in which they were floating as they were before.[108]

The commentator, in other words, discusses the cycle in terms of elemental configurations closely identified with a pantheistic god. Although nothing is said of elements in the *Derveni Theogony*, here as elsewhere the commentator and poet appear to agree. Indeed, whether we are talking about repeated and eternal configurations of air or the cyclical entwined and paradoxical birth of Zeus, the same idea applies.

Recreating the cosmos

Following his ingestion of the cosmos, Zeus recreates everything afresh. The details, as usual, are sparse but there is a clear emphasis on the underlying order of the cosmos. The poem does not seem to recount the recreation of every single god in detail but those who are specifically mentioned appear to be strategically used as descriptions of Zeus' ordered creation. These include Aphrodite, Peitho and Harmonia. In the commentary these figures are said to be aspects of Zeus, parts 'of the same god' (col. 21.7) and extensions of his power. While there is no indication that this particular idea was expressed by the poet, a similar notion appears earlier when the commentator notes: 'Orpheus calls this breath Moira' (col. 18.34). This may suggest that the poem itself identified Moria with the breath of Zeus. On the other hand, the line itself is not part of the poem and Betegh considers it as the commentator's own interpretation.[109] Although we cannot say with any confidence whether the identification of these gods as aspects of Zeus is part of the poem or the commentator's philosophy, this ambiguity is as much a part of the papyrus' fragmented condition as it is an expression of the blurry edges between Orphic poetry and Presocratic philosophy. At any rate, the issue of identification aside, the poet did not arbitrarily choose to describe the divine triad Aphrodite, Persuasion and Harmony but selected these figures as expressions of Zeus' creative and orderly cosmos. This idea is strengthened by an obscure reference to the sun (25.10), the 'equal limbed' (ἰσομελὴς) moon (cols. 24.2) and the cosmic boundary Okeanos (col. 23.4), all of which reflect the ordered nature of the cosmos. Moreover, cosmic order is again stressed when the poet tells us not simply that Zeus gave birth to these things, but that he contrived them (col. 25.14):

[αὐτ]ὰρ [ἐ]πεὶ δ[ὴ πάν]τα Διὸ[ς φρὴν μή]σατ[ο ἔ]ργα.

When the mind of Zeus contrived all things.[110]

Zeus' ordering of the cosmos in this passage is expressed by the word μήδομαι.[111] Leitao argues the term in a theogonical context means 'think into existence' or more generally 'contrive'.[112] Either way, the word, which is also found in later Orphic poetry (OF 155 I-III B),[113] carries a certain amount of philosophical weight and the related term μητίομαι appears, for example, in a similar position in Parmenides' cosmology (DK 28 B 13):

πρώτιστον μέν Ἔρωτα θεῶν μητίσατο πάντων.

First of all the gods, she [the goddess] contrived Eros.[114]

That Parmenides uses this term to begin his cosmology and Orpheus to end his is of little significance. Not only should we recall that in later poetry both Eros and Metis are names for Protogonos, but more importantly, as Parmenides' goddess enigmatically states (DK 28 B 5):

ξυνὸν δέ μοί ἐστιν ὁππόθεν ἄρξωμαι τόθι γὰρ πάλιν ἵξομαι αὖθις.

It is the same to me, whence I begin, for there again shall I come back.[115]

How this very Heraclitean phrase applies to Parmenides' account is unclear,[116] but it nicely encapsulates Zeus' repetition of Protogonos' reign as the closing of a circle. This is the interpretative key to Orpheus' narrative and his radically pantheistic conception of god. Indeed, Orphic gods are not static beings separate from the world; they are intimately connected to it, even identical to the trees, rivers and springs. In this respect, Protogonos–Zeus is best described not in terms of a concrete set of features but in an excessive list of paradoxical attributes and names, an idea Heraclitus immortalized in (DK 22 B 67):

ὁ θεὸς ἡμέρη εὐφρόνη, χειμὼν θέρος, πόλεμος εἰρήνη, κόρος λιμός. ἀλλοιοῦται δὲ ὅκωσπερ ὁκόταν συμμιγῇ θυώμασιν, ὀνομάζεται καθ' ἡδονὴν ἑκάστου.

God is day night, winter summer, war peace, surfeit hunger. It alters as when mingled with perfumes, it gets named according to the pleasure of each.[117]

Heraclitus' and Orpheus' god in their close identification with the world are in some respects typically Presocratic. They too, however, show an important difference from the divine conceptions of philosophers such as Xenophanes. Indeed, Heraclitus and Orpheus, by characterizing their god in terms of motion, excess and change in place of stability, negation and wholeness, create a very different idea of the cosmos.

Conclusion

To date no single reading of the *Derveni Theogony* has offered an account free from contradictions. Indeed, given the fragmented nature of the text, this may not even be possible. What I have, however, attempted in this chapter is to present a plausible reconstruction of the main events and an analysis of their underlying meaning.[118] Some of my reconstructions will not convince everyone, yet even if we cannot offer a complete account, we can still, as Bernabé has argued elsewhere, point towards important general details that characterize Orphic poetry.[119] This chapter has argued that Orpheus rewrote Hesiod's *Theogony* in pantheistic terms where the many-named gods are really refractions of a single deity and divinely ordered cosmos. In the commentary this was expressed through etymologizing divine names as aspects of a divine Mind/Air/

God in a world based on flux. In the poem this same message was achieved through omissions and additions which transformed Hesiod's original narrative in pantheistic terms. These details included placing the creator god Protogonos as the first principle in the cosmos, describing incestuous genealogies where the gods confusingly fold in upon themselves, and in Zeus' swallowing of Protogonos and recreation of the cosmos. For Orpheus, however, this act is not the end of the narrative. Indeed, where Hesiod is happy to end with Zeus, Orpheus' god continues to grow and develop and just as Protogonos was not content to reign supreme in an ordered cosmos, following the kingship of Zeus Orpheus introduces a new contender for the throne: Dionysus. Dionysus is not only the most important of all Orphic gods, he is also the strangest being in Orphic mythology, the immortal who dies. Dionysus' role in early Orphism and his intimate association with the birth of humanity is the subject of the next chapter.

4

Dionysus Dismembered

The allusions and sparse quotations found in the *Derveni Theogony*, though rarely as rich as we would like, facilitate a rough reconstruction of a narrative documenting Protogonos' early birth, the transfer of power through a single genealogy, and finally Zeus' impressive ingestion and recreation of the cosmos. Unfortunately, what follows is far less clear, as the papyrus abruptly ends with a reference to Zeus' encounter with his mother Rhea (col. 26). Although we may never know with certainty how this narrative continued, in later poems this union leads to the birth of Persephone, and in turn to Dionysus, who in the Orphic tradition is both the successor to Zeus and the progenitor of humanity. Olympiodorus, though late, remains the most lucid formulation of a uniquely Orphic myth known as the Orphic anthropogony (OF 220):[1]

παρὰ τῷ Ὀρφεῖ τέσσαρες βασιλεῖαι παραδίδονται. πρώτη μὲν ἡ τοῦ Οὐρανοῦ, ἣν ὁ Κρόνος διεδέξατο ἐκτεμὼν τὰ αἰδοῖα τοῦ πατρός· μετὰ δὲ τὸν Κρόνον ὁ Ζεὺς ἐβασίλευσεν καταταρταρώσας τὸν πατέρα· εἶτα τὸν Δία διεδέξατο ὁ Διόνυσος, ὅν φασι κατ' ἐπιβουλὴν τῆς Ἥρας τοὺς περὶ αὐτὸν Τιτᾶνας σπαράττειν καὶ τῶν σαρκῶν αὐτοῦ ἀπογεύεσθαι. καὶ τούτους ὀργισθεὶς ὁ Ζεὺς ἐκεραύνωσε, καὶ ἐκ τῆς αἰθάλης τῶν ἀτμῶν τῶν ἀναδοθέντων ἐξ αὐτῶν ὕλης γενομένης γενέσθαι τοὺς ἀνθρώπους. οὐ δεῖ οὖν ἐξάγειν ἡμᾶς ἑαυτούς, οὐχ ὅτι, ὡς δοκεῖ λέγειν ἡ λέξις, διότι ἔν τινι δεσμῷ ἐσμεν τῷ σώματι (τοῦτο γὰρ δῆλόν ἐστι, καὶ οὐκ ἂν τοῦτο ἀπόρρητον ἔλεγεν), ἀλλ' ὅτι οὐ δεῖ ἐξάγειν ἡμᾶς ἑαυτοὺς ὡς τοῦ σώματος ἡμῶν Διονυσιακοῦ ὄντος· μέρος γὰρ αὐτοῦ ἐσμεν, εἴ γε ἐκ τῆς αἰθάλης τῶν Τιτάνων συγκείμεθα γευσαμένων τῶν σαρκῶν τούτου.

According to Orpheus there were four cosmic reigns. First was the reign of Uranus, then Cronus received the kingship, having cut off his father's genitals. Zeus ruled after Cronus, having cast his father into Tartarus. Next, Dionysus succeeded Zeus. They say that through Hera's treachery, the Titans who were around Dionysus tore him to pieces and tasted his flesh. And Zeus, being angry at this, struck the Titans with thunderbolts, and from the soot of the vapours that arose from [the incinerated Titans] came the matter from which humanity came into existence. Therefore, we must not commit suicide – not because, as [Socrates] seems to say, we are in our body as if in a prison, since that is obvious and [Socrates] would not call such an idea secret, but rather because our bodies are Dionysiac. We are, indeed, part of Dionysus if we are composed from the soot of the Titans who tasted Dionysus' flesh.[2]

Having discussed the controversial dating of this myth, this chapter will analyse this extraordinary narrative and describe how it adapts and rewrites Hesiod's Promethean division of the sacrificial ox within Orpheus' pantheist assumptions. Drawing comparisons with Empedocles' tale of the fallen daimon, I will discuss how the Orphic anthropogony describes the creation of human beings through a primordial act of sacrifice. I will argue that although the association between sacrifice and the creation of humanity's role in the cosmos is traditional and shared with earlier poets such as Hesiod, the Orphics interpreted this ritual in very different terms. Indeed, rather than emphasizing the creative potential of sacrifice as a means of connecting humans and ontologically distinct gods, the Orphics understood sacrifice negatively as an act that distances humanity from their divine kin and severs the very soul of the cosmos.

Early Orphism and circumstantial evidence

Few stories in antiquity were surrounded with such caution as the death of Dionysus. The sources for the myth are few and far between and in connecting these disparate threads the historian frequently finds themself dealing with misleading witnesses and cover-ups. Some sources provide incongruent and even misleading details; others are reluctant to specify even what they know.[3] Diodorus (3.62.6–8), one of the first ancient witnesses to discuss the myth in any detail, is typical in this regard:

> παραδεδωκότων δὲ τῶν μυθογράφων καὶ τρίτην γένεσιν, καθ' ἥν φασι τὸν θεὸν ἐκ Διὸς καὶ Δήμητρος τεκνωθέντα διασπασθῆναι μὲν ὑπὸ τῶν γηγενῶν καὶ καθεψηθῆναι, πάλιν δ' ὑπὸ τῆς Δήμητρος τῶν μελῶν συναρμοσθέντων ἐξ ἀρχῆς νέον γεννηθῆναι, εἰς φυσικάς τινας αἰτίας μετάγουσι τοὺς τοιούτους λόγους ... σύμφωνα δὲ τούτοις εἶναι τά τε δηλούμενα διὰ τῶν Ὀρφικῶν ποιημάτων καὶ τὰ παρεισαγόμενα κατὰ τὰς τελετάς, περὶ ὧν οὐ θέμις τοῖς ἀμυήτοις ἱστορεῖν τὰ κατὰ μέρος.

> And though the writers of myths have handed down the account of a third birth as well, at which, as they say, the Sons of Gaia tore to pieces the god, who was a

son of Zeus and Demeter, and boiled him, but his members were brought together again by Demeter and he experienced a new birth as if for the first time, such accounts as this they trace back to certain causes found in nature … And with these stories the teachings agree which are set forth in the Orphic poems and are introduced into their rites, but it is not lawful to recount them in detail to the uninitiated.[4]

The bare bones of the myth are there, yet Diodorus out of piety refuses to divulge it in its entirety. However, if the Greeks were reluctant to speak about such matters, they failed to anticipate the desecration of their final resting places. From the nineteenth century until the present day, archaeologists continue to unearth mysterious gold tablets dating between the fifth century BCE and second century CE describing underworld journeys and divine kinship. A South Italian tablet (L 10b; OF 490) from the fourth century BCE reads:

Ἔρχομαιἐ‹κ› καθαρῶ‹ν› καθ‹αρά, χθ›ο‹νίων› βασίλ‹ε›α,
Εὐκλε{υα} κα‹ὶ› Εὐβο‹υ›λεῦ καὶ θεοὶ ‹καὶ› {ὅσοι} δ‹αί›μονες ἄλλοι·
καὶ γὰρ ἐ‹γ›ὼ‹ν› ὑ‹μῶν› γένος εὔχομα‹ι ὄλβιον› εὐ‹›να‹ι› {ὄλβιο}
ποινὰν ‹δ'› ἀνταπέτει‹σ'› ἔργω‹ν ἕνεκ'› ο‹ὔ›τι δικα‹ί›ων.
ε‹ἴ›τ‹ε› με Μοῖρα ‹ἐδάμασσ'› ε‹ἴ›τε ἀσ‹τ›εροπῆτα {κη} κεραυνῶ‹ν›.
νῦν δὲ ‹ἱ›κ‹έτις› ἥκω {ιικω} παρ‹αὶ› ἁ‹γ›νὴν Φ‹ερ›σε‹φ›όνειαν‹›,
ὥς {λ} με ‹π›ρόφ‹ρων› πέ[μ]ψ‹ηι› {μ} ἕδρας ἐς εὐ‹α›γ‹έων›.

Pure I come from the pure, Queen of those below the earth,
And Eukles and Eubouleus and the other gods and daimons;
For I also claim that I am of your blessed race.
Recompense I have paid on account of deeds not just;
Either Fate mastered me or the lightning bolt thrown by the thunderer.
Now I come, a suppliant, to holy Phersephoneia,
That she, gracious, may send me to the seats of the blessed.[5]

Italian polymath Domenico Comparetti, drawing on sources as diverse as Pindar (fr. 133) and the Neoplatonist Olympiodorus quoted above (OF 220 K),[6] concluded that the events described in this confusing gold tablet were a cryptic reference to the Orphic anthropogony.[7] Though certainly possible, this is a remarkable conclusion considering that the six gold tablets from which Comparetti made this deduction say absolutely nothing about Orpheus, the Titans or Dionysus. Nor do any of the extant classical sources directly refer to this event. Even the Hellenistic sources are few and confusing. Comparetti had, however, access to the later Neoplatonist tradition which showed less reticence in discussing these matters and through these fragments Comparetti pieced together a chilling tale, beginning with Zeus ceding his kingship to his son Dionysus (OF 296–300).[8] The child-king's rule, however, is short-lived and lured by the Titans with toys and a mirror, the god is killed and eaten (OF 312–13).[9] Zeus in retaliation strikes the Titans with a thunderbolt and from their remains mankind is born (OF 318, 320).[10]

Despite Comparetti's reliance on late material, his arguments were quickly adopted by a generation of scholars who not only agreed that the Orphic dismemberment was referred to in the gold tablets but that it was the central pivot on which the Orphic theogonical narrative rotated.[11] Unsurprisingly, not everyone was convinced by Comparetti's elegant but fragile reconstruction. Wilamowitz-Moellendorff and later Linforth attempted to shatter this image, arguing that Comparetti's Orphic myth simply assumed the object of its study.[12] In other words, the gold tablets could be interpreted in terms of Dionysus' murder, but the vague allusions only become obvious when viewed through an already assumed Neoplatonist framework. Linforth, for this reason, rejected the Orphic identification of the gold tablets and inaugurated a general attitude of scepticism which set the tone for the following forty or so years.[13]

Dionysus, however, has a talent for resurrection and soon after Linforth laid him to rest, new evidence reinvigorated the ancient murder case. The most impressive finds include the bone plaques from Olbia, featuring the self-designation Orphikoi and perhaps Dionysus (tab. A) as early as the fifth century BCE. The Derveni papyrus, though it omits the key details, provided a clear link between the late Orphic theogonies and those of the archaic period. Finally, a stream of impressive gold tablets was discovered, some of which offered striking confirmation for Comparetti's hypothesis. A fifth-century tablet from Hipponium (L 1; OF 474) referring to the deceased as among the 'initiates and bacchoi' (μύσται καὶ βάχχοι), that is as members of the Dionysiac mysteries, provides the pivotal cultic context required for interpreting the tablets. Another tablet from Pelinna (L7a–b; OF 485–6) describes how the deceased boldly declares 'tell Persephone that Bacchus (Dionysus) himself released you' (εἰπεῖν Φερσεφόναι σ' ὅτι Β<άκ>χιος αὐτός ἔλυσε).[14] With these new finds the older scepticism receded and an increasing number of scholars now agree that Comparetti was at least in part correct in his interpretation.[15] However, despite this growing consensus, others continue to speak of the 'so-called Orphics' in inverted commas. Indeed, in an extreme position Radcliffe Edmonds even insists that the myth as it is discussed in Orphic scholarship is a modern invention of the scholarly imagination 'not told until 1879'.[16]

On the surface, the claim that the myth is a 'modern invention' is not convincing.[17] Olympiodorus' account alone provides a clear indication that the narrative is indeed ancient. Furthermore, although Olympiodorus may add new details to his telling of the myth, the bulk of his account was likely adapted from what Damascius calls the standard narrative of the time, the *Rhapsodies*, which Bernabé argues may date to the first century BCE.[18] While the *Rhapsodies* do not survive, a number of summaries and direct quotations facilitate a reconstruction of their version of the anthropogony. Although the presence of the myth in the *Rhapsodies* provides no definite proof that it existed earlier that the first century BCE, the overall consistency between the *Rhapsodies* and the *Derveni Theogony* in other episodes at the very least makes this a credible possibility. This possibility is further strengthened by clear allusions to the myth in Platonist sources spanning from Damascius to Plato's pupil Xenokrates.[19] Furthermore, some telling fragments from Philodemus suggest that the key mythical details appear to be well known outside Neoplatonist circles and date to as early as the third century BCE.[20] In short, the evidence is not only richer than often realized, but when taken collectively, presents clear testimony for the existence of the key details of the myth as early as the Hellenistic period – and if we accept Plato's veiled allusions, earlier still.[21] Edmonds' arguments, however, present a more significant challenge when it comes to interpreting the classical and archaic evidence. Indeed, despite the apparent wealth of early Orphic sources, including Pindar (fr. 133), the Derveni papyrus, the gold tablets and the Olbian bone plaques, Edmonds rightly argues that no clear reference to the myth can be found in any of them. In fact, neither the relevant Pindaric fragments nor the *Derveni Theogony* say anything about Dionysus, and the ever-increasing number of gold tablets, although suggestive of the dismemberment myth, do not even mention the name Orpheus. In short, despite a great deal of new evidence and over a century of scholarship, the case for the myth in early Orphism remains largely as Comparetti found it: a fragile assemblage of circumstantial claims which may or may not cohere.

Although I will not discuss every strand of the debate, I suggest that the circumstantial nature of the early evidence may not be as fatal as the critics suggest. Indeed, although we should certainly not confuse circumstantial and direct claims, we should by no means dismiss the latter as mere coincidence. As Arthur Maurice Hocart argues in his classic study on Indo-European kingship:

> There is a popular but natural delusion that direct evidence is necessarily better than circumstantial, in fact that it is the only satisfactory kind of evidence. A learned judge in summing up a famous murder trial rebutted this opinion. He pointed out that direct evidence might be the weaker of the two: the witness might be lying or biased; his memory might be at fault, or his imagination be

playing tricks. Even two witnesses might mislead. There are countries where fifty eyewitnesses all telling the same story could not be trusted. On the other hand, when a hundred little details which no man could have premeditated or arranged all point in one direction, and one direction only, the certainty is as great as is ever to be attained in human affairs. Probably no man has ever been hanged in the last hundred years on direct evidence unsupported by circumstantial. Many have been on circumstantial evidence alone.[22]

Following Hocart, I argue that we cannot simply dismiss the early evidence because it is circumstantial. Rather, the task falls to the historian to make sense of the circumstances and if the evidence coheres in surprising and unexpected details, which cannot be dismissed as mere coincidence, it is our job to assess whether these details provide sufficient grounds for assuming the early presence of the Orphic anthropogony.

The richest potential source for the early presence of the Orphic myth is found in the gold tablets. These small golden sheets buried with initiates of the mysteries are part of a continuing tradition spanning the Greek world from South Italy to Macedonia and dating from the fifth century BCE to the third century CE. If the gold tablets are accepted as Orphic, this continuity in time and space makes them one of the most powerful statements on the endurance of the Orphic tradition. The earliest tablet is from Hipponion, South Italy, and dates to the fifth century BCE (L 1; OF 474). The tablet does not mention Orpheus or offer any hint regarding the dismemberment myth. It does, however, refer to the deceased tellingly as going the same way as the other Bacchoi (βάχχοι) – a clear indication that the tablets relate to the Bacchic mysteries. Apart from being the oldest gold tablet, the Hipponion tablet also boasts the longest text which in its details proves that the Cretan, Thessalian and Italian variants are part of a single lineage.[23] It is not surprising that the oldest gold tablet was discovered in South Italy as the region is repeatedly associated with unusual eschatological claims. Plato reportedly travelled in South Italy and Sicily (Cic. *De Rep.* i. 16) and some of his Orphicesque myths are referred to specifically as by a Sicilian or an Italian (*Gorg.* 493a). Pindar's fragment recorded in the *Meno*, whatever we make of it, may well have been from an Italian or Sicilian poem and shows similarities to his *Second Olympian Ode*. This ode was composed for Theron of Acragas and, like the *Meno* fragment, discusses rebirth and salvation.[24] Given South Italy's rich and unusual mythic background, it is not surprising that scholars such as Domenico Comparetti drew these sources together and in particular focusing on Pindar's reference to a blood price paid to Persephone for an ancient grief, claimed that the reference to unjust crimes in the Thurii tablet (L 10b; OF 490) alluded to the Titans' murder of Dionysus.[25] Moreover, while the Orphic reading has not been and perhaps cannot be definitively confirmed, the major alternatives such as those proposed by Zuntz have been rejected, whereas Comparetti's thesis has been repeatedly confirmed. Indeed, the evidence from the Hipponion, Thurii, and the direct message of the Pelinna (L7a–b; OF 485–6) tablet stating 'tell Persephone that Bacchus (Dionysus) himself released you' would be striking coincidences if Comparetti was totally off the mark.[26] Despite these plausible allusions to the anthropogony, the clearest weakness of the gold tablets is found in their lack of a theogonical context associated with the name Orpheus.

The *Derveni Theogony*, on the other hand, presents us with an almost inverted situation. The papyrus clearly states that it is a commentary on a poem by Orpheus and has also been shown to be part of the same theogonic tradition preserved in the *Rhapsodies*. However, while later Orphic theogonies give a central role to the dismemberment myth and anthropogony, the extant passages of the Derveni papyrus say absolutely nothing about Dionysus. It is certainly possible that had more of the papyrus survived the myth would have been recounted, yet there is no evidence in the papyrus itself to establish this claim.[27] And at this point we seem to reach a dead end. The gold tablets and the *Derveni Theogony* approach each other. They even promise to shed light on each other's deficits. Yet they fail to meet in the middle. One source is found in South Italy, the other in Northern Greece. One suggests the dismemberment myth and human guilt in a Bacchic context, the other provides the greater theogonical context in which this episode, at least in later poems, was located. Yet despite these clear problems, there is strong circumstantial evidence for understanding the gold tablets and the papyrus as part of a single tradition. While no gold tablets were discovered in Derveni, many have been found in Northern Greece, and both the gold tablets and the papyrus were found in a funeral context.[28] Furthermore, although the papyrus does not discuss the dismemberment myth, its abrupt ending describing Zeus' contemplation of divine incest is far from a coherent conclusion. Whether the papyrus continued on another roll or not is impossible to say, yet from the literary context alone it is clear that the mythic world of the poem did not end at this point. Zeus' incest with Rhea must lead somewhere and we know of only one tradition that continues this narrative. As later Orphic sources describe it, this union leads to the birth of Persephone, who in turn, with Zeus, begets Dionysus. The presence of this unusual pairing, also likely known to philosopher Xenokrates, is in itself good reason to infer Dionysus' presence in the mythic world of the Derveni poet, if not within the *Derveni Theogony* itself.[29]

The circumstantial claims discussed up to this point may seem weak and would undoubtedly fail to convince a sceptic. The case, however, gains considerable traction when we consider the theogonical context of the gold tablets. Indeed, although the tablets are frequently considered in terms of the dismemberment myth, it is important to stress that they too mention a pantheon of sorts. Apart from the goddess Persephone and Bacchus, the gold tablets repeatedly discuss a group of unusual gods including Brimo, Eukles and Eubouleus.[30] While these are not exclusively Orphic gods, they frequently appear in Orphic and mystery settings. Brimo likely refers to Persephone.[31] Eukles, good fame, may refer to Hades.[32] Eubouleus in the (L 11) gold tablets refers to the son of Zeus, and in the *Orphic Hymns* usually refers to Dionysus (29.6; 30.6; 52.4).[33] The most important link between the theogonical tradition of the Derveni papyrus and that of the gold tablets, however, appears in the Timpone Grande gold tablet (L 12; OF 492).[34] The tablet is anomalous even by Orphic standards and was found wrapped around a smaller standard gold tablet (OF 488). The text of the Timpone Grande is for the most part composed of random letters interspersed with Greek words. These may be part of a single hymn or ritual narrative, yet even if we take the clear words in isolation the tablet is of pivotal importance. Some of the terms such as moira, air and fire suggest a similar obsession with the favourite cosmological elements mentioned in the Derveni papyrus.[35] Nestis, the Sicilian name for Persephone, and the name favoured by Empedocles for the wife of Hades, is also present. One of the most important sequences for my argument appears in line 7:

ἀέρ πῦρ Μᾶτερ Νῆστι νύξ ἡμέρα

Air, fire, Mother, Nestis, night, day.

Bernabé and Jiménez San Cristóbal point out an intriguing overlap with a later Orphic *Hymn to Zeus* recorded by Porphyry (OF 243):

ἓν δὲ δέμας βασίλειον, ἐν ὧι τάδε πάντα κυκλεῖται,
πῦρ καὶ ὕδωρ καὶ γαῖα καὶ αἰθήρ νύξ τε καὶ ἦμαρ.

unique sovereign body, in which all things complete their cycle,
fire, water, earth and ether; night and day.[36]

This reference has even more to tell us and not only does it point to a link between a gold tablet and an Orphic poem known in later antiquity, it points towards a connection with the *Derveni Theogony*. Indeed, the Orphic *Hymn to*

Zeus quoted above also describes in almost identical terms to the Derveni poem[37] how Zeus eats the cosmos and becomes, as Porphyry (OF 243) records:

Ζεὺς πρῶτος γένετο, Ζεὺς ὕστατος ἀργικέραυνος
Ζεὺς κεφαλή, Ζεὺς μέσσα, Διός δ' ἐκ πάντα τέτυκται·

Zeus was the first, Zeus last, the lightning lord,
Zeus head, Zeus centre, all things are from Zeus.[38]

In other words, Porphyry's hymn includes almost identical lines with the poem preserved in the Derveni papyrus and closely approximates lines from the Timpone Grande gold tablet. This strongly suggests that both the tablets and the papyrus draw either on a very similar *Hymn to Zeus* or even on one and the same poem. This striking coincidence is all the more relevant when we consider that the first and incontestable word in the Timpone Grande gold tablet is Protogonos.[39] At this point, the strands quickly come together. Indeed, the presence of the god Protogonos in a gold tablet citing lines likely from a *Hymn to Zeus*, which moreover was literally enveloped by a smaller gold tablet associated with the Bacchic mysteries, is the single clearest testament that the gold tablets and the Derveni papyrus are part of a shared theogonical tradition. This, in other words, is the smoking gun which, in the words of Hocart, 'no man could have premeditated'.[40]

Of course, when dealing with these circumstantial claims, we must be clear on what the evidence does and does not say. First, this complex set of details does not directly say that the crime committed against Persephone in the gold tablets refers to the dismemberment of Dionysus. Nor does it provide a clear testimony to the presence of the anthropogony in either the gold tablets or the *Derveni Theogony*. The critics of early Orphism are entirely correct in this regard. The evidence does, however, link a number of diverse elements into a complex web of associations which are very difficult to dismiss as purely coincidental. The gold tablets are part of a Bacchic tradition linked to a theogonical narrative which features an impressive pantheistic Zeus and Protogonos. They also refer to crimes and payments made to Persephone that are somehow related to Dionysus. Later comparative evidence dating as early as Xenokrates in the fourth century BCE suggests a context for reading these elements in tandem as part of a single theogonical narrative involving murder and the birth of human beings. This narrative, moreover, is the same as that seen in later theogonies such as the *Rhapsodies* from the same Orphic tradition, which begins as early as the *Derveni Theogony*. This is not, of course, direct proof and it may not convince a hardened sceptic. However, this long list of improbable coincidences is, as Hocart puts it, 'as great as is ever to be attained in human affairs' or at the very least in Orphic ones.[41]

Making sense of murder

What emerges from this intricate web of circumstantial claims is the early existence of a myth describing the union of Zeus and Persephone, the birth of Dionysus, and his death at the hands of the Titans. Humanity's existence in turn is something closely intertwined with this event and initiates must now pay a penalty to Persephone to expiate themselves for the crimes of their ancestors. This basic narrative is not only supported by the circumstantial evidence, it is entirely in tune with new religious narratives occurring in sixth-century BCE Greece. The Pythagoreans, for example, may also have discussed rebirth in terms of crime and punishment through the sufferings of Apollo. The myth as recounted in Hesiod's *Catalogue of Women* describes how Apollo, angered by Zeus' murder of his son Asclepius, kills the cyclopes who forged Zeus' thunderbolt, and is punished by Hera by being forced to serve as a slave to the mortal Admetus.[42] Pindar also alludes to a similar idea, if not the Orphic myth itself, in a passage cited in Plato's *Meno* (81b–c; Pind. fr. 133 Bergk):

> Φερσεφόνα ποινὰν παλαιοῦ πένθεος
> δέξεται, εἰς τὸν ὕπερθεν ἅλιον κείνων ἐνάτῳ ἔτεϊ
> ἀνδιδοῖ ψυχὰς πάλιν,
> ἐκ τᾶν βασιλῆες ἀγαυοὶ
> καὶ σθένει κραιπνοὶ σοφίᾳ τε μέγιστοι
> ἄνδρες αὔξοντ': ἐς δὲ τὸν λοιπὸν χρόνον ἥρωες ἁγνοὶ
> πρὸς ἀνθρώπων καλεῦνται.

> Persephone will return to the sun above in the ninth year
> the souls of those from whom
> she will exact punishment for old miseries,
> and from these come noble kings,
> mighty in strength and greatest in wisdom,
> and for the rest of time men will call them sacred heroes.[43]

This fragment does not directly refer to Dionysus and the Titans. However, the discussion of Persephone's reception of 'a requital for an ancient wrong' and in particular the use of the words ποινή and πένθος closely resonates with Orphic mythology.[44]

While some of these alternate mythic traditions are only partially known, the presence of a rich contemporary parallel is found in the philosophical poetry of Empedocles (c. 495–435 BCE).[45] Born in the Sicilian city of Acragas, Empedocles was raised in an environment closely associated with Orphic ideas and artefacts. Indeed, the Orphicesque elements found in Pindar's paean for Theron of Acragas (*Olympian Two* 65–70), for example, were almost certainly known to the twenty-year-old aspiring poet and philosopher.[46] Although it is impossible to specify a direct link between Empedocles and Orphism, both emerged from a similar religious setting and shared important doctrinal views including vegetarianism and perhaps reincarnation.[47] They also shared very similar cosmological and mythical accounts which focused on an interchange of the one and the many. For example, displaying clear similarities to the *Derveni Theogony*'s portrayal of Zeus eating and becoming one with the cosmos, Empedocles' cosmic account describes a homogeneous and divine Sphere that alternately unites and separates under the powers of Love and Strife (DK 31 B 28):

ἀλλ' ὅ γε πάντοθεν ἶσος <ἑοῖ> καὶ πάμπαν ἀπείρων
Σφαῖρος κυκλοτερὴς μονίηι περιηγέι γαίων.

Equal to itself in all directions and completely boundless
a rounded Sphere rejoicing in circular solitude.[48]

This harmonious condition is not, however, destined to last and the divisive force referred to by Empedocles as Strife intervenes, tearing this original unity to plurality. In an account no less impressive than Zeus' creation of the cosmos, Empedocles explains (DK 31 B 21.9–14):

ἐκ τούτων γὰρ πάνθ' ὅσα τ' ἦν ὅσα τ' ἔστι καὶ ἔσται,
δένδρεά τ' ἐβλάστησε καὶ ἀνέρες ἠδὲ γυναῖκες,
θῆρές τ' οἰωνοί τε καὶ ὑδατοθρέμμονες ἰχθῦς,
καί τε θεοὶ δολιχαίωνες τιμῇσι φέριστοι.
αὐτὰ γὰρ ἔστιν ταῦτα, δι' ἀλλήλων δὲ θέοντα
γίγνεται ἀλλοιωπά· τόσον διὰ κρῆσις ἀμείβει.

From them all things that were, that are and that will be
sprang – trees, men, women,
beasts, fowls, water-nourished fish,
and long-lived gods foremost in honours.
for these are the very things that are, which running through other
become different; so much does blending change them.[49]

Although there are clear echoes in Empedocles' and the *Derveni Theogony*'s accounts of creation, the most striking parallels are found in the Sicilian's extensive description of a primordial murder among a society of divine beings known as daimones (DK 31 B115):

ἔστιν Ἀνάγκης χρῆμα, θεῶν ψήφισμα παλαιόν,
ἀίδιον, πλατέεσσι κατεσφρηγισμένον ὅρκοις·
εὖτέ τις ἀμπλακίηισι φόνωι φίλα γυῖα μιήνηι,
ὅς καὶ ἐπίορκον ἁμαρτήσας ἐπομόσσηι,
δαίμονες οἵτε μακραίωνος λελάχασι βίοιο,
τρίς μιν μυρίας ὥρας ἀπὸ μακάρων ἀλάλησθαι,
φυομένους παντοῖα διὰ χρόνου εἴδεα θνητῶν
ἀργαλέας βιότοιο μεταλλάσσοντα κελεύθους.
αἰθέριον μὲν γάρ σφε μένος πόντονδε διώκει,
πόντος δ' ἐς χθονὸς οὖδας ἀπέπτυσε, γαῖα δ' ἐς αὐγὰς
ἠελίου φαέθοντος, ὁ δ' αἰθέρος ἔμβαλε δίναις·
ἄλλος δ' ἐξ ἄλλου δέχεται, στυγέουσι δὲ πάντες.
τῶν καὶ ἐγὼ νῦν εἰμι, φυγὰς θεόθεν καὶ ἀλήτης,
νείκεϊ μαινομένωι πίσυνος.

> There is an oracle of necessity, an ancient decree of the gods,
> everlasting, sealed by broad oaths:
> when one in his crimes stains his own limbs with innocent blood
> or wrongfully forswears himself,
> one of those deities who have gained long life,
> thrice ten thousand seasons he is exiled from the blessed gods,
> through time growing to be all kinds of creatures,
> going from one grievous path of life to another.
> For mighty aether drives him into sea,
> sea spews him onto the surface of the earth, and earth to the rays
> of shining sun, who casts him into the whirls of aether.
> One takes him from another, but all abhor him.
> Of these I too am now one, a fugitive and a wanderer from the gods,
> a devotee of raving Strife.[50]

Like Orpheus' description of the Titans, Empedocles outlines a society of homogenous divine beings known as daimones. We are told that these divine beings have sworn an oath against defiling themselves with an act of Strife, the cannibalistic murder (DK 31 B 139) of one of their own. This divisive act, it transpires, has indeed occurred and at least one daimon, Empedocles himself, has been expelled from the society of divine beings and is currently shifting between various forms of animal, plant and human for a period of 30,000 years until he can return to his previously blessed life.[51] In short, this passage, which could justifiably be referred to as Empedocles' anthropogony, describes how an original act of murder and cannibalism among a society of gods results in the creation of hybrid beings composed of mortal frames inhabited by divine daimones.

Despite the presence of a number of striking similarities, Empedocles and Orpheus do not agree on every detail. For a start, it may be pointed out that Empedocles does not in fact describe a true anthropogony. Indeed, it is a perplexing possibility that humans and animals lacking daimones somehow existed prior to this act of bloodshed.[52] Furthermore, not only is there no being comparable to Protogonos in Empedocles' myth, as noted in the previous chapter, his insistence that (DK 31 B 29) 'two branches do not shoot out of his back [i.e. the Sphere], nor feet or swift knees, neither generative organs' may be a critical reimagining of the Orphic god. Finally, in B128, Empedocles even insists on demoting Zeus' authority in favour of Aphrodite. However, whether we attribute the similarities between Orpheus and Empedocles to direct influence or general cultural trends is not essential to my argument. In either case, these shared orientations provide striking testimony to the emergence of a new cosmological and sacrificial narrative in the sixth or fifth century BCE describing creation as an interchange between the one and the many, an early homogenous society comprised of divine beings, and an act of violence committed against a divinity that leads to the creation of mortal life as we know it today.

As was common with Orphic myth, many of these elements are as traditional as they are innovative. Indeed, while certain ideas are without precedent in early Greek poetry, others improvise upon older Hesiodic themes and an ancient Indo-European narrative I discussed in Chapter 2 as 'creation by sacrifice'. Creation by sacrifice myths, as noted, involve a scenario where 'a primordial being is killed and dismembered, and from his body the cosmos is fashioned'.[53] Empedocles is a particularly striking example of this myth type, as sacrifice occupies a prominent role in both his cosmology and his tale of the fallen daimon.[54] For the daimones, this sacrificial theme is obvious and found in the literal act of bloodshed and the daimon's trust in Strife. Furthermore, and in contrast to the ordered Orphic creation by Zeus, a similar emphasis on creation and sacrifice may also be alluded to in Empedocles' (DK 31 B 31) cosmology and description of how prior to its dissolution 'the limbs of the god [the Sphere] shuddered in turn' (πάντα γὰρ ἑξείης πελεμίζετο γυῖα θεοῖο).[55]

Not only is this act reminiscent of the shuddering of the animal before sacrifice,[56] in DK 31 B 20 the divisive action of Strife is also associated with the verb διατέμνω or cutting up, a term which Empedocles elsewhere (DK 31 B 4) associates with innards or σπλάγχνα. As Mackenzie argues, the language in these fragments is evocative of animal sacrifice and at least hints at the idea that Empedocles envisioned Strife's dissection of the Sphere, the very creation of the cosmos, as a sacrificial act.[57]

The Orphic myth presents a different take on this shared theme. Although allegorically the Titans' murder was sometimes associated with cosmic creation,[58] the *Derveni Theogony* does not link sacrifice with the creation of the cosmos itself. Instead, creation is attributed to Zeus and sacrifice appears as a later aberration associated with establishing humanity's place in the cosmos. This detail not only echoes Empedocles' description of the fallen daimon, it is also reminiscent of Hesiod's Promethean division at Mekone. In both Hesiod's Mekone and the Orphic myth, the first sacrifice not only involves the Titans and the Olympians, but both agree that sacrifice is an act that defines humanity's cosmic role. However, these shared details belie a greater debate. As Detienne rightly points out, even as Orpheus develops upon Hesiodic details, he reverses and rewrites Hesiod's ontological assumptions.[59] The most important example of the Orphic rewriting of Hesiod's narrative is found in how Orpheus uses overtly similar details to cast doubt on Hesiod's key ritual means of relating to the gods: sacrifice. Indeed, in the Orphic myth, what results from the first act of sacrifice is not a clear demarcation between a society of humans and gods, but a radically new understanding of selfhood and the creation of human beings who are ontologically similar to gods. This new conception of selfhood was in turn applied to an innovative criticism of animal sacrifice. In the following sections, I will discuss both of these ideas in turn.

Body and soul in early Orphism

In comparison to the usual absence of Orphic evidence, Orphic notions of selfhood are surprisingly well documented by the ancient sources. The most striking and repeatedly stressed claim is that initiates are directly related to the gods. The owner of the A2 gold tablet, for example, claims to be 'of your blessed race' (A2, A3). In B1 and B11, the initiates state 'my race is heavenly'. Finally, if we include the claim:

Γῆς παῖς εἰμι καὶ Οὐρανοῦ ἀστερόεντος

I am the child of Earth and starry Heaven (B1)[60]

we can detect a divine kinship claim in nearly every tablet with a substantial text. Indeed, some tablets even go beyond kinship and claim ontological identity with the gods.[61] A gold tablet from Thurii promises its initiate that:

ὄλβιε καὶ μακαριστέ, θεὸς δ' ἔσηι ἀντὶ βροτοῖο.

Happy and most blessed one, a god you shall be instead of a mortal. (A1)

A similar statement is seen in Thurii A4:

θεὸς ἐγένου ἐξ ἀνθρώπου·

A god you have become from a man. (A4)

Finally, in a second-century CE tablet we are told:

Καικιλία Σεκουνδεῖνα, νόμωι ἴθι δῖα γεγῶσα.

Caecilia Secundina, come, having become a goddess by the custom. (A5)

When attempting to make sense of early Orphic kinship claims, scholars have predominantly tended to understand Orphic man as a dualistic being, a composite where 'the soul, immortal, corresponds to the Dionysian element; the body, to the Titanic nature'.[62] That the Orphics would propose a dualistic conception of body and soul is not surprising. Dualism in a loose sense can refer to any distinction between body and soul and in this respect, the majority of Greek thinkers can be called dualists. Indeed, even Heraclitus, despite proposing a single underlying monistic world view, in his differentiation of body and soul could be understood as a dualist (DK 22 B 96). This is again apparent in Empedocles' body and soul language, which discusses the fallen daimon entering the body as into an alien cloak (DK 31 B 126). While these 'ghost in the machine'-like descriptions could be described as dualistic in so far as they distinguish the body from the soul, it is important to stress that this general opposition is not necessarily the same as the dualism commonly attributed to the Orphics. Rather, Orphic dualism is more closely aligned with a view often attributed to Plato and later Descartes, which expresses an absolute opposition between the corporeal body and the incorporeal soul. As Plato puts in the *Phaedo* (80a–b):

σκόπει δή, ἔφη, ὦ Κέβης, εἰ ἐκ πάντων τῶν εἰρημένων τάδε ἡμῖν συμβαίνει, τῷ μὲν θείῳ καὶ ἀθανάτῳ καὶ νοητῷ καὶ μονοειδεῖ καὶ ἀδιαλύτῳ καὶ ἀεὶ ὡσαύτως κατὰ ταὐτὰ ἔχοντι ἑαυτῷ ὁμοιότατον εἶναι ψυχή, τῷ δὲ ἀνθρωπίνῳ καὶ θνητῷ καὶ πολυειδεῖ καὶ ἀνοήτῳ καὶ διαλυτῷ καὶ μηδέποτε κατὰ ταὐτὰ ἔχοντι ἑαυτῷ ὁμοιότατον αὖ εἶναι σῶμα.

Then see, Cebes, if this is not the conclusion from all that we have said, that the soul is most like the divine and immortal and intellectual and uniform and indissoluble and ever unchanging, and the body, on the contrary, most like the human and mortal and multiform and unintellectual and dissoluble and ever changing.[63]

It is certainly possible that the Orphics understood humanity in this way. Plato is one of our best sources on the early Orphic view of self and clearly emphasizes a distinction by describing how the Orphic body is a prison (*Phaedo* 62b; *Cratylus* 400c).[64] Furthermore, Plato and Orpheus show a number of close correspondences in their descriptions of the soul, noting how once freed from the body it can speak and defend itself, navigate underworld pathways and drink or refrain from drinking water.[65] However, if Plato likely borrowed elements from Orpheus, the early Orphics did not borrow from Plato. Indeed, although the Orphic soul prefigures aspects of its Platonic counterpart, in many other respects it shows a greater debt to Presocratic views of self which focus on an essential continuity between body, soul and indeed the entire cosmos.[66]

The Presocratic insistence on the continuity of body and soul may initially seem counter-intuitive. Indeed, for many Christians such as Eusebius it was outright ridiculous:

σῶμα δὲ ὁ ἀὴρ καὶ πολὺ πρότερον ὁ αἰθήρ … καὶ πῶς ἂν ταὐτὸν ἐπινοηθείη σῶμα καὶ νοῦς κατὰ διάμετρον ταῖς φύσεσι διεστῶτα;

The air is body and the aither a much more primitive kind of body … but how can body and mind be conceived the same, since in their natures they are diametrically opposed?[67]

However, despite Eusebius' disbelief, this view of self was precisely what many Presocratics and indeed later Greeks thought. Although the early Presocratic sources survive in fragments that usually provide less detail than we would like, some key points on the soul can be observed. First, rather than viewing the soul as the true immaterial centre of self, the earliest sources tend to describe the soul as material and part of a wider network connecting the cosmos. Thales, according to some testimonies, argued that the soul was a force mixed throughout the cosmos (DK 11 A 22).[68] Anaximenes discussed the soul as air and conceived of it as both an inner part of man and something that surrounds the whole world

(DK 13 B2). Heraclitus may have been the first Greek philosopher to argue that the ψυχή was the centre of the self.[69] However, this new meaning did not overwrite earlier understandings. On the contrary, for Heraclitus the soul remained a physical element related to a cosmic soul stuff sometimes called the world soul.[70] Nor did Heraclitus' lofty view of the soul (DK 22 B 45) devaluate the body and in a number of fragments he describes how body and soul mutually influence each other. Drinking too much alcohol, for example, makes the soul wet and binds it closer to the body (DK 22 B117). This was more than a causal relation. Indeed, for Heraclitus souls were bodies and bodies souls, entities coexisting as a part of a series of elemental transformations (DK 22 B 36):

> ψυχῇσιν θάνατος ὕδωρ γενέσθαι, ὕδατι δὲ θάνατος γῆν γενέσθαι, ἐκ γῆς δὲ ὕδωρ γίνεται ἐξ ὕδατος δὲ ψυχή.
>
> For souls it is to die to become water, for water it is to die to become earth, from earth water is being born, from water Soul.[71]

In this fragment, the process of transformations is described in terms of birth and death. Water dies and is transformed into earth, just as earth gives birth to water. However, rather than the expected element, air or perhaps fire, Heraclitus ends this process with soul. This entails, as Kahn argues, that 'there can be no fundamental discontinuity between the realm of the psyche and the realm of elemental transformations'.[72] In other words, body and soul are part of a continuous series of transformations. Indeed, so great is the emphasis on becoming in this passage that it has been argued that Heraclitus did not consider water, soul and earth as substances at all but as processes. Lloyd, for example, has compared Heraclitus' view with the phases of becoming in Chinese thought and in particular *qi*, the underlying and ever-becoming 'substance'.[73] In relation to *qi*, Matthews describes how body and soul exist within what he refers to as a homological system:

> predicated on a single substance (or energy-substance), of which all phenomena, including physicality and interiority, are specific configurations, with a single origin. This extends to separable components of a person. This substance is self-generating and continually transforming.[74]

This monistic emphasis does not, however, eliminate the body and soul distinction, nor eradicate the idea of an independent existence of the soul after it has separated from the body. Rather *qi* is able to exist in two different states to form a single person. As Matthews puts it: 'while the person is separable into "body" and "soul" this separation is not ontological in character, as both constitute alternate configurations of *qi*.[75] A similar idea has been applied to Aztec dualism by Maffie who, again referring to *qi*, likens the configuration of the Aztec body and soul to ice with water inside.[76]

The idea that body and soul were physical entities, as intimately related as ice and water, was not only widespread among early Greek thinkers, its adoption in a similar form by the Stoics ensured its central place in Greek debates for centuries to come. The Orphic sources also point in this direction. For example, the Thurii gold tablet that describes the soul's journey through the underworld was itself wrapped in a larger gold tablet discussing elemental transformations including air and fire (L 12; OF 492). The precise physical view expressed in the Timpone Grande gold tablet is unclear but given the repetition of terms such as fire, air and Protogonos, it shows a broad continuity with the kind of theorizing present in the Derveni commentary, which describes a divine air that controls, unites and, at least at times, is identical with the cosmos.[77] Like the gold tablets, the Derveni commentator also writes extensively, albeit obscurely, on rituals concerning souls.[78] The discussion appears to form the basis of the early columns but can only be reliably reconstructed in column 6, which speaks of hindering souls that are also called daimones (col. 6.3–4). It is not clearly stated in the papyrus, but it is likely that the commentator also identifies these souls with divine Air and therefore Zeus and Mind. This was a common idea, and the Pythagoreans notebooks describe an upper air filled with souls that are also called daimones and heroes.[79] Diogenes of Apollonia (DK 64 B5) also describes Air as Mind, Soul and God. Diogenes may not be the author of the papyrus, as Janko argues,[80] yet the idea that divine Air and souls surround us is not only a common idea of the time, it is demonstrably Orphic and vouched for by Aristotle (*De An.* 410b 27–11a 2):

> τοῦτο δὲ πέπονθε καὶ ὁ ἐν τοῖς Ὀρφικοῖς καλουμένοις ἔπεσι λόγος· φησὶ γὰρ τὴν ψυχὴν ἐκ τοῦ ὅλου εἰσιέναι ἀναπνεόντων, φερομένην ὑπὸ τῶν ἀνέμων, οὐχ οἷόν τε δὲ τοῖς φυτοῖς τοῦτο συμβαίνειν οὐδὲ τῶν ζῴων ἐνίοις, εἴπερ μὴ πάντα ἀναπνέουσιν· τοῦτο δὲ λέληθε τοὺς οὕτως ὑπειληφότας.

> The doctrine contained within the poems called 'Orphic' suffers from this very thing, for it says that the soul comes in from the universe when breathing takes place, borne in upon the winds. However, it is not possible for this to happen to plants, nor to certain animals, for not all of them breathe. But those who hold this view overlooked this fact.[81]

Variant forms of the idea also appear in later Orphic fragments. Proclus (OF 339) quotes a fragment describing

αἱ μὲν δὴ θηρῶν τε καὶ οἰωνῶν πτεροέντων
ψυχαί ὅτ' ἀίξωσι, λίπῃ δέ μιν ἱερός αἰών
τῶν οὔ τις ψυχὴν παράγει δόμον εἰς Ἄιδαο,
ἀλλ' αὐτοῦ πεπότηται ἐτώσιον εἰς ὅ κεν αὐτήν
ἄλλο ἀφαρπάζῃι μίγδην ἀνέμοιο πνοῇσιν
ὁππότε δ' ἄνθρωπος προλίπῃ φάος ἠελίοιο,
ψυχὰς ἀθανάτας κατάνει Κυλλήνιος Ἑρμῆς
γαίης ἐς κευθμῶνα πελώριον.

when the souls of beasts or winged birds flit forth, and the sacred life leaves them, for them there is not one to lead the soul to the house of Hades, but rather it flutters vainly about itself until, mingled with the breath of the wind, another body snatches it in. But when a human being leaves the light of the sun, Kyllenian Hermes leads the immortal souls to the enormous depths of the earth.[82]

And Vettius Valens describes how (OF 436)

ἀέρα δ' ἕλκοντες ψυχὴν θείαν δρεπόμεσθα.

it is by drawing in the air that we acquire a divine soul.[83]

Although these sources may not form a single coherent doctrine, we can at least point to a set of repeated tropes that suggest that the Orphic soul is entirely in tune with its Presocratic counterparts, including the idea that the soul is identified as divine Air which both surrounds all beings and forms the inner self when inhaled by animals, plants and humans.[84]

The Orphic evidence for how precisely the body interacts with the soul is slim, yet we can infer some basic points. If the soul is a fine kind of airy substance, the body is likely to be, as with almost all Presocratics, a heavier material form.[85] Alongside the possible fifth-century BCE work *Physica*, the Suda reports that the Orphics referred to the body as a net which West argues suggests a close relationship where the 'the soul is air occupying the interstices of a material body'.[86] Like the majority of Orphic books, this work does not survive. Ancient authors, however, were impressed by the Orphic position and according to Clement of Alexandria, it not only closely overlapped with Heraclitus' view, the philosopher actually plagiarized his model from Orpheus himself. Clement presents the original Orphic idea as (DK 22 B 36; Clem. *Strom.* 6.2.17):

ἔστιν ὕδωρ ψυχῇι θάνατος, χὐδάτεσσι δὲ γαῖα·
ἐκ δ' ὕδατος ⟨πέλε⟩ γαῖα, τὸ δ' ἐκ γαίας πάλιν ὕδωρ,
ἐκ τοῦ δὴ ψυχὴ ὅλον αἰθέρα ἀλλάσσουσα.

Water is death for the soul; for the waters, earth.
From water the earth is born and from earth, in turn, water,
and from the latter, the soul, that becomes universal ether.[87]

The common consensus is that this passage is post-Heraclitean and a further example of the Orphic appropriation of Heraclitus along Stoicizing lines.[88] However, in light of the discovery of the Derveni papyrus, the idea of later Orphic Stoicizing needs to be reappraised. In any case, even if the Orphics adopted this particular idea, they arguably did so because it was compatible with their existing orientations.[89] Moreover, if early Orphic views on the body remain obscure, we can posit the presence of a similar processual view in their early discussions of mortal and immortal becomings. Indeed, the gold tablets repeatedly speak of the death of the body as the birth of the soul. Two tablets from fourth-century BCE Pelinna (L7 a–b; OF 485–6) describe 'now you have died and now you have been born'.[90] A similar transition appears in the fifth-century BCE bone plaques from Olbia, which describe the triple movement between 'life–death–life'.[91] The phrasing is particularly reminiscent of Heraclitus' enigmatic phrase (DK 22 B 62):

> Ἀθάνατοι θνητοί, θνητοὶ ἀθάνατοι, ζῶντες τὸν ἐκείνων θάνατον τὸν δὲ ἐκείνων βίον τεθνεῶτες.
>
> Immortals mortals, mortals immortals, living the others' death, dying the others' life.[92]

The discussion of births and deaths in this passage recalls the birth and death of the soul in DK 22 B 36 and suggests that gods and men, like earth, water and soul, are not antitypes so much as phases within a process of exchange.[93] That mortals can become immortal and immortals mortal was, as Kahn notes, an 'extraordinarily shocking' idea.[94] The idea, however, was no more shocking than the Orphic claim (Thurii 3; OF 488) that the soul will be a god instead of a mortal (θεὸς δ' ἔσηι ἀντὶ βροτοῖο) or, for that matter, the myth of the dying and reviving god, Dionysus. Indeed, although these ideas are rare in Greek thought, they are early and appear in three key thinkers from this period, Orpheus, Heraclitus and Empedocles, all of whom describe mortals and immortals in very organic terms as learning to grow mortal and immortal. As Empedocles puts it (DK 31 B 35.14):

> αἶψα δὲ θνήτ' ἐφύοντο, τά πρὶν μάθον ἀθάνατ' εἶναι.
>
> And suddenly those things grew mortal which before learned to be immortal.[95]

Conversely those that are mortal can, as Empedocles himself aspires, learn to grow into gods (DK 31 B 112).[96] What emerges from this discussion is a view where life and death, immortality and mortality, are not absolute oppositions but perpetual becomings, a world which continuously breaks down rigid dichotomies between gods and men, bodies and souls.

What remains to be discussed is how these philosophical ideas can be related to a mythical narrative involving the Titans and sacrifice. Although no conclusive claims can be made, I suggest that a monistic interpretation of body and soul also offers a more convincing reading of the anthropogony than a dualistic one. While it is certainly possible that humanity is derived from a combination of Dionysus and the Titans, it must be conceded that any Dionysiac element would necessarily be small. Indeed, where specified, the god is not so much eaten by the Titans as he is tasted (γεύω). Furthermore, in most versions of the myth, Dionysus' body is later reassembled and revived by the gods after the act.[97] As West notes:

> The Dionysus who now exists grew from what the Titans did not eat. What they did eat cannot easily be imagined to have affected the quality of the puff of smoke that stayed hanging in the air when they were smashed into Tartarus. Nor is there anything to show that poet had any such notion in his head.[98]

Although it may be insisted that a small Dionysiac element is present in human beings, the significance of this component is unclear and hardly suggests an immortal divine soul and an ontologically distinct earthy Titanic body. Indeed, as both the Titans and Dionysus are divine, it seems arbitrary to imagine they would constitute separate mortal and immortal parts. Rather, whether it is exclusively through the Titans or a composite of the Titans and Dionysus, the myth describes how humanity has a single divine origin. Two possible objections, however, might be raised against this reading. The first appears in the famous epitaph of the gold tablets: 'I am a child of Earth and Starry Heaven?'[99] This phrase could be read in terms of a dualistic earthly and Titanic body and a heavenly Dionysiac soul. However, the most likely reading follows its common Hesiodic usage and refers to the lineage of the Titans themselves, that is, the divine children of Gaia and Ouranos.[100] The second possible objection arises from the Orphic saying that the body was a prison (*Crat.* 400c). This claim again could be read in terms of Platonic dualism, but it certainly does not mean that the body is Titanic. Xenokrates, it is true, refers to the φρουρά as Titanic (fr. 20 Heinze), yet whatever his precise meaning was, it is unlikely that he considers the body as Titanic and the soul as Dionysiac. Indeed, the majority of Platonists, many of whom develop upon Xenokrates' readings, see the soul as moving between Titanic and Dionysiac states.[101] Nor is it surprising why they claim this. Indeed, the idea that the body is Titanic leads to the rather absurd consequence that the soul is innocent and the prison itself, that is, the Titanic element, is guilty. The major sources, however, stress the very opposite. Plato in the *Cratylus* 400c describes how the soul is guilty and the body, rather than intrinsically evil in nature, is what holds the soul. A similar image emerges from Empedocles' parallel myth. Again, rather than the body being seen as a criminal, it is the daimon or soul that is punished for his crimes. This moreover is precisely what we see in the Orphic gold tablets (L 10a–b; OF 488–9) where the soul, rather than the body, claims to 'have paid a penalty for unjust deeds'. In all these examples, the soul, far from being a pure Dionysiac element, is the Titanic criminal serving his time in a bodily prison. What then is this body composed of? Neither Orpheus' nor Empedocles' myths explain this. Elsewhere, however, Empedocles explains how the body is a less perfect mixture of the same basic stuff as the daimon.[102] There is a great deal of innovation in Empedocles' poetry, but by viewing the body and the daimon or soul as emerging simultaneously, he was simply following Hesiod. Indeed, the closest parallel for the Orphic anthropogony is Hesiod's (*Theog.* 184) description of the Erinyes and Giants who are born from the blood of Ouranos' severed phallus. These beings emerge in a single act as composites of body and soul, and there is no reason to doubt that the Orphic creation myth imagined mankind's birth any differently.

From soul to sacrifice

The Orphic's innovative conception of self was not merely cosmic speculation, it was a myth woven into the fabric of life. Indeed, like Hesiod's Promethean tale, the anthropogony was a simultaneous description of what humans and gods are, an aetiology on sacrifice, and an explanation for the current state of the cosmos. However, although Orpheus and Hesiod agree that sacrifice is something implicated in defining what humanity is, the poets disagree profoundly on what sacrifice actually accomplishes. For Hesiod, sacrifice was a key means of connecting ontologically distinct tribes of gods and humans. For the Orphics, on the other hand, sacrifice separates ontologically similar beings.

The Orphics were not the only Greeks to reject animal offerings. Indeed, the idea may have begun with the Pythagoreans. However, Pythagorean views on sacrifice reveal a great deal of inconsistency.[103] Some sources such as Eudoxus,

Alexis and Strabo suggest that Pythagoras shunned eating ensouled beings altogether.[104] Other testimonies point towards more complex attitudes where meat eating is restricted to certain animals or particular parts.[105] Some scholars even doubt whether the Pythagoreans should be considered to have rejected sacrifice at all.[106] Although complexity in early religious practices is to be expected, early Orphic sources, though few, are clearer and more consistent than their Pythagorean counterparts.[107] The earliest reference to a rejection of sacrifice may appear in Herodotus' discussion of the Orphic ban on wool and an enigmatic reference to a ἱρὸς λόγος ('sacred story').[108] Whether this ἱρὸς λόγος refers to the dismemberment myth remains a possible but elusive testimony.[109] There are, however, some strong sources for this rejection from the classical period. Euripides, for example, describes the Orphic diet in the *Hippolytus* (948–54):

σὺ δὴ θεοῖσιν ὡς περισσὸς ὢν ἀνὴρ
ξύνει; σὺ σώφρων καὶ κακῶν ἀκήρατος;
οὐκ ἂν πιθοίμην τοῖσι σοῖς κόμποις ἐγὼ
θεοῖσι προσθεὶς ἀμαθίαν φρονεῖν κακῶς.
ἤδη νυν αὔχει καὶ δι' ἀψύχου βορᾶς
σίτοις καπήλευ' Ὀρφέα τ' ἄνακτ' ἔχων
βάκχευε πολλῶν γραμμάτων τιμῶν καπνούς.

Are you, then, the companion of the gods, as a man beyond the common? Are you the chaste one, untouched by evil? I will never be persuaded by your vauntings, never be so unintelligent as to impute folly to the gods. Continue then your confident boasting, take up soulless foods and play the showman with your food, make Orpheus your lord and enter a Bacchic state (βάκχευε), holding the smoke of many books in honour.[110]

This passage presents a condensed summary of early Orphism and alludes to a diet of 'food lacking souls' (ἀψύχου βορᾶς), Bacchic rites involving the burning of books, and the idea that a particular lifestyle, pure from evil, makes its practitioners companions of the gods. Plato's description of the Orphic life gives their unusual diet an even more central role (*Leg.* 782c–d):

τὸ δὲ μὴν θύειν ἀνθρώπους ἀλλήλους ἔτι καὶ νῦν παραμένον ὁρῶμεν πολλοῖς
καὶ τοὐναντίον ἀκούομενέν ἄλλοις, ὅτε οὐδὲ βοὸς ἐτόλμων μὲν γεύεσθαι,
θύματά τε οὐκ ἦν τοῖς θεοῖσι ζῷα, πέλανοι δὲ καὶ μέλιτι καρποὶ δεδευμένοι
καὶ τοιαῦτα ἄλλα ἁγνὰ θύματα, σαρκῶν δ' ἀπείχοντο ὡς οὐχ ὅσιον ὂν ἐσθίειν
οὐδὲτοὺς τῶν θεῶν βωμοὺς αἵματι μιαίνειν, ἀλλὰ Ὀρφικοί τινες λεγόμενοι
βίοι ἐγίγνοντο ἡμῶν τοῖς τότε, ἀψύχων μὲν ἐχόμενοι πάντων, ἐμψύχων δὲ
τοὐναντίον πάντων ἀπεχόμενοι.

The custom of men sacrificing one another is, in fact, one that survives even now among many peoples; whereas amongst others we hear of how the opposite custom existed, when they were forbidden so much as to taste an ox, and their offerings to the gods consisted, not of animals, but of cakes of meal and grain steeped in honey, and other pure offerings, and from flesh they abstained as though it were unholy to eat it or to stain with blood the altars of the gods; instead of that, those of us men who then existed lived what is called an 'Orphic life,' keeping wholly to soulless food and, contrariwise, abstaining wholly from ensouled beings.[111]

Plato in this passage is discussing the contrasting attitudes towards sacrifice found in different societies spanning from human sacrifice to a total abstinence from blood rites and replacement with pure offerings. The latter he calls an Orphic life (ὀρφικος βίος) and, confirming Euripides' view, adds that a major prerequisite is abstinence from ensouled beings. Another possible reference is found in Aristophanes' *Frogs* (1032):

Ὀρφεὺς μὲν γὰρ τελετάς θ' ἡμῖν κατέδειξε φόνων τ' ἀπέχεσθαι.

Orpheus showed us rites and to refrain from murder.

The passage does not explicitly mention the killing of animals but a more general refrain from murder. The parallel evidence from Empedocles, however, suggests that murder and sacrifice are synonyms (DK 31 B 134), and it is unlikely that Orpheus is being credited with introducing a prohibition on murdering humans.

The Orphic view that animals possess souls presents a stark contrast with that of the early poets. For Hesiod and Homer, animals may possess some interior qualities similar to humans such as a θυμός, yet they lack key inner dispositions such as a νόος and a ψυχή.[112] Indeed, far from agents, animals appear more as objects which can be used. For the early Orphics and philosophers such as Empedocles, on the other hand, animals possess interiorities like our own and in some cases, this assumption even led to new theogonic myths where animals and humans were once said to have existed side by side as equals. An early example is found in Empedocles' (DK 31 B 128) description of the Golden Age where humanity, animals and the goddess Cypris or Aphrodite live in blissful harmony.[113] Empedocles (DK 31 B 130) notes of animals that:

ἦσαν δὲ κτίλα πάντα καὶ ἀνθρώποισι προσηνῆ
Θῆρές τ' οἰωνοί τε, φιλοφροσύνη τε δεδήει.

They were all tame and gentle to men,
both beasts and fowl, and friendly feelings radiated.[114]

Empedocles' stress on peaceful interspecies relations is emphasized by the terms φιλόφρων ('kindly,' 'disposed,' 'friendly'), κτίλος, ('tame', or perhaps better 'cherished')[115] and προσηνής ('soft', 'gentle'). These ideas were taken even further in Plato's variation of Empedocles' prehistory in the *Statesman*. In this myth, animals were not only friendly,[116] they could also speak (*Plt.* 272b–c):

> εἰ μὲν τοίνυν οἱ τρόφιμοι τοῦ Κρόνου, παρούσης αὐτοῖς οὕτω πολλῆς σχολῆς καὶ δυνάμεως πρὸς τὸ μὴ μόνον ἀνθρώποις ἀλλὰ καὶ θηρίοις διὰ λόγων δύνασθαι συγγίγνεσθαι, κατεχρῶντο τούτοις σύμπασιν ἐπὶ φιλοσοφίαν, μετά τε θηρίων καὶ μετ' ἀλλήλων ὁμιλοῦντες, καὶ πυνθανόμενοι παρὰ πάσης φύσεως εἴ τινά τις ἰδίαν δύναμιν ἔχουσα ᾔσθετό τι διάφορον τῶν ἄλλων εἰς συναγυρμὸν φρονήσεως, εὔκριτον ὅτι τῶν νῦν οἱ τότε μυρίῳ πρὸς εὐδαιμονίαν διέφερον.

> Well, then, if the foster children of Cronus, having all this leisure and the ability to converse not only with human beings but also with beasts made full use of all these opportunities with a view to philosophy, talking with the animals and with one another and learning from every creature that, through possession of some peculiar power he may have had in any respect beyond his fellows perceptions tending towards an increase of wisdom, it would be easy to decide that the people of those old times were immeasurably happier than those of our epoch.[117]

Whether this detail was present in Empedocles' myth or an unknown Orphic variant is uncertain. Nevertheless, the possibility of talking animals was one that emerged from the kinship and mutual recognition which developed from the attribution of souls to animals.[118] It was also the same presence of souls in animals that problematized sacrifice. As Empedocles describes it (DK 31 B 137):

> μορφὴν δ' ἀλλάξαντα πατὴρ φίλον υἱὸν ἀείρας
> σφάζει ἐπευχόμενος μέγα νήπιος· οἱ δ' ἀπορεῦνται
> λισσόμενον θύοντες, ὁ δ' αὖ νήκουστος ὁμοκλέων
> σφάξας ἐν μεγάροισι κακὴν ἀλεγύνατο δαῖτα.
> ὡς δ' αὕτως πατέρ' υἱὸς ἑλὼν καὶ μητέρα παῖδες
> θυμὸν ἀπορραίσαντε φίλας κατὰ σάρκας ἔδουσιν.

> The father lifting up his own son in a changed form
> slaughters him with a prayer in his great folly, and they are lost
> as they sacrifice the suppliant. But he, not heedful of their rebukes,
> having made slaughter has prepared in his halls a ghastly banquet.
> Just so the son laying hold of the father and the children of the mother
> after depriving them of life devour their own kindred flesh.[119]

In this passage, developing upon his doctrine of reincarnation Empedocles suggests that animal sacrifice may potentially lead to the literal eating of one's relatives. Given the absence of any specific arguments in the Orphic fragments, it is tempting to apply this logic here as well.[120] Although the evidence remains controversial, reincarnation may have been included in Orphic interpretations from an early date.[121] However, to assume that reincarnation somehow explains Empedocles' and the Orphics' resistance to animal sacrifice may obscure as much as it elucidates their underlying motivation. Indeed, while sacrifice may in some cases lead to the murder of kin, it is clear that both Empedocles and Orpheus considered sacrifice a 'ghastly banquet' from the very beginning of the cosmos when gods murdered and ate other gods. What I propose instead is that the rejection of sacrifice had little to do with the presence of reincarnation and that both reincarnation and the rejection of sacrifice are secondary phenomena which potentially emerge from the older and more basic assumption of ontological continuity between humans, animals and gods.

The connection between ontology and sacrifice is a point I adopt from Descola's argument that animist and totemist ontologies lack sacrifice because given humanity's existing connection to non-humans in terms of shared interiorities, the institution would be 'pointless and incongruous'.[122] The same is logically true of pantheist ontologies and to understand the redundancy of sacrifice within the Orphic cosmos, it will be useful to reiterate my position on Hesiodic sacrifice. In Chapter 2, I outlined that for Hesiod sacrifice was based on a fundamental ontological distinction between human and gods. In this world, sacrifice was the central means of communication with ambiguous divine affines. My general argument was illustrated by Plato's *Symposium*, which speaks of a daimonic realm that acts as an intermediary connecting ontologically distinct mortals and immortals (202e–203a):

> ἑρμηνεῦον καὶ διαπορθμεῦον θεοῖς τὰ παρ' ἀνθρώπων καὶ ἀνθρώποις τὰ παρὰ θεῶν, τῶν μὲν τὰς δεήσεις καὶ θυσίας, τῶν δὲ τὰς ἐπιτάξεις τε καὶ ἀμοιβὰς τῶν θυσιῶν, ἐν μέσῳ δὲ ὂν ἀμφοτέρων συμπληροῖ, ὥστε τὸ πᾶν αὐτὸ αὑτῷ συνδεδέσθαι. διὰ τούτου καὶ ἡ μαντικὴ πᾶσα χωρεῖ καὶ ἡ τῶν ἱερέων τέχνη τῶν τε περὶ τὰς θυσίας καὶ τελετὰς καὶ τὰς ἐπῳδὰς καὶ τὴν μαντείαν πᾶσαν καὶ γοητείαν. θεὸς δὲ ἀνθρώπῳ οὐ μείγνυται, ἀλλὰ διὰ τούτου πᾶσά ἐστιν ἡ ὁμιλία καὶ ἡ διάλεκτος θεοῖς πρὸς ἀνθρώπους <καὶ πρὸς θεοὺς ἀνθρώποις>, καὶ ἐγρηγορόσι καὶ καθεύδουσι.

> Interpreting and transporting human things to the gods and divine things to men; entreaties and sacrifices from below, and ordinances and requitals from

above: being midway between, it makes each to supplement the other, so that the whole is combined in one. Through it are conveyed all divination and priestcraft concerning sacrifice and ritual and incantations, and all soothsaying and sorcery. God with man does not mingle: but the daimon is the means of all society and converse of men with gods and of gods with men, whether waking or asleep.[123]

This passage, as noted, encapsulates a sacrificial logic involving three components: humans, the animal victim, and gods. Within this triad, the animal acts as an intermediary between two ontologically separated categories and allows mortals and immortals to communicate without threatening their ontological status. What emerges is an understanding of sacrifice where, as Descola notes, 'the characteristic feature of sacrifice is precisely the fact that it establishes a link between two terms initially unconnected'.[124] The idea of connecting opposites, of course, makes perfect sense in a world based on ontological difference. If, however, the cosmos was already connected, there would be no need for an intermediary and consequently no need for sacrifice itself. In other words, rather than the unlikely possibility of eating one's parents, it was precisely the presence of ontological continuity or cosmic kinship that removed the *raison d'être* of the most widespread religious institution in Greece; the institution was obsolete. Indeed, for the Orphics and Empedocles we can take Descola's claims even further; the presence of shared kinship made sacrifice not merely a redundant act, it made it a potentially dangerous one – an act that threatens to dissolve the very bond that connects us to gods and the cosmos as a whole. As Sextus Empiricus puts in *Against the Physicists* (1.126-9):

> οἱ μὲν οὖν περὶ τὸν Πυθαγόραν καὶ τὸν Ἐμπεδοκλέα καὶ τῶν Ἰταλῶν πλῆθος φασὶ μὴ μόνον ἡμῖν πρὸς ἀλλήλους καὶ πρὸς τοὺς θεοὺς εἶναί τινα κοινωνίαν, ἀλλὰ καὶ πρὸς τὰ ἄλογα τῶν ζώων. ἓν γὰρ ὑπάρχειν πνεῦμα τὸ διὰ παντὸς τοῦ κόσμου διῆκον ψυχῆς τρόπον, τὸ καὶ ἑνοῦν ἡμᾶς πρὸς ἐκεῖνα. διόπερ καὶ κτείνοντες αὐτὰ καὶ ταῖς σαρξὶν αὐτῶν τρεφόμενοι ἀδικήσομέν τε καὶ ἀσεβήσομεν ὡς συγγενεῖς ἀναιροῦντες. ἔνθεν καὶ παρῄνουν οὗτοι οἱ φιλόσοφοι ἀπέχεσθαι τῶν ἐμψύχων.

> So then, according to Pythagoras and Empedocles, and the rest of the Italian crowd, not only do we have a certain communion with the gods but also with the irrational animals. For there is one breath that pervades everything in the universe, in the manner of a soul, and this unites us with them. Because of this, to kill them and eat their flesh is a sacrilege as it is a destruction of our own kindred. From this reasoning the philosophers recommended abstaining from living things.[125]

Although this passage may at first seem to simply repeat Empedocles' warnings about sacrificing kin, it also emphasizes a deeper underlying issue. Indeed, while it is true that in a world pervaded by a divine breath, all creatures are related, Sextus stresses that sacrifice more than the murder of relatives involves the very destruction of the 'one breath that pervades everything in the universe, in the manner of a soul, and this unites us'. In other words, sacrifice involves the destruction of a connection. Although Sextus is a late source, the idea that sacrifice is something that dissolves ties elaborates on themes found in Empedocles' depiction of the ideal Golden Age which was lost through the sacrifice of one of these animal agents (DK 31 B 128):

οὐδέ τις ἦν κείνοισιν Ἄρης θεὸς οὐδὲ Κυδοιμός
οὐδὲ Ζεὺς βασιλεὺς οὐδὲ Κρόνος οὐδὲ Ποσειδῶν,
ἀλλὰ Κύπρις βασίλεια.
τὴν οἵ γ' εὐσεβέεσσιν ἀγάλμασιν ἱλάσκοντο
γραπτοῖς τε ζῴοισι μύροισί τε δαιδαλεόδμοις
σμύρνης τ' ἀκρήτου θυσίαις λιβάνου τε θυώδους,
ξανθῶν τε σπονδὰς μελίτων ῥίπτοντες ἐς οὖδας·
ταύρων δ' ἀκρήτοισι φόνοις οὐ δεύετο βωμός,
ἀλλὰ μύσος τοῦτ' ἔσκεν ἐν ἀνθρώποισι μέγιστον,
θυμὸν ἀπορραίσαντας ἐέδμεναι ἠέα γυῖα.

They had no Ares as their god, nor Tumult,
not Zeus the king, nor Cronus nor Poseidon,
but Cypris the queen ...
whom they propitiated with reverent statues,
with pained pictures, delicate perfumes,
and offerings of undiluted myrrh and fragrant frankincense,
pouring to the ground libation of yellow honey,
the altar was not moistened with the pure blood of bulls,
but this was the greatest abomination to men,
to take away their life and devour their goodly limbs.[126]

In this passage, rather than emphasizing the literal eating of a close relative, Empedocles outlines how sacrifice and the following feast resulted in weakening an existing tie and distancing humans, gods and even animals. Through sacrifice, humans are separated from the rule of Cypris, animals who were once peaceful and friendly become wild, and tensions are introduced among the divinities Kronos, Ares, Tumult, Poseidon and Zeus.[127] All of which stresses a single point: sacrifice has no place in a pantheist world. Far from uniting discontinuous beings, the act destroys an existing connection between animals, humans and gods. Indeed, speculating on an extreme but logical conclusion, Augustine argues in *City of God* (4.12) that for pantheists sacrifice could even be interpreted as the literal slaughter of God himself:

> si mundi animus Deus est eique animo mundus ut corpus est, ut sit unum animal constans ex animo et corpore, atque iste Deus est sinu quodam naturae in se ipso continens omnia, ut ex ipsius anima, qua uiuificatur tota ista moles, uitae atque animae cunctorum uiuentium pro cuiusque nascendi sorte sumantur, nihil omnino remanere, quod non sit pars Dei. Quod si ita est, quis non uideat quanta impietas et inreligiositas consequantur, ut, quod calcauerit quisque, partem Dei calcet, in omni animante occidendo pars Dei trucidetur? Nolo omnia dicere, quae possunt occurrere cogitantibus, dici autem sine uerecundia non possunt.

> if God is the soul of the world, and the world is as a body to Him, who is the soul, He must be one living being consisting of soul and body, and that this same God is a kind of womb of nature containing all things in Himself, so that the lives and souls of all living things are taken, according to the manner of each one's birth, out of His soul which vivifies that whole mass, and therefore nothing at all remains which is not a part of God. And if this is so, who cannot see what impious and irreligious consequences follow, such as that whatever one may trample, he must trample a part of God, and in slaying any living creature, a part of God must be slaughtered? But I am unwilling to utter all that may occur to those who think of it, yet cannot be spoken without irreverence.[128]

Augustine's argument that sacrifice in a pantheist world is no less than the destruction of God does not appear in any Orphic source.[129] However, the horror of sacrificing a god is something abundantly clear in early Orphic myth. Indeed, Empedocles and Orpheus simply express this position from the opposite end, describing how sacrifice from its origins involves the murder of a god or daimon. It is from this primordial murder that mortals possess their souls. And it is through their refusal to kill that they may once again become immortal.

Appropriate offerings to the gods

What I have presented in this chapter is a holistic reading of the Orphic evidence where mythology, philosophical speculation on airy souls, and the rejection of animal offerings mutually reinforce each other as part of a pantheist ontology based on the continuity of physicalities and interiorities. While the idea that Orphism expresses pantheistic ideas may not be controversial, that the Orphic rejection of sacrifice is best understood as part of an underlying pantheist ontology may not prove persuasive to all scholars. Betegh for one argues that 'this is exactly where problems erupt; indeed, it is highly doubtful whether one can justifiably speak about "systems" to describe either Orphism or Pythagoreanism'.[130] Systems, as Betegh understands them, refer to an explicitly held sets of ideas, that is, a kind of theology which locates the rejection of sacrifice as part of a more coherent set of practices. The alternative is to understand ideas such as airy souls and abstinence from animal offerings as part of a piecemeal history where certain ideas are adopted, and others rejected in a more chaotic fashion. Betegh is not alone in this assessment. Indeed, one of the most cogent and detailed arguments for this position has been posed by James B. Rives, who also argues that no new theology was entailed in the Orphic rejection of sacrifice and that

> the thinkers of the late archaic and classical period who are commonly said to have rejected animal sacrifice were in fact not concerned with animal sacrifice as a cultic practice intended to establish a connection between the human and divine spheres; their concern was instead with the practice of eating meat, which they regarded as problematic because of their belief in the transmigration of souls between humans and animals.[131]

Moreover, Rives argues that the basic relationship between humans and gods assumed by Hesiod and Homer remained intact in early Orphism and that sacrifice continued to be offered in an almost identical fashion. What did change, he argues, was the kind of offerings that were deemed appropriate to the gods. Animals were considered unsuitable because of the presence of ensouled animals and especially the doctrine of metempsychosis, but Empedocles, the Pythagoreans and the Orphics simply offered substitute offerings in their place.

Although the assumption that the Orphics held a doctrine of reincarnation is debated, on some points Rives is entirely correct.[132] Indeed, gifts to the gods by no means stopped with the rejection of meat, and the sources continue to use the common word θύω or sacrifice to describe Orphic offerings of cakes and libations of milk and honey.[133] This is an important point and if both Hesiod and the Orphics can refer to an offering made to a god involving similar ritual actions by the verb θύω, what reason do we have for understanding the word as sacrifice in only one of these contexts? Comparatively speaking, that a vegetable sacrifice could be part of the same theological view as animal sacrifice would hardly be surprising. The Nuer, for example, famously sacrifice cucumbers, which they assured Evans-Pritchard were really oxen.[134] Empedocles' (D.L.8.53) probable apocryphal sacrifice of an ox made of spices requires even less imagination. However, our acceptance of Rives' argument that sacrifice continued in a similar way depends on whether we understand ritual acts as piecemeal accretions or meaningful theologies. For Rives, the latter is unlikely because in his view 'systematic theologies' only occur in the Imperial period.[135] This allows him to claim that the rejection of animal sacrifice was not based on a new theology but emerged in relation to the introduction of metempsychosis, a new idea added to the existing messy reality of Greek rituals.

Despite a number of valid points, Rives' argument that the early Greeks lacked systematic theologies is problematic. Indeed, even if we ignore the contested status of metempsychosis in early Orphism, I do not understand how Rives can divorce the presence of ensouled animals from a new theology. On the contrary, the very idea that animals can possess souls is itself evidence of a theological shift. It is a revolution that fundamentally changes how we understand a wide range of theological concepts including gods, humans, souls and sacrifice. In this respect, the continuity of the word θύω provides no clear indication that the practice was understood in an identical or even similar way. Indeed, very few scholars would assume that the Zeus of Homer is the same as the Zeus of Heraclitus and that no theological shift is evident because they use the same name and I see no reason why we should treat sacrifice any differently. Therefore, rather than assume continuity with what went before, we must, as far as possible, investigate how sacrifice was understood in Orphic contexts. A useful point of departure towards this end is found in Hesiod's understanding of the ritual. In Chapter 2, I discussed that Hesiodic sacrifice was based on a series of complex hierarchal subdivisions including special shares for gods, aristocrats, commoners and priests. The ritual was practised in order to communicate with ontologically distinct gods. If Rives is correct in asserting that the Orphics merely substituted the offering but continued to sacrifice to the gods in the same way, this emphasis on hierarchy and distinctions should also apply to the Orphic offerings of cakes and spices. The available evidence, though slim, suggests that they neither divided their offerings nor worshipped their gods in a similar fashion.[136] For example, Empedocles' Cyprian myth, though not strictly Orphic, presents a detailed description which contrasts pure offerings of incense, reverent statues, painted pictures and libations of honey against blood offerings (DK 31 B 134). These offerings were made in a spirit of unity where even wild beasts were friendly (DK 31 B 136). The myth in this respect describes an ideal offering based on shared kinship between beings who are similar or even identical to each other. Another important element of Empedocles' ideal sacrifice is the offering of incense, a substance which was also of pivotal importance in Orphic rites.[137] The *Hymns*, for example, frequently begin by allocating a particular perfume appropriate to each god.[138] Protogonos (*OH* 6), for example, receives myrrh and Zeus (*OH* 15) storax. Recent studies of the *Hymns* stress their status as ritual evocations and that the incense mentioned in each hymn may constitute the core offering.[139] This would be fitting. Indeed, incense frequently appears as a direct substitute for meat and Theophrastus, in his moralizing narrative on the history of animal sacrifice, locates incense as the original offering made to the gods before animal meat was wrongly introduced (Porph. *Abst.* 2.5.3). A similar idea also appears in the spice ox supposedly offered by Empedocles (D.L. 8.53). Although Empedocles does not explain the significance of this substitute, Philostratus' *Life of Apollonious* (5.25) not only discusses a very similar bull made of spices, it offers an interpretation of why such an offering is appropriate:

> Ἀνελθόντι δὲ αὐτῷ ἐς τὸ ἱερὸν ὁ μὲν κόσμος ὁ περὶ αὐτὸ καὶ ὁ ἐφ' ἑκάστῳ λόγος θεῖός τε ἐφαίνετο καὶ κατὰ σοφίαν ξυντεθείς, τὸ δὲ τῶν ταύρων αἷμα καὶ οἱ χῆνες καὶ ὁπόσα ἐθύετο, οὐκ ἐπῄνει τὰ τοιάδε, οὐδὲ ἐς δαῖτας θεῶν ἦγεν· ἐρομένου δ' αὐτὸν τοῦ ἱερέως, τί μαθὼν οὐχ οὕτω θύοι, 'σὺ μὲν οὖν' εἶπεν 'ἀπόκριναί μοι μᾶλλον, τί μαθὼν οὕτω θύεις;' εἰπόντος δὲ τοῦ ἱερέως 'καὶ τίς οὕτω δεινός, ὡς διορθοῦσθαι τὰ Αἰγυπτίων;' 'πᾶς' ἔφη 'σοφός, ἢν ἀπ' Ἰνδῶν ἥκῃ. καὶ βοῦν' ἔφη 'ἀπανθρακιῶ τήμερον καὶ κοινώνει τοῦ καπνοῦ ἡμῖν, οὐ γὰρ ἀχθέσῃ περὶ τῆς μοίρας, εἰ κἀκείνην οἱ θεοὶ δαίσονται.'

> When Apollonius had climbed to the sanctuary, its decoration and the lore attached to every part he considered inspired and arranged with wisdom, but he did not approve of the bull's blood, the geese, and all the things offered for sacrifice, nor did he consider them feasts for the gods. The priest asked him on what ground he did not practice this kind of sacrifice, and he replied, 'Rather you should answer me on what ground you practice it.' The priest replied, 'Who is so clever as to correct the customs of Egypt?' 'Any wise man,' said Apollonius, 'if he comes from India. I will roast a bull today,' he continued, 'and you can join with us in tasting the smoke. You will not complain about your portion, since that is what the gods devour too.'[140]

It is notable that the bull does not appear in this passage simply as an alternative to meat, rather its function, despite its form, is very different. Apollonius remarks that the spice bull is superior to the real thing precisely because it cannot be divided and humans and gods enjoy equal communion in the indivisible portions of smoke. This equal division among mortals and immortals, in other words, is a true equal feast that Homer could never have dreamt of. Of course, it could be argued that this act is still referred to using the term sacrifice or θύω, and in this respect we might for consistency's sake wish to retain the same word in our translation. This can be done, provided we understand that the term shifts from hierarchy to equality and ontologically distinct shares to identical shares – in other words, if we understand that θύω has been entirely transformed within a new theological system.

Conclusion: Sacrifice as the pivot of the world

In the previous chapter, I described pantheism in terms of a creative and in some cases a destructive potential. There is no better illustration of this dynamic than the Orphic dismemberment myth where a homogonous society of gods kills and eats one of their own. From this destructive act, mankind and, in some versions, animals and plants are born. For the Orphics, this myth provides the promise of salvation and those who reject animal sacrifice and attempt to purify their souls may hope to return to their divine origins. However, the myth also emphasizes the central role sacrifice occupies in the creation of the cosmos. Indeed, it is not misleading to say that the Orphic world pivots upon sacrifice – an act that perpetuates difference and expands and enlivens the surrounding communities of animals, gods and humans. A vivid, if hypothetical, window on this cosmos is provided in Plato's *Phaedrus* and his rich description of the rise and fall of daimones within a 10,000-year cycle.[141] Plato (248a–b) memorably describes this sequence as a kind of divine carousel where some souls ascend and

> αἱ δὲ δὴ ἄλλαι γλιχόμεναι μὲν ἅπασαι τοῦ ἄνω ἕπονται, ἀδυνατοῦσαι δὲ ὑποβρύχιαι ξυμπεριφέρονται, πατοῦσαι ἀλλήλας καὶ ἐπιβάλλουσαι, ἑτέρα πρὸ τῆς ἑτέρας πειρωμένη γενέσθαι. θόρυβος οὖν καὶ ἅμιλλα καὶ ἱδρὼς ἔσχατος γίγνεται, οὗ δὴ κακίᾳ ἡνιόχων πολλαὶ μὲν χωλεύονται, πολλαὶ δὲ πολλὰ πτερὰ θραύονται.

> the other souls follow after, all yearning for the upper region but unable to reach it, and are carried round beneath, trampling upon and colliding with one another, each striving to pass its neighbour. So there is the greatest confusion and sweat of rivalry, wherein many are lamed, and many wings are broken through the incompetence of the drivers.[142]

How much of Plato's dialogue is Orphic is uncertain, but the animism of its description nicely captures the Orphic cycle of life and death, rising and falling, that results from mortal and immortal choices and their abstinence or acceptance of animal flesh. Plato's description also captures the tangible nature of Orphic divinities. These beings are not like Hesiod's analogously similar yet ontologically distinct Olympians, rather the Orphic gods are fine material beings made of the same essential stuff as the cosmos as a whole. Indeed, in this respect pantheism makes divinity more concrete than Hesiod's anthropomorphic beings ever were and perhaps somewhat akin to the malevolent daimones discussed by Porphyry (*Abst.* 2.42) whose 'pneumatic part grows fat' from the rising smoke of sacrifice. Although Porphyry is a late source, the imagery of a physical daimon greedily eating animal flesh, or vapours, is no more unusual than the myth described by Empedocles, and certainly no more horrifying than the image of the Titans gathering, killing and eating the flesh of Dionysus. Animal sacrifice, in this respect, was rejected not because it did nothing, but because it did too much. It was an act that both destroyed and created the world as we know it.

CONCLUSION

Protagoras and Greek Naturalism

ἀλλ', ὦ Σώκρατες, ἔφη, οὐ φθονήσω: ἀλλὰ πότερον ὑμῖν, ὡς πρεσβύτερος νεωτέροις, μῦθον λέγων ἐπιδείξω ἢ λόγῳ διεξελθών;
πολλοὶ οὖν αὐτῷ ὑπέλαβον τῶν παρακαθημένων ὁποτέρως βούλοιτο οὕτως διεξιέναι.
δοκεῖ τοίνυν μοι, ἔφη, χαριέστερον εἶναι μῦθον ὑμῖν λέγειν.

'I wouldn't think of begrudging you an explanation, Socrates', he replied. 'But would you rather that I explain by telling you a myth, as an older man to a younger audience, or by exposition in a *logos*?'
The consensus was that he should proceed in whichever way he wished.
'I think it would be more pleasant', he said, 'if I told you a myth.'[1]

Plato, *Protagoras* 320c.

These are the words of the great sophist Protagoras – or at least how Plato describes them.[2] Arriving in Athens, Protagoras finds himself in a heated debate with Socrates on whether virtue can be taught. Yet rather than defend himself by way of a λόγος, or an argumentative demonstration, standing amid the intellectual elite with a voice like Orpheus (315a), Protagoras recites a myth narrating the birth of humanity, animals, and their struggle to survive in an unforgiving world.[3] The narrative begins with nameless gods moulding mortal creatures out of a mixture of fire and earth.[4] These animals are difficult to imagine and lacking any distinguishing features, they appear as homogenous beings in potential. Having finished their work, the unnamed gods recede, leaving the task of differentiation to the Titans Prometheus ('Forethought') and Epimetheus ('Afterthought'). Epimetheus sets to providing each animal with the necessary skills for survival. To some creatures he gives strength, to others speed, and so on, ensuring that each is provided with a 'nature' (φύσις) to be able to protect themselves. However, when it comes to humanity, Epimetheus realizes that he has squandered his resources and left man a being in potential, naked, unshod, unbedded and unarmed. When Prometheus discovers Epimetheus' mistake, he is furious. Wishing to help mankind and correct his brother's error, he steals the arts and fire from the Olympian gods. The effects are revolutionary. Armed with the divine spark of cultural know-how, humanity establishes (ἐνόμισεν) the worship of the gods, altars and divine statues, begins speaking, and invents all the necessary attributes he lacks by nature. Despite these new-found skills, humanity still lacks justice and is unable to live in stable communities. Zeus, fearing that mankind may destroy itself once and for all, presents it with a final gift, 'justice' (δίκη) and 'reverence/shame' (αἰδώς), and prescribes the death penalty for those who fail to obey (320c–322e).

Protagoras' myth must have seemed both familiar and strange to his listeners. It may still seem that way to us today. It was a tale where traditional ideas such as Prometheus' theft of fire were juxtaposed with contemporary politics and a teleological cosmic design.[5] Yet, despite these innovative elements, Protagoras does not claim to be inventing a new tradition. Rather he considers his myth to be a variation, a strand of an illustrious lineage of sophists including Homer, Hesiod and Orpheus (315a). Whether Hesiod and Orpheus considered themselves to be sophists is unlikely, but there are nonetheless some clear continuities between Protagoras' cosmology and those of the early poets. Indeed, Hesiod, Orpheus and Protagoras all focus on the struggle between the Titans and the Olympians as something integral for understanding humanity's ontological standing among the gods and animals. Yet, it is equally apparent that all three use these details to describe very different worlds. In Hesiod's Promethean myth, humanity is part of a hierarchal chain above animals and below superior gods.[6] The Orphic myth presents a similar triadic hierarchy. However, rather than separating the individual links, the ontological boundaries are far more permeable. Man is born from divine ashes and retains a divine element within himself. Indeed, in Orphic thought, even animals are considered to be part of a single continuous divine whole. Protagoras' view presents another important configuration of the ontological furniture; rather than describe a continuous realm or a hierarchal chain, his Promethean tale is framed in terms of a struggle between a 'nature' (φύσις) shared with animals and a divine spark 'custom' (νόμος), which raises mankind above his bestial nature.

Naturalism and sophistic thought

The final ontology I will discuss in this book is also the one that many of us are most familiar with: naturalism. Descola's dominant ontology of the West is based on a continuity of physicalities or bodies and a distinction in terms of interiorities or minds. It may help to understand this dualism in terms of the widespread idea that although humans and animals possess similar physical bodies, the possession of mind and consciousness is something reserved for humanity alone. Naturalism is also an idea intimately related to a particular cosmological vision. Indeed, as the name suggests, naturalism emerges from the taken-for-granted assumption that nature is an autonomous realm shared by animals, plants and humans. Humanity, however, through their distinctive minds, ingenuity and cultural practices can to some extent rise above and even beyond nature.

The influence of the nature/culture divide is so pervasive in Western thought that we may easily take it for granted. Indeed, for much of the twentieth century scholars were content to designate the natural world as the prerogative of the sciences and relegate cultural representations to the humanities.[7] However, this distinction, though initially intuitive and attractive, on closer inspection often proves more elusive. Marilyn Strathern, for example, famously argued that the Hagen of Papua New Guinea have no concept of culture and nature.[8] This is not to say that they have no concept of the regularity of growth in plants, seasons, animals and people, nor that they lack classificatory systems. The Hagen, like all human societies, classify the world in complex ways. They even possess a distinction between the cultivated (*mbo*) and the wild (*rømi*) that in some respects approximates the terms nature/culture. However, these terms also show important differences to the Protagorean dichotomy. Strathern explains that '*rømi* in Hagen comprises neither a domain of given features in the environment, nor innate propensities in people'.[9] In other words, there is no idea of nature as an independent entity, no notion of humanity as a dualistic compromise between an innate savagery and an imposed culture, and no vision of spirits as supernatural beings living outside of this order.[10] The Hagen are by no means alone in this and Descola has also questioned the presence of the dichotomy among the animist Amazonian community, the Achuar, where rituals and speech are characteristics held by humans, spirits and animals alike.[11] This model is in many ways the very opposite of Protagoras' sophistic account. For the Achuar, humans and animals differ in terms of their bodies but share a 'common inner disposition [where] nonhumans behave as full social beings: they abide by kinship rules and ethical codes, engage in ritual activity, organize feasts, and procure their subsistence, just like humans'.[12] A related and more radical view called perspectivism has been proposed by Viveiros de Castro. Perspectivism starts from the assumption that animals and spirits possess shared cultural traits such as speech and rituals.

However, because animals differ in their physical forms, these traits are not visible from the human's perspective. Rather they exist from the animal's point of view. Viveiros de Castro explains:

> In normal conditions, humans see humans as humans, animals as animals and spirits (if they see them) as spirits; however animals (predators) and spirits see humans as animals (as prey) to the same extent that animals (as prey) see humans as spirits or as animals (predators). By the same token, animals and spirits see themselves as humans: they perceive themselves as (or become) anthropomorphic beings when they are in their own houses or villages and they experience their own bodies and characteristics in the form of culture – they see their food as human food (jaguars see blood as manioc beer, vultures see the maggots in rotting meat as grilled fish, etc.), they see their bodily attributes (fur, feathers, claws, beaks, etc.) as body decorations or cultural instruments, they see their social system as organized in the same way as human institutions are (with chiefs, shamans, ceremonies, exogamous moieties, etc.). This 'to see as' refers literally to percepts and not analogically to concepts, although in some cases the emphasis is placed more on the categorical rather than on the sensory aspect of the phenomenon.[13]

To summarize a complex idea in simple terms, perspectivism requires that we see the world in terms of perspectives rather than in terms of substances with fixed properties. It might help to consider how one would explain the English term brother to someone who has no such concept.[14] If I say that John is a brother, I will have explained very little. John does not possess any individual qualities which make him a brother but is a brother only in relation to someone else. In a related way, perspectivism invites us to imagine that not only brothers but also everything – beer, jaguars, spirits, salmon – are perspectival terms. They make sense only from the point of view of the other. These examples may seem remote, yet alternative configurations of the nature/culture dichotomy are as common in large empires as they are in small societies. Lloyd and Sivin point out that until quite recently there was no word which corresponded to nature in Chinese. Some terms such as '*tzu-jan*' have been often translated as 'nature' but, as Lloyd and Sivin note, '*tzu-jan*, meant simply something that exists or is the case (*jan*) without something else causing it (*tzu*)'.[15] This in turn is related to a very different configuration of relations between gods, animals and humans. As Sterckx argues, 'the classic Chinese perception of the world did not insist on clear categorical or ontological boundaries between animals, human beings, and other creatures such as ghosts and spirits', rather these beings 'were viewed as part of an organic whole in which the mutual relationship among the species were characterized as contingent, continuous, and interdependent'.[16] In short, the dichotomy once found everywhere has become increasingly idiosyncratic.

Protagoras' myth, of course, is a clear testament that a similar position to modern naturalism existed in fifth-century BCE Greece and we should not exclude that other non-Western societies may have developed analogous positions, or that West will one day undergo a future change. Indeed, the presence of the divide by no means suggests its permanence and in Greece, as we have seen, sophistic naturalism remained one idea among many. Moreover, we should not forget that the distinction itself had a history. As Lloyd argues, in Homer and Hesiod there was 'no overarching concept or category that picks out the domain of nature as such – as opposed either to "culture" or to the "supernatural"'.[17] This assertion requires some additional explanation. Indeed, in early poetry we do find loose equivalents for both in the words νόμος and φύσις. Φύσις, as noted in the Introduction, appears once in Homer in reference to a magical plant where the god Hermes (*Od.* 10.303) outlines the colour of its flower and roots and its divine name, Moly.[18] Νόμος in Classical Greek is usually translated as custom or law. This meaning seems to have first emerged with the poet Hesiod (*WD* 276) where it refers to a law ordained by Zeus. As with the Hagen's conception of the cultivated (*mbo*) and the wild (*rømi*), it may seem a small step from νόμος and φύσις to nature and culture, yet it is important to note that ancient usage is quite distinct from modern understandings. In Archaic Greece, φύσις is a term very much used in the plural. Everything from men, gods and plants possess a φύσις, yet nowhere do we see nature in the singular as an autonomous realm.[19] Νόμος, on the other hand, is equally idiosyncratic. In Hesiod's early usage of the term, rather than refer to a set of customs that distinguishes one society from another, Zeus' law applies to humanity as a whole.[20] The idea that all humans practise – or should practise – similar customs is in fact common in early poetry. Indeed, in almost every society described in early poetry, including that of the Olympians, we see that people abide by nearly identical cultural practices. Homer's Trojans, for example, worship the same gods and practise similar customs to the Greeks. Odysseus, too, in his travels is shocked whenever Greek customs are flouted by hubristic societies like the Cyclopes.[21] In this respect, culture does not appear to be something acquired or something that distinguishes human societies, but an expected standard of behaviour proscribed by the gods.

If nature writ large is not found in early epic, its discovery is usually attributed to the sixth century BCE and the philosophers Aristotle (*Eth. Eud.* 1235a) referred to as the φυσιολόγοι or 'investigators of nature'.[22] As the name suggests, these thinkers inquired into the nature of the world as a whole, describing its complex workings and underlying order. The natural philosophers did not, however, oppose φύσις to cultural institutions or propose any radical separation of human beings from nature.[23] On the contrary, they viewed these terms as part of a continuum. Heraclitus (DK 22 B114), for example, describes how

τρέφονται γὰρ πάντες οἱ ἀνθρώπειοι νόμοι ὑπὸ ἑνὸς τοῦ θείου.

All human laws are nurtured by the One law of the god.

The phrase suggests a more organic view where a diversity of νομοί flourishes from a single underlying unity. Laws are recognized to vary but, as Long puts it, for Heraclitus there is no split between νόμος and φύσις, rather 'divine law *is* a law of nature'.[24] In other words, far from divorcing nature from culture, we see a kind of monistic culture–nature totality.

However, by the fifth century BCE the ontological recipe for naturalism existed and the split between nature and culture was drawing near. When precisely this occurs is unclear. The earliest formulation of a culture/nature divide may appear in the strikingly modern cosmology of Democritus or the sophistic writing of Antiphon.[25] For Democritus, nature was comprised of atoms and void. This, however, had little to do with how the world was experienced by humans. To account for this, Democritus introduced the idea of subjective distinctions made according to νομοί such as taste, colour and temperature (DK 68 B 125).[26] By sharply distinguishing between the natural world and the world of subjective and inconsistent experience, Democritus' views may have paved the way for the νόμος/φύσις divide adopted by his compatriot and in some traditions his student (Diog. Laert. 8.50), the sophist Protagoras of Abdera.

What emerged with sophists such as Antiphon and Protagoras was a new understanding of humanity where φύσις existed in polar opposition to νόμος. In this schema, φύσις reflects the raw material and dispositions that all mortal beings, humans and animals alike, share. Νόμος, on the other hand, reflects the human difference, the additional element that differentiates humans from animals.[27] These conceptions were not only part of a new psychology, they were part of a transformation of Hesiod's mythology, adapting and transforming the illustrious shared table of gods and men into a pessimistic narrative on humanity's original struggle to survive in their natural state.[28] There could hardly be a more drastic reinterpretation of Hesiod's early humans and their affinal ties with the gods and in place of an ideal and innately cultured human race, Protagoras describes early man as wild folk plagued by ignorance and war. Indeed, Protagoras argues that even the most wicked man 'reared by human customs' (ἐν νόμοις καὶ ἀνθρώποις τεθραμμένων) would appear a saint compared to a those living in this bestial condition. As Protagoras insists (327c–d):

> οὕτως οἴου καὶ νῦν, ὅστις σοι ἀδικώτατος φαίνεται ἄνθρωπος τῶν ἐν νόμοις καὶ ἀνθρώποις τεθραμμένων, δίκαιον αὐτὸν εἶναι καὶ δημιουργὸν τούτου τοῦ πράγματος, εἰ δέοι αὐτὸν κρίνεσθαι πρὸς ἀνθρώπους οἷς μήτε παιδεία ἐστὶν μήτε δικαστήρια μήτε νόμοι μηδὲ ἀνάγκη μηδεμία διὰ παντὸς ἀναγκάζουσα ἀρετῆς ἐπιμελεῖσθαι, ἀλλ᾽ εἶεν ἄγριοί τινες οἷοίπερ οὓς πέρυσιν Φερεκράτης ὁ ποιητὴς ἐδίδαξεν ἐπὶ Ληναίῳ.

> likewise in the present case you must regard any man who appears to you the most unjust person ever reared among human laws and society as a just man and a craftsman of justice, if he had to stand comparison with people who lacked education and law courts and laws and any constant compulsion to the pursuit of virtue, but were a kind of wild folk such as Pherecrates the poet brought on the scene at last year's Lenaeum.[29]

Protagoras' portrait of a time before culture presents a grim view of humanity and a natural world forever on the brink of destruction. And it is upon this cruel and bestial reality that the Titan Prometheus appears. However, this is not the Prometheus we know from Hesiod or Orpheus. Indeed, far from Hesiod's ambiguous trickster, and even further from Orpheus' murderous Titan, Protagoras' Prometheus appears as a saviour and culture bringer bestowing upon wild beings a divine dispensation (θείας μοίρας) in the form of cultural knowledge.[30] What resulted from Prometheus' gift was the creation of a new anthropology, a new hybrid being, joined to the world by a common nature, and distinguished from the world by the heavenly gift of culture.

Protagoras' legacy

That Greek philosophers such as Protagoras helped shape Western naturalism is not in doubt. However, we should be cautious in assuming an identical naturalism in the ancient and modern worlds. Indeed, although sophistic thought approaches modern naturalism, the νόμος/φύσις dichotomy in ancient Greece resulted in a plurality of views. Protagoras, for example, was very much an advocate for the importance of νόμος. It is the presence of this divine spark that allows man to flourish as a cultural being and create all that he lacks by nature

(322a). Other philosophers took the opposite path and discarded the artifice of νόμος in favour of living according to nature itself. Antiphon the Sophist (DK 87 B 44b) turned this into a noble ideal, describing how cultural differences are only superficial, and by nature humanity is one. Others understood living by nature in more morally suspect terms.[31] The sophists Callicles (Pl. *Grg.* 482d–484b) and Thrasymachus (Pl. *Resp.* 338c), for example, argued that νόμος was for the weak and that strong natures will live according to nature. Others still embraced νομοί in all their diversity. Herodotus (3.38), seemingly unperturbed by the plurality of cultures, at times appears to adopt a multicultural attitude based on the tolerance of difference. Although there are significant differences in these sophistic narratives, all remain naturalists in their agreement that man is a dualistic being united with animals by 'nature' (φύσις) and separated, for better or worse, by 'culture' (νόμος).

Alongside the diversity of naturalism in ancient Greece, the sophists also had to contend with the continuity of older ontological positions and the ongoing development of new ones. Diogenes of Apollonia and the Derveni commentator, for example, continued to engage with the pantheism and monism found in Orphic poetry and the philosophy of Heraclitus. Nor was analogism by any means out of the running. Indeed, for the majority of the Greeks, philosophers such as Protagoras were of minor importance and Homer and Hesiod remained the cornerstone of an ancient education. This coexistence of competing ideas is central to how I understand the ontological debates I have discussed in this book. Indeed, although I have traced the mythic material through their historical developments, the approach should not be confused with a developmental history. Hesiod, of course, did not have the same notions regarding νόμος and φύσις as the sophists and could not have written a myth identical to those proposed by Protagoras or Orpheus. In this respect, each myth can be viewed as a particular child of its time, developing from particular ideas, language and mythical themes of the period. This historical specificity, however, should not be equated with a teleological narrative where one superior narrative replaces what went before. Rather what we see is a proliferation of variations and debates leading to a world where Hesiod, Orpheus and Protagoras coexisted as part of an ongoing argument that continued throughout antiquity and beyond.

The presence of debate in ancient Greece is not in itself surprising. Indeed, to a greater or lesser extent, all societies, at all times, debate and innovate upon traditional ideas. The West is no exception and the rich ontological speculation of the ancient world continued long after the introduction of Christianity. However, if the argument was ongoing, its precise terms changed. A pantheism of sorts continued with some Neoplatonist philosophers into the sixth century CE. However, for most Christians pantheism was something viewed with suspicion and unlikely to survive the demise of paganism.[32] Analogism, on the other hand, had a more successful run during the Middle Ages. Indeed, it was even during the Renaissance that Descola argues 'analogism shone most brightly'.[33] However, pantheism and analogism were increasingly overshadowed by the ever-growing dominance of naturalism. As with all intellectual debates, the roots of this view are complex.[34] Certainly some strands can be traced to Greece and sophists such as Protagoras, whereas others draw on the Abrahamic religious traditions and a view of God as a being ontologically separate from the world.[35] However, whatever the precise origins of Western naturalism, once it took root, it flourished. One of the most influential examples of this new orientation appears in the writing of Descartes, who, much like the sophists, argued for a view of nature that encompassed the whole world, including human bodies and animals. However, in his *Sixth Meditation*, he famously separated mind from body, describing the former as a divine substance reserved for man alone. In other words, man is an animal by nature, but also possesses a divine spark in common with a transcendental God. Descartes did not write a speculative biography on the origins of mankind, yet just ten years after his *Meditations* (1641), Hobbes published his *Leviathan* (1651), describing, in strikingly sophistic terms, his social contract:

> Hereby it is manifest, that during the time men live without a common Power to keep them all in awe, they are in that condition which is called Warre; and such a warre, as is of every man, against every man. For WARRE, consisteth not in Battell onely, or the act of fighting; but in a tract of time, wherein the Will to contend by Battell is sufficiently known: and therefore the notion of Time, is to be considered in the nature of Warre; as it is in the nature of Weather. For as the nature of Foule weather, lyeth not in a showre or two of rain; but in an inclination thereto of many dayes together: So the nature of War, consisteth not in actuall fighting; but in the known disposition thereto, during all the time there is no assurance to the contrary. All other time is PEACE.
>
> Whatsoever therefore is consequent to a time of Warre, where every man is Enemy to every man; the same is consequent to the time, wherein men live without other security, than what their own strength, and their own invention shall furnish them withall. In such condition, there is no place for Industry; because the fruit thereof is uncertain; and consequently no Culture of the Earth; no Navigation, nor use of the commodities that may be imported by Sea; no commodious Building; no Instruments of moving, and removing such things as require much force; no

Knowledge of the face of the Earth; no account of Time; no Arts; no Letters; no Society; and which is worst of all, continuall feare, and danger of violent death; And the life of man, solitary, poore, nasty, brutish, and short.[36]

As in the Protagoras myth, the way out of this state of nature was through the development of cultural practices and a social contract among men. It is not coincidental that Hobbes' vision echoes the sophistic myths.[37] Indeed, Hobbes, like most thinkers of the time, was aware of his ancient predecessors and even translated the first English language edition of the often-sophistic history of Thucydides.[38]

It is, of course, important not to over-homogenize the ontological assumptions of the West. For example, it could be argued that Hobbes, like Protagoras, was one voice among many and counterbalanced by philosophers such as Rousseau and de Montaigne.[39] Indeed, Michel Serres, adopting Descola's framework, has argued for an even greater diversity of ontological positions associating Leibniz with analogism, Proust with animism, and Flaubert with totemism.[40] However, while ontological debate certainly existed and continues to do so, from the seventeenth century on naturalism increasingly occupied a dominant influence upon the West and its engagement with other societies in a way that never occurred in ancient Greece.[41] As Descola outlines, 'what now came into existence was a notion of Nature as an autonomous ontological domain, a field of inquiry and scientific experimentation, an object to be exploited and improved; and very few thought to question this'.[42]

Living in Protagoras' world

The rise of naturalism is a familiar tale of science, technology, oppression, benefits and loss. Yet, the heaviest price paid for humanity's elevation was the one paid by nature. While few are willing to abandon the benefits of Prometheus' flame, with an ever-growing ecological threat on the horizon, theorists are increasingly looking beyond naturalism for alternate ontological conceptions through which to rethink our relationship with the world and its non-human inhabitants. Anthropological discussions often focus on the potential of animist ontologies, which are found in many of the indigenous philosophies of America and elsewhere. For advocates of animist ontologies, the idea that animals possess souls like those of humans potentially offers a way of sharing our world, rather than exploiting it. As Harvey describes it:

Animists' contribution to ecological thinking and acting are rooted in the firm insistence that not only is all life inescapably located and related, but also that the attempt to escape is at the root of much that is wrong with the world today. Animism's alternative promise is a celebratory engagement of embodied persons with a personal and sensual world.[43]

There is no doubt that the West stands to benefit from the wisdom of animists, yet alternate traditions are equally promising. Indeed, with the humanities' increasing engagement with the ecological turn, it was only a matter of time until scholars also asked what the Classical world may offer. Jula Wildberger, for example, argues that the Stoics present a potential 'starting point for a eudaemonist environmental ethics'.[44] Joel Schlosser similarly argues that Herodotus' emphasis on 'how cooperation can create new and powerful responses to overwhelming problems' may provide hope for a possible escape from the existential threats posed by the Anthropocene.[45] The recent scholarly engagement between the ancient world and modern problems is welcome and at times insightful. However, it may well be the case that neither the Stoics, Herodotus, nor even the illustrious Orpheus hold the solution to our current ecological crisis. Yet rather than the letter of their text or practices, it is perhaps the spirit of the ancient Greeks and their propensity for debate that offers a potential lesson. The Greeks above all else understood the importance of creativity, of continuously reinventing their worlds, and of offering a plurality of answers to perennial problems. And here, at least, we can learn something.

Appendix: Some Key Orphic Texts

In this Appendix I have listed some of the key texts which I refer to in my reconstructions of the early Orphic theogonies:

1. The preserved fragments from the sixth-century BCE *Derveni Theogony*

In this section, I have listed the longest surviving lines from the poem in the order they appear in the commentary.

The poem starts with an oath of secrecy and outlines that the poem will glorify the rule of Zeus and those born from him:

[φθέγξομαι οἷς θέμις ἐστί: θ]ύρας δ ἐπίθε[σθε βέβηλοι]

I shall proclaim to those for whom it is proper; close the doors, profane ones (col. 7.)[1]

[ο]ἳ Διὸς ἐξεγένοντο [ὑπερμεν]έος βασιλῆος.

who were born from Zeus the mighty king (8.2).

Ζεὺς μὲν ἐπεὶ δὴ πα[τρὸς ἑο]ῦ πάρα θέ[σ]φατον ἀρχὴν
[_____] [ἀ]λκήν τ' ἐν χείρεσσι ἔ[λ]αβ[εν κ]α[ὶ] δαίμον[α] κυδρόν.

and when Zeus took from his father the prophesied rule
and the strength in his hands and the glorious daimon (8.4-5).

Columns 11–13 discuss oracles Zeus receives from Night and Kronos advising him on how to secure his rule:

[ἡ δὲ] ἔχρησεν ἅπαντα τά οἱ θέ[μις ἦν ἀνύσασ]θαι.

she (Night) proclaimed an oracle about all that was right for him to hear (11.10).

ὡς ἂν ἔ[χοι κά]τα καλὸν ἕδος νιφόεντος Ὀλύμπου.

so that he may rule on the lovely abode of snowcapped Olympus (12.2).

Ζεὺς μὲν ἐπεὶ δὴ πατρὸς ἑοῦ πάρα [θ]έσφατ' ἀκούσα[ς.

Zeus when he heard the prophecies from his father (13.1).

The passage quoted in Column 13.4 is confusing from the point of view of the narrative and seems to anticipate the action in Column 16.3–6.

αἰδοῖον κατέπινεν, ὃς αἰθέρα ἔκθορε πρῶτος.

he swallowed the reverend one, who sprang from the aither first (13.4).

Columns 14–15 describe Zeus' succession of Kronos and offers some background information on previous rulers:

ὃς μέγ' ἔρεξεν.

(he) (Kronos?) who did a great deed (14.5).

Οὐρανὸς Εὐφρονίδης, ὃς πρώτιστος βασίλευσεν.

Ouranos son of Night, who first of all ruled (14.6).

ἐκ τοῦ δὴ Κρόνος αὖτις, ἔπειτα δὲ μητίετα Ζεύς.

from him in turn Kronos, and then wise Zeus (15.6).

μῆτιν κα[ὶ μακάρων κατέχ]εν βασιληίδα τιμ[ήν].

(Zeus?) Holding wisdom and royal honour over the blessed gods (15.13).

Column 16 presents the longest passage preserved from the poem and describes the swallowing of Protogonos:

Πρωτογόνου βασιλέως αἰδοίου· τῶι δ' ἄρα πάντες
ἀθάνατοι προσέφυν μάκαρες θεοὶ ἠδὲ θέαιναι
καὶ ποταμοὶ καὶ κρῆναι ἐπήρατοι ἄλλα τε πάντα,
_____ ἄσσα τότ' ἦν γεγαῶτ', αὐτὸς δ' ἄρα μοῦνος ἔγεντο.

[with?] reverend king Protogonos, onto which all
the immortals grew (or: clung fast), blessed gods and goddesses
and rivers and lovely springs and everything else
that had been born then; and he himself became solitary (16.3–6).

Columns 16–19 describe the glory of Zeus as first, middle and last:

[νῦν δ' ἐστὶ]ν βασιλεὺς πάντ[ων καί τ' ἔσσετ' ἔπ]ειτα.

Now he is king of all and will always be (16.14).

Ζεὺς κεφα[λή, Ζεὺς μέσ]σα, Διὸς δ' ἐκ [π]άντα τέτ[υκται.

Zeus the head, Zeus the middle, and from Zeus all things have their being (17.13).

Ζεὺς βασιλεύς, Ζεὺς δ' ἀρχὸς ἁπάντων ἀργικέραυνος.

Zeus the king, Zeus who rules all with the bright bolt (19.10).

Columns 23–24 describe how Zeus recreates the cosmos including goddesses, rivers and the moon:

Ἀφροδίτη Οὐρανία, Πειθώ, Ἁρμονία

Aphrodite Ourania, Persuasian, Harmony (21.5-7).

ἶνας δ' ἐγκατ[έλε]ξ' Ἀχελωΐου ἀργυ[ρ]οδίνε[ω.

he placed in it the sinews of the silver-eddying Achelous (23.11).

ἢ πολλοῖς φαίνει μερόπεσσι ἐπ' ἀπείρονα γαῖαν.

(the moon)which shines for many articulate-speaking humans on the boundless earth (24.3).

Columns 25–26 describe how Zeus plans to mate with Rhea and anticipates the birth of Persephone:

[αὐτ]ὰρ [ἐ]πεὶ δ[ὴ πάν]τα Διὸ[ς φρὴν μή]σατ[ο ἔ]ργα.

But once [? the heart] of Zeus devised all deeds (25.14).

μητρὸς ἑᾶς ἤθελεν μιχθήμεναι ἐν φιλότητι

He wished to lie in love with his own mother (col. 26)

The *Derveni Theogony* shows similarities with both later Orphic Theogonies such as the *Rhapsodies* and Orphic hymns to Zeus. I offer the Orphic *Hymn to Zeus* (OF 243)[2] known to Porphyry as an example of the latter genre:

Ζεὺς πρῶτος γένετο, Ζεὺς ὕστατος ἀργικέραυνος
Ζεὺς κεφαλή, Ζεὺς μέσσα, Διὸς δ' ἐκ πάντα τέτυκται·
Ζεὺς ἄρσην γένετο, Ζεὺς ἄφθιτος ἔπλετο νύμφη·
Ζεὺς πυθμὴν γαίης τε καὶ οὐρανοῦ ἀστερόεντος
Ζεὺς βασιλεύς, Ζεὺς αὐτὸς ἁπάντων ἀρχιγένεθλος.
ἓν κράτος, εἷς δαίμων, γένετο, μέγας ἀρχὸς ἁπάντων,
ἓν δὲ δέμας βασίλειον, ἐν ὧι τάδε πάντα κυκλεῖται,
πῦρ καὶ ὕδωρ καὶ γαῖα καὶ αἰθὴρ νύξ τε καὶ ἦμαρ.

καὶ Μῆτις πρῶτος γενέτωρ καὶ Ἔρως πολυτερπής
πάντα γὰρ ἐν μεγάλου Ζηνός τάδε σώματι κεῖται.
τοῦ δή τοι κεφαλὴ μὲν ἰδεῖν καὶ καλὰ πρόσωπα
οὐρανὸς αἰγλήεις, ὅν χρύσεαι ἀμφὶς ἔθειραι
ἄστρων μαρμαρέων περικαλλέες ἠερέθονται,
ταύρεα δ' ἀμφοτέρωθε δύο χρύσεια κέρατα,
ἀντολίη τε δύσις τε, θεῶν ὁδοὶ οὐρανιώνων,
ὄμματα δ' ἠέλιός τε καὶ ἀντιόωσα σελήνη·
νοῦς δέ οἱ ἀψευδὴς βασιλήιος ἄφθιτος αἰθήρ,
ὧι δὴ πάντα κλύει καί φράζεται· οὐδέ τίς ἐστιν
αὐδὴ οὐδ' ἐνοπὴ οὐδε κτύπος οὐδέ μὲν ὄσσα,
ἣ λήθει Διός οὖας ὑπερμενέος Κρονίωνος·
ὧδε μὲν ἀθανάτην κεφαλὴν ἔχει ἠδὲ νόημα.
σῶμα δέ οἱ περιφεγγές, ἀπείριτον, ἀστυφέλικτον,
ἄτρομον, ὀβριμόγυιον, ὑπερμενὲς ὧδε τέτυκται ·
ὦμοι μὲν καὶ στέρνα καὶ εὐρέα νῶτα θεοῖο
ἀὴρ εὐρυβίης, πτέρυγες δέ οἱ ἐξεφύοντο,
τῇις ἐπὶ πάντα ποτᾶθ', ἱερὴ δέ οἱ ἔπλετο νηδὺς
γαῖά τε παμμήτωρ ὀρέων τ' αἰπεινὰ κάρηνα
μέσση δὲ ζώνη βαρυηχέος οἶδμα θαλάσσης
καὶ πόντου πυμάτη δὲ βάσις, χθονὸς ἔνδοθι ῥίζαι,
Τάρταρά τ' εὐρώεντα καὶ ἔσχατα πείρατα γαίης.
πάντα δ' ἀποκρύψας αὖθις φάος ἐς πολυγηθὲς
μέλλεν ἀπὸ κραδίης προφέρειν πάλι, θέσκελα ῥέζων.

Zeus was the first, Zeus last, the lightning lord,
Zeus head, Zeus centre, all things are from Zeus.
Zeus born a male, Zeus virgin undefiled;
Zeus the firm base of earth and starry heaven;
Zeus sovereign, Zeus alone first cause of all:
One power divine, great ruler of the world,
One kingly form, encircling all things here,
Fire, water, earth, and ether, night and day;
Metis, first parent, and delightful Eros:[3]
For in Zeus' mighty body these all lie.
His head and beauteous face the radiant heaven
Reveals and round him float in shining waves
The golden tresses of the twinkling stars.
On either side bulls' horns of gold are seen,
Sunrise and sunset, footpaths of the gods.
His eyes the Sun, the Moon's responsive light;

His mind immortal ether, sovereign truth,
Hears and considers all; nor any speech,
Nor cry, nor noise, nor ominous voice escapes
The ear of Zeus, great Kronos' mightier son:
Such his immortal head, and such his thought.
His radiant body, boundless, undisturbed
In strength of mighty limbs was formed thus:
The god's broad-spreading shoulders, breast and back
Air's wide expanse displays; on either side
Grow wings, wherewith throughout all space he flies.
Earth the all-mother, with her lofty hills,
His sacred belly forms; the swelling flood
Of hoarse resounding Ocean girds his waist.
His feet the deeply rooted ground upholds,
And dismal Tartarus, and earth's utmost bounds.
All things he hides, then from his heart again
In godlike action brings to gladsome light.[4]

2. Some key gold tablets

Here I reproduce the first and longest tablet from Hipponion, the Thurii tablet referring to the payment of a penalty, the Pelinna tablet mentioning Bacchus and Persephone, and the fragment of Pindar on which Comparetti based much of his argument.

Fifth-century BCE Hipponion gold tablet (L1 OF 474).

Μναμοσύνας τόδε †ἐριον†· ἐπεὶ ἄμ μέλληισι θανεῖσθαι
εἰς Ἀίδαο δόμους εὐηρέας, ἔστ' ἐπὶ δ⟨ε⟩ξιὰ κρήνα,
πὰρ δ' αὐτὰν ἑστακῦα λευκὰ κυπάρισ⟨σ⟩ος·
ἔνθα κατερχόμεναι ψυχαὶ νεκύων ψύχονται.
ταύτας τᾶς κράνας μηδὲ σχεδὸν ἐγγύθεν ἔλθηις.
πρόσθεν δὲ εὑρήσεις τᾶς Μναμοσύνας ἀπὸ λίμνης
ψυχρὸν ὕδωρ προρέον· φύλακες δ' ἐπύπερθεν ἔασι.
οἳ δέ σε εἰρήσονται ἐν⟨ὶ⟩ φρασὶ πευκαλίμαισι
ὅτ⟨τ⟩ι δὴ ἐξερέεις Ἄϊδος σκότος ὀρφ⟨ν⟩ήεντος.
εἶπον· Γῆς παῖ⟨ς⟩ ἤμι καὶ Οὐρανοῦ ἀστερόεντος.
δίψαι δ' εἰμ' αὖος καὶ ἀπόλλυμαι· ἀλ⟨λ⟩ὰ δότ' ὦκα
ψυχρὸν ὕδωρ πιέναι τῆς Μνημοσύνης ἀπὸ λίμ⟨νης⟩.
καὶ δή τοι ἐρέουσιν ὑποχθονίωι βασιλῆι·

καὶ {δή τοι} δώσουσι πιεῖν τᾶς Μναμοσύνας ἀπ[ὸ] λίμνας,
καὶ δή καὶ σὺ πιὼν ὁδὸν ἔρχεα⟨ι⟩ ἄν τε καὶ ἄλλοι
μύσται καὶ βάχχοι ἱερὰν στείχουσι κλε⟨ε⟩ινοί.

This is the work of Memory, when you are about to die
down to the well-built house of Hades. There is a spring at the right side,
and standing by it a white cypress.
Descending to it, the souls of the dead refresh themselves.
Do not even go near this spring!
Ahead you will find from the Lake of Memory,
cold water pouring forth; there are guards before it.
They will ask you, with astute wisdom,
what you are seeking in the darkness of murky Hades.
Say, "I am a son of Earth and starry Sky,
I am parched with thirst and am dying; but quickly grant me
cold water from the Lake of Memory to drink."
And they will announce you to the Chthonian King,
and they will grant you to drink from the Lake of Memory.
And you, too, having drunk, will go along the sacred road on
which other glorious initiates and Bacchoi travel.[5]

Fourth-century BCE Thurii tablet (L 10b; OF 490)

Ἔρχομαι ἐ⟨κ⟩ καθαρῶ⟨ν⟩ καθ⟨αρά, χθ⟩ο⟨χνίων⟩ βασίλ⟨ει⟩α,
Εὔκλε{υα} κα⟨ὶ⟩ Εὐβο⟨υ⟩λεῦ καὶ θεοὶ ⟨καὶ⟩ {ὅσοι} δ⟨αί⟩μονες ἄλλοι·
καὶ γὰρ ἐ⟨γ⟩ὼ⟨ν⟩ ὑ⟨μῶν⟩ γένος εὔχομα⟨ι ὄλβιον ε⟨ἶ⟩να⟨ι⟩ {ὄλβιο}
ποινὰν ⟨δ'⟩ ἀνταπέτεισ'⟩ ἔργω⟨ν⟩ ἕνεκ' ο⟨ὔ⟩τι δικα⟨ί⟩ων.
εὔτ⟨ε⟩ με Μοῖρα ⟨ἐδάμασσ'⟩ ε⟨ἴτε ἀσ⟩τεροπῆτα {κη} κεραυνῶ⟨ν⟩.
νῦν δὲ ⟨ἱ⟩κ⟨έτις⟩ ἥκω {ιικω} παρ⟨αὶ⟩ ἁ⟨γνὴν⟩ Φ⟨ερ⟩σε⟨φόνειαν⟩,
ὥς {λ} με ⟨π⟩ρόφ⟨ρων⟩ πέ[μ]ψ⟨ηι⟩ {μ} ἕδρας ἐς εὐ⟨α⟩γ⟨έων⟩.

Pure I come from the pure, Queen of those below the earth,
And Eukles and Eubouleus and the other gods and daimons;
For I also claim that I am of your blessed race.
Recompense I have paid on account of deeds not just;
Either Fate mastered me or the lightning bolt thrown by the thunderer.
Now I come, a suppliant, to holy Phersephoneia,
That she, gracious, may send me to the seats of the blessed.[6]

Fourth-century BCE ivy-shaped tablet from Pelinna Thessaly (L 7a,b OF 485-6):

νῦν ἔθανες καὶ νῦν ἐγένου, τρισόλβιε, ἄματι τῶιδε.
εἰπεῖν Φερσεφόναι σ' ὅτι Β⟨άκ⟩χιος αὐτὸς ἔλυσε.

τα{ι}ῦρος εἰς γάλα ἔθορες.
αἶψα εἰς γ⟨ά⟩λα ἔθορες.
κριὸς εἰς γάλα ἔπεσ⟨ες⟩.
οἶνον ἔχεις εὐδ⟨α⟩ίμονα τιμὴ⟨ν⟩
καὶ σὺ μὲν εἶς ὑπὸ γῆν τελέσας ἅπερ ὄλβιοι ἄλλοι.

Now you have died and now you have come into being, O thrice happy one, on this same day.
Tell Persephone that Bacchus himself released you.
Bull, you jumped into milk.
Quickly, you jumped into milk.
Ram, you fell into milk.
You have wine as your fortunate honor.
And below the earth there are ready for you the same prizes [or rites] as the other blessed ones.[7]

The Pindar fragment (fr. 133 Bergk):

Φερσεφόνα ποινὰν παλαιοῦ πένθεος
δέξεται, εἰς τὸν ὕπερθεν ἅλιον κείνων ἐνάτῳ ἔτεϊ
ἀνδιδοῖ ψυχὰς πάλιν,
ἐκ τᾶν βασιλῆες ἀγαυοὶ
καὶ σθένει κραιπνοὶ σοφίᾳ τε μέγιστοι
ἄνδρες αὔξοντ᾽· ἐς δὲ τὸν λοιπὸν χρόνον ἥρωες ἁγνοὶ
πρὸς ἀνθρώπων καλεῦνται

For from whomsoever Persephone shall accept requital for ancient wrong, the souls of these she restores in the ninth year to the upper sun again; from them arise glorious kings and men of splendid might and surpassing wisdom, and for all remaining time are they called holy heroes amongst mankind.[8]

The fourth-century BCE *Timpone Grande gold tablet (C1) and Bernabé and Jiménez San Cristóbal's (2008) interpretation and translation:*

ΠΡΩΤΟΓΟΝΟΤΗΜΑΙΤΙΕΤΗΓΑΜΜΑΤΡΙΕΠΑΚΥΒΕΛΕΙΑΚΟΡΡΑΟΣ ΕΝΤΑΙΗΔΗΜΗΤΡΟΣΗΤ
ΤΑΤΑΙΤΤΑΤΑΠΤΑΖΕΥΙΑΤΗΤΥΑΕΡΣΑΠΤΑΗΛΙΕΠΥΡΔΗΠΑΝΤΑΣΤΗΙΝΤΑΣΤΗΝΙΣΑΤΟΠΕΝΙΚΑΙΜ
ΣΗΔΕΤΥΧΑΙΤΕΦΑΝΗΣΠΑΜΜΗΣΤΟΙΜΟΙΡΑΙΣΣΤΗΤΟΙΓΑΝΝΥΑΠΙΑΝΤΗΣΥΚΛΗΤΕΔΑΡΜΟΝΔΕΥΧΙ
ΣΠΑΤΕΡΑΤΙΚΙΠΑΝΤΑΔΑΜΑΣΤΑΠΑΝΤΗΡΝΥΝΥΝΤΑΙΣΕΛΑΒΔΟΝΤΑΔΕΠΑΝΤΕΜΟΙΒΤΗΣΛΗΤΕΑΣΩ
ΤΗΜΜΑΕΡΙΠΥΡΜΕΜΜΑΤΕΡΛΥΕΣΤΙΣΟΙΣΛ·ΕΝΤΑΤΟΝΗΣΣΙΝΝΥΞΙΝΗΜΕΦΗΜΕΡΑΝΕΓΛΧΥΕΣ
ΕΠΠΗΜΑΡΤΙΝΗΣΤΙΑΣΤΑΝΖΕΕΥΕΝΟΡΘΤΤΙΕΚΑΙΠΑΝΟΠΤΑΑΙΕΝΑΙΜΙΘ·ΜΑΤΕΡΜΑΣΕΠ
ΩΥΣΟΝΕΟΕΥΧΑΣΤΑΚΤΑΠΥΑΡΣΥΟΛΚΑΠΕΔΙΩΧΑΜΑΤΕΜΑΝΚΑΛ ΗΑΔΙΕΡΑΔΑΜΝΕΥΔΑΜΝΟΙ
ΩΤΑΚΤΗΡΙΕΡΑΜΑΡΔΗΜΗΤΕΡΠΥΡΖΕΥΚΑΡΗΧΦΟΝΙΑΤΡΑΒΔΑΗΤΡΟΣΗΝΙΣΤΘΟΙΣΤΝ

ΗΡΩΣΝΗΓΑΥΝΗΓΑΟΣΕΣΦΡΕΝΑΜΑΤΑΙΜΗΤΝΝΤΗΣΝΥΣΧΑΜΕΣΤΩΡΕΙΛΕΚΟΙΡΗΝ
ΑΙΑΦΗΡΤΟΝΟΝΣΣΜΜ'ΟΕΣΤΟΝΑΕΡΤΑΙΠΛΝΙΛΛΥΕΣΦΡΕΝΑΜΑΡ· ΤΩΣ.

As interpreted by Bernabé and Jiménez San Cristóbal (2008) with nonsense letters in capitals:

Πρωτογόνω‹υ› ΤΗΜΑΙΤΙΕΤΗ Γᾶι ματρί ΕΠΑ Κυβελεία‹υ› Κόρρα‹υ› ΟΣΕΝΤΑΙΗ Δήμητρος ΗΤ ΤΑΤΑΙΤΤΑΤΑΠΤΑ Ζεῦ ΙΑΤΗΤΥ ἀέρ ΣΑΠΤΑ Ἥλιε, πῦρ δὴ πάντα ΣΤΗΙΝΤΑΣΤΗΝΙΣΑΤΟΠΕ νικᾶι Μ ΣΗΔΕ Τύχα ΙΤΕ Φάνης, πάμνηστοι Μοῖραι ΣΣΤΗΤΟΙΓΑΝΝΥΑΠΙΑΝΤΗ σὺ κλυτὲ δαῖμον ΔΕΥΧΙ Σ πάτερ ΑΤΙΚ παντοδαμάστα ΠΑΝΤΗΡΝΥΝΤΑΙΣΕΛΑΒΔΟΝΤΑΔΕΠ ἀνταμοιβή ΣΤΛΗΤΕΑΣΤΛ ΤΗΜΗ ἀέρ ι πῦρ ΜΕΜ Μᾶτερ ΛΥΕΣΤΙΣΟΙΛ-ΕΝΤΑΤΟ Νῆστι Ν νύξ ΙΝΗΜΕΦ ἡμέρα ΜΕΡΑΝΕΓΛΧΥΕΣ ἑπτῆμαρ ΤΙ νήστιας ΤΑΝ Ζεῦ ἐνορύττιε(?) καὶ πανόπτα. αἰέν ΑΙΜΙΥ*μᾶτερ, ἐμᾶς ἐπάκουσον ΕΟ εὐχᾶς ΤΑΚΤΑΠΥΑΡΣΥΟΛΚΑΠΕΔΙΩΧΑΜΑΤΕΜΑΝ καλ{η}ὰ Δ ἱερά ΔΑΜΝΕΥΔΑΜΝΟΙ ΩΤΑΚΤΗΡ ἱερά ΜΑΡ Δημῆτερ, πῦρ, Ζεῦ, Κόρη Χθονία ΤΡΑΒΔΑΗΤΡΟΣΗΝΙΣΤΗΟΙΣΤΝ ἥρως ΝΗΓΑΥΝΗ φάος ἐς φρένα ΜΑΤΑΙΜΗΤΝΝΤΗΣΝΥΣΧΑ μήστωρ εἶλε Κούρην αἶα ΦΗΡΤΟΝΟΣΣΜΜΟ-ΕΣΤΟΝ ἀέρ ΤΑΙΠΛΝΙΛΛΥ ἐς φρένα ΜΑΡ*ΤΩΣ

To the First-Born, to Mother Earth, to Cybelea, daughter of Demeter.
Zeus, Air, Sun. Fire conquers all.
Avatars of fortune and Phanes. Moirai that remember all. You, O illustrious demon.
Father who subdues all. Compensation.
Air, fire, Mother, Nestis, night, day
Fasting for seven days. Zeus who sees all. Always. Mother, hear my prayer. Fine sacrifices.
Sacrifices. Demeter. Fire. Zeus, the Underground Girl.
Hero. Light to the intelligence. The adviser seized the Girl.
Earth. Air. To the intelligence.[9]

Notes

Introduction

1 Trans. Verity 2007.
2 Gerber (1999) 43. Lourenço (2011) 67–8.
3 For a more detailed discussion on Greek conceptions of nature, see Chapter 5.
4 In *Isthmian Four* (49–50), the athlete, Mellissus, is contrasted with Orion in terms of his φύσις. Pindar explains: 'οὐ γὰρ φύσιν Ὠαριωνείαν ἔλαχεν' (Mellisus did not have the φύσις of Orion). Pindar elaborates 'ἀλλ' ὀνοτὸς μὲν ἰδέσθαι' (He looks awful). Φύσις in this case appears to refer to Mellissus' physical appearance.
5 Gerber (1999) 47.
6 Trans. Evelyn-White (1914). On the closely related meanings of ἐναλίγκιος and ὅμοιος see Nagy (2010).
7 The problem is further exacerbated by a textual variant where the order is reversed. See scholium on Eur. *Med.* 1224 (ii.207) Schwartz. See Gerber (1999) 46.
8 Gerber (1999) notes the 'intransitive προσφέρω with dative and accusative of respect cf. fr. 43.1–3' should be translated as 'resemble' (46).
9 Trans. Lattimore (1951) modified.
10 In terms of interiorities, Zeus is described by Hesiod in similar terms to humans and possesses a θυμός (*Theog.* 551) and a νόος (*Theog.* 613). It is more difficult to speak of the presence of a ψυχή in the gods. In early poetry, ψυχή usually appears only at death as the soul departs to Hades (e.g. Hom. *Il.*13) and for this reason, even if present in the immortals, it is not something very likely to be described.
11 Trans. Lattimore (1951).
12 Vernant (1989) 39.
13 Trans. Arnson Svarlien (1990).
14 Trans. Verity 2007.
15 Trans. Verity 2007.
16 Trans. Grube (1997).
17 Lourenço (2011) 70.
18 Trans. Tredennick (1989).
19 How accurate Aristotle's reports are is difficult to say. It is possible that Aristotle's testimony is entirely faithful to the early Greek thinker. Yet, equally, Aristotle's descriptions may tell us more about his own understanding of philosophy than those of Thales. See Warren (2007) 26.

20 The literature on Heraclitus is vast. For a general introduction to his thought see Hussey (1999). For his collected fragments and a commentary see Kahn (1979). My own reading is closest to that of Finkelberg (2017).
21 DK 22 A 6: Pl. *Crat.* 402a8–10. The fragment possesses multiple variations. See Finkelberg (2017) 154–6. Heraclitus' theory of flux is among the most-debated issues in his philosophy. See Graham (2013); Taran (1989) for general discussions. The controversy is based on a distinction between radical and moderate theories of flux. The radical flux doctrine described by Plato in the *Theaetetus* holds that all things are in motion all the time (180 b–c). This radical view is more of a straw man argument than a genuine summary of Heraclitus' position. Nevertheless, it has become a key focus of criticism in Heraclitean studies. Adamson (2014), for example, states that 'the flux interpretation of Heraclitus is wrong and it's all Plato's fault' (33). KRS (1957) also questions the radical flux thesis and asks, 'can Heraclitus really have thought that a rock or a bronze cauldron, for example, was invariably undergoing invisible changes of material' (197). Both Adamson and KRS then attempt to reformulate a moderate thesis of flux. However, the distinction between moderate flow and extreme flow is not something I find entirely clear. Flux whether moderate or extreme is a matter of degree and the debate, especially as KRS formulate it, says more about the difficulty many people have with process philosophy. Lloyd (2012) 23, on the other hand, compares Heraclitean change to the Chinese phases where rather than stable elements, water, for example, is better understood as soaking downwards, fire flaming upwards, etc. Heraclitus' cosmos as a whole is based on a similar idea. From the surviving fragments of Heraclitus, it is abundantly clear that flow and change are essential to his views. As Guthrie (1980) argues 'his main purpose seems to be to show that all stability in the world is merely apparent, since if observed with understanding as well as with the senses it proves to be only a resultant of unremitting strife and tension. This is the tenor both of the fragments and of other testimony, in particular that of Plato, whose remarks consort well with the fragments themselves. Perhaps the strongest evidence of all is the primacy given to fire' (466).
22 Trans. Betegh (2007). See Chapter 4 for a further discussion of this passage.
23 Heraclitus probably did not specifically direct this statement at the genealogical relation between Night and Day in Hesiod's poem and may have had Hesiod's description of the gates of Night and Day (*Theog.* 748–67) in mind. See Kahn (1979) 108–9. Elsewhere Heraclitus criticizes Hesiod alongside Pythagoras (DK 22 B40) as a polymath without understanding.
24 Drozdek (2007) 28. This emphasis on flow is not only seen as the most distinctively Heraclitean idea, but it is often stressed as an exception in a Greek world obsessed with substance and stasis. In particular, the idea is often opposed to Parmenides whose rigid monism supposedly denied change and becoming altogether. As

Graham (2013), for example, notes, 'whereas they attempt to explain change in terms of constant realities and their modifications, Heraclitus attempts to explain constancy in terms of ongoing change. Whereas in some metaphysical sense they are all philosophers of stasis, for whom (especially from Parmenides on) stability is fundamental and change problematic, Heraclitus is a philosopher of process, for whom change is fundamental and stability problematic' (319). Heraclitus' thought was, however, more widespread and influential in the Greek world than is usually stressed. This is not to deny the originality of his thought. Heraclitus certainly makes flow central to his thought and draws our attention to the consequences of a world in motion in a way unmatched by anyone else. However, Heraclitus should be thought of more as a particular development of Milesian thought and many of his central ideas, including an underlying pantheistic unity in motion, are not unparalleled, either before or after. Anaximenes' stress on substance change, rarefaction and condensation (and the same, I suspect, applies to the other Milesians) is after all a kind of process. See Finkelberg (2017) 247. Furthermore, while no later philosopher appears to have adopted Heraclitus' views in every respect, this emphasis on flow and unity enjoyed widespread influence in the history of philosophy both among his immediate contemporaries and throughout antiquity, especially among the Stoics. See Long (1996).

25 Nestle cited in Morales (2007) 58.
26 Kirk, Raven and Schofield (1957) 73-4.
27 Guthrie (1953), 7.
28 Sassi (2018) 9.
29 The literature on the subject is expanding quickly. For a general criticism and some new perspectives on the transition from myth to reason see Buxton (1999) and especially the contribution by Most (1999). Other good general surveys are Osborne, R. (2006) and Osborne, C. (2006). On the mystical side of Pythagoras and the Pythagoreans see Burkert (1972). On Empedocles and Parmenides see Kingsley (1995, 2003). On Heraclitus see Leon Ruiz (2007).
30 Burkert (1992).
31 Clark (2013) 12.
32 On Parmenides see Tor (2017) 250-77. For a discussion of the poetics of Presocratic philosophy see Mackenzie (2021).
33 Drozdek (2007) 7.
34 Trans. Graham (2010) modified.
35 Trans. Kahn (1981). The reconstruction of the text is debated. Diels supplies πῦρ. My reading follows Kahn (1981).
36 See Jaeger 2002 [1936]; Drozdek 2007; Finkelberg 2017.
37 Finkelberg (2017) 302.
38 Lloyd (1990) 52 quoted in Clark (2010) 10.

39 As Finkleberg (1986) 334 describes it, 'in the 6th century Orphic lore and Presocratic speculation were kindred teachings, differences between which resulted from different shaping of current religious and moral ideas rather than from any real divergence in the basic outlook'.
40 Schrempp (1992) 11. Indeed, countless works on indigenous philosophy adapt creation stories as the basis for reconstructing underlying views. See for example Farella's (1984) discussion of Navajo philosophy or Maffie's (2014) discussion of Aztec pantheism.
41 Scott (2007) 4. See also Sahlins (1985); Valeri (2004); Scott (2007).
42 Scott (2007) 10.
43 Smith (1978) 100 quoted in Puett (2012) 122.
44 According to Descola (2013a), 'relative universalism takes as its starting point ... the relations of continuity and discontinuity, identity and difference, resemblance and dissimilarity that humans everywhere establish between existing beings, using the tools that they have inherited from their phylogenesis: a body, an intentionality, an aptitude for discerning differential gaps, an ability to weave with any human or nonhuman relations of attachment or antagonism, domination or dependence, exchange or appropriation, subjectivization or objectivization' (305).
45 Morgan's *Ancient Society* (1877) is perhaps the most famous example of such an evolutionary model. For one of the better modern examples see Bellah (2011).
46 This is a major assumption and for many a point of contention. Indeed, adherents of the embodiment approach such as Damasio (1994) have repeatedly criticized this body/soul dualism. It may also seem strange that having spent so long criticizing the Cartesian-like split between nature and culture, Descola simply adopts another dualism here. Descola (2013a) argues 'a proof of this would be that there is no known case of a conception of the ordinary living human person that would be based on interiority alone – let us call it a mind without a body – or on physicality alone – a body without a mind – or not at least, in the latter case, until the advent of materialist theories of consciousness of the late twentieth century. Rather than reducing the distinction between interiority and physicality to an ethnocentric prejudice, one should instead apprehend the specific forms this distinction was given in Europe by philosophical and theological theories as local variants of a more general system of elementary contrasts that can be studied comparatively'(79).
47 Bloom (2004) 155–89.
48 Descola (2013a) 116.
49 Descola (2013a) 38.
50 Although Descola elsewhere (2014b: 436–7) specifically refers to the Greeks as analogists, in *Beyond Nature and Culture* he does not discuss the classification in any detail. The identification, however, is clear and Descola often uses Greek examples to elucidate how analogism works (2013a: 202–4).

51 Descola (2013a) 201.
52 Descola (2013a) 202.
53 Lloyd (2011) 829; Vernant 1980.
54 Burkert (1985) 217.
55 Parker (2011) 94.
56 The debates are somewhat different in anthropology and Sahlins, as early as 1981, successfully navigated a path through structure and history.
57 According to Descola (2013b), 'An ontology is ... an unfolding of the phenomenological consequences of different kinds of inferences about the identities of things around us, inferences which operate by lumping together, or dissociating, elements of the lived world that appear to have similar or dissimilar qualities' (37).
58 Bourdieu (1990) 53.
59 Scott (2014) 3.
60 On homologism see Matthews (2017). For some constructive criticisms of Descola see the various contributions in *HAU*'s (2014) *Colloquia: The Ontological French Turn*. See in addition Ingold (2016a), who argues for the problematic naturalist assumptions behind Descola's ontologies. See also Descola's (2016) rejoinder and in turn Ingold's (2016b) further comments. Arhem and Sprenger (2015) are more sympathetic to Descola's model but have documented its limitations in large parts of Southeast Asia. However, see Scott (2014) and Matthews (2017) for a possible reformulation and remedy to this problem.
61 Parts of this chapter appear in the article 'Hesiod's Theogony and Analogist Cosmogonies' published in *HAU: Journal of Ethnographic Theory*. Vol. 10.1.2020.

Chapter 1

1 Lloyd (1975) 205.
2 Godley (1920).
3 Clay (2003) 3.
4 Trans. Most (2006).
5 Cornford (2009 [1912]); Clay (2003) 2-3.
6 Trans. adapted from Most (2006).
7 See Koning (2010) 195.
8 It appears, for example, in Aristophanes' *Av.* 693 and *Nub.* 424.
9 Trans. Lamb (1967) modified.
10 Lloyd (2000) notes that 'before the first philosophical cosmologies in the 6th century B.C.E., it is doubtful whether we would be correct in speaking of any *unified* concept of the world as such at all. The idea that cosmos, or world order, is such a unity only becomes explicit for the first time with the philosophers' (21). Burkert (1999) further

argues that '"kosmos" is an artificial concept we see evolving at the beginning of Greek philosophy' (88). According to Aetius, Pythagoras 'was the first to call the sum of the whole by the name of the cosmos, because of the order which it displayed' (Aetius 2.1.1 cited in Collins (2007) 59). On the history of the Greek term κόσμος see Finkelberg (1998).

11 West (1999) 64 n. 116.
12 Hesiod the philologist is nicely illustrated in his discussion of Aphrodite (*Theog.* 195–200): τὴν δ᾽ Ἀφροδίτην ἀφρογενέα τε θεὰν καὶ ἐυστέφανον Κυθέρειαν / κικλῄσκουσι θεοί τε καὶ ἀνέρες, οὕνεκ᾽ ἐν ἀφρῷ / θρέφθη: ἀτὰρ Κυθέρειαν, ὅτι προσέκυρσε Κυθήροις: / Κυπρογενέα δ᾽, ὅτι γέντο πολυκλύστῳ ἐνὶ Κύπρῳ / ἠδὲ φιλομμηδέα, ὅτι μηδέων ἐξεφαάνθη. 'Gods and men call her Aphrodite, because she was formed in foam, and Cytherea, because she approached Cythera, and Cyprus-born, because she was born in wave-crested Cyprus, and "genial" because she was appeared out of genitals.' Trans. West (1988). In this case Hesiod points out two etymologies that link Aphrodite's birth from the foamy castrated genitals of Kronos with her personal name and epitaph. The first is based on ἀφρός 'foam' and the second West approximates in his translation 'genial' from φιλομμειδής, literally 'smile loving', which Hesiod links with μῆδος, 'genitals'.
13 See KRS (1957) 36. Elsewhere Aristot. *Xen*. 976b14–19 discusses this as the common view. See Koning (2010) 197.
14 Trans. MacLeod (1967).
15 Tarrant (2002).
16 Hornung (2001) 43.
17 Etymology of course was not the only consideration in this emendation and having established that Chaos was a gap, Cornford and others scoured Hesiod's text to find it. Often attention is drawn to lines 700–5, seen by KRS (1957) 38 as confirmation of Cornford's thesis indicating that Chaos exists as a gap between Ouranos and Gaia. The allusion, however, is far from clear and stands in contradiction to later lines where Chaos is located in the underworld (811–14). Based on these lines, Miller (2001) 3–10 argues that Chaos is the gap between Gaia and Tartarus in the underworld. He also draws attention to a reference to a great chasm (χάσμα μέγ᾽) in 740–3 to propose that Hesiod saw it as a gap. Again, whether this chasm is identical with Chaos or simply in a nearby location, or a general description of the underworld itself as a chasm, is unclear. While I agree that these lines indeed indicate that Chaos is somewhere in the underworld, they hardly justify understanding Chaos specifically as a gap, any more than a space, formlessness, or water. Another more important, but often overlooked, question is not simply to where this description refers but to *when*. As Mondi (1989) points out, 'the fact that the cosmological Chaos, now bounded by the elements of the evolved cosmos, can be viewed as, or as being in, a chasm, would not necessarily imply that the

cosmogonic Chaos, existing alone before the genesis of any other entity, should or could be so viewed' (10). Indeed, it is surely of some small significance that the geography described in these lines, including Poseidon's hefty Bronze Gates which keep Chaos, Night and Day, and everything else in their proper place (732–5), refer to a period of substantial cosmic renovation that has very little to do with the beginning of the cosmos.

18 Cornford (2009 [1912]) 66–7.
19 Ibid.
20 Cornford (1967) 42; see KRS (1957) 238.
21 KRS (1957) 33. Gregory (2007) 23. Miller (2001) is critical of Cornford and KRS. However, he still reiterates the essential gapping nature of Chaos, replacing Ouranos and Gaia with Tartarus and Gaia.
22 Fränkel (1973) 101 saw Chaos as a 'yawning emptiness'. This position was elaborated by Mondi (1989), who notes 'the primary lesson to be drawn from two and a half millennia of exegesis is that it is all too easy to see in Hesiod's Χάος practically anything that one is predisposed to see' (3). He too goes on to propose an alternative root in χαῦνος, insubstantial or formless. Sedley (2009) 250, on the other hand, maintains the idea of gap but stresses a punning connection with χεῖσθαι to flow. Lincoln (2002) presents a more theoretical view, arguing 'Chaos may then be understood as existence in its zero grade, coupled with potentiality at the maximum: the point of departure for all subsequent creation and creativity' (112). Bussanich (1983) similarly stresses 'Chaos symbolizes the initial stage of pre-cosmic reality', a space necessary for creation to exist (214).
23 KRS (1957) 39.
24 Indeed there is no real alternative as, according to KRS (1957), 'it is out of the question that Hesiod or his source was thinking of the originative substance as coming into being out of nothing' (29).
25 See Frankel (1975); Gigon (1945); Diller (1946); Rowe (1983), who are in favour, while KRS see him more reservedly as a step in the right direction. Miller (2001) argues that 'semantically, to begin from Chaos is to affirm the priority of difference to the Undifferentiated' (1). Hyland (2006) also elaborates upon this point, stressing that Chaos indicates that 'difference somehow precedes sameness or identity', adding 'right from the beginning, it seems, ontological difference comes first' (14). While many of these readings appear as quite a radical break from Cornford, there is a more pervasive tendency to align them with proto-Milesian philosophy and especially with Anaximander's ἄπειρον.
26 Koning (2010) 190–9.
27 Clay (2003) 15 refers to Mondi (1989) and Bussanich (1983).
28 Clay (2003) notes 'Hesiod's cosmic vision offers the first systematic presentation of the nature of the divine and human cosmos, of Being and Becoming. Thus,

Janus-like, he synthesizes earlier traditions and at the same time prepares the way for the Pre-Socratics, especially Parmenides, Empedocles, and Heraclitus' (2-3).
29 Ibid. 152.
30 Ibid. 15.
31 Wang (2012) 42.
32 Wang (2012) 44.
33 Valeri (2014) 278-9.
34 Eliade (1965) 114-15.
35 Whether directly influenced by Eliade or not, this kind of cosmological focus has dominated interpretations of mythical cosmologies in both anthropology and comparative religion. Johnston (2012) has interestingly suggested that Eliade was influenced by the works of Plato.
36 Puett (2011) 110.
37 Di Mattei (2016) 7. López-Ruiz (2012) also notes that the account 'presumes the existence of "something" at the moment of creation. First, tohu-wa-wohu ("welter and waste") is not "nothing", and is immediately characterized as some mass of waters, very much in the Mesopotamian tradition. Then, the very first words can be read in a way that underscores even more the fact that the narrative is about the starting point of God's creation, not of the universe itself' (35).
38 This striking opening was also the product of a richer history of debated beginnings. In Psalm 74, for example, we see disordered forces play a more prominent part and Yahweh must defeat a dragon-like Leviathan. See López-Ruiz (2012) 37.
39 Assmann (2003) 189. Traunecker (2001) notes 'because all life emerged from him, Nun was a place of regeneration but also an emanation of the uncreated and thus, a dangerous intrusion of the unorganized into the ordered world' (73-4).
40 Assmann (2014) elsewhere argues for a great deal of diversity in Egyptian cosmological speculation.
41 Plato too fits within this schema and contrasts an initial period of disorder (ἄμετρος) followed by a demiurge to help things get started (διακοσμέω) (*Tim.* 53a). Yet Plato's flirtation with disorder seems like a light prelude compared with Hesiod's gigantic overture and it is questionable how comparable these systems really are. For a detailed comparison of the two see Boys-Stones (2009).
42 Burkert (2004); López-Ruiz (2010).
43 These have been usefully compiled and compared alongside the Greek material by López-Ruiz (2010).
44 Trans. Dalley (2008).
45 Sonik (2013) has adopted Assmann's distinction between different kinds of chaos in a Babylonian context, though I am not convinced. The narrative of the *Enûma Eliš* is one of repeated fighting, changes of rule, where only at its very end Sky is separated from Earth.

46 Hermann Gunkel's idea of *chaoskampf* or 'struggle against chaos' has long since been recognized as a pivotal focus in Mesopotamian religion. See Frankfort (1978) 232. Rochberg (2005) also notes 'as forces and agents within natural objects, the gods brought order to the cosmos through authority and law. The cosmos was not seen as a self-governing body, but as ruled by divine law' (319).
47 Trans. Tarrant (2002).
48 Tarrant (2002) 349.
49 Burkert (2004); López-Ruiz (2010).
50 Vernant (1982) 107. See also Sassi (2018) 41–51; Valeri (2014) 276–80.
51 Vernant (1982) 115.
52 Vernant (1982) 117.
53 As Buxton (1999) 8 discusses, Vernant later revised his general position by replacing mythic with alternate forms of rationality.
54 Trans. Tredennick (1933).
55 Sassi (2018) 48–50.
56 Scott (2007)10.
57 Descola (2013a) 131.
58 Ibid. 163.
59 Ibid. 15.
60 Puett (2011) has recently argued that alongside monistic myths 'alternative religious views and practices, as well as modes of dealing with the divine, are at least as common' (123).
61 See Almqvist (2020) for a more theoretical focus on the ontological foundations of analogist mythology.
62 Scott (2007) 12.
63 Valeri (2001) 293. See also Scott (2007) 12–17.
64 Bateson (1972) 10.
65 Bateson (1972) 10.
66 See Descola (1996).
67 Matthews (2017) 280.
68 Compare the line with Odysseus' contrast between his account and the deceitful tales of others in his predictions to Eumaeus (*Od.* 14.160): ἦ μέν τοι τά δε πάντα τελείεται ὡς ἀγορεύω.
69 The combination of πρώτιστα and αὐτὰρ ἔπειτα is also common in Homer. For example (*Il.* 9.168–9): Φοῖνιξ μὲν πρώτιστα Διῒ φίλος ἡγησάσθω,/αὐτὰρ ἔπειτ' Αἴας τε μέγας καὶ δῖος Ὀδυσσεύς. See also *Il.* 2.5–6; *Od.* 4.456–7.
70 If KRS ignore this, Miller (2001) describes that πρώτιστα is simply an honorary position. Gaia and Tartarus are originally fused in one mass and hence primary 'Chaos, the "gap" or "yawning space" that, as the differentiation of each from the other, first lets earth and Tartara be, precedes them' (21).

71 On αὐτὰρ ἔπειτα as indicative of a temporal succession see Hyland (2006) 13.
72 Miller (2001) 21.
73 The debate is longstanding. The triadic view is currently the most common and adopted by Clay (2003) 16; Sedley (2007) 3 n 3. Miller (2001), however, argues for an Gaia/Tartarus dichotomy at the heart of the *Theogony*. Chaos is relocated as the gap between Gaia and Tartarus, which he sees as an original mass separated by Chaos. Eros is positioned as a force of attraction. The understanding of Chaos as a gap introduces a similar weakness to Cornford and KRS' position. Secondly, the pivotal role Miller gives to Tartarus is questionable. The arguments for seeing Tartarus as a space within Gaia rather than a primal deity hinge on whether we read Tartarus as a specifically named primal god or a recess within Gaia. In later passages, Tartarus is grouped alongside Gaia, Ouranos and Pontus (*Theog.* 807) and even in the opening passages Tartarus does not appear as a separate being, like Eros and Chaos, but is described as a nook within Gaia. Beall (2009) argues that Tartarus is not in the nominative but in the accusative and the object of ἔχουσι. This shifts the meaning from a primal god to a space within Gaia, i.e. the gods who hold Olympus and Tartarus.
74 Clay (2003) 15.
75 Since Aristotle, there has a been a tendency to see Pherecydes as more philosophical than Hesiod, yet the two show more overlap than is usually acknowledged. Pherecydes' Chthonie, the chthonic aspect of Earth, is similar to Hesiod's Gaia. Both represent the mother of the gods, men and most other beings. Chronos, punning on Hesiod's Kronos, is an abstract force: time. It is certainly possible that Hesiod was aware of this wordplay, though the later appearance of the god and his characterization suggests he was not utilized in the same way. While Pherecydes does not include Eros in his triad, Proclus (DK 7 B 3) notes that Zas when the situation calls for it can transform into Eros. In general see Schibili (1990). It is however, important to note that Pherecydes places his version of Zeus at the very outset of his cosmology rather than as a latecomer.
76 Clay (2003) 13.
77 See for example Aristotle's views on Eros in *Met.* 1.984b. See also Sedley (2007) 3.
78 Calame (1999) 181.
79 This sometimes involves displacing Chaos in favour of Eros as occurs in Pl. *Symp.* (178b) and (195c) and Aristot. *Met.* (984b23–31). See Koning (2015) 198.
80 Valeri (2014) 271.
81 Rowe (1983) 134–5; Miller (1983) 141. See Bussanich (1983). Clay (2003) deals with this at length but incorporates this violence and excess as part of an overarching teleology.
82 Ibid. 16.
83 Clay (2003) 15.

84 For a general approach to personifications in Greek religion see Stafford (2000). Whether abstract gods are differentiated from anthropomorphic ones does not appear to be a major concern to most Greeks. Farella discusses a similar phenomenon among the Navajo Indians in relation to the term 'nayéé'. Nayéé is usually translated as monster. However, while monstrous beings are included in this category, so too are abstractions such as old age, poverty, disease, etc. Farella (1984) argues: 'Navajos use nayéé to refer to and describe anything that gets in the way of a person living his life. It refers more to the subjective than to the objective, more to the internal than to the external' (51).

85 Miller (2001) 16. I depart from Miller, however, when he incorporates this duality into a neatly unfolding cosmology. In doing so he effectively neutralizes Hesiod's starting point, merging initial difference into a greater unity. I should also point out that Clay (2003), who characteristically devotes ample attention to Hesiodic concerns, points out a similar Eris/Eros conflict: 'we can now detect more clearly the operation of two cosmic forces, Eros, which brings things together, and Eris, who forces them apart. It bears emphasizing, however, that they do not simply correspond to the male and female principles, yet both are necessary for the coming-to-be of the cosmos' (16). This position again argues for a greater unity behind the only apparent presence of cosmic strife. Lincoln (2012a) 111 adopts a similar position but argues for a central opposition between the lineages of Gaia as 'substantial' and Chaos as 'non-material' deities which never intersect. Prier (1976) 45, in a related model, argues that Gaia is the antithesis of Chaos and mediated by a third term Eros. This interpretation, though compelling in so far as it accounts for the twin genealogies of Gaia and Chaos, is problematic in other respects. Indeed, Gaia and Chaos are not simply opposed in terms of substantiality and non-substantiality but in terms of form and relation. For this reason, I consider Miller's reading more convincing.

86 West (1966) 31.

87 Rowe (1983) 134–5; Miller (1983) 141. See Bussanich (1983).

88 See discussion by Tor (2017) 17.

89 Clay (2003) 152 also treats the narrative as a whole but, as argued above, considers it part of a complex teleological development.

90 The most extensive comparative treatment is López-Ruiz (2010). She also includes the *Derveni Theogony* which I will discuss at length in Chapters 3 and 4. For a brief but useful summary see Littleton (1969).

91 Littleton (1969) 82.

92 Clay (2001) 151. For a more extensive catalogue of hybrids see especially Clay (2001) 150–75.

93 It may be helpful to draw a parallel here between the hybrids of the *Theogony* and those in Empedocles' (DK 31 B 61) zoogony characterized by man-faced oxen and wandering limbs. See Sedley (2007) 33–52.

94 Versnel (1994) 94.
95 See Versnel (1994) 90–136 for a comprehensive discussion of Kronos and the Kronia.
96 Clay (2001) 26.
97 I draw inspiration for this approach from Schrempp (1992) 36, who points out the close intersection between philosophy, myth and riddles in the problems of Zeno and elsewhere.
98 Trans. Frazer (1921).
99 Detienne and Vernant (1991) 55–131.
100 See Clay (2003) 28; Detienne and Vernant (1991) 55–131; Nelson (1998) 101.
101 Hesiod's account may show a good deal of originality in his specific wordplays, yet the idea of a storm god eating something and consolidating power occupies an important place in Near Eastern and Greek myths and in particular the Hurro-Hittite Kumarbi myth (c. 1200 BCE). López-Ruiz (2010) 91 also includes the Orphic *Derveni Theogony*. As I will discuss at length in Chapter 3, the similarities depend very much on the reconstruction and interpretation of the papyrus. Despite their differences and often-debated reconstructions, in all these poems the act of eating appears as a means of expressing a particular configuration of difference. In the Kumarbi myth Anu, the equivalent of Ouranos, is castrated by Kumarbi (Kronos), who swallows the phallus of his father. After the act Kumarbi, a male god, becomes pregnant and gives birth to Teshub. The ending is fragmented but seems to involve the eating of a stone and the coronation of Teshub as the new ruler and arranger of the cosmos. When we examine the variations in tandem we can see how both the *Theogony* and Kumarbi cosmologies show a similar structure and focus on, as López-Ruiz (2010) notes, 'the swallowing of a divinity or part of a divinity by another in order to consolidate power'(142). For a more comprehensive summary of the Kumarbi myth, see López-Ruiz (2010) 91–4. While neither the *Enûma Eliš* nor the Kumarbi myth have the same specific kinship relations as Hesiod, the narrative structure of the successions and many of the attributes of the respective gods permit rough identifications. I do not, however, imply that all are the same. Indeed, the model is even more general and Faraone and Teeter (2004) add Egypt to this, proposing that the imagery of the pharaoh swallowing Maat (order) may have influenced Hesiod. I do not think that there is any need, however, to propose such a direct route, given the widespread prevalence of the idea.
102 Sahlins (1985b) 99.
103 Dumont (1980) 239.
104 Ibid. 239–40.
105 According to Sahlins (1985b), 'Such mythical exploits and social disruptions are common to the beginnings of dynasties and to successive investitures of divine

kings. We can summarily interpret the significance something like this: to be able to put the society in order, the king must first reproduce an original disorder. Having committed his monstrous acts against society, proving he is stronger than it, the ruler proceeds to bring system out of chaos. Recapitulating the initial constitution of social life, the accession of the king is thus a recreation of the universe' (80).

106 While it may become reductionist to take the parallels too far, I am not proposing a historical connection extending between Greece and Fiji, but rather that both societies address in their myths the common analogical problem of difference.
107 Descola (2013) 228 discusses Dumont's hierarchies in terms of analogism.
108 Clay (2003) 13: 'the *Theogony* constitutes an attempt to understand the cosmos as the product of a genealogical evolution and a process of individuation that finally leads to the formation of a stable cosmos and ultimately achieves its telos under the tutelage of Zeus.'
109 Clay (2003) 26; Nelson (1998) 101–4.
110 This is stressed in terms such as ἑξῆς (738) one after another, in order, in a row. The term is common in Homer, e.g.: "ἐς δ'ἦλθον μνηστῆρες ἀγήνορες. οἱ μὲν ἔπειτα ἑξείης ἕζοντοκατὰ κλισμούς τε θρόνους τε' (*Od.*1.145).
111 Lincoln (2012a) 116.
112 Clay (2003) 29.
113 See Solmsen's (1949) 36–8 defence of Hesiod's deliberate introduction of the two generations of the Moirai.
114 Clay (2003) 29.
115 Clay (2003) 26; Nelson (1998) 103. See Yasumura (2013) for an extensive treatment of the early challenges to Zeus.
116 Somer (2000) 95. Smith (1976) has criticized this dominant interpretation, seeing the Akitu as a reactionary development established by the Hellenistic kings. His argument is far from conclusive. See Somer (2000) for a discussion and argument in favour of the traditional interpretation.

Chapter 2

1 The claim is widespread. See for example Kirk (1970) 228; Wirshbo (1982) 109; Dillon (1992) 98–9; Gera (2003) 47; Dougherty (2003) 36.
2 Lévi-Strauss (1969) 155.
3 Eliade (1959) 88. For a discussion of Eliade's Golden Age and Greek myth see Chlup (2008).
4 Kramer (1963) 147–8.

5 Leeming (2005) notes that paradise myths are 'marked by qualities that humans all long for: opulence, fertility, pleasure, freedom, peace, and full communication among all species'.
6 Eliade (1959) 56.
7 Dillon (1992) 29.
8 Trans. Graham 2010.
9 Trans. Most (2006).
10 For the Christian apologist Clement of Alexandria the Greek sacrificial shares were nothing less than a thinly disguised act of gluttony and an affront to their non-existent gods (Strom 7.6.30). See Detienne and Sissa (2000) 71. West (1961) 138 even posits that Hesiod departs from an earlier version of the myth where Zeus was deceived.
11 Detienne and Sissa (2000) 75; Stocking (2017) 58.
12 Parker (2011) 140. See Wirshbo (1982) 103 n. 8 for a list of different interpretations.
13 Burkert (1966) 104.
14 Vernant (1989).
15 Ibid. 21.
16 Ibid. 43.
17 Wirshbo (1982) 109.
18 Dougherty (2003) 36.
19 Gera (2003) 47.
20 Dillon (1992) 25.
21 Wirshbo (1982) argues that we understand Prometheus as a trickster. However as early as the fifth century Prometheus as a culture bringer occupied a pivotal role in tragedies such as Aeschylus' *Prometheus Bound* (436–506) and the *Homeric Hymn to Hephaestus* which describe Prometheus, and sometimes Hephaestus, as a defiant benefactor who helps differentiate humans from animals through cultural gifts. See Chapter 5.
22 Clay (2003) 95–9.
23 See Versnel (1994) 90–136 for a comprehensive discussion of Kronos and the Kronia.
24 Trans. Most (2006) altered. Verdenius (1985) 132 notes that ἐν θαλίῃσι in the dative suggests an equation with feasts.
25 On ἀκηδέα θυμὸν, see *Theog.* 61 where the phrase is applied to the Muses and *Theog.* 489 where it is used of Zeus.
26 Revised following Irwin (2005) 37.
27 Versnel (1994); Chlup (2008) 100.
29 Versnel (1994) 121; Chlup (2008) 98; Clay (2003) 97–8.
20 Garcia (2013) 168.
30 The word ὁμόθεν (from the same place) seems to carry a double burden and Hesiod by calling it 'another story' (ἕτερόν λόγον) intends that both the Promethean myth from the *Theogony* and the new myth of the Golden Age can be understood by this term.

31 Van Noorden (2014), following Peabody (1975) 248–50, argues that 'the phrase emphasizes not so much the single origin of gods and men but their respective differentiation into dissimilarity and conflict' (71).
32 σοῖς τε κασιγνήτοις, οἵ τοι ὁμόθεν γεγάασιν (135). This is similar to Euripides' (*IA* 502–3) usage: τὸν ὁμόθεν πεφυκότα/στέργων μετέπεσον.
33 Garcia (2013) 168.
34 Graf and Johnston (2007) 114. Van Noorden (2014) 69 offers a useful summary.
35 Indeed, it is likely that ὁμόθεν refers not so much to blood as to the place of origin. These can and often do coincide, but in Sophocles, for example, the two appear as complementary but differentiated forms of relating (*El.* 157).
36 See Loraux (2000) 1–12. The wider Greek tradition provides more details, yet little clarification. In some cases, human beings may appear as part of a single larger genealogy (Pindar, *Nem.* 6). This is not, however, the case with Hesiod, who clearly describes that men and women are made by the gods in an unspecified way (Hesiod *WD* 70; 110). In the *Theogony* an obscure reference to humans and ash trees may suggest that humanity was a descendent of the Melian Nymphs (*Theog.* 187; 563; *WD* 145). See Van Noorden (2015) 69 and Clay (2003) 97–8. However, the significance of this phrase is unclear, and the most likely assumption is that humans, like Pandora (*WD* 61; *Theog.* 571), were simply moulded by the gods out of clay or some other substance.
37 A similar idea can also be gleaned from an almost antithetical scene where Hesiod describes in detail how the gods weaken without their immortal food (*Theog.* 793–803). It is worth noting that weakened gods come eerily close not simply to descriptions of mortals, but, as Heath (2005) 61 points out, to dying mortals. The nearly dead Odysseus, for example, is described as 'breathless and voiceless' (ἄπνευστος καὶ ἄναυδος *Od.* 5.456). These scenes show the extreme ends of immortality and mortality, their limitations and potentials. In some respects, they indicate just how flexible the concepts of man and god can be; in others, that gods and mortals retain an essential difference.
38 Revised following Irwin (2005) 37.
39 Lanfer (2012) 97 also argues that in Genesis there is a clear suggestion that the fall introduces death.
40 Trans. Jones (1918) modified.
41 Sahlins (2013) ix.
42 Self-willed (αὐτόματος) objects are often divine and those who eat them close to the gods. See *Il.* 5.749 for a description of the self-opening gates in Olympus or *Il.* 18.376 for the self-moving tripods of Hephaestus. It is also worth noting a contrast with the ephemeral fruits fed to Thyphon in Apollodorus (1. 6. 3).
43 Trans. Fagles (1996) modified.
44 The literature is vast. See for example Sahlins (2013) 6; Carsten (1995); Vilaça (2010); Janowski and Kerlogue (2007).

45 Vilaça (2010) 48.
46 Fustel de Coulanges (1956) 62.
47 Robertson Smith (1889) 257.
48 Stowers (1995); Stocking (2017). As Jay (1992) argues, 'it is the social relations of reproduction, not biological reproduction, that sacrificial ritual can create and maintain. Where the state and social relations of production are not separable from a patrilineally organized social relations of reproduction, the entire social order may be understood as dependent on sacrifice' (37). Cited in Stocking (2017) 13.
49 See Parker (2005) 13.
50 Aristotle attributes the term ὁμοσίπυος to the law-giver Charondas and ὁμόκαποι to the miracle worker and poet Epimenides.
51 See Parkes (2005). The phenomenon is evident in Greek myths where Herakles is suckled by Hera (Diodorus 4.9.6–7; Pausanias 9. 25.2). The modern Greek practice is discussed by Kenna (2001) 89 where Parkes (2005) notes 'it is still treated as an impediment to marriage' (591–2).
52 Bremmer (1999) 2.
53 For example *WD* 82; 146; *Od.* 8.222.
54 See Onians (1951) 200–6. Hesiod understands αἰών in this way in his reference to gods and men not possessing ἰσαίωνες 'equal aeons' (*Cat.* 7). The line is reconstructed. See Irwin (2005) 39.
55 See Onians (1951) 200–6; Clarke (1999) agrees that αἰών is an 'essence that is tantamount to vitality' (113). Clay (1982) takes the position further and argues, based on the nearly identical term βροτός 'mortal' and Homer's rare term for 'blood' or 'gore' (βρότος), that mortals' blood was created through the bread they ate. Thus mortals are 'those who have blood in their veins', and 'this blood is conceived of as produced by their eating of grain' and because of this 'blood, the consumption of grain, and mortality are thus linked to form a definition of human life' (114).
56 Trans. Fagles (1996).
57 Stocking (2017) notes 'each type of being gets the food that is proper to each one's ontological status' (124).
58 See Detienne and Sissa (2000) 29–30.
59 See West (2007) 158.
60 Trans. Lattimore (1951) modified.
61 Almqvist (2020) 184.
62 The idea is common and appears for example in the Norse Apples of Idun. For more examples from the Indo-European tradition see West (2007) 157–60.
63 For example, when the αἰών is slain from Patroklos and his body risks decay, Thetis preserves the flesh with ambrosia and nectar (*Il.* 19.38). See Onians (1951) 204. Clay (1981), on the other hand, argues that for 'Homer, nectar and ambrosia do not by themselves make the gods immortal, but they prevent them from aging and exempt

them from the natural cycle of growth and decay' (115). Clay tackles the problematic differences between agelessness and immortality and argues that ambrosia only prevents decay in archaic literature. However, this sense is not always clear and at least at times ambrosia appears to make men immortal. See, for example, Theocritus (*Id.* 15.106–8).

64 Although ὁμοτράπεζοι can at times can be used for the household (οἶκος) or those who share the same table, it is generally reserved for relations among aristocrats at the shared feast. See for example Pl. *Euthphr.*4c; Pl. *Leg.* 9.868e. Gould (2001) defines supplicants and ξένοι as 'social institutions which permit the acceptance of the outsider within the group and which create hereditary bonds of obligation between the parties' (55). See also Belfiore (2000) 6.

65 Affinity is usually understood in a weak sense as the affiliation of two previously unrelated groups through marriage. The term, however, also has a broader meaning and may refer to moieties, tribes or more generally to non-consanguineous kin who enter into social relationships. See Helms (2010) 8–9.

66 Vernant (1969) 147. Indeed, at times the two overlap and Odysseus appears as both a ξένος and a potential son-in-law to the Phaeacian king. Herman (1987) 36 notes there is even some debate regarding which was the stronger association and when Hiero of Sicily and Pyrrhus decided to strengthen their ξενία tie with the marriage of their children, marriage appeared as a kind of afterthought.

67 Isocrates (5.122) too lists crimes against ξενία alongside patricide, fratricide and incest. See also Eur. *Hec.* 710; Dio Sic. 20.70. 3–4. See Herman (1987) 66, 125.

68 Herman (1987) 29. For a different view see Fragoulaki's (2013) 3–11 study of kinship in Thucydides.

69 The most famous example appears in Apollo's rejection of the child's relation to the mother in Aeschylus' *Eumenides* (657–61). That ξενία could be inherited is clear from the ancestral ξενία of Glaucos and Diomedes (*Il.* 6.215) which was originally formed by their ancestors. Indeed, the idea of inheriting what we would see as socially acquired characteristics was common in the Greek world and Aristotle, for example, discusses the commonly held idea that scars and tattoos could be passed down through the generations (*Gen. An.* 724a).

70 Indeed, the Greeks held nurture alongside nature to be of central importance in child development and practices such as shaping new-born infants abound. See Martin's (1995) discussion on the Greek body, esp. 26. Xenophon's (*Cyr.* 8.7.14) Cyrus captures a similar dynamic in his description of what unites a city and starting from a seed (σπέρματος), he describes an ongoing incorporative process based on those nourished together (τραφέντες). It also includes non-kin, who share a tie through eating together (σύσσιτος) and sharing the same house (οἰκειότεροι), before encompassing all male citizens.

71 Wilgaux (2010).

72 Vilaça (2010) 48.
73 Sahlins (2013) 54.
74 Helms (2010) 58.
75 Lyons (2012) 2–3 deals at length with the problem of wives, exchange, and incorporating outsiders in Greek myth and practice. On marriage rituals and the incorporation of women into the house see Vernant (1983). Hesiod also discusses how choosing one's affines is always problematic. His answer is a happy medium, proposing that the ideal wife, in a phrase that echoes Homer's discussion of the gods' relationship to the Phaeacians (*Od.* 7.201–205), is someone who lives near, an ἐγγύθι or a neighbour (*WD* 700). More precisely this is the daughter of the neighbour, or the potential affine, who shares in your feasts (*WD* 343)
76 See Benveniste's (2016) 61–75 discussion of Indo-European hospitality and especially his discussion of the Latin term *hostis*.
77 Helms (2010) 8.
78 Viveiros de Castro (2015) 101.
79 Although Benveniste (2016) has argued ξένος lacked 'the same sense of "enemy" as did *hostis* in Latin' (69), Belfiore (2000) 63–81, for example, in her study of Sophocles' *Philoktetes* demonstrates how the ambivalence of the term ξένος was often deliberately played upon by the tragedians.
80 Vernant (1989) 27.
81 Ibid. 25; Vernant (1991) 280.
82 Vernant (1989) 43.
83 Ibid. 25.
84 Vernant (1989) 25. See also Clay (2003) 56.
85 Vernant (1981) 61.
86 See Parker (2011) 144, for a discussion of holocaust offerings where the victim was entirely destroyed and the intention appears to be separation full stop.
87 Parker (2011) 141.
88 See Parker (2011) 142. Petridou (2016) notes how 'the deities are invited to feast from these tables and recline on the guest couches specially designed for the divine. In other words, in these rather anthropocentric rites of theoxenia, the gods are imagined as following the protocol of human dining. The divine guests are treated like foreigners, travellers, or strangers who momentarily pose a threat to the well-ordered microcosm of the city; they need to be treated with discretion so as not to be offended' (311). The practice of θεοξένια should not, however, be mistaken as a return to Mekone. Arguably it goes the other way: men do not dine with gods, so much as particular gods dine with men. This also is evident in that the most frequently invited guests are deities with close ties to humans such as Herakles and the Dioskouri.
89 Similarly Athena refers to sacrifice as 'the feast of the gods' (*Od.* 3.336). Bakkar (2013), in his recent study on Greek meat, argues against imposing artificial distinctions

between the sacrificial offerings to the gods and the feast that follows. He notes 'the *dais* is thus always a sacrifice. The gods are always participants in the *dais*' (40).

90 Alongside these examples, Parker (2011) 141 documents a number of further instances where offerings of raw meat and cooked entrails are directly served to gods. The conference *La Cuisine et l'autel* (2005) is dedicated to the subject. Stocking (2017), summarizing the proceedings, concludes 'in light of these important studies, it seems impossible to maintain Vernant's original assumption, which served as the basis for much of his argument, namely that the meat of sacrifice should be considered a "mortal portion"' (6–7). Detienne alongside Sissa (2000) has revised his earlier position and argues 'the Greek gods were carnivorous. Ambrosia and Nectar were of course, their special, Olympian forms of nourishment, but they were by no means averse to the meat of animals, provided it was served up to them in the form of an *odor*' (75).

91 Vernant (1989) 226 n.17.
92 Ibid.
93 Robertson Smith (1889) 251.
94 Hubert and Mauss (1981) 97.
95 Descola (2013b) 42.
96 Trans. Fowler (1925) modified.
97 Although Hesiod's descriptions do not clearly describe how meals were divided during the Golden Age, it is of note that during the shared feasts among the gods and the Phaeacians, these mythical humans both sacrifice to the gods and share the same table (*Od.* 7.201–5).
98 If it is now abundantly clear that gods in the archaic and classical periods were frequently offered meat, Vernant's influence is persistent and a number of scholars continue to insist that they do not eat it. Stocking (2017) 1 makes this central to his discussion of sacrifice and argues that, unlike the Babylonians and the Indians, the Greeks did not imagine that the gods eat their sacrificial portions. Rather the gods receive honour from sacrifice. The main evidence for this claim emerges from a lack of any clear descriptions of meat-eating gods, rather than a clear statement that the gods actually refuse meat. My own assumption is the reverse and unless it is clearly stated that the Olympians do not eat meat, I take it that, like their Babylonian counterparts, they probably eat the food offered to them. However, Stocking does offer some intriguing points of support. In the *Hymn to Demeter* (310–13) for example, when mortals cease to sacrifice to the gods, the gods are described as deprived of honour (τιμή) rather than food. On the other hand, hungry gods deprived of sacrifice were the butt of jokes by Aristophanes (*Av.* 1519) and Lucian (*De Sacr.* 9). Although these examples can hardly be used uncritically, the satirical sketches of Aristophanes are not a far cry from Hesiod's description of oath-breaking gods deprived of ambrosia and nectar in the *Theogony* (793–803). Indeed, the joke arguably works because it refers to actually held views. I am thus suspicious of Stocking's blanket statement that the Greek

gods did not eat meat but persuaded that the issue of hungry gods was problematic for some Greeks. However, the existence of this contested view should not be seen as a major problem and even among those who laughed at hungry gods, the vast majority continued to sacrifice to them. In this respect, how gods received their shares and what they did with them is far from the most significant issue. Sacrifice in all cases entails more than nutrition. As Valeri (1985) stresses regarding Hawaiian divinities, 'to eat is to encompass, to possess, to transform' (56).

99 Valeri (1985) 57.
100 A general theory of sacrifice will inevitably be the subject of criticism and I should add a disclaimer at this point. Parker (2011) notes regarding the complexity of the offerings that 'we fumble in interpreting these variations, and it is very plausible that different Greek communities deployed the repertory of symbols in different ways. The basic components, however – foodstuffs – are always the same' (150). I have attempted to keep my position as flexible as possible, but inevitably my argument will not apply to every case where an animal is ritually killed. One issue, as noted above, is found in holocaust offerings where the victim was entirely destroyed. This does not, however, contradict my model. Rather, holocaust offerings are arguably simply another configuration of an offering, where the emphasis is on creating distance rather than proximity. I have also not discussed the sacrificing of vegetables and cakes. See Stowers (2011) for a survey of these offerings. While every sacrifice needs to be considered in its proper context, I do not see why these offerings cannot behave like meat, that is, as intermediaries which are divided and distributed in different ways.
101 The meal, as Douglas (1991) notes, is both a creative and a structured process where 'the rules of the menu are not in themselves more or less trivial than the rules of verse to which a poet submits' (273). Ekroth (2011) also emphasizes the creativity of sacrifice. I am also indebted to the useful discussion by McClymond (2010) 143–5 who refers to the almost infinite potential of meat divisions and the creation of cosmic relations. These complications are now increasingly recognized in later Greek inscriptions such as the divisions described at Cos (LSCG 151). See Stocking (2017) 46–7.
102 Trans. Fagles (1996). Petropoulou (1987) and Kadletz (1984) interpret this scene as somewhat exceptional. However, as Hitch (2009) 46 argues in her extensive analysis of Homeric sacrifice, 'no single detail can be used in Homer to define an action, even a "typical action"'.
103 Suk Fong Jim (2014) 57.
104 A related idea may appear in Simonides' (fr. 20) enigmatic phrase: 'θύουσι νύμφαις τῶι τε Μαιάδος τόκωι: οὗτοι γὰρ ἀνδρῶν αἷμ᾽ ἔχουσι ποιμένων.' 'They sacrifice to the Nymphs and the son of Maia [Hermes]: for these have the blood of shepherd men.' How to read this passages has perplexed scholars but see Versnel (2011) 369 and Ekroth (2011) 24 for some suggestions.

105 The hierarchical aspect of feasting may appear to contradict Homer's frequent reference to the equal feast. For Seaford (2004) 41 the meaning of this phrase is clear and he argues that equality in the feast means just that – people, though not gods, are treated the same. Hitch (2009) 108, however, has argued that ἴσος does not refer to equality at all but to a share appropriate to each. See also Stocking (2017) 8–9; Bakker (2013) 38–42.
106 The term is adapted from Ekroth's (2011) 36 discussion of the classical material.
107 Chlup (2011) 98.
108 Lincoln (1975).
109 Ibid. 128.
110 Ibid. 123.
111 Trans. Donniger (1981).
112 Lincoln (1975) 139.
113 Parker (2011) 140.
114 Dougherty (2006) 36.
116 See also Seaford's (2004) 39–47 discussion of the shared language and practices surrounding the division of war spoils and sacrificial shares.
116 A similar overlap in language is typical elsewhere. In Homer's description of the quarrel over sovereignty between Zeus, Poseidon and Hades, the brothers agree to draw lots and to decide who will reign respectively over Heaven, Hades and the Sea. The allotment is described through the term δατέομαι 'distribute' and μείρομαι 'apportion the destinies' (*Il.* 15.189). Gods and men are also frequently said to possess different destinies (μοῖρα) or the near equivalent, μόρσιμος. Apollo, for example, warns an overzealous Achilles (*Il.* 22.7–15) that he is not 'μόρσιμος to die'. Aeschylus' Prometheus (933) scorns death for the same reason (933). In both cases the gods express their immortality in terms of their μόρσιμος.
117 Parker (2011) 140. See Wisrhbo (1982) 103 n. 8 for a list of different interpretations.
118 The association between deciding and cutting may seem idiosyncratic, yet it appears in many languages the world over. See Deutscher (2005) 126. Even the English word 'decision' is derived from the Latin *decido* to cut off. This etymology is not transparent in English, but Hesiod appears to be fully aware of the semantic range, describing a literal act of dividing an animal and deciding mankind's destiny.
119 Chlup (2011) argues that a return to the Golden Age 'would mean harmonious co-existence, but one achieved at the expense of abandoning the rules of civilization. The Greeks did not desire to merge with their origins and took care to remind themselves of both faces of Kronus. They knew how difficult origins can be and were grateful enough for their Iron Age, despite bemoaning its hardships once in a while' (98).
120 McClymond (2008) 142.

Chapter 3

1. See Papadopoulou (2014) xi.
2. For a concise comparison of Hesiod's *Theogony* and the *Derveni Theogony*, see Santamaría (2019).
3. Laugrand (1999) 98 cited in Vilaça (2016) 130.
4. Ibycus (fr. 17).
5. See Graf and Johnston (2007) 165–75 for further details on the biography of Orpheus.
6. On the gold tablets see Bernabé and Jiménez San Cristóbal (2008; 2011). On the poetic fragments see Meisner (2018). On Orphism's interaction with philosophy see Betegh (2004).
7. See Betegh (2004) 350–9.
8. Edmonds (2013) 77–82.
9. OF 539. Trans. Herrero de Jáuregui (2015) modified. See also the discussion of this poem in Bernabé (2010). The fragment is often read with the additions of OF 539, 540, 542, 543.
10. Euboules means 'good counsel' while Antauges appears to be a variation on Phanes and means literally 'appear', from ἀνταυγάζω 'expose to the light, illuminate'.
11. This passage is also very Heraclitean and the term exchange ἀμειβομένοιο, for example, recalls Heraclitus DK 22 B 33 and his use of ἀνταμείβομαι. The context of the Heraclitean fragment is also of note. Plutarch (*De E* 388f) also cites Heraclitus as a means of understanding the allegorical meaning of an Orphic myth. See Finkelberg (2017) 140. More than the exact words, the sentiment as a whole is reminiscent of Heraclitus' long list of names for the one god in DK 22 B 67 and in particular the explanation: ἀλλοιοῦται δὲ ὅκωσπερ ὁκόταν συμμιγῇ θυώμασιν, ὀνομάζεται καθ' ἡδονὴν ἑκάστου / it alters as when mingled with perfumes, it gets named according to the pleasure of each. Trans. Kahn (1981). Alongside the similar imagery and sentiment, note that Orpheus' use of ἀλλάσσω is similar to Heraclitus' ἀλλοιόω.
12. This view is not uncommon in Orphic poetry and in an Orphic *Hymn to Zeus*, which is part of the same poetic tradition as the *Derveni Theogony*, Porphyry explains 'they supposed Zeus to be the mind of the world, and that he created all things therein, containing the world in himself' (τὸν γὰρ Δία τὸν νοῦν τοῦ κόσμου ὑπολαμβάνοντες, ὃς τὰ ἐν αὐτῷ ἐδημιούργησεν ἔχων τὸν κόσμον). Eusebius, *Praep. Ev.* 3.9.2 (OF 243 I B = OF 168 K). Trans. Meisner (2015).
13. Rowe (1980) 15.
14. Finkelberg (2017) 258.
15. Betegh (2004) 221.
16. Ibid.

17 Alderink (1981) 30.
18 Burkert (1985) 131 cited in Meisner (2015) 155.
19 Schopenhauer, for example, rejected Spinoza's pantheism because in his view 'to *call the world "God" is not to explain it*; it is only to enrich our language with a superfluous synonym for the word "world."'; cited in Levine (1994) 27. Dawkins (2006) more recently repeats a similar criticism, referring to pantheism as 'sexed up atheism' (40).
20 Drozdek (2007) 41.
21 Owen (1971) 65. See Levine (1994) 2. Another helpful study on poetry and pantheism is Maffie's (2014) study of Aztec pantheism esp. 79–137.
22 Holbraad and Willerslev (2007).
23 China is mentioned by Descola (2013a) 206 based on the work of Granet (1934) as the key example of analogism. He does not, however, develop this idea in much detail. While analogies proliferate in China, many scholars such as Jullien (2015) and Lloyd and Sivin (2002) describe the importance of processes. Puett (2002) posits a dynamic debate present in Chinese philosophy between continuity and discontinuity. China might still resemble an analogistic system in many respects, yet if its fundamental (or at least a major) stress is on continuity, it hardly makes sense to classify it as an ontology defined in terms of discontinuity. Arguably similar 'hybrid systems' occupy a significant presence globally and appear without always dominating in hierarchal societies or emerging hierarchies in India, Greece and perhaps among the Aztecs. It should, however, be noted that these ontologies remain debated. Descola (2013a), for example, describes the Aztecs as analogistic, while Maffie (2014), with no reference to Descola's work, discusses their cosmology as a form of pantheism.
24 Descola (2013a) 365.
25 Scott (2014) continues: 'it is striking, in fact, that Descola's four modes of identification, graphed at intervals throughout the book with increasing elaboration as a grid in four quadrants, does not appear to cognize the possibility of continuity of interiority and continuity of physicality at the scale of an all-inclusive, or indeed, infinite cosmos. In the only mode of identification with double continuity – totemism – this double continuity applies only within each totemic class and not across the totemic system as a whole. Where then might we locate a truly cosmic double continuity on Descola's grid?'(15).
26 Matthews (2017); Scott (2014); Puett (2002).
27 Matthews (2017) 280. This is certainly a possibility and apart from the somewhat arbitrary subdivisions within Descola's otherwise more logical schema, it is worth remembering that analogism and totemism were once merged as a single grouping in Descola's earlier triadic model.
28 Finkelberg (2017) 247 calls this a 'common conceptual scheme'.

29 Finkelberg (1986) 325.
30 Trans. Morand (2015).
31 See Morand (2015) 214–18. The details are very similar to Damascius' description or Protogonos from the *Rhapsodies* (OF 80 I B Damascius, *De Principiis* 123 bis).
32 John Malalas in his *Chronographia* describes it as an 'an eastern word' meaning life-giver, Ζωοδοτήρ (4. 91).
33 As Burkert (2004) 82, this could be read as 'Man-and-boy-thyrsos'.
34 The word Protogonos is clearly legible in the tablet yet there is some debate regarding to whom this title refers. The text is composed of disjointed words, interspersed with unintelligible letters. Crucially, however, the plate begins with a clear reference to Protogonos and later more ambiguously mentions Phanes. This important fourth-century gold tablet until very recently has played a rather marginal role in this debate. Guthrie (1993), for example, notes that Diodorus is the first to mention the god 'unless indeed it is included in the jumble of deities invoked in the weird and unintelligible inscription of the gold tablet unearthed in South Italy and known as the Timpone Grande tablet ... but it must remain doubtful' (96). Betegh and Bernanbé discuss this tablet, but attempt to distance Protogonos from Phanes. Betegh (2011) 222, for example, associates Protogonos with Ouranos. This is in part based on the clear appearance of Gaia and absence of Ouranos in the gold tablet. This argument is not convincing when applied to such a fragmented text and one cannot help feeling that Betegh is attempting to square the Protogonos of the gold tablet with his reading of the *Derveni Theogony*. This forcing of the evidence is also true of Bernabé's (2008) 142–4 identification of Phanes in the Timpone Grande tablet with Dionysus, based on a puzzling reference in Diodorus 1.11.2. Bremmer (2013), on the other hand, considers the tablet as obvious: 'Protogonos needs no illustration, as he is a familiar Orphic figure' (43). Aside from the co-presence of Protogonos and Phanes in the tablet, one of the few legible statements is an epitaph associated with the god in later poetry, σὺ κλυτὲ δαῖμον (OF 140). This recalls Erikapaeus' description as περικλυτός in OF 140 = Proclus *in Plato Tim I*. For the importance of the plate in general see Santamaría (2016a) 208–9.
35 OF 65 = Frag. 758a.1103–8. See West (1983) 111–12. That Orpheus recited the theogony is conjectural, though plausible. He is not only a character in the tragedy but the setting is also in Thrace. As Bremmer (2011) 4 points out, another fragment from the same play discusses how Euneus is given a music lesson by Orpheus. This would be an ideal time to recite a theogony.
36 Trans. O'Neill, Jr. (1938).
37 OF 80.1. See also OF 123.4, 136, 102.3, 143. See Santamaría (2016a) 211. The comparison has not proven convincing to all and Betegh, for example, argues that Aristophanes' cosmology is an eclectic mix where no detail can be securely identified as Orphic or anything else. It is true, as Betegh (2004) 149 points out, that

details such as the egg also appear in Epimenides, yet it should be stressed that if these ideas really were so common at the time, and are clearly a major feature of later Orphic theogonies, they are likely to have been present in early Orphic poetry too.

38 See Santamaría (2016b). The idea is far from conclusive but there are some clear echoes of Orphic poetry, such as Plato's paraphrase of the Orphic oath of secrecy (*Symp.* 218b).
39 See also DK 31 B 134.
40 Cornford (1937) 56 suggests Empedocles has either arms or wings. Rowett (2013) 26 refers to wings but does not explain why. A similar ambiguity appears in Pherecydes and KRS (1957) note in relation to Pherecydes' winged oak tree that 'the oak is winged partly at least because of the spreading, winglike appearance of these same branches' (65).
41 For further possible similarities between Empedocles and Orpheus see Riedweg (1997) and Chapter 4.
42 See Santamaría (2016a). It is difficult to say with any certainty which names and features Protogonos had acquired by this early date. The lack of secure references could be read as implying that Protogonos was only partially developed in early Orphism. It is certainly true that the god acquired more names and features with time, however, rather than endorsing a teleological path towards a supergod fully described in the Hellenistic period or even later, I argue that Protogonos' tendency towards growth both in terms of forms and names is part of his character from the beginning.
43 The most thorough and convincing defence is offered by Santamaría (2016a); however, the controversy is now so entrenched I doubt this will be the last word.
44 Homer uses it, for example, of firstborn lambs (*Il.* 4.101–3).
45 Trans. Betegh (2004).
46 See for example αἰδοίη βασίλεια Hom. *Od.* 18.314; βασιλεῦσιν ἅμ' αἰδοίοισιν Hes. *Theog.* 80. Santamaría (2016a) 149–50 gives many more examples.
47 West (1983) 85 argues that αἰδοῖον in the poem refers to the reverend one and that the commentator's reading is part of his allegorical method, moving between the similar terms 'reverend' and 'phallus' and making the final association with the sun because the phallus is a generative source. Bernabé (2002) 106 considers the three-step identification process too complicated for the commentator. However, while the logic of this identification is difficult, I do not think it is too complicated. The punning of reverend and phallus was already used by his favourite philosopher, Heraclitus (DK 22 B15), and arguably the commentator simply illustrates his ingenuity through this complex identification. Still, we might wonder, why not directly equate the reverend one with the sun, as later authors did, and leave out the phallus altogether. Santamaría (2016) 141–3 has recently attempted to surmount the

problem and preserve the understanding of both poem and commentator by arguing that the commentator does not in fact make an equation with αἰδοῖον but is using an analogy. Thus, when he says αἰδοίωι εἰκάσας τὸν ἥλιο[ν·], 'εἰκάζω means "compare to", not "identify with"'. In other words, the commentator likens the sun to the phallus, he does not identify the two. Rather his aim is simply to identify the reverend one to the sun, by expressing that, like a phallus, it is a generative principle. It should also be pointed out that the understanding of αἰδοῖον in col. 16.1 is entirely dependent on one's interpretation of col. 13.

48 Those who argue for the presence of Protogonos–Phanes include West (1983) 85; Brisson (2003); Kouremenos (2006) 26–8; Laks and Most (1997); Parker (1995); Sider (2014); Santamaría (2016a) and Chrysanthou (2020). In their estimation the firstborn god in the Derveni papyrus is identical or similar to Protogonos–Phanes of the later *Rhapsodies*. The second group take the neuter noun αἰδοῖον meaning phallus and include Burkert (1992) 90–2; Bernabé (2002b); Betegh (2004) 120–2. The reading has also proved more influential in discussions that do not deal specifically with textual problems in the Derveni papyrus, such as Edmonds (2013) 169 and Miguel Herrero de Jaguregui (2010) 298 n. 3.

49 Trans. Betegh (2004) modified.

50 The translation is debated and Laks and Most (1997) translate col. 13. 4 as 'who was the first to leap forth into aether'. Although the term aither is in the accusative, Betegh notes 'the accusative can, in principle, here mean two things. It can either mean the source or the direction of the movement described by the verb ... on either construal, it is clear that the aither must have existed before the birth of the "first-born"' (154–5).

51 OF 124 = Procl. *in Plat. Tim.* I 433.31; OF 125 = Lactant. *Divin. inst.* 1.5.5.

52 OF 121 = Dam. *De princ.* 123. See also OF 123 I = Hermias, *in Plat. Phaedr.* 148.25 Couvr.

53 Betegh (2004) 113.

54 Burkert (2004) 92–3. Bernabé (2007) 107–8 argues for a similar reading. Santamaría (2016a) points out 'this meaning and construction is unparalleled in the extant Greek literature' (150).

55 See Betegh (2004) 155. Santamaría (2016a) 150.

56 OF 174 = (I) Alex. Aphrod. *in Aristot. Metaph.* 821.19. Parker (1995) 491. See also Kouremenos et al. (2006) 28 and West (1983) 233. Betegh (2004) 118–19 points out that in this case the sentence is qualified by saying 'after his mother Night' and that this does not appear in the Derveni papyrus. This is a fair point, yet the idea of ruling 'first' after someone else still has a rather paradoxical ring to it. Firstness in Orphism, at least when applied to Zeus, means something quite different from Hesiodic poems. Brisson (2003) 28 offers a number of potential parallels, including Proclus' (OF 175 = *in Tim. Ill* 176.18–24) reference to an Orphic poem discussing

the very first marriage (πρώτιστος γάμος) in relation to Gaia and Ouranos, despite the fact that earlier unions existed prior to this. Santamaría (2016a) 56–7 points to an intriguing passage referring to a king who does not rule: Μνημονεύουσι δὲ τῶν χρόνων, ἵνα καὶ τῆς ἐπανόδου δηλώσωσι τὸν καιρὸν, καὶ σαφῶς ἡμᾶς διδάξωσι, ὡς τηνικάδε βασιλεὺς Ἑβραῖος οὐκ ἐβασίλευσε (They [sc. Zacharias and Agaeus] make mention of the time (in which their prophecies began) to declare the moment of the return and to clearly teach us that at this time the Hebrew king did not reign) *Interpretatio in xii prophetas minores* MPG 81, 1876, 17, on *Zacharias* 1.1.

57 In the Kumarbi succession after Atum, the equivalent of Ouranos, is castrated, his son Kumarbi swallows his severed phallus. After the act Kumarbi, a male god, becomes pregnant and gives birth to the Hittite Zeus, Teshub. The narrative indeed describes swallowing a severed phallus, but it does not describe how Teshub recreates the cosmos and in many respects the narrative is closer to Hesiod's *Theogony* than the Derveni poem. On the Hurro-Hittite narrative see López-Ruiz (2010) 90–4.

58 Diogenes Laertius (1.5) has also been used to support this reading: ἐγὼ δέ, εἰ τὸν περὶ θεῶν ἐξ ἀγορεύσαντα τοιαῦτα χρὴ φιλόσοφον καλεῖν οὐκ οἶδα,<οὐδὲ>τίνα δεῖ προσαγορεύειν τὸν πᾶν τὸ ἀνθρώπειον πάθος ἀφειδοῦντα τοῖς θεοῖς προστρῖψαι, καὶ τὰ σπανίως ὑπό τινων ἀνθρώπων αἰσχρουργούμενα τῷ τῆς φωνῆς ὀργάνῳ. 'Now, considering the sort of things he said about the gods, I hardly know whether he ought to be called a philosopher; for what are we to make of one who does not scruple to charge the gods with all human suffering, and even the foul crimes wrought by the tongue amongst a few of mankind.' Trans. Hicks (1972). Betegh (2004) 121 notes that Diogenes Laertius' testimony 'is almost compelling' in favour of his view and certainly for others the comparative material has proven extremely memorable. For example, when Edmonds (2013) 169 n. 20 refers to Betegh's 'cogent arguments', it is not his detailed arguments for reading col.13.4 but the Hittite material that he recalls. See also Burkert (2004) 91. However, the passage has a number of serious problems. For a start, it is unclear if swallowing a severed phallus and αἰσχρουργέω really are equivalents. See Kouremenos (2006) 26 n. 68; Sundell Torjussen (2008) 234; Santamaría (2016a) 162. If we accept that they are, we still have to explain how this event was known to Diogenes Laertius while it eluded everyone else. That the detail was too offensive to be repeated by later poets is not a valid explanation, as the Derveni commentator had no problem elaborating on this detail. At the same time, he was very disturbed by the poem's description of divine incest (col. 26). This squeamishness did not lead to the detail being omitted and later poetry even adds increasingly bizarre details. Even if we assume that Diogenes did know of such a narrative, where did he hear it from? The event is not mentioned by any Platonists and even the Christian apologists, who were particularly eager to point out the heresies of pagan myths, make no reference to this act. However,

Christian apologists do refer to another similar act where Zeus pleasures Hera. See Theophillus of Antioch 3.3. Where Theophillus learned of this event is not specified in this passage, but in 3.8 he links it with an allegorical account by the Stoic Chrysippus. While the event is thus not actually identified with Orpheus, Chrysippus, according to Vellius, allegorically interpreted Orphic myths. See Struck (2004) 118. Moreover, not only was this widely cited in the second century CE by Diogenes' near contemporaries, Chrysippus' description of this act was also known to Diogenes himself and described in his life of Chrysippus (D. L. 7.7 187). It is, for these reasons, very likely that this scene is what Diogenes associates with Orpheus' Zeus rather than the swallowing of Ouranos' phallus.

59 Apart from his impressive description in the *Orphic Hymns* (*OH* 6) and presence in the *Hymn to Zeus* known to Porphyry (OF 243), Platonist commentators provide a great deal of information about this figure. Damascius even dedicates two chapters to the firstborn god in Orphic theologies in his *Problems and Solutions Concerning First Principles* (Ahbel-Rappe (2010) 123–4). Here he describes the *Rhapsodies*, which he sees as the standard version, a very brief description of a theogony referred to by Eudemos (a pupil of Aristotle), and finally a fuller description of a theogony by Hieronymus and Hellanicus. The second major source is gleaned from the numerous digressions made by Proclus in his commentaries on Plato. Dates are difficult to specify with any certainty. On these figures see West (1983) 176–8. Damascius wrote in the sixth century BCE; however, the material he quotes from is much earlier. According to Bernabé (2010) 423 the *Rhapsodies* may date to the first century BCE, Hieronymus to the second century BCE, Eudemos to the fourth century BCE.

60 Betegh (2004) 140; Edmonds (2013) 142.

61 West (1983) remains the most ambitious reconstruction of the main Orphic theogonies.

62 See Damascius *de principiis* 123. I am unable to follow West's (1983) 116–39 reasons for constructing the Eudemean theogony based on Plato's *Timaeus* and Apollodorus' *Bibliotheka*.

63 Even the sceptical Edmonds (2013) 72–3 notes a certain family resemblance among the different texts.

64 The initial stage before Protogonos shows the most significant disagreements in the multiple accounts. Hieronymus' version appears to have given a greater role to the god Chronos and to some extent blurred his characteristics with those of Protogonos. See West (1983) 224 for a brief comparison.

65 Ibid. 68–116.

66 Betegh's (2004) 93 methodology excludes this kind of comparison as a vicious circle and argues for a 'close reading of the papyrus itself' and 'preference to the internal evidence in the reconstruction of the poem in all those cases where this procedure does not result in untenable consequences' (93–4). Due to the multiple directions in

which the internal evidence points, this is not in fact possible. It is worth contrasting his position with Rusten (1985), who argues that 'the events of the Derveni Theogony (although not its individual verses) can be assumed to be largely identical with those in the later poem ascribed to Orpheus (called the *Rhapsodies*) which the Neoplatonists Proclus and Damascius quote and summarize at length. Therefore the fragments of these poems have considerable (although not absolute) authority for reconstructing the text of the poem which the commentator had before him' (122).
67 Trans. Parker (1995) modified. OF 241 = Procl. *in Plato. Tim.* I 324.14.
68 Trans. Betegh (2004) modified.
69 I should stress that sharing the phrase 'μάκαρες θεοὶ ἠδὲ θέαιναι' would hardly be compelling if taken in isolation. As Sider (2014) 246 points out, this is a variation on a Homeric phrase appearing for example in *Od.* 8.341. However, when these phrases appear in an identical context, the possibility of shared influence is almost certain.
70 Parker (1995) 491. Meisner (2015) 291 also points out the shared use of [θεῶν] τροφὸς ἀμβροσίη Νύξ Proclus (OF 112 I B = *in Plat. Cratyl.* 92.9).
71 Trans. Betegh (2004).
72 See Santamaría (2016a) 150–1 and n. 56 for further examples.
73 OF 126 = *Et. M.* 287.29–32. See Meisner (2015) 277.
74 There is no evidence in favour or against the idea that Night has multiple births in the *Derveni Theogony*. Meisner (2015) rejects the idea as a Platonist invention (285–97). This is possible, although phrases like 'thrice born' are Orphic and Dionysus is described as such in the *Hymns* (30.2).
75 This figure occupies an important role in the *Rhapsodies* and Hieronymian account. See OF 66 = Procl. *in Plat. Resp.* 2.138.8 Kroll.
76 See Herrero de Jáuregui (2010) 301. The most famous example of this is found in Plato *Ti.* 30a.
77 OF 539 = Macrob. *Sat* 1.23.21.
78 The sequence in the *Rhapsodies* is somewhat complex and involves three Nights. See West (1983) 70; Betegh (2004) 141–2. The first is a primordial goddess, the second Phanes produces by mating with himself. Afterwards, he mates with Night and gives birth to the rest of the next generation, including Ouranos and Gaia. The presence of multiple gods with the same name is not something we can discount in the *Derveni Theogony* and introduces a potential difficulty in reconstructing it on a logical basis.
79 Another, more indirect argument in support of Protogonos as the father of Night emerges in the broad similarities between Protogonos' and Zeus' creations. The Derveni poem describes how Zeus is the son of Rhea (26.9). However, since Zeus has by this stage eaten the cosmos and recreated it, Rhea is in a sense his daughter. He then mates with her and produces Persephone. It is at least a possibility that this

event, like in the *Rhapsodies*, is a doublet of Protogonos' original incestuous acts. Chrysippus (fr. 1078, 1081 SVF) may have made this connection and according to Philodemus he wrote about Orpheus and other poets that ἅπαντά τ' ἐστιν αἰθήρ, ὁ αὐτὸς ὤν καὶ πατὴρ καὶ υἱός, ὥς κἂν τῷ πρώτῳ μὴ μάχεσθαι τὸ τὴν Ῥέαν καὶ μητέρα τοῦ Διὸς εἶναι καὶ θυγατέρα. 'Everything is aither, which itself is both father and son, so that even at the start it does not conflict that Rhea is both the mother of Zeus and his daughter.' Trans. Meisner (2015) 147–8.
80 Santamaría (2019) 49–51.
81 Bernabé (2007) 106; Betegh (2004) 168. Indeed, Night takes the mother-like role further than Hesiod and where Gaia's character is somewhat temperamental, Night is consistently helpful.
82 Damascius' *First Principles* (123–4) is one of the main sources. However, as the book is specifically concerned with first principles, after an excellent discussion of the primordial gods the author loses interest. In the Hieronymian version, Ouranos and Gaia emerge from the two fragments of Protogonos' egg. See West (1983) 180. The detail is derived from Athenagoras (*Leg.* 18.4) This is not the case in either the *Derveni Theogony* (col. 14.6) or the *Rhapsodies*, which both note that Ouranos is the son of Night (OF 149). OF 149 = Herm. *in Plat. Phaedr.* 154.23.
83 Bernabé (2007) 108.
84 See Sider (2014) 243–4.
85 The latter three are all mentioned in the papyrus but their genealogical position can only be guessed.
86 Herrero de Jáuregui (2010) 318. This strategy of identification, as Herrero de Jáuregui points out, is common in the later Orphic *Hymns* where 'typical series of strung-together epithets make it possible to also juxtapose the names of gods, who are thus very tangibly identified with one another, without need for explanation, more by mystical intuition than by logical reasoning'.
87 Trans. Betegh (2013) modified.
88 This does not appear to be from the theogony itself but taken from an early and otherwise unpreserved collection of hymns.
89 Herrero de Jáuregui (2015) notes: 'we must assume, therefore, that the syncretistic strategy that it deploys is also present in early Orphic hymns. In fact, such a strategy is present already in the line quoted by the Derveni commentator from "the Orphic hymns": Δημήτηρ [Ῥ]έα Γῆ Μή[τ]ηρ ⟨τε καὶ⟩ Ἑστία Δηιώι' (240).
90 Betegh (2004) 190. Moreover, the idea that two or more gods are the same is demonstrably early and appears for example in Aeschylus' *P.V.* 311–13. See Seaford (1986).
91 In fact, the commentator disliked the content so much that in col. 26 he attempts unsuccessfully to explain the detail away.
92 Sahlins (2011) 87.

93 Trans. Betegh (2004).
94 The quotation consists of two fragments from the Derveni papyrus: the first half is taken from col. 18.12, while the second line is quoted in full in col. 17.12. The phrase as a whole is repeated in an almost identical form in the Orphic *Hymn to Zeus* preserved in *De Mundo* (401a–b) and it is likely that the phrase as a whole was present in the Derveni poem. The idea of Zeus as the breath of all sounds Stoic, but is already found in the Derveni papyrus (col. 18.2) where air is called breath, and more generally in col. 18 where the commentator identifies the Moira with Zeus and breath.
95 Trans. Betegh (2004).
96 See West (1983) 218; 239.
97 Bernabé (2007) 114.
98 Betegh (2004) 174.
99 Edmonds (2013) 170. See also Betegh (2004), who takes the phallus reading and notes: 'the same logic works also if we take it that Zeus swallows not Ouranos' phallus but Phanes, as Phanes is customarily identified with Eros' (174).
100 There is a tendency to pass over the many obscurities entailed in eating 'a principle of all generation'. While Betegh and Bernabé do not say it directly, I think it is implicit in their arguments that the phallus is a principle of all generation not in a literal sense but a symbolic one. It is a part of Ouranos, a metonymy standing for power and generation. This may be the case and this understanding of the phallus has an early advocate in the commentator himself (col. 13.6–9). I am, however, sceptical whether the poet, if a phallus was present in the poem at all, made the leap from *a* generative power to *the* generation of all.
101 Once again the Orphic poem is very similar, even as it significantly transforms the meaning of Hesiod's text. In Orpheus and Hesiod, both acts of swallowing a divinity occur on the cusp of Zeus' new reign and involve solving a problem in the universe. Indeed, the scenes were so closely associated that Protogonos may even take on the name Metis (col. 15.6) at this point, as occurs in later poems. See Betegh (2005) 113.
102 Like Hesiod, this act is simple but effective. Zeus can be born first, because he literally swallows priority, combining and internalizing the god. Guthrie (1952) in his discussion of the *Rhapsodies* also sees the Orphic answer in such transparent terms. As he puts it, 'there is no subtlety about the answer. Zeus swallows Phanes, and with Phanes, who is the first-born, and origin of all, he may be regarded as taking into himself all things that exist' (81). On the other hand, if the text refers to the phallus of the firstborn god, this idea and our understanding of the coherence of the Orphic narrative is lost. In this respect, scholars who wish to downplay later parallels and adopt the phallus reading have a good deal of work remaining. They cannot assume a neat equivalence between the phallus and creation but must

explain why Zeus becomes first and why this act involves an internalization of the cosmos. In both cases there is nothing obvious in these associations.

103 Note the related expression φύω in the *Rhapsodies* (OF 241). Προσφύω is more specific and West (1983) 88–9 illustrates its meaning with an example from the *Odyssey* (12.433) where Odysseus hangs from a tree. Sider (2014) on the other hand, citing the same Homeric example, gives an almost opposite reading and argues that 'the verb usually indicates close/tight attachment of something that still retains its dissecting nature' (256).

104 West agrees that the passage and vocabulary point in this direction, but rejects the reading because 'whatever Protogonos represents, there is no suggestion that he was identified with the world and with the totality of gods' (89). However, since almost everything we know about the early Protogonos comes from this paragraph, should we not take this suggestion seriously? This idea, it may be noted, has a close parallel in the dialectic between the one and the many in Empedocles. Here too the Sphere's unity and dissolution is described in terms of all things growing together and apart (DK 31 B 17). See Chapter 4.

105 Although the imagery evokes the ourobouros or serpent that eats its own tail, there is no indication that the Derveni author had this specific image in mind. However, later Orphic poems frequently use snake imagery. Athenagoras' summary in *Plea for the Christians*, probably drawing on the Hieronymos theogony, describes the scene in vivid serpentine imagery: 'or who will admit that Phanes himself, being a first-born god (for he it was that was produced from the egg), has the body or shape of a snake, or was swallowed by Zeus, so that Zeus might be infinite?' (18.4) and later describes Zeus' mating with Rhea in similar lines: 'and how he persecuted his mother Rhea when she refused to wed him, and, she becoming a she-snake, and he himself being changed into a snake, bound her with what is called the Heraclean knot, and mated with her – of which the rod of Hermes is a symbol; and again, how he violated his daughter Persephone, in this case also assuming the form of a snake, and became the father of Dionysus' (18.3). Trans. Herrero de Jáuregui (2010).

106 Bernabé (2002b) too describes the scene in time-travelling terms: 'en avalant le phallus du Ciel, suivant les prophéties de la Nuit et de son père Kronos, Zeus remonte dans le temps, il remonte à l'origine et redémarre l'histoire de l'univers, en devenant la « nouvelle mère » de celui qui avait été l'aîné. Si le Ciel a bien été le premier né, Zeus, en quelque sorte, pour avoir introduit le phallus du Ciel dans son sein, devient lui-même l'ascendant de ce premier être, tout en ayant été le dernier-né' (115). An extreme version of the bootstrap paradox, in some respects similar to the Derveni poem, occupies a prominent place in the film *Predestination* (2014). The narrative depicts a woman who gives birth to a child with two sets of genitals and is raised as a girl, Jane. Jane later transitions to a man, John, and is hired as a special agent who prevents terrorist attacks by going back in time. It later turns out

that Jane/John was chosen for this role precisely because of the unusual circumstances surrounding his/her birth. At some point John realizes the story of his birth and having travelled back in time impregnates Jane. The child that is born is Jane/John.

107 West (1983) denies that Zeus should be equated with Phanes in this scene because Zeus has 'two eyes, not four, and no other evident peculiarities; besides, he is called the son of Kronos' (240 n. 23). I do not think that the identification needs to be one-to-one to indicate that Zeus is being deliberately depicted with features associated with the firstborn god in the poem.

108 Trans. Betegh (2004). See Betegh (2004) 258–9 for a discussion of the cyclic cosmos.

109 Betegh (2004) 200–1.

110 Trans. Betegh (2004).

111 The word is also used in reference to Zeus' contriving Okeanos (col. 23.4).

112 See Leitao (2012) 107; Burkert (2004) 95. Proclus uses the same term to describe Protogonos' creation (*in Plat. Tim.* 2.48.15, 2.282.11, 3.142.12; OF 155 I–III B): μήσατό δ' ἄλλην γαῖαν ἀπείριτον, ἥν τε Σελήνην ἀθάνατοι κλήζουσιν, ἐπιχθόνιοι δέ τε Μήνην, ἣ πόλλ' οὔρε' ἔχει, πόλλ' ἄστεα, πολλὰ μέλαθρα. 'And he contrived another boundless earth, which the immortals call Selene, and those who live upon the earth call it Mene (moon), which has many mountains, many cities, and many houses.' Trans. Meisner (2015). See West (1983) 210 n. 111.

113 OF 155 = (I) Procl. *in Plat. Tim.* II 48.

114 Trans. Graham (2010). On the possible connections between Parmenides and Orphism see Ferella (2019).

115 Trans. Graham (2010).

116 For a discussion of this passage see Bicknell (1989).

117 Trans. Kahn (1981). The reconstruction of the text is debated. Diels supplies πῦρ. My reading follows Kahn (1981).

118 My reconstruction is close to West (1983) 100 and notably differs somewhat from the better-known reconstructions of Betegh (2004) and Bernabé (2007). This is in a large part because of the disagreement on where to locate Protogonos. Bernabé argues that Night is a primordial goddess. Night is clearly an early figure but her status as the starting point of the poem is not clear but assumed, based on comparisons with the Eudemian theogony. This assumption is no stronger than the comparison between the Derveni papyrus and the *Rhapsodies*, and in fact considerably weaker in that we know almost nothing about the Eudemian theogony. See Damascius *De principiis* 123. On the other hand, as noted above, we can pinpoint some almost exact parallels from the Derveni poem and the *Rhapsodies*. The primordial place of Night is also problematic because of the clearly important and early presence of Aither.

119 Bernabé (2010).

Chapter 4

1 OF 220 = Olymp. *in Phaed.* I.3 = OF 220K = 227iv + 299vii + 304i + 313ii + 318iii + 320iB).
2 Trans. Graf and Johnston (2007) modified.
3 Burkert (1985) notes: 'one should therefore concede that the myth of the dismemberment of Dionysus is relatively old and well known among the Greeks but was consciously kept secret as a doctrine of the mysteries' (298). Edmonds (2013) 299 is critical of the ancient silence and compares it to a modern conspiracy theory. I find this attitude puzzling, as ancient silence on the mysteries is clearly a real issue, appearing as early as Herodotus (2.171) in his discussion of Egyptian rites. The idea of Orphic secrecy is evident from the opening formula of the *Derveni Theogony* ordering the uninitiated to 'put doors to their ears' (col. 7.9). This oath is also possibly referred to by Plato (*Phd.* 62b) and certainly by Diodorus (3.62.8). The secrecy is also clear from Clement of Alexandria's wish to divulge the Bacchic mysteries in the *Protrepticus* (2.12.1–2–23.1).
4 Trans. Oldfather (1935).
5 Trans. Edmonds (2011).
6 OF 220 = (I) Olymp. *in Plat. Phaed* 1.3.
7 Comparetti (1882).
8 OF 296 = Procl. *in Plat. Tim.* I 408; OF 297 = Procl. *Theol. Plat.* 5; OF 298 = Tzetz. *Ex.* II. p. 26, 1; OF 299 = Procl. *in Plat. Cratyl.* 55; OF 300 = Procl. *in Plat. Tim.* III 316.
9 OF 312 = Clem. Alex. *Protr.* 2, 18, 1; OF 313 = Plut. *De esu carn.* I 7.
10 OF 318 = Clem. Alex. *Protr.* 2, 18, 2; OF 320 = Olymp. *in Plat. Phaed.* 1, 3. For this reconstruction see Graf and Johnston (2007) 67.
11 Harrison (1903); Rohde (1898); Nilsson (1935). For later scholars who support this myth see Guthrie (1952); Detienne (1979); Alderink (1981); Parker (1995); Bernabé (2002a); Graf and Johnston (2007).
12 Wilamowitz-Moellendorff (1931/1932); Linforth (1941).
13 For more on the history of Orphic scholarship see Graf and Johnston (2007) 50–65; Edmonds (2011) 3–14.
14 For the Orphic origin of the tablets and a discussion of the evidence see Bernabé and Jiménez San Cristóbal (2011) 68–101.
15 Parker (1995); Bernabé (2002); Graf and Johnston (2007).
16 Edmonds (1999) 66. Edmonds' position has been repeatedly refined and culminates in (2013).
17 Edmonds' (2013) sceptical attitude is more precisely targeted at what he calls the four elements which he argues define the modern myth. These are 'the dismemberment of Dionysus Zagreus by the Titans, the punishment of the Titans by Zeus, the generation

of human beings from the ashes of the lightning-blasted Titans, and the burden of guilt that human beings inherited from their Titanic ancestors because of this original sin' (297). For two recent evaluations of this position, see Meisner's (2018) 237–78 balanced assessment of Edmond's position and Chrysanthou's (2020) 85–112 more critical approach. Meisner (2015) offers a fair discussion of the strengths and weaknesses of Edmonds' work, concluding in partial agreement, noting: 'despite the claim that the anthropogony is a lynch pin by both Orphic adherents and critics, I propose no such details are necessary. I attempt to explain how the myth fits into the Rhapsodic narrative, so that then we might see how the *Rhapsodies* as a whole fit into Orphism. From this perspective, the story of Dionysus being killed by the Titans is indeed one of the most important episodes of the Rhapsodic narrative, but it might not be the central point; rather, it could be read as the last of a series of episodes that culminate in Zeus securing his royal power' (350).

18 Bernabé (2010) 423.
19 A clear knowledge of the myth and similar allegorical interpretations are found in Damascius' commentary on the *Phaedo* I.4–11; Plotinus' *Enneads* 4.3.12; Plutarch's *On Eating Meat* (996b–c); Dio Chrysostom (30.10); and Xenokrates (*Aët. Plac.* I.7.30), fr. 20 Heinze. Even the sceptical Edmonds (1999) recognizes that 'it seems likely that Xenokrates, like Plutarch, was explaining the myth as an allegory of the punishment of a human soul that eats meat' (46). I intend to treat the importance and coherence of the Neoplatonist evidence elsewhere.
20 Diodorus (3.62.6–8). Philodemus (OF 59 I–II) discusses Euphorion's (275 BCE) discussion of the myth. For a discussion of these sources see Henrichs (2011) and Chrysanthou (2020) 91–2.
21 Indeed, although the evidence is indirect, Plato's engagement with Orphism also suggests knowledge of an Orphic theogony including six generations (*Philib.* 66c), a central obsession with crime and punishment associated with the soul (*Cratylus* 400c), and a poem featuring Zeus as beginning, middle and end (*Leg.* 715e–716a). See Santamaría (2016b) 220.
22 Hocart (1987) 16.
23 See Bernabé and Jiménez San Cristóbal (2008) 68–101.
24 See below for further details.
25 On Comparetti and the history of Orphic scholarship more generally see Graf and Johnston (2007) 50–65; Edmonds (2011) 3–14.
26 Bernabé and Jiménez San Cristóbal (2011) present a nice example of Hocart's methodology: 'all these arguments form a mass of evidence which can neither be associated with any other known religious movement, nor be arbitrarily segmented. On the contrary, it agrees perfectly with the image that we have nowadays of Orphism. The evident conclusion which arises from all these considerations is that the gold leaves can only be Orphic' (101).

27 West (1983) 94 argues that this was a means of ending a papyrus roll and that the text continued on another destroyed papyrus.
28 On the ritual context of the Derveni papyrus see Bernabé (2014). Apart from the rites described by the author, the book itself was probably burned as part of a ritual similar to that alluded to by Euripides (*Hipp.* 952–7).
29 Xenokrates (*Aët. Plac.* I.7.30) in a confusing discussion regarding the partnership between Rhea and Zeus strengthens this claim. The union between Zeus and his mother is not part of mainstream mythology and Dillon (2003) 104 concludes that Xenokrates is relying on an Orphic tradition.
30 See Bremmer (2013); Morand (2009).
31 Bernabé and Jiménez San Cristóbal (2008) 156.
32 Ibid. 102 n. 18.
33 The Hellenistic Gurob papyrus also mentions the dismemberment myth and speaks of Eubouleus (18). The name is not exclusively Orphic and Eubouleus is also associated with the Eleusinian mysteries where the name refers to Chthonic Zeus. See Bernabé and Jiménez San Cristóbal (2008) 103–4.
34 See Bernabé and Jiménez San Cristóbal's (2008) 137–50 reconstruction and interpretations; Betegh (2004) 325–48 also interprets the tablet in Heraclitean terms.
35 Betegh (2004) notes: 'to conclude, the fact that most of the intelligible words of this gold tablet, found in the tomb of a cremated person, are indeed catch-words in the Derveni text (air, fire, sun, Zeus, Moira, Ge, mother, Demeter), makes it at least defensible to evoke the evidence of the gold tablets in the interpretation of the papyrus. I would even venture to say that Tablet C might shed some dim light on a religious lore operating with a theory of elements that lays special stress on air and fire, and from which the cosmological theory developed in the Derveni papyrus may have emerged' (337).
36 OF 243 = (I) Euseb. *Praep. Ev.* 3, 8, 2 (= Porph. *On Statues* fr. 354F Smith) Trans. Bernabé and Jiménez San Cristóbal (2008) 146.
37 Trans. Gifford (1903). Col. 17.12.; 18.12: Ζεὺς πρῶτος γένετο, [Ζεὺς ὕστατος ἀργικέραυνος] / Ζεὺς κεφαλή, Ζεὺς μέσσα, Διὸς δ' ἐκ πάντα τέτυκται. 'Zeus was born first, Zeus bearer of lighting is last. Zeus is the head, Zeus the middle, from Zeus are all things made.' Compare with Ps. Aristot. *Mund.* 401a–b.
38 Compare this with col. 17.12 and col. 18.12 of the Derveni papyrus.
39 See discussion in Chapter 3.
40 Hocart (1987) 16.
41 Hocart (1987) 16.
42 Ps. Hes. fr. 51–2 and 54 a–c Merkelbach/West; Primavassi (2008) concludes: 'thus, Empedocles' cycle of the guilty god' shares with the Pythagorean legend the feature of an Olympian god who passes through a series of incarnations, and with the Hesiodic myth the feature of an Olympian who is sent into an earthly exile as a punishment for bloodshed. In both cases, the god in question is Apollo' (262).

43 Trans. Grube (1997).
44 Parker (2014).
45 See Finkelberg (2017) esp. 126–45, who rightly discusses Empedocles, Heraclitus and the Orphics together; Riedweg (1997); Betegh (2004) 170–2; Gheerbrant (2017). Parker (2014) points out the importance of Empedocles in the discussion, noting: 'a reconstruction based on three words of Pindar, five of Plato, one line of one Gold Leaf and a text written a millennium or so later is manifestly fragile. But an Orphic notion of a primal fall would not be as isolated as Edmonds implies: Empedocles tells in his own words how his journey through a cycle of incarnations was caused by a crime in his past life. The important parallel figure of Empedocles is strangely absent, except on points of detail, from Edmonds' account' (para. 12).
46 Lloyd Jones (1980).
47 Indeed for Plutarch (*De esu carn.* 1.7), Empedocles simply rewrote the Orphic myth and incorporated it into his own model.
48 Trans. Graham (2010). On the comparison between Empedocles' Sphere and the Orphic Zeus see West (1983) 108.
49 Trans. Graham (2010).
50 Trans. Graham (2010). The passage appears in Hippol. *Haer.* 7.29.14–23; Plut. *De Exil.* 607c–d.
51 Important manuscript variations exist and there is a debate on whether the text should read φόβος or φόνος. Picot (2007) 55 argues φόβος is the correct reading but I am sceptical for two reasons. First, while Plutarch's text may have been corrupted, it is clear that he associates the crime with meat eating in in *De esu carn.* and associates this with unspecified lines from Empedocles: 'ἀλληγορεῖ γὰρ ἐνταῦθα τὰς ψυχάς, ὅτι φόνων καὶ βρώσεως σαρκῶν καὶ ἀλληλοφαγίας δίκην τίνουσαι σώμασι θνητοῖς ἐνδέδενται' (1.7.) The idea of a meat-eating daimon is also clear from DK 31 B 139. Sedley (2007) 51 argues that not all humans undergo reincarnation, but this is a minority view.
52 This reading depends on how we understand the relationship between Empedocles' 'two poems'. See note 54 below.
53 Lincoln (1975) 128.
54 The precise relation between Empedocles' daimonic tale and his physical cosmology is fiercely debated. A long-standing interpretation argues that Empedocles recites two distinct narratives: one describing the mixing and separation of the four elements and the other discussing a divine murder and cycle of rebirths. However, more recent scholarship has focused on uniting these two strands as part of a single coherent plot. In this reading, the tale of the daimon, like the sacrifice of Dionysus, takes place shortly after the dissolution of the unity of the Sphere. Others seek even closer correspondences. Primavesi (2008), for example, has proposed 'interpreting the Empedoclean account of the transmigratory daimones as a mythological mirror',

noting: 'We may say, then, that the rule of the Sphairos corresponds to the happy state of the god within the community of the blessed ones, the destruction of the Sphairos to his crime and departure, the movement toward complete separation to his punishment, and the movement toward complete unity to his return' (263). In other words, Empedocles' description of the Sphere and society of daimones are two sides of the same coin. Whether we follow Primaversi's mirror model or simply understand the mythological and cosmological tales as part of a single extended narrative is not central to my reconstruction of the Orphic myth. It is sufficient to note that the events either mirror or echo (see Mackenzie 2021, 150-1) each other and that both emphasize how unity results in the creation of a plurality of different forms. On the relation between the two poems see Kahn (1974); this paper was written before the discovery of the Strasbourg papyrus but remains relevant. For a more updated discussion of the two separate poems see Kingsley (1996) and Primaversi (2008). Osborne (1987) and Sedley (2007) 32, however, attempt to align the fragments into a single narrative.

55 Trans. Graham (2010).
56 See for example Plut. *De Defect.* 435c; Plut. *Quaes. Conv.* 729f.
57 Mackenzie (2021) 150-1.
58 Finkelberg (2017) 137 n. 43 points out that Plutarch associates the onset of Strife with the myth of the Titans at *De. Fac.* 926d-e:

> ὥσθ' ὅρα καὶ σκόπει, δαιμόνιε, μὴ μεθιστὰς καὶ ἀπάγων ἕκαστον ὅπου πέφυκεν εἶναι διάλυσίν τινα κόσμου φιλοσοφῇς καὶ τὸ νεῖκος ἐπάγῃς τὸ Ἐμπεδοκλέους τοῖς πράγμασι μᾶλλον δὲ τοὺς παλαιοὺς κινῇς Τιτᾶνας ἐπὶ τὴν φύσιν καὶ Γίγαντας καὶ τὴν μυθικὴν ἐκείνην καὶ φοβερὰν ἀκοσμίαν καὶ πλημμέλειαν ἐπιδεῖν ποθῇς χωρὶς τὸ βαρὺ πᾶν καὶ χωρὶς <θεὶς πᾶν> τὸ κοῦφον.

'So look out and reflect, good sir, lest in rearranging and removing each thing to its "natural" location you contrive a dissolution of the cosmos and bring upon things the "Strife" of Empedocles – or rather lest you arouse against nature the ancient Titans and Giants and long to look upon that legendary and dreadful disorder and discord when you have separated all that is heavy and all that is light.' Trans. Cherniss (1957).

59 Detienne (1979) 73-84.
60 Translations of the gold tablets follow Edmonds (2011).
61 Johnston and Graf (2007) elaborate: 'Thus, an ancient reader of our tablets would have understood the soul's declaration that it was a "child of Earth and starry Sky" to mean that it was claiming an affinity – based on both lineage and nature – with the gods' (114).
62 Casadesús Bordoy (2013) 174. This view has a long history. Nilsson (1935) argues: 'if the soul is, as it must be, the good, divine principle of man, being the tomb of the

soul, must represent the evil part of man' (205–6). Guthrie (1980) 83 also speaks of man's two-fold nature as earthly titanic versus heavenly Dionysus. Alderink (1981) notes: 'the Orphics taught that humans bear a composite nature – partly Titanic (evil and bodily) and partly Dionysiac (good and of the soul)' (66–7); Finkelberg (1986) notes: 'according to this Dionysus was devoured by the earth-born Titans and recreated anew by Zeus; the Titans were blasted by Zeus' thunderbolt and from the ashes arose the race of human beings who therefore consist of both earthly Titanic and heavenly Dionysiac elements. The myth not only provides an anthropogony, but also expresses the eschatological idea of salvation by purifying the soul of the evil, earthly, Titanic element mingled with it' (326). Bernabé and Jiménez San Cristóbal (2008) write of man's 'dual essence, earthly and heavenly' (42). As one moves outside of specialized literature, this dualism has a tendency to be further increased. Eliade (1982), for example, speaks of what he refers to as 'a dualism (spirit/body) very close to the Platonic dualism' and describes how 'according to this myth, man shared both in the Titanic nature and in divinity, since the ashes of the Titans also contained the body of the infant Dionysus' (189–90).

63 Trans. Fowler (1966). Although this view of Plato is typical, Plato discusses the soul in multiple and conflicting ways. Indeed, it is problematic to make general statements on a philosopher who is claimed as both the founder of Cartesian dualism and an advocate of process philosophy. The dualist interpretation, whatever Plato's true position, has influenced modern interpretations of Orphism and I will for this reason use it to clarify my argument. For a critical discussion of Plato's dualism and Descartes see Broadie (2001).

64 The gold tablets also show some striking similarities with the souls described in Plato's eschatological myths which were probably, in part, inspired by Orphic accounts. See Bernabé (2013) for a survey of probable Platonic mythic borrowings.

65 Compare the descriptions of the underworld in Pl. *Resp.* 10.614b –21 with those of the gold tablets.

66 Renehan (1980) argues this in strong terms: 'the attribution to sixth-century "Orphics" and Pythagoreans of a grasp of spiritual reality "in its full incorporeality" lacks foundation. The fallacy here consists in the unconscious assumption that a soul which is independent of, indeed opposed to, the body is therefore free from matter and incorporeal. Later Greeks were to think that way. But before such concepts had become familiar, the inference was by no means automatic. There is in fact no evidence to suggest that any Greek in the sixth century was in a position to define the soul as an immaterial being' (107).

67 Trans. Meisner (2015). Euseb. *Praep. Ev.* 3.11.3–4.

68 Drozdek (2007) 6–8.

69 See Nussbaum (1972); Kahn (1979) 127; Schofield (1991).

70 Betegh (2007); Finkelberg (2017) esp. 104–25, who points toward Aetius 4.3.12 = DK 22 A 15.
71 Trans. Betegh (2007).
72 Kahn (1981) 238. My discussion also is indebted to Betegh (2007) and Finkelberg (2017).
73 Lloyd (1990) 117.
74 Matthews (2017) 282.
75 Ibid. 276.
76 Maffie (2014) 49. The view he notes is similar to what is known as 'neutral monism' and, again making comparisons with *qi*, describes something similar in his description of Aztec pantheism: 'Aztec constitutional monism affirms that reality consists of a tertium quid, a *third kind* of stuff that is *neither* mind *nor* matter (as customarily conceived by dualists). This third kind of stuff is electricity-like energy or power' (48).
77 Betegh (2004) 332–7 makes a convincing case for Heraclitean influence.
78 On the daimonology of these passages see Bernabé (2014); Burkert (2014); Rodríguez (2019).
79 Diog. Laert. 8.32: εἶναί τε πάντα τὸν ἀέρα ψυχῶν ἔμπλεων· καὶ ταύτας δαίμονάς τε καὶ ἥρωας ὀνομάζεσθαι· (the whole air is full of souls which are called daimones or heroes). See Burkert (2014) 111 for further similarities between the two.
80 Janko (1997) 80–7.
81 Trans. Megino (2011). For a more detailed study of this passage see Megino (2011) 23. Iamblichus (*De An.* 8) in his commentary on Aristotle's passage adds some further detail:

> ὥσπερ Ἀριστοτέλης μὲν ἐν τοῖς Φυσικοῖς ἔπεσί φησι λέγεσθαι τὴν ψυχὴν εἰσιέναι ἐκ τοῦ ὅλου ἀναπνεόντων ἡμῶν φερομένην ὑπὸ τῶν ἀνέμων· 'ἔοικέ γεμὴν αὐτὸς ὁ Ὀρφεὺς χωρὶς ὑπολαμβάνειν εἶναι καὶ μίαν τὴν ψυχήν, ἀφ' ἧς πολλὰς μὲν εἶναι διαιρέσεις, πολλὰς δὲ καὶ ἀμέσους ἐπὶ πνοίας καθήκειν ἐπὶ τὰς μεριστὰς ψυχὰς ἀπὸ τῆς ὅλης ψυχῆς. 'Aristotle, it is said in the *Physika* poem that the soul enters into us from the universe, borne by the winds, when we breathe; and it seems certainly that Orpheus himself considered that the soul was separate and one, and that out of it there spring many divisions, and that many intermediary "breaths" descended to the individual souls from the universal soul.' Trans. Finamore and Dillon (2002). See Gagné (2007) for a longer treatment of this passage.

82 Trans. Edmonds (2013). OF 339 = Proc. *in Resp.* 2.339.20–6.
83 Trans. Edmonds (2013). Valens also adds: ψυχὴ δ' ἀνθρώποισιν ἀπ' αἰθέρος ἐρρίζωται 'for humans, the soul derives its roots from the ether' (OF 422). See discussion in Edmonds (2013) 288. Megino (2012) argues that it 'seems clear that we may consider these two passages as the genuine expression of an Orphic conception of the soul preceding Aristotle's time, which is directly connected to pre-Socratic speculation, as Anaximenes, Diogenes of Apollonia and the Pythagoreans attest' (142).

84 Gagné (2007) 7–9 argues that the position from the gold tablets, Aristotle and the Derveni papyrus may even derive from a fifth-century Orphic book known as the *Physica*. He further notes that 'it is in the context of this natural philosophy that the implicit association of breath and soul was first transferred into a systematic equation of soul with air and wind, and many Presocratics of the later fifth century taught that the individual souls were reflections of a single cosmic whole grounded in one of the physical elements. This is exactly the context in which the *Physika* of Orpheus belongs' (13). Whether we accept the existence of the Orphic *Physica* or not, there is much in common between the Orphic evidence and Presocratic views and Aristotle's description of the Orphic soul has much in common with his account of Heraclitus. Aristotle notes (*De An.* 405a24): 'Heraclitus says that the principle is soul, if indeed soul is the exhalation of which everything else is composed.' Trans. Finkelberg (2013) 149. The correspondence, however, entails that we identify Heraclitus' soul with air/breath/exhalation instead of fire. This view has been supported by Kahn (1981), Betegh (2007) and Finkleberg (2017) but remains debated.

85 Renehan (1980) notes: 'there is in fact no evidence to suggest that any Greek in the sixth century was in a position to define the soul as an immaterial being' (107).

86 West (1983) 10 argues that this poem was probably known by Aristotle (fr. 26 Kern).

87 Trans. Kahle (2011).

88 On this passage see Kahle (2012). Betegh (2013) notes that 'there is of course no guarantee that the Orphic rephrasing of B 36 and the Orphic doctrine reported by Aristotle ever formed parts of a coherent and explicit "Orphic theory of the soul". Yet I find it remarkable that they correspond perfectly to the respective parts of the Heraclitean theory as I have tried to reconstruct it' (260).

89 Betegh (2013) notes: 'some relatively early Orphics were impressed directly by the Heraclitean theory of the soul, both that the ψυχή can be identified with the element that extends from the atmospheric air to the heavenly fire and that we receive shares of it by breathing it in' (260).

90 Seaford (2012) stresses that 'the parallelism together with the repeated "now" implies the simultaneity – even the unity – of the opposites of death and rebirth' (235).

91 West (1982) 18 notes that Plato speaks of a very similar process of life changing into death and vice versa in the *Phaedo* (72a): ὁμολογεῖται ἄρα ἡμῖν καὶ ταύτῃ τοὺς ζῶντας ἐκ τῶν τεθνεώτων γεγονέναι οὐδὲν ἧττον ἢ τοὺς τεθνεῶτας ἐκ τῶν ζώντων, τούτου δὲ ὄντος ἱκανόν που ἐδόκει τεκμήριον εἶναι ὅτι ἀναγκαῖον τὰς τῶν τεθνεώτων ψυχὰς εἶναί που, ὅθεν δὴ πάλιν γίγνεσθαι. 'So by this method also we reach the conclusion that the living are generated from the dead, just as much as the dead from the living; and since this is the case, it seems to me to be a sufficient proof that the souls of the dead exist somewhere, whence they come back to life.' Trans. Fowler (1966). West does not comment on these similarities at any length, but it is possible that Plato is elaborating an Orphic idea in this passage.

92 Trans. Kahn (1981).
93 Kahn (1981) argues that the most likely reading of this is that 'mortals live the death of immortals. Immortals are dead in the life of mortals' (217). Betegh (2013) argues that 'the fragment can be mapped seamlessly on the subjects of B 36' (253).
94 Kahn (1981) 216–20.
95 Trans. Graham (2010) modified.
96 Heraclitus' and Empedocles' views on mortality and immortality are also compared by Kahn (1981) and Betegh (2013) 254.
97 The myth is often discussed in terms of the Titans eating Dionysus, but this is the phrase used by Plut. (*De esu carn.* 1.1) and Olymp. (*in Phd.* 1.3). Clement (*Prot.* 2.12.2) more generally speaks of ὠμοφαγία (the eating of raw flesh). On Dionysus' revival see Olymp. 304 I; Proc *Plat. in Resp. II*, 338; Dio Chrys. *Or.* 30.10.
98 West (1983) 165.
99 E.g. OF 474, L 1; OF 476, L 3; OF 477, L 4.
100 Edmonds (2010) 108. The phrase is repeatedly used by Hesiod as such. See *Theog.* 45, 105–6, 154, 421.
101 Xenokrates perhaps meant more generally that the imprisonment was due to the Titanic crime. At any rate, the idea of a Dionysiac element is said only by Olympiodorus, who proposes it as part of his secret reading. Olympiodorus, however, argues that man's body, not his soul, was part Dionysiac (OF 304 I = (I) Olymp. *in Plat. Phaed* 1.3). The majority of Platonists do not follow this position and argue instead that the soul moves between Dionysiac and Titanic states. The Titans represented disunity and Dionysus the possibility of unity.
102 See Inwood (2001) 61.
103 See Rives (2011) 190. Betegh (2014) differentiates the Orphics from the Pythagoreans in terms of Orphism's 'hardcore' attitude and 'complete avoidance of bloodshed' (155–6) compared with the more selective attitude of the Pythagoreans.
104 For the sources on a strict avoidance of meat see Porphyry, *Vit. Pyth.* 7 = Eudoxus F 325 Lasserre; Mnesimachus F 1 Kassel-Austin = Diog. Laert. 8.37; Antiphanes F 133 Kassel-Austin = Ath. 4.161a; Alexis F 223 Kassel-Austin = Ath. 4.161b.; *FGrHist* 134 F 17 = Strabo, *Geog.* 15.1.63–5, C 715–16. See Rives (2011) 200 n. 14–16.
105 On a more selective attitude see Diog. Laert. (8.19), who cites the authority of Aristotle. See also Aristox. fr. 29a Wehrli (Diog. Laert. 8.20) Porph. *VP* 42–5; *Abst.* 1.26; Iambl. *VP* 85. See Gemelli Marciano (2014); 140–1; Rives (2011) 190.
106 See Rives (2011); Betegh (2014) 154–9; Ullucci (2012) 58–61.
107 On the more complicated and conflicting Pythagorean sources see Bernabé (2013); Rives (2011); Betegh (2014); Ullucci (2012) esp. 31–64. While the Pythagorean

sources show a rather complex and selective attitude to animal food, there is a general agreement that the Orphic and Empedoclean evidence is more consistent. A possible exception, however, appears in Euripides' *Cretans* (fr. 472) which may well use some Orphic material and appears to offer a contradictory attitude. On the one hand, it clearly mentions the avoidance of ensouled food ἐμψύχων βρῶσιν. Equally it points towards feasts of raw flesh. Bernabé (2015) argues the passage should be understood in terms of a transition from meat to pure life and that 'the aorists γενόμην (line 10), τελέσας (line 12), ἀνασχών (line 113), ἐκλήθην, and ὁσιωθείς (line 15) refer to a specific action in the past, the initiation ritual, the only time when it would be permissible to eat meat, but only then. Thereafter, the initiate is totally forbidden to eat meat for the rest of his life (except perhaps during a repetition of the ritual)' (198).

108 Herodotus (2.81): οὐ μέντοι ἔς γε τὰ ἱρὰ ἐσφέρεται εἰρίνεα οὐδὲ συγκαταθάπτεταί σφι· οὐ γὰρ ὅσιον. ὁμολογέουσι δὲ ταῦτα τοῖσι Ὀρφικοῖσι καλεομένοισι καὶ Βακχικοῖσι, ἐοῦσι δὲ Αἰγυπτίοισι καὶ Πυθαγορείοισι· οὐδὲ γὰρ τούτων τῶν ὀργίων μετέχοντα ὅσιον ἐστὶ ἐν εἰρινέοισι εἵμασι ταφθῆναι. ἔστι δὲ περὶ αὐτῶν ἱρὸς λόγος λεγόμενος.

'But nothing woolen is brought into temples, or buried with them: that is impious. They agree in this with practices called Orphic and Bacchic, but in fact Egyptian and Pythagorean: for it is impious, too, for one partaking of these rites to be buried in woolen wrappings. There is a sacred legend about this.' Trans. Godley (1920). The passage is debated and one family of manuscripts reduces the phrase from 'Orphic and Bacchic, but in fact Egyptian and Pythagorean' to 'practices called Orphic and Pythagorean'. This is probably due to a scribal error and the reading I have quoted is generally accepted. See Parker (1995) 502.

109 See Edmonds (2013) 348.
110 Trans. Kovacs (1995). For a more detailed study of this passage see Bernabé (2015).
111 Trans. Bury (1967–8) modified.
112 An exception to this is found in *Od.* 14.426. See Bremmer (1983) 125–32.
113 Animals do not appear to play an important role in most Orphic theogonies. However, it is of note that *Hymn 37* directly implicates the creation of animals into the anthropogony:

Τιτῆνες, Γαίης τε καὶ Οὐρανοῦ ἀγλαὰ τέκνα,
ἡμετέρων πρόγονοι πατέρων, γαίης ὑπένερθεν
οἴκοις Ταρταρίοισι μυχῶι χθονός ἐνναίοντες,
ἀρχαί καί πηγαί πάντων θνητῶν πολυμόχθων,
εἰναλίων πτηνῶν τε καὶ οἵ χθόνα ναιετάουσιν·
ἐξ ὑμέων γάρ πᾶσα πέλει γενεά κατὰ κόσμον.

Titans, glorious children of Sky and Earth,
ancestors of our fathers you dwell down below
in Tartarean homes in the bowels of the earth.
From you are descended all toiling mortals,
the brood of the sea and the birds, and those who live on the land.
From you all generations of the world are born.

Trans. Athanassakis and Wolkow (2013). The *Hymns* are a late source and Athanassakis and Wolkow (2013) x suggest the mid-third century CE. However, the idea may well be earlier and another collection of hymns is mentioned in the Derveni papyrus (col. 22.12).

114 Trans. Graham (2010).
115 Κτίλος is often translated as tame or docile, though the term can also mean cherished, as it does, for example, in Pind. *Pyth.* (2.17): ἱερέα κτίλον Ἀφροδίτας 'Aphrodite's cherished priest'.
116 *Plt.* 271e: ὥστε οὔτ᾽ ἄγριον ἦν οὐδὲν οὔτε ἀλλήλων ἐδωδαί, πόλεμός τε οὐκ ἐνῆν οὐδὲ στάσις τὸ παράπαν. 'so that no creature was wild, nor did they eat one another, and there was no war among them, nor any strife whatsoever.' Trans. Fowler (1921).
117 Trans. Fowler (1921).
118 See Gera (2003) 61–7.
119 Trans. Graham (2010).
120 Rives (2011) 193.
121 Plutarch (*De esu carn.* 1 996b), at any rate, understood it as such. As did Proc. *in Resp.* 2.338.10–339.9 (OF 338 B): οὕνεκ᾽ ἀμειβομένη ψυχὴ κατὰ κύκλα χρόνοιο/ ἀνθρώπων ζώιοισι μετέρχεται ἄλλοθεν ἄλλοις/ἄλλοτε μὲν θ᾽ ἵππος, τότε γίνεται/ ἄλλοτε δὲ πρόβατον, τότε δ᾽ ὄρνεον αἰνὸν ἰδέσθαι,/ἄλλοτε δ᾽ αὖ κύνεόν τε δέμας φωνή τε βαρεία,/καὶ ψυχρῶν ὀφίων ἕρπει γένος ἐν χθονὶ δίῃ. 'on account of this a soul returning according to certain cycles of times goes into different animals from humans at different times. One time it becomes a horse, than [. . .]; another time a sheep, then a bird dreadful to behold; another time a canine body and growling voice, and the race of cold serpents creeps upon the divine earth.' Trans. Edmonds (2013). Whether this refers to an early doctrine is unclear and as is often the case with early Orphism, the evidence is strong but circumstantial. For a start, Orpheus, a figure frequently described as talking to animals himself, attributed souls to animals and, like Empedocles, abstained from their flesh. These ideas do not necessarily entail metempsychosis but are frequently associated with it. Further, the idea of metempsychosis would also help make sense of Aristotle's (*De An.* 410b 27–11a 2) description of the Orphic soul as something inhaled by animals, plants and humans. This idea is also strengthened by the presence of a gold tablet from Thurii (OF 488) which describes the deceased escaping from a heavy and difficult

'circle' or 'cycle' (κύκλος); see Dousa (2011) 123. The term κύκλος, given the context, likely refers to a cycle of births and is understood as such by later Platonists. Bernabé and Jiménez San Cristóbal (2011) 78-9 argue this case and point towards Proc. *in Ti* 3.296.7. The term κύκλος is used in reference to Orpheus, metempsychosis, and cycles of time in Proc. *in Resp.* 2.338.10-339.9 (OF 338). However, Edmonds (2013) 289-90 argues that κύκλος may have a more general meaning. Alongside the Orphic fragments, the idea may also be suggested by a passage where Herodotus (2.123) attributes metempsychosis to the Egyptians. As there is little evidence for this belief in Egyptian texts, it is possible that Herodotus has mistakenly inferred the view based on his assumption that the Pythagoreans and Orphics derived their doctrines from Egypt (2.81). See Burkert (1972) 126-8; Edmonds (2013) 283. Finally, we should not neglect the presence of distinctly Orphic details in Plato's descriptions of metempsychosis. As Bernabé (2013) argues in the Myth of Er (621a), for example, Plato describes an underworld journey and springs of water associated with forgetfulness which closely echo the underworld topography of the gold tablets. The myth furthermore features Orpheus himself who chooses to be reborn as a swan (620a). As with Herodotus, it is likely that Plato understood metempsychosis to be an Orphic doctrine. Nonetheless, the issue remains unclear. Bernabé and Jiménez San Cristóbal (2011) 78-9 accept the presence of metempsychosis in early Orphism. Betegh (2014) 154-9 questions it. Edmonds (2013) 280-6 argues that the idea is one of many ideas compatible with the strangeness of Orpheus. Herrero de Jáuregui (2010) in his discussion of later Orphism notes that 'reincarnation seems to have been an open option that Orphism could develop or pass over, and the scarce Christian critiques treat it as such' (342).

122 Descola (2013a) 229-30.
123 Trans. Fowler (1925).
124 Descola (2013a) 239.
125 Trans. Harden (2013). Sextus does not mention Orpheus here, though given the specification of Empedocles and Pythagoras, it is possible that the Orphics are meant by 'the Italian crowd' (τῶν Ἰταλῶν πλῆθος). Indeed, the idea of soul as shared breath has more in common with Orphism than Empedocles. At any rate, his point applies, logically at least, to all pantheists and is true whether or not animals are viewed as reincarnated kin or simply more generally as part of the same encompassing soul stuff which is spread throughout the cosmos.
126 Trans. Graham (2010).
127 Rangos (2012) argues that the 'names of traditional male gods seem to stand for aspects or particular manifestations of Strife' (320). However, this list defies any easy attempt to describe it in terms of a simple opposition between Love and Strife. In general, see Picot (2012). Porphyry's (*Abst.* 2.22) summary, which may draw on

Theophrastus, only discusses the event in relation to Ares and Battle Din: 'I think that when friendship and perception of kinship ruled everything, no one killed any creature because people thought that other animals were related to them. But when Ares and Battle-noise and all kinds of conflict and sources of war were in control, then for the first time no one spared any related creature at all.' Trans. Clark (2000). It is possible that for Empedocles, Kronos and perhaps Poseidon represent sources of conflict. However, to classify Zeus as an agent of Strife verges on blasphemy. A more plausible interpretation is that these figures represent the birth of the 'long lived gods' described elsewhere. These are neither representative of Love nor Strive but include negative and positive gods.

128 Trans. Dods (2009).

129 The coherence of the position should not be mistaken as an argument that no pantheists sacrifice. Most Stoics, for example, do not reject sacrifice. Augustine (4.12), however, argued that they should. Further Sextus' (*Phys.* 1.126-9) reference to τὰ ἄλογα τῶν ζῴων ('the animals lacking logos') and πνεῦμα ('breath') also suggests a Stoic presence in this argument. This is curious and may suggest that the place of sacrifice was debated among Stoic circles.

130 Betegh (2014) 152. This view is very common and Burkert (1972) also claims that Pythagorean doctrines 'developed from living custom, with all its complexity and paradox, rather than from clearly articulated doctrine' (182).

131 Rives (2011) 193. Rives' position has been adopted by Ullicci (2012) 60 and Naiden (2013) 281.

132 See note 121 above.

133 That the Orphic could use the word θύω for sacrifice is not surprising. As Mikalson (2010) 24 notes, the Greek word is etymologically linked with making smoke and has no intrinsic relation to animal slaughter. Indeed, as the verb is frequently applied to both meat and plant offerings in Greek texts, a number of scholars have criticized the meat-centric bias in the literature on sacrifice. See survey in Stowers (2011); more generally McClymond (2010) 65–92. That the Greeks described plant sacrifices does not, however, change the fact that in Greece the dominant meaning of the term was related to killing animals. This understanding is apparent from poems such as the *Iliad* and myths such as the Promethean division. Moreover, the word's intimate association with meat is clear from Theophrastus' attempt to redefine θύω towards non-meat offerings and criticism that 'we do not hear these aright when, thinking they refer to the later error, we call thusia the supposed worship which uses animals' (Porph. *Abst.* 2.5). Trans. Clark (2000).

134 See Evans-Pritchard (1956) 146.

135 Rives (2011) 187.

136 This may also be the case with the sacrifice of Dionysus himself. In some cases, he is divided into seven shares, in others he is torn apart. In no version of the myth is

there anything like the ordered and hierarchal apportionment we see in Homer and Hesiod. OF 311 = Proc. *in Tim.* II 146, 9. Graf and Johnston (2007) note that 'its crude means of dividing up its victims prevents the careful apportioning of sacrificial meat into shares for the mortals and shares for the gods – much less into a special share for a particular god or priest' (81).
137 For a discussion on the importance of the use of incense and smells in conceptualizing divinity in Greek offerings see Clements (2015).
138 The Derveni papyrus briefly describes offerings of many knobbed cakes, water and milk made to daimones or hindering souls (col. 6.5–8). Very little is said about how the participants and the daimones to which they are offered share these cakes, but one detail that is stressed is the plurality of both the cakes and the recipients.
139 Graf (2011) 207.
140 Trans. Prestige Jones (2005).
141 The myth is attributed to Stesikhoros, although Ryan (2012) 171 notes this may be more a play on his alleged birthplace, Himera (i.e. desire) than a serious designation.
142 Trans. Fowler (1925).

Conclusion

1 Trans. Lombardo and Bell (1997) modified.
2 The common consensus remains that the core details of the myth are genuinely Protagorean. Lampert (2010) 50 n. 54; Morgan (2000) 132; Guthie (1971) 63; de Romilly (1992) 162. The text may be mentioned by Diogenes Laertius (9.55), who refers to a work by Protagoras Περὶ τῆς ἐν ἀρχῇ καταστάσεως. Guthrie (1971) 64 translates this as *On the Original State of Man*.
3 On the history of the Greek terms λόγος and μῦθος see Lincoln (1999).
4 How we should view the gods in Protagoras' myth is debated. Guthrie (1980), for example, argues that divinities such as Prometheus and Hermes should be seen as colourful additions 'to make it more entertaining' (266) rather than active players. This is a fair conjecture when it comes to a man who famously said (DK 80 B 4): περὶ μὲν θεῶν οὐκ ἔχω εἰδέναι οὔθ' ὡς εἰσίν, οὔθ' ὡς οὐκ εἰσίν· πολλὰ γὰρ τὰ κωλύοντα εἰδέναι, ἥ τ' ἀδηλότης καὶ βραχὺς ὢν ὁ βίος τοῦ ἀνθρώπου. 'As to the gods, I have no means of knowing either that they exist or that they do not exist. For many are the obstacles that impede knowledge, both the obscurity of the question and the shortness of human life.' Trans. Hicks (1925) modified. That the gods are 'colourful additions' is certainly possible, yet Drozdek (2007) notes Protagoras does not deny the existences of the gods but rather 'pronounces his inability to have definite knowledge concerning this theological issue, but he leaves

open a possibility that some positive pronouncements about the gods can be made' (109).

5 McNeil (1986) 316 discusses Anaxagorean and Empedoclean influences and Betegh (2009) 93 discusses Platonic teleology. Fire and earth (320d) are also present in Plato's *Timaeus* where the demiurge fashions the universe out of fire, earth, water and air (32b–c). Parmenides' cosmology combines light and dark which Aristotle (*Ph.* 188a) refers to as 'hot and cold, or fire and earth'.
6 See Vernant (1980). See also Lloyd (2012) 8–31.
7 As Martin Holbraad (2008) puts it, 'there exists a world, whose main property is to be single and uniform. And there exist representations of the world, whose main property is to be plural and multifarious depending on who holds them' (34).
8 Strathern (1980).
9 Ibid. 196.
10 Ibid.
11 Descola and Pálson (1996) 7.
12 Descola (2013a) 39.
13 Viveiros de Castro (1998) 470.
14 The term brother is not in fact universal and as Wierzbicka (2014) 36 discusses, many societies do not have words for brothers or sisters but may use words referring to older or younger siblings.
15 Lloyd and Sivin (2002) 200. Another potential contender Tao, sometimes translated as the Way, tended to encompass natural and cultural aspects and in this respect is closer to Heraclitus' understanding of a divine νόμος. On the comparison with Heraclitus, albeit in terms of the phases, see Lloyd (2012) 23. The Tao has also frequently elicited comparisons with Heraclitus' divine Logos. See Yu (2015).
16 Sterckx (2002) 5. China is by no means alone; the use of the opposition nature, culture and supernature has also been questioned in relation to Japan and India. See Descola (2013a) 28–9.
17 Lloyd (2000) 22. Macé (2017).
18 It is not surprising that this example refers to a plant, as φύσις derives etymologically from φύω to grow.
19 Macé (2017) 208.
20 Long (2005) 414.
21 Heath (2005) 62. Homer was not totally unaware of cultural differences and the presence of different languages is introduced at times and even applies to the gods (*Il.* 20.74). The important point, however, is that he consistently chooses to discuss these societies in terms of universal norms.
22 *Eth. Eud.* 1235a: οἱ δὲ φυσιολόγοι καὶ τὴν ὅλην φύσιν διακοσμοῦσιν ἀρχὴν λαβόντες τὸ τὸ ὅμοιον ἰέναι πρὸς τὸ ὅμοιον. 'And the natural philosophers even arrange the

whole of nature in a system by assuming as a first principle that like goes to like.' Trans. Rackham (1981). See Macé (2017) 206–7.
23 Many of the Presocratics did not discuss νόμος at all. However, their new concept of order was frequently discussed in terms of δίκη (justice). Anaximander (DK 12 B 1), for example, describes how existing things διδόναι γάρ αὐτά δίκην καί τίσιν ἀλλήλοις τῆς ἀδικίας κατὰ τὴν τοῦ χρόνου τάξιν; 'pay penalty and retribution to one another for their injustice, according to the assessment of time'. Trans. Long (2005). Long (2005) 416–17 also notes the place of justice in Parmenides (DK 28 B 8.14–15) and Heraclitus (DK 22 B 94).
24 Long (2015) 418.
25 The dating is difficult and Democritus may have been the younger of the two. See Lavery (2008) 42 n. 2.
26 Νόμωι γάρ φησι γλυκύ, (καὶ) νόμωι πικρόν, νόμωι θερμόν, νόμωι ψυχρόν, νόμωι χροιή, ἐτεῇι δὲ ἄτομα καὶ κενόν. 'For by convention he says sweet, by convention bitter, by convention hot, by convention colour, but in reality atoms and void.' Trans. Graham (2010).
27 As de Romilly (1992) puts it, 'there exists on the one hand the domain of nature, on the other the artificial rules which are imposed by human beings and which run contrary to the state of nature' (114). In sophistic thought these terms are often strongly polarized. Elsewhere in the dialogue Hippias states this view in crystalline terms (337e–d): οἱ παρόντες, ἡγοῦμαι ἐγὼ ὑμᾶς συγγενεῖς τε καὶ οἰκείους καὶ πολίτας ἅπαντας εἶναι φύσει, οὐ νόμῳ· τὸ γὰρ ὅμοιον τῷ ὁμοίῳ φύσει συγγενές ἐστιν, ὁ δὲ νόμος, τύραννος ὢν τῶν ἀνθρώπων, πολλὰ παρὰτὴν φύσιν βιάζεται. 'Those who are here present, I regard you as kin and family and fellow-citizens by nature, not by convention: for like is akin to like by nature, whereas convention, despot of mankind, often constrains us against nature.' Trans. Lamb (1967) modified. The phrase 'fellow citizens by nature' may sound paradoxical, but as it encompasses Athenians and foreigners such as Protagoras, it is likely intended as reference to a more abstract citizenship of the world, to be contrasted with the limitations of legal citizenship. The phrase echoes the words of the fifth-century sophist Antiphon (DK 87 B 44 b) and probably should be read in the same way.
28 One of the earliest versions of this myth could have been associated with the atomist and compatriot of Protagoras, Democritus. See Cole (1967). A parallel sophistic example of the transition from a state of nature to culture is preserved in the fragments of the fifth-century philosopher Prodicus. Prodicus, however, offers an innovative twist on the place of the gods in society. In Protagoras' myth, the gods create culture. It is a gift bestowed on men by Prometheus and later Zeus. Prodicus inverts this position and argues that it is precisely culture that creates the gods. For Prodicus (DK 85 B 5) the immortal gods were fabricated by men with the introduction of cultural practices and the deification of the skills and resources

considered useful to the survival of the human race. Similar myths also appear in a number of later accounts including Diodorus (1.7–8) and Lucretius (5.925–1436), who discuss these events as a stage within wider cosmologies, including the formation of the earth and animal life. For a collection of the antiprimitivist fragments see Lovejoy and Boas ([1935] 1997).

29 Trans. Lamb (1967). Although these people are mentioned as part of Protagoras' later philosophical discussion, a similar opposition appears in his Promethean myth in terms of the distinction between animals who by nature are equipped to protect themselves (320e) and man as a dualistic being who 'partakes of a divine share' (θείας μετέσχε μοίρας) through which he acknowledges (νομίζω) the gods and builds their altars.

30 Although the authorship of Protagoras' myth remains disputed, the ideas Plato ascribes to him are indisputably old. Indeed, similar views of Prometheus occupied a pivotal role in tragedies such as Aeschylus' *Prometheus Bound* (436–506) and the Homeric *Hymn to Hephaestus*, which describe Prometheus, and sometimes Hephaestus, as a defiant benefactor who helps differentiate man from the animals through cultural gifts.

31 *Discourses on Livy* (c. 1517).

32 See for example Augustine *City of God* 4.12.

33 Descola (2013) 205.

34 See Foucault ([1966] 1989); Descola (2013a); Sahlins (2008).

35 See Sahlins (1996).

36 Hobbes (1651) 1.13.

37 For the social contract reading see Guthrie (1971) 136; Kerferd (1981) 147; de Romilly (1992) 166. Although Protagoras does not call it a social contract, de Romilly (1992) notes: 'the seed of what was, centuries later, to be known as "the social contract" is clearly detectable in his thinking' (166). Guthrie (1971) is similar: 'The records of Protagoras do not contain the actual word "compact", but when the gods are removed from his parable (as in view of his agnosticism they must be), we have a picture of men perishing for lack of the art of living together in cities and by hard experience learning to act justly and respect the rights of others and so founding political communities' (136–7).

38 Sahlins (2008) 87.

39 Rousseau's *The Social Contract* (1762) and Montaigne's earlier sixteenth-century work *Of Cannibals* (1570–92).

40 Serres (2009).

41 On the presence of an innate selfishness in man's nature as the dominant theme in Western history see Sahlins (2008).

42 Descola (2013a) 69.

43 Harvey (2017) 186.

44 Wildberger (2019) 63.
45 Schlosser (2020) 18.

Appendix

1 The text and reconstruction follows Betegh (2004) with alterations.
2 OF 243 = (I) Euseb. *Praep. Ev.* 3.8. 2 (= Porphyr. Περί ἀγαλμ. fr. 354 F).
3 Both Eros and Metis are common names for Protogonos. See Procl. *In Tim II*, 102; Macro. *Sat.* 1.23.21.
4 Trans. Gifford (1903).
5 Trans. Graf and Johnston (2007).
6 Trans. Edmonds (2011).
7 Trans. Graf and Jonhston (2007) modified.
8 Trans. Lamb (1967).
9 Trans. Bernabé and Jiménez San Cristóbal (2008).

Bibliography

Adamson, P. (2014). *Classical Philosophy: A History of Philosophy Without Any Gaps.* Vol. 1. Oxford University Press.
Ahbel-Rappe, S. (2010). *Damascius' Problems and Solutions Concerning First Principles.* Oxford University Press.
Albinus, L. (2000). *The House of Hades.* Aarhus University Press.
Alderink, L. (1981). *Creation and Salvation in Ancient Orphism.* American Classical Studies 8, The American Philological Association.
Alduri, V. (2013). *Philosophy, Salvation, and the Mortal Condition.* De Gruyter.
Allan, W. (2006). 'Divine Justice and Cosmic Order in Early Greek Epic.' *The Journal of Hellenic Studies* 126: 1–35.
Almqvist, O. (2020). 'Hesiod's *Theogony* and Analogist Cosmogonies.' *HAU: Journal of Ethnographic Theory.* Vol. 10, No. 1.
Andersen, O. (1981). 'A Note on the Mortality of the Gods.' *Greek, Roman, and Byzantine Studies* 22: 323–7.
Arhem, K. and Sprenger, G. (2015). *Animism in Southeast Asia.* Routledge.
Assmann, J. (2014). *From Akhenaten to Moses: Ancient Egypt and Religious Change.* American University in Cairo.
Assmann, J. (2003). *The Mind of Egypt.* Harvard University Press.
Athonassakis, A. N. and Wolkow B. M. (2013). *The Orphic Hymns.* The Johns Hopkins University Press.
Atran, S. (2004). *In Gods We Trust: The Evolutionary Landscape of Religion.* Oxford University Press.
Austin, N. (1973). 'The One and the Many in the Homeric Cosmos.' *Arion* 1.2: 219–74.
Babbitt, F. (1936). *Plutarch, Moralia.* Harvard University Press.
Badalanova Geller, F. (2008). *Qur'ān in Vernacular: Folk Islam in the Balkans.* Max Planck Institute for the History of Science (Preprint 357).
Bakkar, G. J. (2013). *The Meaning of Meat and the Structure of the Odyssey.* Cambridge University Press.
Basore, J. (1975). *Seneca, Moral Essays.* Harvard University Press.
Bateson, G. (1972). *Steps Towards an Ecology of the Mind.* Chicago University Press.
Beall, E. F. (2009). 'Once More on Hesiod's Supposed Tartarus Principle.' *The Classical World* 102.2: 159–61.
Belfiore, E. (2000). *Murder Among Friends: Violation of Philia in Greek Tragedy.* Oxford University Press.

Bellah, R. (2011). *Religion in Human Evolution: From the Paleolithic to the Axial Age.* Harvard University Press.

Benveniste, E. 2016. *Dictionary of Indo-European Concepts and Society.* Chicago University Press.

Berdeslee, J. W. (1918). *The use of 'Phusis' in Fifth Century Greek Literature.* Chicago University Press.

Bernabé, A. (2002a). 'La toile du Penelope: A-t-il Existé un Mythe Orphique sur Dionysos et les Titans?' *RHR* 219(4): 401–33.

Bernabé, A. (2002b). 'La Theogonie Orphique du Papyrus de Derveni.' *Kernos*, 91–129.

Bernabé, A. (2004). *Orphicorum et Orphicis Similiumtestimonia et Fragmenta. Poetae Epici Graeci.* Pars II. Fasc. 1–3. Bibliotheca Teubneriana.

Bernabé, A. (2010). 'The Gods in Later Orphism.' In Bremmer, J. and Erskine, A. *The Gods of Ancient Greece.* Edinburgh University Press. 422–41.

Bernabé, A. (2013a). 'Orphics and Pythagoreans: the Greek Perspective.' In Cornelli G., McKirahan, R. and Macris, C. eds. *On Pythagoreanism.* De Gruyter. 117–53.

Bernabé, A. (2013b). 'Plato's Transposition of Orphic Netherworld Imagery.' In Adluri, V. ed. *Philosophy and Salvation in Greek Religion.* De Gruyter. 117–49.

Bernabé, A. (2014). 'On the Rites Described and Commented upon in the Derveni Papyrus.' In Papadopoulou, I. and Muellner, L. C. eds. *Poetry as Initiation: The Center for Hellenic Studies Symposium on the Derveni Papyrus.* Harvard University Press. 19–53.

Bernabé, A. and Jiménez San Cristóbal, A. I. (2008). *Instructions for the Netherworld.* Brill.

Bernabé, A. and Jiménez San Cristóbal, A. I. (2011). 'Are the "Orphic" gold leaves Orphic?' In Edmonds, R. ed. *The 'Orphic' Gold Tablets and Greek Religion.* Cambridge University Press. 68–101.

Betegh, G. (2004). *The Derveni Papyrus: Cosmology, Theology and Interpretation.* Cambridge University Press.

Betegh, G. (2007a). 'On the Physical Aspect of Heraclitus' Psychology.' *Phronesis* 52: 3–32.

Betegh, G. (2007b). 'The Derveni Papyrus and Early Stoicism.' *Rhizai* 4: 133–52.

Betegh, G. (2011). 'The Great Tablet from Thurii (OF 492).' In Herrero de Jáuregui, M ed. *Tracing Orpheus: Studies of Orphic Fragments in Honour of Alberto Bernabé.* De Gruyter. 219–27.

Betegh, G. (2013). 'On the Physical Aspect of Heraclitus' Psychology. With New Appendices.' In Sider, D. and Obbink, D. eds. *Doctrine and Doxography: Studies on Heraclitus and Pythagoras.* De Gruyter. 225–63.

Betegh, G. (2014). 'Pythagoreans, Orphism and Greek Religion.' In Huffman, C. ed. *A History of Pythagoreanism.* Cambridge University Press. 149–66.

Bicknell, P. J. (1989). 'Parmenides, DK 28 B5.' *Apeion* 13.1: 9–12.

Bierl, A, (2014). '"Riddles over Riddles": "Mysterious" and "Symbolic" (Inter)textual Strategies. The Problem of Language in the Derveni Papyrus.' In Papadopoulou, I.

and Muellner L. C. eds. *Poetry as Initiation: The Center for Hellenic Studies Symposium on the Derveni Papyrus*. Harvard University Press. 187–211.

Biernacki, L. and Clayton, P. (2014). *Panentheism Across the World's Traditions*. Oxford University Press.

Blacker, C. and Loewe, M. (1975). *Ancient Cosmologies*. Allen & Unwin.

Bloch, M. (2012). *Anthropology and the Cognitive Challenge*. Cambridge University Press.

Bloom, P. (2004). *Descartes' Baby*. Random House.

Boyd, J. W. and Crosby, D. A. (1979). 'Is Zoroastrianism Dualistic or Monotheistic?' *Journal of the American Academy of Religion* 47.4: 557–88.

Boyer, P. (2001). *Religion Explained: The Evolutionary Origins of Religious Thought*. Basic Books.

Boys-Stones, G.R. Haubold J. H. (2009). *Plato and Hesiod*. Oxford University Press.

Bourdieu, P. (1977). *Outline of a Theory of Practice*. Cambridge University Press.

Bourdieu, P. (1990). *The Logic of Practice*. Stanford University Press.

Boyancé, P. (1974). 'Remarques sur le Papyrus de Derveni.' *Revue des Études Grecques* 87: 90–110.

Boylston, (2013). 'Food, Life and Material Religion in Ethiopian Orthodox Christianity.' In Lambeck, M. ed. *A Companion to the Anthropology of Religion*. Blackwell-Wiley. 257–73.

Bossi, B. (2011). 'Heraclitus B 32 Revisited in the Light of the Derveni Papyrus.' *Anales del Seminario de Historia de la Filosofía* Vol. 28: 9–22.

Bremmer, J. (1983). *The Early Greek Concept of the Soul*. Princeton University Press.

Bremmer, J. (1999). 'Rationalisation and Disenchantment in Ancient Greece – Max Weber among the Pythagoreans and the Orphics?' In Buxton, R. ed. *From Myth to Reason?* Oxford University Press. 71–83.

Bremmer, J. (2002). *The Rise and Fall of the Afterlife*. Routledge.

Bremmer, J. (2006). 'The Rise of Hero Cult and the New Simonides.' *Zeitschrift für Papyrologie und Epigraphik* 158: 15–26.

Bremmer, J. (2011). 'The Place of Performance in Orphic Poetry (OF 1).' In Herrero de Jáuregui, M. ed. *Tracing Orpheus: Studies of Orphic Fragments in Honour of Alberto Bernabé*. De Gruyter. 1–7.

Bremmer, J. (2013). 'Divinities in the Orphic Gold Leaves: Euklês, Eubouleus, Brimo, Kybele, Kore and Persephone.' *ZPE* 187: 35–48.

Bremmer, J. and Erskine, A. (2010). *The Gods of Ancient Greece*. Edinburgh University Press.

Brisch, N. (2008). *Religion and Power: Divine Kingship in the Ancient World and Beyond*. Chicago University Press.

Brisson, L. (1992). 'Le Corps "Dionysiaque": L'Anthropogonie Décrite dans le *Commentaire sur le Phédon de Platon* (1, par. 3–6) Attribué a Olympiodore est-elle Orphique?' In Goulet-Cazé, M. O., Madec, G. and O'Brien, D. eds. Ζοφίης μαιήτορες *Chercheurs de Sagesse: Hommage á Jean Pépin*. Série Antiquité, 131. Paris: Institut d'études augustiniennes. 481–99.

Brisson, L. (2003). 'Sky, Sex and Sun: The Meaning of αιδοισ/αιδοιον in the Derveni Papyrus.' *ZPE* 144: 19–23.

Brisson, L. (2004). *How Philosophers Saved Myths. Allegorical Interpretation and Classical Mythology.* Chicago University Press.

Brisson, L. (2009). 'Zeus did not Commit Incest with his Mother: An Interpretation of Column XXVI of the Derveni Papyrus.' *ZPE* 168: 27–39.

Broadie, S. (2001). 'Soul and Body in Plato and Descartes.' *Proceedings of the Aristotelian Society* 10: 295–308.

Burkert, W. (1966). 'Greek Tragedy and Sacrificial Ritual.' *GRBS* 7: 87–112.

Burkert, W. (1972). *Lore and Science in Ancient Pythagoreanism.* Harvard University Press.

Burkert, W. (1977). 'Orphism and Bacchic Mysteries: New Evidence and Old Problems of Interpretation.' *The Center for Hermeneutical Studies* 28: 1–47.

Burkert, W. (1982). 'Craft versus Sect: The Problems of Orphics and Pythagoreans.' In Meyer B. F. and Sanders E. P. eds. *Jewish and Christian Self-definition III.* Fortress Press. 1–22.

Burkert, W. (1983). *Homo Necans: The Anthropology of Ancient Greek Sacrificial Ritual and Myth.* University of California Press.

Burkert, W. (1985). *Greek Religion.* Cambridge University Press.

Burkert, W. (1987). *Ancient Mystery Cults.* Cambridge University Press.

Burkert, W. (1996). *Creation of the Sacred: Tracks of Biology in Early Religions.* Harvard University Press.

Burkert, W. (1999). 'The Logic of Cosmogony.' In Buxton, R. ed. *From Myth to Reason? Studies in the Development of Greek Thought.* Oxford University Press. 87–106.

Burkert, W. (2004). *Babylon, Memphis, Persepolis: Eastern Contexts of Greek Culture.* Harvard University Press.

Burkert, W. (2011). 'The Derveni Papyrus on Heraclitus (col IV).' In Herrero de Jáuregui, M. ed. *Tracing Orpheus: Studies of Orphic Fragments in Honour of Alberto Bernabé.* De Gruyter. 361–5.

Burkert, W. (2014). 'How to Learn About Souls: The Derveni Papyrus and Democritus.' In Papadopoulou, I. and Muellner, L. C. eds. *Poetry as Initiation: The Center for Hellenic Studies Symposium on the Derveni Papyrus.* Harvard University Press. 107–15.

Burton, D. (2001). 'The Death of Gods in Greek Succession.' In Budelmann, D. and Michelakis, P. eds. *Homer, Tragedy and Beyond: Essays in Honour of P.E. Easterling.* Society for the Promotion of Hellenic Studies. 43–56.

Burtt, J. O. (1962). *Minor Attic Orators.* Harvard University Press.

Bussanich, J. (1983). 'A Theoretical Interpretation of Hesiod's Chaos.' *Classical Philology* 78.3: 212–19.

Buxton, R. (1999). *From Myth to Reason? Studies in the Development of Greek Thought.* Oxford University Press.

Buxton, R. (2013). *Myths and Tragedies in their Ancient Greek Contexts.* Oxford University Press.
Calame, C. (2007). 'Gardens of Love and Meadows of the Beyond: Ritual Encounters with the Gods and Poetical Performances in Ancient Greece.' In Conan M. ed. *Sacred Gardens and Landscapes: Ritual and Agency.* University of Washington Press.
Calame, C. (2011). 'Funerary Gold Lamellae and Orphic Papyrus Commentaries: Same Use, Different Purpose.' In Edmonds, R. ed. *The 'Orphic' Gold Tablets and Greek Religion.* Cambridge University Press. 203–18.
Calame, C. (2013). *The Poetics of Eros in Ancient Greece.* Princeton University Press.
Caldwell, R. (1989). *The Origin of the Gods: A Psychoanalytic Study of Greek Theogonic Myth.* Oxford University Press.
Carsten, J. (1995). 'The Substance of Kinship and the Heat of the Hearth: Feeding, Personhood, and Relatedness among Malays in Pulau Langkawi.' *American Ethnologist* 22.2: 223–41.
Cartledge, P. (1993). *The Greeks: A Portrait of Self and Others.* Oxford University Press.
Casadesús Bordoy, F. (2013). 'On the Origin of the Orphic-Pythagorean Notion of the Immortality of the Soul.' In Cornelli, G., McKirahan, R. and Macris, C. eds. *On Pythagoreanism.* De Gruyter. 153–79.
Chaniotis, A. (2003). 'The divinity of the Hellenistic rulers.' In Erskine, A. ed. *A Companion to the Hellenistic World.* Oxford University Press.
Chernis, H. and Helmbold, W. (1957). *Plutarch, Moralia.* Harvard University Press.
Chlup, R. (2008) 'Illud tempus in Greek myth and ritual,' *Religion* 38.4: 355–65.
Chrysanthou, A. (2020). *Defining Orphism: The Beliefs, the Teletae and the Writings.* De Gruyter.
Clark, G. (2000). *Porphyry, On Abstinence from Killing Animals.* Duckworth.
Clark, S. (2013). *Ancient Mediterranean Philosophy: An Introduction.* Bloomsbury.
Clarke, M. (1995). 'The Wisdom of Thales and the Problem of the Word *Hieros*.' *Classical Quarterly* 45: 196–317.
Clarke, M. (1999). *Flesh and Spirit in the Poetry of Homer.* Oxford University Press.
Clay, J. (1981). 'Immortal and Ageless Forever.' *The Classical Journal* 77.2: 112–17.
Clay, J. (1983). *The Wrath of Athena.* Princeton University Press.
Clay, J. (2003). *Hesiod's Cosmos.* Cambridge University Press.
Clements, A. (2014). 'Divine Scents and Presence.' In Bradley, M. ed. *Smell and the Ancient Senses.* Acumen. 46–60.
Cohoon, J. W. (1932). *Dio Chrysostom.* Harvard University Press.
Cole, T. (1967). *Democritus and the Sources of Greek Anthropology.* The Press of Western Reserve University for the American Philological Association.
Collins, J. (2007). 'Cosmology: Time and History.' In Johnston, S. ed. *Ancient Religions.* Cambridge University Press. 59–71.
Colomo, D. (2004). 'Herakles and the Eleusinian Mysteries. P.Mil.Vogl. I 20, 18–32 Revisited.' *ZPE* 148: 87–98.

Colvin, M. (2007). 'Heraclitean Flux and Unity of Opposites in Plato's Theaetetus and Cratylus.' *Classical Quarterly* 57.2: 759–69.
Comparetti, D. (1882). 'The Petelia Gold Plate.' *JHS* 3: 111–18.
Cook, E. (1995). *The Odyssey in Athens: Myths of Cultural Origins*. Cornell University Press.
Cornford, F. M. (1903). 'Plato and Orpheus.' *Classical Review* 17.9: 433–45.
Cornford, F. M. (1937). *Plato's Cosmology*. Routledge.
Cornford, F. M. (2009[1912]). *From Religion to Philosophy: A Study of the Origins of Western Speculation*. Princeton University Press.
Cosmides, L. and Tooby, J. (1992). *The Adapted Mind: Evolutionary Psychology and the Generation of Culture*. Oxford University Press.
Curd, P. (1998). *The Legacy of Parmenides: Eleatic Monism and Later Presocratic Thought*. Princeton University Press.
Currie, B. (2005). *Pindar and the Cult of Heroes*. Oxford University Press.
Dalley, S. (2008). *Myths from Mesopotamia: Creation, the Flood, Gilgamesh*. Oxford University Press.
Damásio, A. (1994). *Descartes' Error: Emotion, Reason, and the Human Brain*. Putnam Publishing.
Dawkins, R. (2006). *The God Delusion*. Bantam Books.
de Coppet, D. and Iteanu, A. (1995). *Cosmos and Society in Oceania*. Berg Publishers.
de Heusch, L. (1997). 'The Symbolic Mechanisms of Sacred Kingship: Rediscovering Frazer.' *The Journal of the Royal Anthropological Institute*. 3.2: 213–32.
de Romilly, J (1992). *The Great Sophists in Periclean Athens*. Trans. Lloyd, J. Clarendon Press.
Descola, P. (2013a). *Beyond Culture and Nature*. Chicago University Press.
Descola, P. (2013b). 'Presence, Attachment, Origin: Ontologies of "Incarnates".' In Lambeck, M. ed. *A Companion to the Anthropology of Religion*. Blackwell-Wiley. 35–50.
Descola, P. (2013c). *The Ecology of Others*. Chicago University Press.
Descola, P. (2014). 'The Grid and the Tree: Reply to Marshall Sahlins' Comment.' *HAU* 4.1: 295–300.
Descola, P. (2016). 'Biolatry: A Surrender of Understanding (Response to Ingold's "A Naturalist Abroad in the Museum of Ontology").' *Anthropological Forum* 26.3: 321–8.
Descola P. and Pálson G. (1996). *Nature and Society: Anthropological Perspectives*. Routledge.
Detienne, M. (1979). *Dionysos Slain*. Trans. Muellner M. and Muellner L. The Johns Hopkins University Press.
Detienne, M. (1994). *The Gardens of Adonis*. Trans. Lloyd J. Princeton University Press.
Detienne, M. (2002). *The Writing of Orpheus*. Trans. Lloyd, J. The Johns Hopkins University Press.
Detienne, M. and Sissa, G. (2000). *The Daily of the Greek Gods*. Trans. Lloyd, J. Stanford University Press University Press.

Detienne, M. and Vernant, P. (1991). *Cunning and Intelligence in Greek Culture and Society*. Chicago University Press.

Deutscher, G. (2005). *Through the Language Glass: Why The World Looks Different in Other Languages*. Random House.

Dietrich, B. C. (1979). 'Views of Homeric Gods and Religion.' *Numen* 26.2: 129-51.

Dignas, B. and Trampedach, K. (2008). *Practitioners of the Divine: Greek Priests and Religious Officials from Homer to Heliodorus*. Harvard University Press.

DiMattei, S. (2016). *Genesis 1 and the Creationism Debate: Being Honest to the Text, Its Author and His Beliefs*. Wipf & Stock.

Dodds, E. R. (1997 [1951]). *The Greeks and the Irrational*. University of California Press.

Dods, M. (2009). *Augustine, City of God*. Hendrickson.

Doniger, W. (1981). *The Rig Veda*. Penguin Books.

Donlon, W. (1985). 'The Social Groups of Dark Age Greece.' *Classical Philology*. 80.4: 293-308.

Donlon, W. (2007). 'Kin-Groups in the Homeric Epics.' *The Classical World*. 101.1: 29-39.

Domaradzki, M. (2012). 'Theological Etymologizing in the Early Stoa.' *Kernos. Revue Internationale et Pluridisciplinaire de Religion Grecque Antique* 25: 143-7.

Douglas, M. (1991). *Implicit Meanings*. Routledge.

Dousa, T. (2011). 'Common Motifs in the Orphic B tablets and Egyptian Funerary Texts: Continuity or Convergence?' In Edmonds, R. ed. *The 'Orphic' Gold Tablets and Greek Religion*. Cambridge University Press. 120-65.

Drozdek, A. (2007). *Greek Philosophers as Theologians: The Divine Arche*. Ashgate Publishing.

Dumézil, G. (1988[1948]). *Mitra Varuna: An Essay on Two Indo-European Representations of Sovereignty*. Zone Books.

Durkheim, E. (2001[1912]). *The Elementary Forms of Religious Life*. Oxford University Press.

Earle, R. (2012). *The Body of the Conquistador: Food, Race and the Colonial Experience in Spanish America, 1492-1700*. Cambridge University Press.

Edmonds, R. G. (1999). 'Tearing apart the Zagreus Myth: A Few Disparaging Remarks on Orphism and Original Sin.' *Classical Antiquity* 19: 35-73.

Edmonds, R. G. (2004). *Myths of the Underworld Journey: Plato, Aristophanes, and the 'Orphic' Gold Tablets*. Cambridge University Press.

Edmonds, R. G. (2010). 'The Children of Earth and Starry Heaven.' In Bernabé, A, Casadesús, F. Santamaría, M. eds. *Orfeo y el Orfismo: Nuevas Perspectivas*. Alicante: Biblioteca Virtual Miguel de Cervantes. 98-121.

Edmonds, R. G. (2011). *The 'Orphic' Gold Tablets and Greek Religion*. Cambridge University Press.

Edmonds, R. G. (2013). *Redefining Ancient Orphism: A Study in Greek Religion*. Cambridge University Press.

Ekman, P. (1999). 'Basic Emotions.' In Dalgleish, T. and Power, M. eds. *Handbook of Cognition and Emotion*. Wiley. 45–60.

Ekroth, G. (2007). 'Meat in Ancient Greece: Sacrificial, Sacred or Secular?' *Food & History* 5.1: 249–72.

Ekroth, G. (2009). 'Thighs or Tails? The Osteological Evidence as a Source for Greek Ritual Norms.' *La Norme en Matière Religieuse Kernos Supplement* 21: 125–51.

Ekroth, G. (2011). 'Meat for the gods.' *Nourrir les dieux? Sacrifice et Représentation du Divin Kernos Supplément* 26: 15–41.

el-Aswad, el-Sayed (1994). The Cosmological Belief System of Egyptian Peasants.' *Anthropos* 89.4/6: 359–77.

el-Aswad, el-Sayed (1997). 'Archaic Egyptian Cosmology.' *Anthropos* 92.1/3: 69–81.

Eliade, M. (1965). *The Two and the One*. Harvill Press.

Eliade, M. (1967). 'Cosmogonic Myth and Sacred History' *Religious Studies* 2.2: 171–83.

Eliade, M. (1982). *A History of Religious Ideas Vol. 2*. Chicago University Press.

Emlyn-Jones, C. J. (1976). 'Heraclitus and the Identity of Opposites.' *Phronesis* 21: 89–114.

Emlyn-Jones, C. J. (1992). 'The Homeric gods: poetry, belief and authority.' In Emlyn Jones, C. J., Hardwick, I. and Purkis, J. eds. *Homer: Readings and Images*. Duckworth Press. 90–103.

Endsjø, D. (2009). *Greek Resurrection Beliefs and the Success of Christianity*. Springer.

Evans, V. and Levinson, S. (2010). 'The Myth of Language Universals: Language Diversity and its Importance for Cognitive Science.' *Behavioral and Brain Sciences* 32: 429–92.

Evans Pritchard, E. E. (1956). *Nuer Religion*. Oxford University Press.

Evelyn-White, H. G. (1914). *Hesiod, the Homeric Hymns and Homerica*. Harvard University Press.

Everett, C. (2013). *Linguistic Relativity: Evidence Across Languages and Cognitive Domains*. De Gruyter.

Everett, D. (2016). *Dark Matter of the Mind: The Culturally Articulated Unconscious*. Chicago University Press.

Fagles, R. (1996). *Homer, The Odyssey*. Penguin.

Faraone, C. (2008). 'Household Religion in Ancient Greece.' In Bodel, J. and Olyan, S. eds. *Household and Family Religion in Antiquity*. Oxford University Press. 210–28.

Faraone, C. (2011). 'The Many and the One: Imagining the Beginnings of Political Power in the Hesiodic Theogony.' *Archiv für Religionsgeschichte* 13.1: 37–50.

Farella, J. R. (1991). *The Main Stalk: A Synthesis of Navajo Philosophy*. The University of Arizona Press.

Feldman Barrett, L. (2017). *How Emotions Are Made: The Secret Life of the Brain*. Macmillan.

Ferella, C. (2019). 'Ζεὺς μοῦνος and Parmenides' What-is.' In Santamaría, M. *The Derveni Papyrus: Unearthing Ancient Mysteries*. Brill. 65–77.

Ferrari, G. (2008). *Alcman and the Cosmos of Sparta*. Chicago University Press.

Finamore, J. F. and Dillon, J. (2002). *Iamblichus, De Anima*. Brill.
Finkelberg, A. (1986). 'On the Unity of Orphic and Milesian Thought.' *The Harvard Theological Review* 79.4: 321–35.
Finkelberg, A. (1989). 'The Milesian Monistic Doctrine and the Development of Presocratic Thought.' *Hermes* 117.3: 257–70.
Finkelberg, A. (1998). 'On the History of the Greek Kosmos.' *Harvard Studies in Classical Philology* 98: 103–36.
Finkelberg, A. (2013). 'Heraclitus, the Rival of Pythagoras.' In Sider, D. and Obbink, D. eds. *Doctrine and Doxography: Studies on Heraclitus and Pythagoras*. De Gruyter. 147–52.
Finkelberg, A. (2017). *Heraclitus and Thales' Conceptual Scheme: A Historical Study*. Brill.
Foley, H. (1994). *The Homeric Hymn to Demeter: Translation, Commentary, and Interpretive Essays*. Princeton University Press.
Fontaine, P. F. M. (1986). *The Light and the Dark: A Cultural History of Dualism. Vol 1. Dualism in the Archaic and Early Classical Periods of Greek History*. Brill.
Foucault (1989 [1966]). *The Order of Things*. Routledge.
Fowler, R. (2004). *The Cambridge Companion to Homer*. Cambridge University Press.
Fragoulaki, M. (2013). *Kinship in Thucydides: Intercommunal Ties and Historical Narrative*. Oxford University Press.
Fränkel, H. (1938). 'Heraclitus on God and the Phenomenal World.' *Transactions and Proceedings of the American Philological Association*. 69: 230–44.
Frankfort, H. (1978[1948]). *Kingship and the Gods*. Chicago University Press.
Frazer, J. (1995). *Apollodorus, The Library*. Harvard University Press.
Frazer, J. (2009 [1990]). *The Golden Bough*. Oxford University Press.
Freidenreich, D. (2011). *Foreigners and Their Food: Constructing Otherness in Jewish, Christian, and Islamic Law*. University of California Press.
Funkenstein, A. (1982). *Theology and the Scientific Imagination: From the Middle Ages to the Seventeenth Century*. Princeton University Press.
Funkenstein, A. (1994). 'The Polytheism of William James.' *Journal of the History of Ideas*. 55.1: 99–111.
Fustel de Coulanges, N. (1956 [1864]). *The Ancient City*. Doubleday Anchor.
Gagné, R. (2007). 'Winds and Ancestors: The Physika of Orpheus.' *Harvard Studies in Classical Philology* 103: 1–23.
Garani, M. (2013). 'Lucretius and Ovid on Empedoclean Cows and Sheep.' In Lehoux, D. Morrison, A. D. Sharrock, A. *Lucretius: Poetry, Philosophy, Science*. Oxford University Press. 233–59.
Garcia, L. F. (2013). *Homeric Durability Telling Time in the Iliad*. Hellenic Studies Series 58. Harvard University Press.
Gemelli Marciano, M. L. (2014). 'The Pythagorean Way of Life and Pythagorean Ethics.' In Huffman, C. ed. *A History of Pythagoreanism*. Cambridge University Press. 131–48.

Georgoudi, S., Piettre, R. and Schmidt, F. (2005). *La Cuisine et l'Autel: Les Sacrifices en Questions dans les Sociétés de la Méditerranée Ancienne*. BEHESR 124 Turnhout. Brepols.

Gera, D. L. (2003). *Ancient Greek Ideas on Speech, Language, and Civilization*. Oxford University Press.

Gerber, D. (1984). *Greek Poetry and Philosophy: Studies in Honour of Leonard Woodbury*. Scholars Press.

Gerber, D. (1999). 'Pindar, *Nemean Six*: A Commentary.' *Harvard Studies in Classical Philology* 99: 33–91.

Gertz, S. R. P. (2011). *Death and Immortality in Late Neoplatonism: Studies on the Ancient Commentaries on Plato's Phaedo Studies in Platonism*. Brill.

Gheerbrant, X. (2017). *Empédocle: Une Poétique Philosophique*. Classiques Garnier.

Gifford, E. H. (1903). *Eusebius, Praeparatio Evangelica*. Harvard University Press.

Godley, A. D. (1920). *Herodotus, The Histories*. Harvard University Press.

Gould, J. (1985). 'On Making Sense of Greek Religion.' In Easterling, P. and Muir, J. V. eds. *Greek Religion and Society*. Cambridge University Press. 1–33.

Gould, J. (2001). 'Hiketeia.' In *Myth, Ritual, Memory, and Exchange: Essays in Greek Literature and Culture*. Oxford University Press. 22–74.

Gradel, I. (2002). *Emperor Worship and Roman Religion*. Oxford University Press.

Graf, F. (2011). 'A Satirist's Sacrifices: Lucian on Sacrifices and the Contestation of Religious Traditions.' In Knust, J. W. and Varhelyi, Z. eds. *Ancient Mediterranean Sacrifice*. Oxford University Press. 203–13.

Graf, F. and Iles Johnston, S. (2007). *Ritual Texts for the Afterlife: Orpheus and the Bacchic Gold Tablets*. Routledge.

Graham, D. W. (2005). 'Once more into the stream.' *Symposium Philosophiae Antiquae*. Samos.

Graham, D. W. (2006). *Explaining the Cosmos: The Ionian Tradition of Scientific Philosophy*. Princeton University Press.

Graham, D. W. (2010). *The Text of the Early Greek Philosophy Part I*. Cambridge University Press.

Granet, M. (1934). *La Pensée Chinoise*. La Renaissance du Livre.

Granger, H. (2007). 'The Theologian Pherecydes of Syros and the Early Days of Natural Philosophy.' *Harvard Studies in Classical Philology* 103: 135–63.

Graziosi, B. and Haubold J. (2005). *Homer: The Resonance of Epic*. Duckworth Press.

Gregory, A. (2013). *The Presocratics and the Supernatural: Magic, Philosophy and Science in Early Greece*. Bloomsbury.

Griffin, J. (1983a). 'The Divine Audience and the Religion of the *Iliad*.' *The Classical Quarterly* 28.1: 1–22.

Griffin, J. (1983b). *Homer on Life and Death*. Oxford University Press.

Gros, A. (2016). 'Jean-Pierre Vernant et l'Analyse Structurale: le Mythe Hésiodique des Races.' *L'Homme* 218: 219–38.

Guthrie, W. (1980a [1962]). *A History of Greek Philosophy, Vol. I: The Earlier Presocratics and the Pythagoreans*. Cambridge University Press.
Guthrie, W. (1980b [1965]). *A History of Greek Philosophy, Vol. II: The Presocratic Tradition from Parmenides to Democritus*. Cambridge University Press.
Guthrie, W. (1980c [1971]). *A History of Greek Philosophy, Vol. III: The Fifth Century Enlightenment*. Cambridge University Press.
Guthrie, W. (1993 [1952]). *Orpheus and Greek Religion: A Study of the Orphic Movement*. Princeton University Press.
Halbmayer, E. (2012). 'Amerindian Mereology: Animism, Analogy, and the Multiverse.' *Indiana* 29: 103–25.
Halloday, C. (1996). *Fragments from Hellenistic Jewish Authors, Vol. IV, Orphica*. Scholars Press.
Hallowell, A. I. (1960). 'Ojibwa Ontology, Behavior, and World View.' In Diamond, S. ed. *Culture in History: Essays in Honor of Paul Radin*. Columbia University Press. 19–52.
Hamilton, J. R. (1984). 'The Origins of Ruler Cult.' *Prudentia* 16: 3–16.
Harden, A. (2013). *Animals in the Classical World: Ethical Perspectives from Greek and Roman Texts*. Palgrave Macmillan.
Harrison, J. (1903). *Prolegomena to the Study of Greek Religion*. Cambridge University Press.
Harrison, J. (1976 [1912]). *Themis: A Study of the Social Origins of Greek Religion*. Cambridge University Press.
Harvey, G. (2017). *Animism: Respecting the Living World*. Hurst and Company.
Harvey, P. (2000). *An Introduction to Buddhist Ethics*. Cambridge University Press.
Heath, J. (2005). *The Talking Greeks*. Cambridge University Press.
Heidel, A. (1942). *The Babylonian Genesis*. Chicago University Press.
Heiden, B. (2007). 'The Muses' Uncanny Lies: Hesiod, "Theogony" 27 and Its Translators.' *The American Journal of Philology* 128.2: 153–75.
Helms, M. (2010). *Access to Origins: Affines, Ancestors, and Aristocrats*. The University of Texas Press.
Henrich, J., Heine, S. J. and Norenzayan, A. (2010). 'The Weirdest People in the World?' *Behavioral and Brain Sciences* 33: 61. 18.
Henrichs, A. (2010). 'What is a Greek God?' In Bremmer, J. and Erskine, A. eds. *The Gods of Ancient Greece*. Edinburgh University Press.
Henrichs, A. (2011). 'Dionysos Dismembered and Restored to Life: The Earliest Evidence (OF 59 I–II).' In Herrero de Jáuregui, M ed. *Tracing Orpheus: Studies of Orphic Fragments in Honour of Alberto Bernabé*. De Gruyter. 61–8.
Herman, G. (1987). *Ritualised Friendship and the Greek City*. Cambridge University Press.
Hermann, A. (2004). *To Think Like God*. Parmenides Publishing.
Herrero de Jáuregui, M. (2010). *Orpheus and Christianity in Late Antiquity*. De Gruyter.
Herrero de Jáuregui, M. (2011). *Tracing Orpheus: Studies of Orphic Fragments in Honour of Alberto Bernabé*. De Gruyter.

Herrero de Jáuregui, M. (2015). 'The poet and his addressee in Orphic Hymns.' In Faulkner, A. Hodkinson, O. eds. *Hymnic Narrative and the Narratology of Greek Hymns*. Brill. 224–44.

Hershbell, J. P. (1970). 'Hesiod and Empedocles.' *The Classical Journal* 65.4: 145–61.

Hicks. R. D. (1925). *Diogenes Laertius, Lives of the Eminent Philosophers*. Harvard University Press.

Hitch, S. (2009). *King of Sacrifice: Ritual and Royal Authority in the Iliad*. Harvard University Press.

Hocart, M (1987 [1936]). *Kings and Councillors*. Chicago University Press.

Holbraad, M. (2008). 'Ontology is just another word for culture. Motion tabled at the 2008 meeting of the Group for Debates in Anthropological Theory (GDAT).' University of Manchester.

Holbraad, M. (2012). *Truth in Motion: The Recursive Anthropology of Cuban Divination*. Chicago University Press.

Holbraad, M. and Pedersen M. (2017). *The Ontological Turn: An Anthropological Exposition*. Cambridge University Press.

Holbraad, M. and Willerslev, R. (2007). 'Afterword. Transcendental Perspectivism: Anonymous Viewpoints from Inner Asia.' *Inner Asia* 9.2: 329–45.

Holmes, B. (2010). *The Symptom and the Subject: The Emergence of the Physical Body in Ancient Greece*. Princeton University Press.

Holmes, B. (2017). 'The Body of Western Embodiment: Classical Antiquity and the Early History of a Problem.' In Smith, J. E. H. ed. *Embodiment: A History*. 17–53.

Hordern J. (2000). 'Notes on the Orphic Papyrus from Gurôb.' *ZPE* 129: 131–40.

Hornung, E. (1983 [1971]). *Conceptions of God in Ancient Egypt*. Routledge and Kegan Paul.

Howell, S. (2014). 'Metamorphosis and Identity: Chewong Animistic Ontology.' In Harvey, G. ed. *The Handbook of Contemporary Animism*. Acumen. 101–12.

Hubert, H. and Mauss, M. (1964 [1898]). *Sacrifice: Its Nature and Function*. Chicago University Press.

Hussey, E. (1999). 'Heraclitus.' In Long. A. A. ed. *The Cambridge Companion to Greek Philosophy*. Cambridge University Press. 88–112.

Hussey, E. (2000). 'The Milesians.' In Brunschwig, J. and Lloyd, G. E. R. eds. *Greek Thought: A Guide to Classical Knowledge*. 882–93.

Hyland, D. A. (2006). 'First of All Came Chaos.' In Hyland, D. A. and Panteleimon Manoussakis, J. eds. *Heidegger and the Greeks: Interpretive Essays*. Indiana University Press. 9–23.

Ingold, T. (2011). *Being Alive: Essays on Movement, Knowledge and Description*. Routledge.

Ingold, T. (2016a). 'A Naturalist Abroad in the Museum of Ontology: Philippe Descola's *Beyond Nature and Culture*.' *Anthropological Forum* 26.3: 301–20.

Ingold, T. (2016b). 'Rejoinder to Descola's "Biolatry: A Surrender of Understanding."' *Anthropological Forum* 26.3: 329–32.

Iribarren, L. (2018). *Fabriquer le Monde: Technique et Cosmogonie dans la Poésie Grecque Archaique*. Classiques Garnier.

Irwin, E. (2005). 'Gods Among Men? The Social and Political Dynamics of the Hesiodic Catalogue of Women.' In Hunter, R. ed. *The Hesiodic Catalogue of Women*. Cambridge University Press. 35–84.

Jacobs, A. (2012). 'Was an "Orphic Anthropogony" Known to Plato?' *Mouseion* 12.3: 297–323.

Jaeger, W. (2002 [1936]). *The Theology of the Early Greek Philosophers*. Wipf & Stock Pub.

Janko, R. (1997). 'The Physicist as Hierophant: Aristophanes, Socrates and the Authorship of the Derveni Papyrus.' *ZPE* 118: 61–94.

Janko, R. (2001). 'The Derveni Papyrus (Diagoras of Melos, Apopyrgizontes Logoi?): A New Translation.' *Classical Philology* 96: 1–32.

Janko, R. (2008). 'Reconstructing (Again) the Opening of the Derveni Papyrus.' *ZPE* 166: 37–51.

Janko, R. (2010). 'Orphic Cosmogony, Hermeneutic Necessity and the Unity of the Derveni Papyrus.' In Bernabé, A., Casadesús, F. and Santamaría, M. A. eds. *Orfeo y el orfismo: Nuevas perspectivas*. 178–92.

Janowski, M. and Kerlogue, F. (2007). *Kinship and Food in South East Asia*. Nias Press.

Jay, N. (1988). 'Sacrifice, Descent and the Patriarchs.' *Vetus Testamentum* 38: 52–70.

Jay, N. (1992). *Throughout Your Generations Forever: Sacrifice, Religion, and Paternity*. Chicago University Press.

Jiménez San Cristóbal, A. I. (2009). 'The Meaning of βάκχος and βακχεύειν in Orphism.' In Cassadio, G. and Johnston, P. eds. *Mystic Cults in Magna Graecia*. University of Texas Press. 46–60.

Jiyuan Yu (2015). '*Logos* and *Dao*: Conceptions of Reality in Heraclitus and Laozi.' In Li, C. and Perkins, F. eds. *Chinese Metaphysics and its Problems*. Cambridge University Press. 105–20.

Johnston, S. (2011). 'In Praise of the Disordered: Plato, Eliade and the Ritual Implications of a Greek Cosmogony.' *Archiv für Religionsgeschichte* 13.1: 51–68.

Jones, C. P. (1999). *Kinship Diplomacy in the Ancient World*. Cambridge University Press.

Jullien, F. (2015). *The Book of Beginnings*. Yale University Press.

Kadletz, E. (1984). 'The Sacrifice of Eumaios the Pig Herder.' *GRBS* 25: 99–105.

Kahle, M. (2011). 'OF 437 and the Transformation of the Soul.' In Herrero de Jáuregui, M. ed. *Tracing Orpheus: Studies of Orphic Fragments in Honour of Alberto Bernabé*. De Gruyter. 153–8.

Kahn, C. (1981). *The Art and Thought of Heraclitus: An Edition of the Fragments with Translation and Commentary*. Cambridge University Press.

Kahn, C. (1974). 'Religion and Natural Philosophy in Empedocles' Doctrine of the Soul.' In Mourelatos, A. P. D. ed. *The Pre-Socratics: A Collection of Critical Essays*. Princeton University Press. 426–56.

Kahn, C. (1994). *Anaximander and the Origins of Greek Cosmology*. Indianapolis University Press.
Kahn, C. (1997). 'Was Euthyphro the Author of the Derveni Papyrus?' In Laks, A. and Most, G. eds. *Studies on the Derveni Papyrus*. Oxford University Press. 55–63.
Kahn, C. (2001). *Pythagoras and Pythagoreans*. Hackett Publishing Company.
Kapferer, B. (2014). 'Back to the Future: Descola's Neostructuralism.' *HAU* 4.3: 389–400.
Kenna, M. E. (2001). *Greek Island Life: Fieldwork on Anafi*. Harwood Academic Publishers.
Kerferd, G. B. (1981). *The Sophistic Movement*. Cambridge University Press.
Kindt, J. (2012). *Rethinking Greek Religion*. Cambridge University Press.
Kingsley, P. (1995). *Ancient Philosophy, Mystery and Magic*. Clarendon Press.
Kingsley, P. (1996). 'Empedocles' Two Poems.' *Hermes* 124.1: 108–11.
Kingsley, P. (2003). *Reality*. Golden Sufi Center.
Kingsley, P. (2010). *A Story Waiting to Pierce You: Mongolia, Tibet and the Destiny of the Western World*. Golden Sufi Center.
Kirk, G. S. (1954). *Heraclitus: The Cosmic Fragments*. Cambridge University Press.
Kirk, G. S. (1970). *Myth: Its Meaning and Functions in Ancient and Other Cultures*. Cambridge University Press.
Kirk, G. S., Raven, J. E. and Schofield, M. (1957). *The Presocratic Philosophers: A Critical History with a Selection of Texts*. Cambridge University Press.
Koning, H. (2010). *Hesiod: The Other Poet: Ancient Reception of a Cultural Icon*. Brill.
Kotwick, M. (2014). 'Reconstructing Ancient Constructions of the Orphic Theogony: Aristotle, Syrianus and Michael of Ephesus on Orpheus' Succession of the First Gods.' *Classical Quarterly* 64.1: 75–90.
Kouromenos, T. Parssoglou G. M. and Tsantsanoglou, K. (2006). *The Derveni Papyrus. Edited with Introduction and Commentary*. Casa Editrice Leo S. Olschki.
Kovacs, D. (1995). *Euripides, Hippolytus*. Harvard University Press.
Kullmann, W. (1985). 'Gods and Men in the *Iliad* and the *Odyssey*.' *Harvard Studies in Classical Philology* 89: 1–23.
Laks, A. (1997). 'Between Religion and Philosophy: The Function of Allegory in the Derveni Papyrus.' *Phronesis* 42.2: 121–42.
Laks, A. (1999). 'Soul, Sensation and Thought.' In Long, A. A ed. *The Cambridge Companion to Greek Philosophy*. Cambridge University Press.
Laks, A. and Most, G. W. (1997). *Studies on the Derveni Papyrus*. Oxford University Press.
Lambert, W. G. (1963). 'The Great Battle of the Mesopotamian Religious Year: The Conflict in the Akītu House (a Summary).' *Iraq* 25.2: 189–90.
Lampert, L. (2010). *How Philosophy Became Socratic*. Chicago University Press.
Lanfer, P. (2012). *Remembering Eden: The Reception History of Genesis 3:22-24*. Oxford University Press.
Lardinois, A. (1998). 'How the Days Fit the Works in Hesiod's *Works and Days*.' *The American Journal of Philology* 119.3: 319–36.

Larson, J. (1995). *Greek Heroine Cults.* Routledge.
Larson, J. (2007). *Ancient Greek Cults: A Guide.* Routledge.
Larson, J. (2016). *Understanding Greek Religion.* Routledge.
Lattimore, R. (1951). Homer, *The Iliad.* Chicago University Press.
Laugrand, F. (1999). 'Le Mythe comme Instrument de Mémoire: Remémoration et Interprétation d'un Extrait de la Genèse par un Aîné inuit de la Terre de Baffin.' *Études/Inuit/Studies* 23.1/2: 91–115.
Lavery, J. (2008). 'Protagoras.' In O'Grady, P. ed. *The Sophists: An Introduction.* Bloomsbury. 30–45.
Leach, E. (1961). 'Rethinking Anthropology Malinowski Memorial Lecture.' In *Rethinking Anthropology.* The Athlone Press. 1–28.
Leitao, D. (2012). *The Pregnant Male as Myth and Metaphor in Classical Greek Literature.* Cambridge University Press.
Leon Ruiz, N. E. (2007). *Heraclitus and the Work of Awakening.* State University of New York.
Levaniouk, O. (2007). 'The Toys of Dionysos.' *Harvard Studies in Classical Philology* 103: 165–202.
Levine, M. (2002). *Pantheism: A Non-Theistic Concept of Deity.* Routledge.
Levinson, S. (2003). *Space in Language and Cognition: Explorations in Cognitive Diversity.* Cambridge University Press.
Lévi-Strauss, C. (1966). *The Savage Mind.* Chicago University Press.
Lévi-Strauss, C. (1969). *The Raw and the Cooked.* Chicago University Press.
Lévi-Strauss, C. (1977). 'How Myths Die.' *Structural Anthropology, vol. II.* Allen Lane. 256–68.
Lévi-Strauss, C. (1995). *The History of Lynx.* Chicago University Press.
Lévi-Strauss, C. (2001). 'Hourglass configurations.' In Maranda, P. ed. *The Double Twist: From Ethnography to Morphodynamics.* Toronto University Press. 15–32.
Levy, H. (1979). 'Homer's Gods: A Comment on Their Immortality.' *GRBS* 20: 215–18.
Lincoln, B. (1999). *Theorizing Myth: Narrative, Ideology, and Scholarship.* Chicago University Press.
Lincoln, B. (2011). 'The One and the Many in Iranian Creation Myths: Rethinking "Nostalgia for Paradise".' *Archiv für Religionsgeschichte* 13.1: 15–30.
Lincoln, B. (2012a). 'In Praise of Chaos.' In *Gods and Demons Priests and Scholars.* Chicago University Press. 109–21.
Lincoln, B. (2012b). 'From Bergaigne to Meuli: How Animal Sacrifice Became a Hot Topic.' In Faraone, C. and Naiden, F. S. eds. *Greek and Roman Animal Sacrifice: Ancient Victims, Modern Observers.* Cambridge University Press. 13–31.
Linforth, I. M. (1973 [1941]). *The Arts of Orpheus.* Arno Press.
Littleton, S. (1969). 'Lévi-Strauss and the "Kingship in Heaven": A Structural Analysis of a Widespread Theogonic Theme.' *Journal of the Folklore Institute* 6.1: 70–84.
Littman, R. (1990). *Kinship and Politics in Athens 600–400 B.C.* Peter Lang Publishing.

Litwa, M. (2012). *We Are Being Transformed: Deification in Paul's Soteriology.* De Grutyer.
Litwa, M. (2013). *Becoming Divine: An Introduction to Deification in Western Culture.* Wipf & Stock.
Litwa, M. (2016). *Desiring Divinity: Self-deification in Early Jewish and Christian Mythmaking.* Oxford University Press.
Lloyd, A. (2009). *What is a God? Studies on the Nature of Greek Divinity.* David Brown Book Company.
Lloyd, G. E. R. (1962). 'Right and Left in Greek Philosophy.' *The Journal of Hellenic Studies* 82: 56–66.
Lloyd, G. E. R. (1966). *Polarity and Analogy.* Cambridge University Press.
Lloyd, G. E. R. (1975). 'Greek Cosmologies.' In Blacker, C. and Loewe, M. eds. *Ancient Cosmologies.* Allen and Unwin. 198–224.
Lloyd, G. E. R. (1983). *Science, Folklore and Ideology: Studies in the Life Sciences in Ancient Greece.* Cambridge University Press.
Lloyd, G. E. R. (1990). *Demystifying Mentalities.* Cambridge University Press.
Lloyd, G. E. R. (1996). *Adversaries and Authorities.* Cambridge University Press.
Lloyd, G. E. R. (1999). *Magic, Reason, and Experience: Studies in the Origins and Development of Greek Science.* Duckworth Press.
Lloyd, G. E. R. (2000). 'Images of the World.' In Brunshwig, J. and Lloyd, G. E. R. eds. *Greek Thought: A Guide to Classical Knowledge.* Harvard University Press.
Lloyd, G. E. R. (2004). *Ancient Worlds, Modern Reflections: Philosophical Perspectives on Greek and Chinese Science and Culture.* Oxford University Press.
Lloyd, G. E. R. (2009). *Cognitive Variations: Reflections on the Unity and Diversity of the Human Mind.* Oxford University Press.
Lloyd, G. E. R. (2011). 'Humanity Between Gods and Beasts? Ontologies in Question.' *Journal of the Royal Anthropological Institute* 17.4: 829–45.
Lloyd, G. E. R. (2012). *Being, Humanity, and Understanding: Studies in Ancient and Modern Societies.* Oxford University Press.
Lloyd, G. E. R. (2013). 'Response to Comments on Being, Humanity, and Understanding.' *HAU* 3.1: 204–9.
Lloyd, G. E. R. (2015). *Analogical Investigations.* Cambridge University Press.
Lloyd, G. E. R. and Sivin, N. (2002). *The Way and the Word: Science and Medicine in Early China and Greece.* Yale University Press.
Lloyd-Jones, H. (1990). 'Pindar and the Afterlife.' In *Greek Epic, Lyric, and Tragedy.* Oxford University Press. 80–109.
Lombardo, S. and Bell, K. (1997). 'Protagoras.' In Cooper, J. ed. *Plato, Complete Works.* University of Indianapolis Press. 746–91.
Loney, A. and Scully, S. (2018). *The Oxford Handbook of Hesiod.* Oxford University Press.
Long, A. A. (1963). 'The Principles of Parmenides' Cosmogony.' *Phronesis* 8.2: 90–107.
Long, A. A. (1996a). 'Heraclitus and Stoicism.' *Stoic Studies.* Cambridge University Press. 35–57.

Long, A. A. (1996b). 'Soul and Body in Stoicism.' *Stoic Studies*. Cambridge University Press. 224–49.
Long, A. A. (1999). *The Cambridge Companion to Greek Philosophy*. Cambridge University Press.
Long, A. A. (2005). 'Law and Nature in Greek Thought.' In Gagarin, M. and Cohen, D. eds. *The Cambridge Companion to Ancient Greek Law*. Cambridge University Press. 412–30.
Long, A. A. (2015). *Greek Models of Mind and Self*. Harvard University Press.
López-Ruiz, C. (2010). *When the Gods Were Born: Greek Cosmogonies and the Near East*. Harvard University Press.
López-Ruiz, C. (2012). 'How to Start a Cosmogony: On the Poetics of Beginnings in Greece and the Near East.' *Journal of Ancient Near Eastern Religions* 12: 30–48.
Loraux, N. (2000). *Born of the Earth: Myth and Politics in Athens*. Cornell University Press.
Lourenço, F. (2011). 'A "Cloud of Metaphysics" in Pindar: The Opening of *Nemean 6*.' *Humanitas* 63: 61–73.
Lovejoy, A. O. (1936). *The Great Chain of Being: A Study of the History of an Idea*. Cambridge University Press.
Lovejoy, A. O. and Boas, G. C. (1997 [1935]). *Primitivism and Related Ideas in Antiquity*. Johns Hopkins Press.
Lyons, D. (2003). 'Dangerous Gifts: Ideologies of Marriage and Exchange in Ancient Greece.' *Classical Antiquity* 22.1: 93–134.
Macchioro, V. (1930). *From Orpheus to Paul*. Constable and Company Limited.
Macé, A. (2016). 'Nature among the Greeks: Empirical Philology and the Ontological Turn in Historical Anthropology.' In Skafish. P. and Charbonnier, P. *Comparative Metaphysics: Ontology After Anthropology*. Rowman & Littlefield. 201–21.
Mackenzie, T. (2021). *Poetry and Poetics in the Presocratic Philosophers*. Cambridge University Press.
MacLeod, M. (1967). *Lucian, Amores*. Harvard University Press.
Maffie. J. (2014). *Aztec Philosophy: Understanding a World in Motion*. University Press of Colorado.
Martin, D. (1999). *The Corinthian Body*. Yale University Press.
Martinez, L. (2011). 'Aristotle, *Metaphysics* 13.4: a Problematic Reference to Orphism (OF 20 IV).' In Herrero de Jáuregui, M. ed. *Tracing Orpheus: Studies of Orphic Fragments in Honour of Alberto Bernabé*. De Gruyter. 41–9.
Matthews, W. (2017). 'Ontology with Chinese Characteristics: Homology as a Mode of Identification.' *HAU* 7.1: 265–85.
McClymond, K. (2008). *Beyond Sacred Violence*. The Johns Hopkins University Press.
McNeil, R. (1986). 'Protagoras the Historian.' *History and Theory* 25.3: 299–318.
McWhorter, J. (2014). *The Language Hoax*. Oxford University Press.
Megino C. (2011). 'Presence in Stoicism of an Orphic Doctrine of the Soul quoted by Aristotle (*de Anima* 410b 27 = OF 421).' In Herrero de Jáuregui, M. ed. *Tracing*

Orpheus: Studies of Orphic Fragments in Honour of Alberto Bernabé. De Gruyter. 139–47.

Meisner, D. A. (2015). *'Zeus the Head, Zeus the Middle': Studies in the History and Interpretation of the Orphic Theogonies.* University of Western Ontario Press.

Meisner, D. A. (2018). *Orphic Tradition and the Birth of the Gods.* Oxford University Press.

Mihai A. (2010). 'Soul's Aitherial Abode According to the Poteidaia Epitaph and the Presocratic Philosophers.' *Numen* 57: 553–82.

Mikalson, J. (2010). *Greek Popular Religion in Greek Philosophy.* Oxford University Press.

Miller, M. (1983). 'The Implicit Logic of Hesiod's Cosmogony: An Examination of Hesiod's *Theogony*, 116–133.' *Independent Journey of Philosophy* 4: 131–42.

Miller, M. (2001). 'First of All: On the Semantics and Ethics of Hesiod's Cosmogony.' *Ancient Philosophy* 21: 251–76.

Miller, P. L. (2011). *Becoming God: Pure Reason in Early Greek Philosophy.* Continuum.

Mitchell-Boyask, R. (2013). *Aeschylus: Eumenides.* Bloomsbury.

Mondi, R. (1986). 'Tradition and innovation in the Hesiodic Titanomachy.' *TAPh/A* 116: 25–48.

Mondi, R. (1989). 'Χαος and the Hesiodic Cosmogony.' *Harvard Studies in Classical Philology* 92: 1–41.

Morales, H. (2007). *Classical Mythology: A Very Short Introduction.* Oxford University Press.

Morand, A. F. (2009). 'Orphic Gods and Other Gods.' In Lloyd, A. (2009). *What is a God? Studies on the Nature of Greek Divinity.* David Brown Book Company. 169–83.

Morand, A. F. (2010). 'Etymologies of divine names in Orphic texts.' In Bernabé A. Casadesús, F. Santamaría Á. M. eds. *Orfeo y el Orfismo Nuevas Perspectivas.* Alicante. 157–76.

Morand, A. F. (2015). 'The Narrative Techniques of the *Orphic Hymns*.' In Faulkner, A. Hodkinson, O. *Hymnic Narrative and the Narratology of Greek Hymns.* Brill. 209–24.

Morgan, K. (2000). *Myth and Philosophy from the Presocratics to Plato.* Cambridge University Press.

Morgan, M. (1990). *Platonic Piety: Philosophy and Rituals in Fourth-Century Athens.* Yale University Press.

Morgan, T. (2013). 'Divine-Human Relations in the Aesopic Corpus.' *Journal of Ancient History* 1.1: 3–26.

Morris, I. (1986). 'The Use and Abuse of Homer.' *Classical Antiquity* 5.1: 81–138.

Most, G. W. (1997). 'The Fire Next Time: Cosmology, Allegoresis and Salvation in the Derveni Papyrus.' *The Journal of Hellenic Studies* 117: 117–35.

Most, G. W. (1999). 'From Logos to Mythos,' In Buxton, R. ed. *From Myth to Reason? Studies in the Development of Greek Thought.* Oxford University Press. 25–47.

Most, G. W. (2013). 'Heraclitus on Religion.' *Rhizomata* 1.2: 1–15.

Most, G. W. (2018). *Hesiod, Theogony. Works and Days. Testimonia*. Harvard University Press.
Murray, G. (1925). *Five Stages of Greek Religion*. Oxford University Press.
Nagler, M. N. (1988). 'Toward a Semantics of Ancient Conflict: Eris in the *Iliad*.' *The Classical World* 82.2: 81–90.
Nagy, G. (2010). 'The Meaning of Homoios (ὁμοῖος) in Verse 27 of the Hesiodic *Theogony* and Elsewhere.' In Mitsis, P. and Tsagalis, C. eds. *Allusion, Authority, and Truth: Critical Perspectives on Greek Poetic and Rhetorical Praxis*. De Gruyter. 153–67.
Naiden, F. S. (2012). 'Blessed are the Parasites.' In Faraone, C. and Naiden, F. S. eds. *Greek and Roman Animal Sacrifice: Ancient Victims, Modern Observers*. Cambridge University Press. 55–84.
Naiden, F. S. (2013). *Smoke Signals for the Gods: Ancient Greek Sacrifice from the Archaic through Roman Periods*. Oxford University Press.
Nelson, S. (1998). *God and the Land: The Metaphysics of Farming in Hesiod and Vergil*. Oxford University Press.
Nestle, W. 1940. *Vom Mythos zu Logos: Die Selbstentfaltung des griechischen Denkens von Homer bis auf dis Sophistik und Sokrates*. Kröner.
Newmyer, S. (2017). *The Animal and the Human in Ancient and Modern Thought: The 'Man Alone of Animals' Concept*. Routledge.
Nilsson, M. P. (1935). 'Early Orphism and Kindred Religious Movements', *The Harvard Theological Review* 28.3: 181–230.
Nilsson, M. P. (1955). *Geschichte der Griechischen Religion*. Munich.
Nussbaum, M. (1972). 'ΨΥΧΗ in Heraclitus I.' *Phronesis* 17.1: 1–16.
Obbink, D. (2003). 'Allegory and Exegesis in the Derveni Papyrus: The Origin of Greek Scholarship.' In Boys-Stones, G. R. ed. *Metaphor, Allegory, and the Classical Tradition: Ancient Thought and Modern Revisions*. Oxford University Press. 177–88.
Oldfather, C. H. (1933). *Diodorus, The Library of History*. Harvard University Press.
Osborne, C. (1987). 'Empedocles Recycled.' *Classical Quarterly* 37: 24–50.
Osborne, C. (2006). 'Was There an Eleatic Revolution in Philosophy?' In Goldhill S. and Osborne, R. eds. *Rethinking Revolutions through Ancient Greece*. Cambridge University Press. 218–45.
Osborne, C. (2009). *Dumb Beasts and Dead Philosophers*. Oxford University Press.
Osborne, R. (2006). *Rethinking Revolutions through Ancient Greece*. Cambridge University Press.
Otto, W. F. (1954). *The Homeric Gods*. Thames and Hudson.
Owen, H. P. (1971). *Concepts of Deity*. Macmillan.
Padel, R. (1992). *In and Out of the Mind: Greek Images of the Tragic Self*. Princeton University Press.
Papadopoulou, I. and Muellner, L. C. (2014). *Poetry as Initiation: The Center for Hellenic Studies Symposium on the Derveni Papyrus*. Harvard University Press.

Parker, R. (1995). 'Early Orphism.' In Powell, A. ed. *The Greek World*. Routledge. 483–510.
Parker, R. (1997). *Athenian Religion: A History*. Oxford University Press.
Parker, R. (2005). *Polytheism and Society at Athens*. Oxford University Press.
Parker, R. (2011). *On Greek Religion*. Cornell University Press.
Parker, R. (2014). 'Redefining Ancient Orphism: A Study in Greek Religion.' *Bryn Mawr Classical Review*. 2014.07.13.
Parkes, P. (2004). 'Fosterage, Kinship, and Legend: When Milk Was Thicker than Blood?' *Comparative Studies in Society and History* 46.3: 587–615.
Parkin, R. (2009). *Louis Dumont and Hierarchical Opposition*. Berghahn Books.
Peabody, B. (1975). *The Winged Word: A Study in the Technique of Ancient Greek Oral Composition as Seen Principally through Hesiod's Works and Days*. State University of New York Press.
Petropoulou A. (1987). 'The Sacrifice of Eumaeus Reconsidered.' *GRBS* 28: 135–49.
Picot, C. (2007). 'Empedocles, fragment 115.3: Can One of the Blessed Pollute his Limbs with Blood?' In Stern S. and Corrigan, K. eds. *Reading Ancient Texts I: Presocratics and Plato—Essays in Honour of Denis O'Brien*. Brill. 41–56.
Picot, C. (2012). 'Empédocle fr. 128 – Cronos, Poséidon, Cypris, Hadès – Mythe hésiodique des races.' *RMM* 3: 339–56.
Pinker, S. (1994). *The Language Instinct*. William Morrow and Company.
Price, S. (1984). *Rituals and Power: The Roman Imperial Cult in Asia Minor*. Cambridge University Press.
Price, S. (1999). *Religions of the Ancient Greeks*. Cambridge University Press.
Prickard, A. O. (1918). *Plutarch, The E at Delphi*. Harvard University Press.
Prinz, J. (2012). *Beyond Human Nature: How Culture and Experience Shape Our Lives*. Penguin Books.
Pritzl, K. (1985). 'On the Way to Wisdom in Heraclitus.' *Phoenix* 39.4: 303–16.
Pucci, P. (1994). 'Gods' Intervention and Epiphany in Sophocles.' *The American Journal of Philology* 115.1: 15–46.
Puett, M. (2002). *To Become a God: Cosmology, Sacrifice and Self Divinization in Early China*. Harvard University Press.
Puett, M. (2008). 'Ritual and the Subjunctive.' In Seligman, A., Weller, R. and Simon, B. eds. *Ritual and its Consequences: An Essay on the Limits of Sincerity*. Oxford University Press. 17–42.
Puett, M. (2011). 'Social Order or Social Chaos.' In Orsi, R. ed. *The Cambridge Companion to Religious Studies*. Cambridge University Press. 109–30.
Pusey, E. B. (1838). *Augustine, The Confessions*. Oxford University Press.
Quigley, D. (2005). *The Character of Kingship*. Bloomsbury.
Rackham, H. (1981). *Aristotle, Eudemian Ethics*. Harvard University Press.
Rangos S. (2012). 'Empedocles on divine nature.' *RMM* 75: 315–38.
Redfield, J. (1975). *Nature and Culture in the Iliad: The Tragedy of Hector*. Chicago University Press.

Redfield, J. (2003). *The Locrian Maidens: Love and Death in Greek Italy*. Princeton University Press.
Remes, P. (2014). *Neoplatonism*. Routledge.
Renehan, R. (1980). 'On the Greek Origins of the Concept of Incorporeality and Immateriality.' *GRBS* 21: 105–38.
Riedweg, C. (1997). 'Orfismo en Empédocles.' *Taula* 27–8: 33–59.
Risjord, M. and Palecek, M. (2012). 'Relativism and the Ontological Turn Within Anthropology.' *Philosophy of the Social Sciences* 43.1: 3–23.
Rives, J. B. 'The Theology of Animal Sacrifice in the Ancient Greek World.' In Wright Knust, J. and Varhelyi, Z. eds. *Ancient Mediterranean Sacrifice*. Oxford University Press. 187–203.
Robbins, J. (2004). *Becoming Sinners: Christianity and Moral Torment in a Papua New Guinea Society*. University of California Press.
Robertson Smith, W. (1889). *Lectures on the Religion of the Semites*. A. and C. Black.
Robinson, T. (1986). 'Heraclitus on the Soul.' *The Monist* 69.3: 305–14.
Rochberg, F. (2005). 'Mesopotamian Cosmology.' In Snell, D. eds. *A Companion to the Near East*. Blackwell. 316–29.
Rodríguez, C. M. (2019). 'Daimons in the Derveni Papyrus and Early Stoicism.' In Santamaría, M. *The Derveni Papyrus: Unearthing Ancient Mysteries*. Brill. 30–47.
Rohde, E. (2000[1925]). *Psyche*. Routledge and Kegan Paul.
Rosaldo, R. (1980). *Ilongot Headhunting 1883–1974: A Study in Society and History*. Stanford University Press.
Rose, H. J. (1936). 'The Ancient Grief: A Study of Pindar, Fr. 133 (Bergk).' In Bailey, C. ed. *Greek Poetry and Life: Essays Presented to Gilbert Murray on His Seventieth Birthday, January 2, 1936*. Oxford University Press. 79–96.
Rowe, C. J. (1980). 'One and Many in Greek Religion.' In Portman, A. and Ritsema, R. eds. *Oneness and variety*. Brill. 54–67.
Rowe, C. J. (1983). 'Archaic Thought in Hesiod.' *The Journal of Hellenic Studies* 103: 124–35.
Rowett, C. (2016). 'Love, Sex and the Gods: Why things have divine names in Empedocles' poem, and why they come in pairs.' *Rhizomata*. 4.1: 80–110.
Rowett, C. (2017). 'On being reminded of Heraclitus by the motifs in Plato's *Phaedo*.' In *Heraklit in Kontext*. Fantino, E., Muss, U., Schubert, C. and Sier, K. eds. De Gruyter. 373–413.
Roy, J. (1999). '"*Polis*" and "*Oikos*" in Classical Athens.' *Greece & Rome* 46.1: 1–18.
Rusten, J. S. (1985). 'Interim Notes on the Papyrus of Derveni.' *Harvard Studies in Classical Philology* 89: 121–40.
Ryan, P. (2012). *Plato's Phaedrus: A Reader's Commentary for Greek Readers*. University of Oklahoma Press.
Sahlins, M. (1981a). *Historical Metaphors and Mythic Reality: Structure in the Early History of the Sandwich Islands Kingdom*. University of Michigan Press.
Sahlins, M. (1981b). 'The Stranger-King: Or Dumézil Among the Fijians.' *The Journal of Pacific History* 16.3: 107–32.

Sahlins, M. (1985). *Islands of History*. Chicago University Press.
Sahlins, M. (1995). *How Natives Think: About Captain Cook, for example*. Chicago University Press.
Sahlins, M. (1996). 'The Sadness of Sweetness: The Native Anthropology of Western Cosmology.' *Current Anthropology* 37.3: 395–428.
Sahlins, M. (2002). *Waiting for Foucault, Still*. Prickley Paradigm Press.
Sahlins, M. (2004). *Apologies to Thucydides: Understanding History as Culture and Vice Versa*. Chicago University Press.
Sahlins, M. (2008). *The Western Illusion of Human Nature*. Prickly Paradigm Press.
Sahlins, M. (2011). 'Twin-Born with greatness, the dual kingship of Sparta.' *HAU: Journal of Ethnographic Theory* 1: 56–70.
Sahlins, M. (2013). *What Kinship Is – and Is Not*. Chicago University Press.
Santamaría, M. A. (2016a). 'A Phallus Hard to Swallow: the meaning of αἰδοῖος/-ον in the Derveni Papyrus.' *Classical Philology* 111.2: 139–164
Santamaría, M. A. (2016b). 'Did Plato Know of the Orphic God Protogonos?' In Martín Velasco, J. and García Blanco, J. eds. *Greek Philosophy and Mystery Cults*. Cambridge University Press. 205–31.
Santamaría, M. A. (2017). 'The Sceptre and the Sickle. The Transmission of Divine Power in the Orphic *Rhapsodies*.' In Fotini Viltanioti, I. and Marmodoro, A. eds. *Divine Powers in Late Antiquity*. Oxford University Press. 108–24.
Santamaría, M. A. (2019). The Orphic Poem of the Derveni Papyrus and Hesiod's *Theogony*. In Santamaría, M. *The Derveni Papyrus: Unearthing Ancient Mysteries*. Brill. 47–65.
Sassi, M. (2001). *The Science of Man in Ancient Greece*. Chicago University Press.
Schiappa, E. (2003). *Protagoras and Logos: A Study in Greek Philosophy and Rhetoric*. University of South Carolina Press.
Schibili H. S. (1990). *Pherekydes of Syros*. Clarendon Press.
Schlosser, J. (2020). *Herodotus in the Anthropocene*. The University of Chicago Press.
Schmidt, N. (1920). 'Bellerophon's Tablet and the Homeric Question in the Light of Oriental Research.' *Transactions and Proceedings of the American Philological Association* 51: 56–70.
Schopenhauer, A. (1951). 'A Few Words on Pantheism.' *Essays from the Parerga and Paralipomena*. Allen and Unwin. 40–1.
Schrempp, G. (1992). *Magical Arrows: The Maori, the Greeks, and the Folklore of the Universe*. University of Wisconsin Press.
Scott, M. W. (2007). *The Severed Snake: Matrilineages, Making Place, and a Melanesian Christianity in Southeast Solomon Islands*. Carolina Academic Press.
Scott, M. W. (2014). 'Book Review: Anthropological Cosmochemistry.' *Anthropology of This Century* (11).
Scully, S. (2015). *Hesiod's Theogony: From Near Eastern Creation Myths to Paradise Lost*. Oxford University Press.

Seaford, R. (1981). 'Dionysiac Drama and the Dionysiac Mysteries.' *The Classical Quarterly* 31.2: 252–75.
Seaford, R. (1986). 'Immortality, Salvation, and the Elements.' *Harvard Studies in Classical Philology* 90: 1–26.
Seaford, R. (1989). 'Homeric and Tragic Sacrifice.' *Transactions of the American Philological Association* 119: 87–95.
Seaford, R. (2004). *Money and the Early Greek Mind: Homer, Philosophy, Tragedy*. Cambridge University Press.
Seaford, R. (2006). *Dionysus*. Taylor and Francis.
Seaford, R. (2012). *Cosmology and the Polis: The Social Construction of Space and Time in the Tragedies of Aeschylus*. Cambridge University Press.
Sedley, D. (1999). 'The Ideal of Godlikeness.' In Fine, G. ed. *Plato Vol. 2*. Oxford University Press. 309–29.
Sedley, D. (2003). *Plato's Cratylus*. Cambridge University Press.
Sedley, D. (2007). *Creationism and Its Critics in Antiquity*. University of California Press.
Serres, M. (2009). *Ecrivains, Savants et Philosophes Font le Tour du Monde*. Le Pommier.
Sfameni Gasparro, G. (2015). 'Daimonic Power.' In Eidinow, E. Kindt, J. *The Oxford Handbook of Ancient Greek Religion*. Oxford University Press. 413–29.
Shorey, P. (1969). *Plato, Laws*. Harvard University Press.
Sider, D. (1997). 'Heraclitus in the Derveni Papyrus.' In Laks, A. and Most, G. eds. *Studies on the Derveni Papyrus*. Oxford University Press. 129–48.
Sider, D. (2014). 'The Orphic Poem of the Derveni Papyrus.' In Papadopoulou, I. and Muellner, L. C. eds. *Poetry as Initiation: The Center for Hellenic Studies Symposium on the Derveni Papyrus*. Harvard University Press. 225–55.
Smith, B. K. (1994). *Classifying the Universe: The Ancient Indian Varṇa System and the Origins of Caste*. Oxford University Press.
Smith, J. Z. (1972). 'The Wobbling Pivot.' *The Journal of Religion* 52.2: 134–49.
Smith, J. Z. (1978). *Map Is Not Territory: Studies in the History of Religion*. Chicago University Press.
Smyth, H. W. (1926). *Aeschylus, Prometheus Bound*. Harvard University Press.
Snell, B. (1953). *The Discovery of the Mind in Greek Philosophy and Literature*. Oxford University Press.
Snell, D. A. (2005). *A Companion to the Ancient Near East*. Blackwell.
Solmsen, F. (1949). *Hesiod and Aeschylus*. Cornell University Press.
Somer, B. D. (2000). 'The Babylonian Akitu Festival: Rectifying the King or Renewing the Cosmos?' *JANES* 27: 82–95.
Sommerstein, A. H. (1989). *Aeschylus, Eumenides*. Harvard University Press.
Sonik, K. (2013). 'From Hesiod's Abyss to Ovid's rudis indigestaque moles: Reading Chaos into the Babylonian "Epic of Creation."' In Scurlock, J. and Beal, R. eds. *Creation and Chaos: A Reconsideration of Herman Gunkel's Chaoskampf Hypothesis*. Winona Lake. 21–45.

Stafford, E. (2000). *Worshipping Virtues: Personification and the Divine in Ancient Greece*. Duckworth.

Stafford, E. (2002). 'Herakles between Gods and Heroes.' In Bremmer, J. and Erskine, A. eds. *The Gods of Ancient Greece*. Edinburgh University Press. 228–44.

Sterckx, R. (2002). *The Animal and the Daemon in Early China*. State University of New York Press.

Stewart, D. J. (1966). 'Hesiod and the Birth of Reason.' *The Antioch Review* 26.2: 213–31.

Stocking, C. H. (2009). *Bones, Smoke and Lies: Hellenizing Burnt Sacrifice*. University of California.

Stocking, C. H. (2017). *The Politics of Sacrifice in Early Greek Myth and Poetry*. Cambridge University Press.

Stocking, D. (2007). '"Res Agens": Towards an Ontology of the Homeric Self.' *College Literature* 34.2: 56–84.

Stoddard, K. (2004). *The Narrative Voice in the Theogony of Hesiod*. Brill.

Stokes, M. C. (1962). 'Hesiodic and Milesian Cosmogonies.' *Phronesis* 7.1: 1–37.

Stowers, S. T. (1995). 'Greeks who Sacrifice and those who do not: Towards an Anthropology of Greek Religion.' In White, L. and Yarbrough, O. eds. *The Social World of the Frist Christians: Essays in Honor of Wayne A. Meeks*. Fortress Press. 299–333.

Strathern, M. (1980). 'No Nature, No Culture: The Hagen Case.' In MacCormack C. and Strathern, M. eds. *Nature, Culture and Gender*. Cambridge University Press. 174–222.

Strenski, I. (2008). *Dumont on Religion Difference, Comparison, Transgression*. Equinox.

Struck, P. T. (2004). *Birth of the Symbol: Ancient Readers at the Limits of Their Texts*. Princeton University Press.

Suk Fong Jim, T. (2014). *Sharing with the Gods: Aparchai and Dekatai in Ancient Greece*. Oxford University Press.

Sundell Torjussen, S. (2008). *Metamorphoses of Myth: A Study of the "Orphic" Gold Tablets and the Derveni Papyrus*. University of Tromso.

Tambiah, S. J. (1968). 'The Magical Power of Words.' *Man* 3.2: 175–208.

Tambiah, S. J. (1990). *Magic, Science, Religion and the scope of Rationality*. Cambridge University Press.

Taran, L. (1999). 'Heraclitus: The River Fragments and their Implications.' *Elenchos* XX.1: 9–52.

Tarrant, R. J. (2002). 'Chaos in Ovid's *Metamorphoses* and its Neronian influence.' *Arethusa* 35: 349–60.

Taylor, A. C. (2013). 'Distinguishing Ontologies.' *HAU* 3.1: 201–4.

Tcherkézoff, S. (1994). 'On Hierarchal Reversals Ten Years Later.' *Journal of the Historical Society of Oxford* 25.2: 133–67.

Thomson, G. (1953). 'From Religion to Philosophy.' *The Journal of Hellenic Studies* 73: 77–83.

Tor, S. (2017). *Mortal and Divine in Early Greek Epistemology*. Cambridge University Press.

Toren, C. (1994). 'All Things Go in Pairs, or the Sharks Will Bite: The Antithetical Nature of Fijian Chiefship.' *Oceania* 64.3: 197–216.

Traill, D. A. (1989). 'Gold Armor for Bronze and Homer's Use of Compensatory TIMH.' *Classical Philology* 84.4: 301–5.

Trapp, M. (2002). 'Plato in Dio.' In Swain, S. ed. *Dio Chrysostom: Politics, Letters, and Philosophy.* Oxford University Press. 213–39.

Traunecker, C. (2001). *The Gods of Egypt*. Cornell University Press.

Tuck, R. (2003). *Leviathan*. Cambridge University Press.

Ullucci, D. (2012). *The Christian Rejection of Animal Sacrifice*. Oxford University Press.

Vacca, R. (1991). 'The Theology of Disorder in the *Iliad*.' *Religion & Literature* 23.2: 1–22.

Valeri, V. (1986). *Kingship and Sacrifice: Ritual and Society in Ancient Hawaii*. Chicago University Press.

Valeri, V. (2000). *The Forest of Taboos: Morality, Hunting, and Identity among the Huaulu of the Moluccas*. The University of Wisconsin Press.

Valeri, V. (2001). *Fragments from Forests and Libraries: A Collection of Essays*. Carolina Academic Press.

Vamvacas, C. (2009). *The Founders of Western Thought: The Presocratics*. Springer.

van den Berg, R. M. (2001). *Prolcus' Hymns. Essays, Translations, Commentary*. Brill.

van Gennep, A. (1960). *The Rites of Passage*. (1909). Chicago University Press.

van Noorden, H. (2014). *Playing Hesiod: The Myth of the Races in Classical Antiquity*. Cambridge University Press.

Verdenius, W. J. (1985). *A Commentary on Hesiod, Works and Days, vv. 1–382*. Brill.

Vergados, A. (2013). *The Homeric Hymn to Hermes: Introduction, Text and Commentary*. De Gruyter.

Vernant, J.-P. (1981). 'Sacrificial and Alimentary Codes in Hesiod's myth of Prometheus.' In Detienne, M. and Gordon, R. L. eds. *Myth, Religion and Society*. Cambridge University Press. 57–79.

Vernant, J.-P. (1983). 'Hestia–Hermes: The Religious Expression of Space and Movement in Ancient Greece.' In *Myth and Thought Among the Greeks*. 127–75.

Vernant, J.-P. (1984). *The Origin of Greek Thought*. Cornell University Press.

Vernant, J.-P. (1989). 'At Man's Table: Hesiod's Foundation Myth of Sacrifice.' In Detienne, M. and Vernant, J.-P. eds. *The Cuisine of Sacrifice Among the Greeks*. Chicago University Press. 23–89.

Vernant, J.-P. (1991). *Mortals and Immortals: Collected Essays*. Princeton University Press.

Versnel, H. S. (1994). *Inconsistencies in Greek and Roman Religion: Transition and Reversal in Myth and Ritual*. Brill.

Versnel, H. S. (2011). *Coping with the Gods: Wayward Readings in Greek Theology*. Brill.

Vilaça, A. (2010). *Strange Enemies: Indigenous Agency and Scenes of Encounter in Amazonia*. Duke University.
Vilaça, A. (2016). *Praying and Preying: Christianity in Indigenous Amazonia*. University of California Press.
Visala, A. (2011). *Naturalism, Theism and the Cognitive Study of Religion: Religion Explained*. Ashgate.
Vishwa, A. (2012). *Philosophy and Salvation in Greek Religion*. De Gruyter.
Viveiros de Castro, E. (1992). *From the Enemy's Point of View: Humanity and Divinity in an Amazonian Society*. Chicago University Press.
Viveiros de Castro, E. (1998). 'Cosmological Deixis and Amerindian Perspectivism.' *The Journal of the Royal Anthropological Institute* 4.3: 469–88.
Viveiros de Castro, E. (2007). 'The Crystal Forest: Notes on the Ontology of Amazonian Spirits.' *Inner Asia* 92.2: 153–72.
Viveiros de Castro, E. (2012). 'Cosmological Perspectivism in Amazonia and Elsewhere.' *Masterclass Series 1 HAU: Journal of Ethnographic Theory* 45–168.
Viveiros de Castro, E. (2015). The Relative Native. In *The Relative Native: Essays on Indigenous Conceptual Worlds*. HAU Books.
Vlastos, G. (1947). 'Equality and Justice in Early Greek Cosmologies.' *Classical Philology* 42.3: 156–78.
Vlastos, G. (1952). 'Theology and Philosophy in Early Greek Thought.' *The Philosophical Quarterly* 2.7: 97–123.
Vlastos, G. (1953). 'Isonomia.' *The American Journal of Philology* 74.4: 337–66.
von Brandenstein, C. G. (1978). 'Identical Principles Behind Australian Totemism and Empedoclean Philosophy.' In Hiatt, L. R. ed. *Australian Aboriginal Concepts*. Australian Institute of Aboriginal Studies. 134–45.
Wang, R. (2012). *Yinyang; the Way of Heaven and Earth in Chinese Thought and Culture*. Cambridge University Press.
Warren, J. (2007). *Presocratics*. Acumen.
Waterfield, R. (2000). *The First Philosophers*. Oxford University Press.
West, M. (1961). 'Hesiodea.' *Classical Quarterly* 11: 130–45.
West, M. (1966). *Hesiod, Theogony*. Oxford University Press.
West, M. (1976). 'Graeco-Oriental Orphism in the Third Century BC.' *Travaux du VIe Congrès International d'Études Classiques* 221–6.
West, M. (1978). *Hesiod, Works and Days*. Oxford University Press
West, M. (1982). 'The Orphics of Olbia.' *Zeitschrift für Papyrologie und Epigraphik* 45: 17–29.
West, M. (1983). *The Orphic Poems*. Oxford University Press.
West, M. (2007). *Indo-European Poetry and Myth*. Oxford University Press.
Westerink, L. G. (2009). *Damascius, The Greek Commentaries on Plato's 'Phaedo'*. Prometheus Trust.
Westerink, L. G. (2009). *The Greek Commentaries on Plato's 'Phaedo': Olympiodorus*. Prometheus Trust.

Wierzbicka, A. (2014). *Imprisoned in English: The Hazards of English as a Default Language*. Oxford University Press.
Wildberger, J. (2019). 'Cosmic Beauty in Stoicism: A Foundation for an Environmental Ethic as Love of the Other?' In Hunt, A. and Marlow, A. eds. *Ecology and Theology in the Ancient World*. Bloomsbury. 63–75.
Wilgaux, J. (2011). 'Consubstantiality, Incest, and Kinship in Ancient Greece.' In Rawson, B. ed. *A Companion to Families in the Greek and Roman Worlds*. Wiley-Blackwell. 217–30.
Wilson, B. (1970). *Rationality*. Blackwell.
Yasumura, N. (2013). *Challenges to the Power of Zeus in Early Greek Poetry*. Bloomsbury.
Zaidman, L. B. and Pantel, P. S. (2011). *Religion in the Ancient Greek City*. Trans. Cartledge, P. Cambridge University Press.
Zeitlin, F. I. (1978). 'The Dynamics of Misogyny in the Oresteia.' *Arethusa* 11: 149–84.
Zhmud L. (1992). 'Orphism and Grafitti from Olbia.' *Hermes* 120.2: 159–.
Zhmud L. (2012). *Pythagoras and the Early Pythagoreans*. Oxford University Press.
Zuntz, G. (1971). *Persephone: Three Essays on Religion and Thought in Magna Graecia*. Oxford University Press.

Index Locorum

This index includes references to passages quoted and discussed. Passages that are merely referred to as parallels or examples are generally omitted.

Anaximander
   DK 12 B 1: 203 n.23
Anaximenes
   DK 13 B 2: 10
Apollodorus
   The Library 3.5.8: 41
Aristophanes
   Birds 693–7: 80
   Frogs 1032: 122
Aristotle
   De Anima 410b–11a: 116
   De Anima 405a: 195 n.84
   Eudemian Ethics 1235a: 202–3 n.22
   Metaphysics 983b: 7
   Metaphysics 14.1091b: 31
   Politics 1.1252b: 58
Athenagoras
   Plea for the Christians 18.3–4: 186 n.105
Augustine
   City of God 4.12: 127

Chrysippus
   Fr. 1078, 1081 SVF: 183–4 n.79

Derveni Papyrus
   col. 13.4: 82, 85–6, 91
   col. 14.6: 81
   col. 14.7: 88
   col. 16.3–6: 85, 86, 91
   col. 17.7–9: 94
   col. 17.12: 91
   col. 18.12: 91
   col. 18.34: 95
   col. 22.12: 89
   col. 25.14: 95
Diodorus
   Library of History 3.62.6–8: 100–101
Diogenes Laertius
   Lives of Eminent Philosophers 1.5: 181 n.58

Lives of Eminent Philosophers 8.32: 194 n.79

Empedocles
   DK 31 B 21: 109
   DK 31 B 29: 81, 111
   DK 31 B 28: 109
   DK 31 B 31: 111
   DK 31 B 35.14: 118
   DK 31 B 115: 110
   DK 31 B 128: 126
   DK 31 B 128: 48
   DK 31 B 130: 122
   DK 31 B 137: 123
Eusebius
   Praeparatio evangelica 3.11.3–4: 114
Euripides
   Hippolytus 948–54: 121
   Hypsipyle, Frag. 758a: 80

Heraclitus
   DK 22 A6:, 8
   DK 22 B 36: 8, 115, 117
   DK 22 B 57: 8
   DK 22 B 62: 118
   DK 22 B 67: 10, 76, 96, 176 n.11
   DK 22 B 114: 138
Herodotus
   Histories, 2.53: 21
   Histories, 2.81: 197 n.108
Hesiod
   Catalogue of Women Fr. 1.1–7 M.W.: 52
   Theogony 31–4: 22
   Theogony 116–20: 22, 34
   Theogony 195–200: 160 n.12
   Theogony 210–40: 87
   Theogony 226–30: 37
   Theogony 296–9: 40
   Theogony 535–47: 49

Works and Days 109: 54
Works and Days 116: 55
Works and Days 109–18: 51
Works and Days 129: 3
Homer
　Iliad 5.339–42: 4, 59
　Iliad 5.441–2: 4
　Iliad 9.168–9: 163 n.69
　Odyssey 1.145: 167 n.110
　Odyssey 5.196–9: 59
　Odyssey 7.201–5: 57
　Odyssey 8.546–7: 60
　Odyssey 10.303: 137
　Odyssey 14.418–38: 66–6
Homeric Hymns
　To Delian Apollo 119: 86

Iamblichus
　De Anima 8: 194 n.81

Lucian (Pseudo)
　Amores 32: 24

Macrobius
　Saturnalia 1.23.21: 75

Orphic Fragments
　OF 174: 83
　OF 220: 99
　OF 241: 84–5
　OF 243: 106–7
　OF 243 I B: 176 n.12
　OF 338: 198 n.121
　OF 339: 116–17
　OF 436: 117
　OF 422: 194 n.83
　OF 474: 102
　OF 485–6: 102
　OF 488: 106
　OF 490: 101
Orphic Hymns
　Protogonos: 79–80

Zeus: 91, 106
Titans: 197–8 n.113
Ovid
　Metamorphosis 1.7–9: 24, 30

Parmenides
　DK 28 B 13:, 95
　DK 28 B 5: 96
Pausanias
　Description of Greece 8.2.4: 56
Philostratus
　Life of Apollonius 5.25: 130
Pindar
　Fr. 133 Bergk: 6, 108
　Isthmian Five 14–16: 4–5
　Nemean Six 1–7: 54
　Olympian Two 65–70: 5
　Pythian Three 59–62: 5
Plato
　Gorgias 507e–8d: 23
　Laws 782c–d: 121–2
　Phaedo 72a: 195 n.91
　Phaedo 80a–b: 113–14
　Phaedrus 248a–b: 131
　Protagoras 320c: 133
　Protagoras 327c–d: 139
　Protagoras 337e–d: 203 n.27
　Statesman 271e: 198 n.116
　Statesman 272b–c: 123
　Symposium 202e–3a: 65, 124–5
Plutarch
　On the Face in the Moon 926d–e: 192 n.58
Protagoras
　DK 80 B 4: 201–3 n.4

Sextus Empiricus
　Against the Physicists 1.126–9: 125
Simonides
　Fr. 20: 175 n.104

Xenophanes
　DK 21B 23: 3

General Index

Achuar 13, 15, 135
Aeschylus 45
ambrosia 59–60, 63
analogism 14–16, 32–4, 64, 77–8, 140–2
Anaximander 8, 27
Anaximenes 8, 10, 75, 114
animism 13–15, 32, 77, 124, 135, 142–3
animals
    agency 48–9, 123, 126
    Descola's ontologies 14–15
    Empedocles, *see* Empedocles: animals
    Protagoras 133–4
    sacrifice 62–5, 123–6
    souls 116–17, 120–2
Antiphon the Sophist 140
Aphrodite/Cypris 4, 48, 88, 95, 111, 122
Apollo 4, 44, 59, 74, 86, 88, 108
Apollodorus 21, 41, 55
Aristophanes 24, 80–1, 122
Aristotle
    Chaos 24
    early poets 31–2, 37–8
    kinship 58, 61
    Orphic soul 116
    Presocratics 7–9, 137
Asclepius 108
Athena 23, 45

Babylon 7, 10, 29, 38, 45
Bacchic mysteries 74, 102, 104–5, 121
bone plaques 102–3, 118
blood (kinship) 4, 54, 56, 58–61

Chaos
    Babylonian religion 45
    birth 34–5
    Cornford, *see* Cornford
    Eros 35–8
    etymology 23–4
    genealogy 37
    Nun 24
    Orphic theogonies 86

China 27, 77, 115, 136
Cornford 25–7, 30–3
creation by sacrifice 69–71, 111–12
culture and nature 135–9
cyclical cosmos 93–4

daimones 110–11, 116, 120, 124–5, 131–2
Demeter 88–9, 100–1
Derveni papyrus
    discovery 73
    Hesiod, comparison with 88–90
    gold tablets, relation to 105–8
    philosophic commentary 73, 75–6, 82, 88, 89, 92, 95, 116
    Protogonos, *see* Protogonos: presence in the *Derveni Theogony*
    Zeus, *see* Zeus: *Derveni Theogony*
Descartes, René 113, 141
Descola, Philippe
    analogism, *see* analogism
    animals, *see* animals: Descola's ontologies
    animism, *see* animism
    cosmology 32–4
    four ontologies 13–16
    mind-body relation 14, 158 n.46
    sacrifice 64–55, 124–7
Diodorus 100–1
Diogenes of Apollonia 116, 140
dualism 8, 14, 87, 13, 119

Egypt 9–10, 24, 27, 29–30, 83, 130
Eliade, Mircea 28, 48
Empedocles
    animals 110–12, 122–3
    comparison with Orphism 111
    cosmology 109
    daimon 110–11
    sacrifice 123–6
    two poems 191 n.54
Enûma Eliš 7, 29–30, 33, 38
Erikapaios 80

General Index

Eros
   Hesiod 17, 22, 24, 35–8, 44, 65
   Orphic poetry 75–6, 79–81, 95
etymologising
   Chaos, *see* Chaos: etymology
   Orphic commentator 73, 88, 96–7
   Orphic poetry 76, 80, 86
Eukles 101, 106
Euripides 27, 80, 81, 121–2
Eubouleus 76, 101, 106
Eudemus/Eudemean theogony 75, 84

Gaia
   Hesiod 2, 17, 22, 25–6, 35–40, 53–4
   Orphic poetry 79, 87–9, 92, 100, 119
Genesis 28–9, 48, 51
gold tablets 74, 80–1, 101–8, 112–13, 116, 118–20

Hades 106, 117
Hagen 135, 137
Hera 45, 59, 108
Heraclitus
   cosmology 8–10
   flux 156 n.21
   Hesiod 8
   Orpheus 75–6, 96, 117–18
   phusis 138
   soul 113–15
Hermes 3, 68, 88, 117, 137
Herodotus 21, 121, 140, 143
Hesiod
   Aristotle 31
   biography 21–2
   golden age 51–3, 57, 61
   Mediterranean cosmologies 28–30
   Mekone, *see* Prometheus: Mekone
   myth of races 53
   Orpheus 73–4
   Presocratics, *see* Presocratics: Hesiod
   Heraclitus, *see* Heraclitus: Hesiod
Hestia 89
Hieronymus and Hellanicus 84
Hobbes, Thomas 141–2
Homer
   cosmology 7, 23–4, 73
   Ethiopians and Phaeacians 55, 57
   food and kinship 58–60
   immortals and mortals 3–4

phusis 2–3, 137
sacrifice 63–4, 66–9
homologism 17, 78, 115
Hundred-Handers 39, 41
hybrid beings 39–40

Iatmul creation myth 33

Kumarbi epic 29, 38, 83
Kronos
   defeat by Zeus 41
   depictions in *Theogony* and *Works and Days* 53–4
   Empedocles 126
   Kronos and Humanity 48, 51, 57
   Orphic Kronos 88, 91
   rule 38–40

Lévi-Strauss 47, 64

Marduk 29, 45
Mekone
   Callimachus 70
   creation by sacrifice 69–71
   human mortality 54–5
   interpretations 50
   sacrifice 59–61, 62–4
metempsychosis 124, 198 note 121
Metis 41–3, 91–3, 95
Moirai 44, 88, 95

nature, *see phusis*
Night (goddess)
   Hesiod 31, 37, 40
   Orphic 80, 82–4, 86–8

Oedipus 41, 61
Okeanos 7, 24, 73, 88, 95
Olympiodorus 99–103
Orpheus
   Bacchic Rites, *see* Bacchic Mysteries
   biography 74
   bone plaques, *see* bone plaques
   gold tablets, *see* gold tablets
   Heraclitus, *see* Heraclitus: Orpheus
   Orphic *Hymns* 79–80, 89, 91, 106
   Rhapsodies 84, 87, 103
   soul 116–19
   works attributed to Orpheus 74–5

Ouranos
    Cornford 25–6, 36
    gold tablets 119–20
    Hesiod 37–40
    Orphic 73, 81–3, 87–90
Ovid 21, 24, 30

Pangu Kaitian 27–8, 32
Pantheism
    ontology definition 77–8
    Orphic poetic pantheism 74–6
    relationship with analogism 140–1
Perspectivism 135–6
Purusha-Sutka 69–70
Parmenides 10, 35, 95–6
Pausanias 56, 60
Persephone 6, 89, 99, 102, 104, 105–8
Pherecydes 11, 23, 31, 35, 73, 90
Philon of Byblos 29, 38
phusis
    Presocratics 7–10, 137–8
    Heraclitus, *see* Heraclitus: *phusis*
    Homer, *see* Homer: *phusis*
    sophists 138–9
Pindar
    Homer 4–5
    Nemean Six 1–6
    Orphism 6, 101, 108–9
Plato
    body and soul 113–14, 131
    early humans 123
    Orphism 103–4, 108, 119–20, 121–2
    Protagoras 133–4
    sacrifice 124–5
Porphyry 94, 107–8, 132
Presocratics
    cosmology 7–11
    Hesiod 26–7, 30–1, 35
    nature, *see phusis*: Presocratics
    Orpheus 74–8
    soul 114–16
Prometheus
    culture bringer 139
    Mekone 49–51, 62–3
    trickster 51
    Protagoras 133–4, 139
Protagoras
    culture and nature 138–9
    influence 139-42

myth 133–4
Plato, *see* Plato: Protagoras
Protogonos
    birth 86–8
    classical sources 80–1
    gold tablets 107
    hymns 75–6, 79–80
    presence in the *Derveni Theogony* 81–5
    Zeus, relationship to 91–3
Pythagoreans 6, 31, 108, 116, 120–1, 125, 128

qi 115–16

reincarnation, *see* metempsychosis
Rhea 38, 41, 88–9, 99, 105
Robertson Smith 18, 58, 64

Sahlins, Marshall
    divine incest 89–90
    kinship 56, 61
    stranger king 42–3
sophists 134, 138–40
Stoics 23, 76–7, 116, 118, 143
structuralism 15

Tenetehara myth 47–8
Tethys 7, 24, 73
Thales 7–12, 78, 114
Theophrastus 130
Typhoeus 40, 43

vegetarianism 120–2
Vernant, Jean-Pierre
    Hesiod's *Theogony* 30–1
    Metis 41–3
    sacrifice 50, 62–4

woman 43, 48, 63

xenia
    creation of kinship 60–1
    definition 60
    Pausanias 56
    rituals 63
    stranger 61–2, 68
Xenophanes 3, 10, 90, 96

Zeus
    analogist cosmologies 31

challenges to authority 45
Derveni Theogony
   creation 94–6
   destruction of the Titans 99–102
   eating of the cosmos 91–3
   and Rhea 105
Empedocles 126
Hesiod's *Theogony*
   battle against Typhoeus 40
   birth 41–2
   and Metis 41–3
   organization of the cosmos 43–4, 70–1
   and Prometheus 49–50
Heraclitus 129
hymns to Zeus 91, 94, 106–7
Protagoras' myth 134
Rhapsodies 84–5